# FINAL APPROACHES

# FINAL APPROACHES

## A MEMOIR

*Gerald Hensley*

AUCKLAND UNIVERSITY PRESS

First published 2006
Reprinted 2006

Auckland University Press
University of Auckland
Private Bag 92019
Auckland
New Zealand
www.auckland.ac.nz/aup

ISBN-10: 1 86940 378 9
ISBN-13: 978 1 86940 378 2

**National Library of New Zealand Cataloguing-in-Publication Data**
Hensley, G. C. (Gerald Christopher)
Final approaches : a memoir / Gerald Hensley.
Includes index.
ISBN-13: 978-1-86940-378-2
ISBN-10: 1-86940-378-9
1. Hensley, G. C. (Gerald Christopher) 2. Diplomats–New
Zealand–Anecdotes. 3. New Zealand–Officials and
employees–Anecdotes. I. Title.
327.93–DC 22

Publication is assisted by the History Group, Ministry for Culture and Heritage.

Cover design: Sarah Maxey
Printed by Printlink Ltd, Wellington

# CONTENTS

*Foreword*                              *vii*

*One* An Apprentice in Samoa            1

*Two* Manhattan and Other Islands       40

*Three* The Commonwealth Divided        70

*Four* War in Nigeria                   104

*Five* A Washington Spectator           132

*Six* New Zealand Adrift                165

*Seven* Tropical Asia                   191

*Eight* The Last Years of Muldoon       224

*Nine* The Elusive David Lange          266

*Epilogue*                              310

*Index*                                 313

Years ago I sat in an aircraft preparing to land and listened to the practised rattle of the air hostess: 'As we are now on our final approaches, would you please ensure that your seat back is upright . . .' A natural title for memoirs, I thought – looking back over a journey as you prepare to come down, with the landing lights sweeping over the landscape. It was an idle thought; I had no intention of writing a memoir. Recollections of official life have a limited appeal, the joys of bureaucratic battles often not being as apparent to the reader as they are to the author. The diplomatic memoir has even greater pitfalls, tending to exploits with rod and gun and fruity reminiscences. There are awkward moments in diplomatic life but they can seem rather technical to those not in the business. All I remember now of the memoirs of the British ambassador in Russia at the start of the First World War was when the Tsar at dinner proposed a toast to the Kaiser. The ambassador could not stand to drink to his country's enemy, nor could he insult the Tsar by remaining seated: he solved the problem by rising to a half crouch.

Those who do write memoirs often explain that they have done so only at the insistent urging of their friends. Unfortunately this was not so in my case. My mind was changed by the accident of helping a political science student with his research. The resulting thesis was admirable. All the relevant documents had been consulted, all the citations were correct, but reading it I thought, *It wasn't like this*. The files often lack the human thumbprints of those who made them, all the muddle and misgivings, the arguments and atmospherics, which precede what actually happened. What is now history was once the future, with all its possibilities open, and the memories of those who were present can convey some sense of how the pattern came to be fixed.

There are limits to the memoir. 'Pray take away this pudding,' said Winston Churchill to a waiter at the Savoy Hotel, 'it has no theme.' This is the difficulty with a life; it is as shapeless as the Savoy's pudding. I have not therefore attempted an autobiography but instead have tried to focus the lens of memory on a series of episodes from my first thirty years of service with the New Zealand government from 1959 to 1989, excluding both youthful reminiscences and my later years as Secretary of Defence. The episodes are confined to those in which I was involved and had some first-hand knowledge to set down. So this is not a history of my times; many important events are passed over simply because they were outside my direct experience. It is keyhole history, with the narrow field of vision which comes from recording only one person's point of view.

Inevitably keyhole history exaggerates the writer's part in the events he is recording. Churchill demonstrates this as well. 'Winston', said a tart lady, 'has written a perfectly enormous book about himself and called it *The World Crisis.*' Quite. The memoir is an egocentric form of history and all that can be done in mitigation, apart from humbly apologising in advance, is to check memory against as much as possible of the available documentation. I have never kept a diary but over the years a considerable mass of papers, cables, notes of meetings and letters has accumulated in boxes in the attic. These are the basis of what follows but framed and checked by consulting the relevant official files.

So I am grateful to James Kember and John Mills for arranging access to the files of the Ministry of Foreign Affairs and Trade, and to David Kersey, Brent Anderson and Paula Dymond, who did the same for me in the Department of the Prime Minister and Cabinet. Archives New Zealand were most helpful in finding everything I asked for, as were Archives Canada in Ottawa, with kind encouragement from Professor Norman Hilmer and Ryan Shackleton, and the Commonwealth Secretariat Library in London. Cartoons and photographs were generously made available by Garry Linnell and Bill Leak of the *Bulletin* and Tim Pankhurst, Frank Stefanski and Eric Heath of the *Dominion Post*. Finally I owe the warmest thanks to Elizabeth Caffin, Director of the Auckland University Press, who first suggested this book and whose encouragement chapter by chapter helped overcome my doubts.

Then there are the apologies. I decided at the outset to keep names to an absolute minimum to avoid clogging the narrative, but this has meant passing over in silence the work of many friends and colleagues to whom I can only offer this explanation. I think after writing these chapters that I may also owe an apology to my dear children – it looks as if I did not spend as much time at home as I thought when they were growing up. Finally there is my wife Juliet whose careful judgement and attention to detail made up for my own shortcomings. But that is the least of it: neither the book nor the life it records would have been worthwhile without her.

*Kahu Vineyard, Martinborough*

# CHAPTER ONE

# An Apprentice in Samoa

THE FLYING-BOAT LANDED IN A CURTAIN OF SPRAY. THROUGH the open hatch I could see across a wide lagoon to a distant line of palms waving silver-green in the steady trade wind. The sun was flickering on the turquoise-coloured water and the heat was like a blow. It was my first sight of Western Samoa, a country whose future had preoccupied my short working life for four months. By the time I had landed and been driven to Apia through villages little changed since Robert Louis Stevenson's time, I knew that I had found what I wanted to do in life.

The romance of the tropics and the diplomatic life had begun to take hold early in this journey at the beginning of May 1959. At the small airport at Nadi, surrounded by sugar-fields, I crossed the sun-baked tarmac to join the immigration queue. A police inspector asked if anyone had a diplomatic passport and clutching my newly issued one I went to the head of the queue. This was a gratifying introduction to diplomatic life but it proved to be misleading. Though I subsequently went through four or five such passports, this never happened again.

Nevertheless it was a promising start, made more promising by staying a night in the old Grand Pacific Hotel in Suva. This was a place patronised years earlier by Somerset Maugham, with ceiling fans, a half acre of white wicker chairs and tables, and circling waiters summoned by a clap of the hands. I sampled all this to the extent permitted by Treasury regulations and in the rather spartan bedroom first encountered that distinctive damp smell which ever afterwards has brought back nostalgia for the tropics.

At dawn the next morning the Solent flying-boat was to take off for Samoa. The lagoon at Laucala Bay, however, was as smooth as a pond and the surface suction would not allow the aircraft to lift off. We had to taxi about like a powerboat racer until the water was sufficiently choppy for the plane to become airborne. The flight thereafter was a leisurely one. At 2000 feet there were views of islands like the Vava'u Group in northern Tonga; the seats tilted back to become beds; and you could go downstairs and order a drink at the bar. As an introduction to international air travel this too proved misleading.

I had started at the New Zealand Department of External Affairs the previous December and held the most junior rank as a 'diplomatic trainee'. After abandoning a law degree and graduating from the University of Canterbury with honours in history I was assumed to be an historian. With the help of a postgraduate scholarship it was arranged that I should go to Magdalen College at Oxford to do a doctorate on early Stuart parliaments. However historical research palled as I wanted to have a hand in events rather than simply write about them. This was reinforced by another urge: a deepening interest in a Christchurch journalist, Juliet Young. Even the most self-absorbed young man had to accept that so beautiful a girl would be unlikely to remain unattached during his three-year absence at Oxford. The answer to that, and to a future approach to her father, was clearly paid employment. I went to Wellington, saw the Secretary of External Affairs, Alister McIntosh, and asked him whether he preferred to have me with or without a doctorate. This rather dodged the issue of whether he wanted to have me at all but after some understandable fencing he plumped for an early start and I resigned the scholarship.

He may have wondered about his decision. My first task in the Department was writing a speech for the Prime Minister, Walter Nash, who was opening a Commonwealth Conference in Palmerston North, the first Commonwealth gathering held in New Zealand. I had never written a speech before and laboured over an academic and painful draft ('Commonwealth ties are very often old school ties'). McIntosh called me in and said, 'This will never do'. My heart sank. 'The Prime Minister', said Mac, 'likes to speak in this fashion.' He called in his stenographer and began to dictate. It was a brilliant imitation of Walter Nash's style, teetering on the verge of parody but never quite overbalancing. It meandered back and forth; it repeated itself; it was reminded of other things only to be reminded of earlier thoughts. Above all it breathed the distinctive aroma of what I was later to recognise as Bomfog (the Brotherhood of Man and the Fatherhood of God), which permeated all of Nash's utterance. I was listening entranced when to my horror Mac broke off half way through and said, 'You get the idea. Now go and finish it.'

A second effort at speech-writing also led to embarrassment. With this instruction I had grasped the elements of the prime-ministerial style and my draft, for another occasion, was suitably sentimental and wreathed in trailing clouds of the required Bomfog pieties. Finishing it late at night in high spirits I added the words '(Laughter and fruit-throwing)' at the end. By some mischance it was typed, and went straight through to Mac, who returned it with these words crossed out and a note beside them: 'True, but better omitted'.

After this it was a relief to me, and perhaps to others, that my speech-writing career was interrupted. The newly returned Deputy Secretary, Frank Corner, sent for me in early January 1959 and said, 'Do you want to get your hands dirty?' New Zealand had, he said, invited a high-ranking United Nations Mission to go to the Trust Territory of Western Samoa in March but we had not yet started work on what proposals to put to them about the territory's future. With time short we would have to work hard. I returned to my room as Samoan Desk Officer, running my finger back and forth over a map of the Pacific until I was able to establish where Samoa was.

As a trust territory under New Zealand administration Western Samoa (the smaller eastern part was an American territory) had for some years been on a path of constitutional development under the guidance of an able High Commissioner (in fact Governor), G. R. Powles. In 1954 a Constitutional Convention had laid down a timetable for the remaining steps which it thought would be completed in the early 1960s. Samoa would then have full internal self-government, with New Zealand responsible only for external affairs and defence, and the trusteeship would be ended. The example in everyone's mind was neighbouring Tonga, a British protected state, and hence the goal was usually referred to as the 'Tongan solution'.

The trouble was that since 1954 no one had given this any further thought. We had asked for a special Visiting Mission (all four members of ambassadorial rank) to discuss the ending of trusteeship but had not worked out the details of what we wanted to discuss with them. But with two months in hand and the outline of Samoan and New Zealand thinking well agreed, drafting a formal memorandum to present to the Mission did not seem too difficult a task even for a trainee.

For some weeks I read all the files and books on Samoa that I could find and listened to the experiences of members of the Department of Island Territories, which administered all New Zealand's responsibilities in the South Pacific. Almost every day I went back and forth to Frank Corner's office with notes for him to read, extracts from books, documents from the files and anything else which seemed relevant. Although Frank was busy (he was among other things Secretary-General of an impending SEATO Conference), we had lengthy discussions, very characteristic of his way of working, of the 'what if' kind. He would think out loud, what if we did this, why were we so sure of that, and stimulated by this I would go away and think again. As we delved more deeply into the issues in this way our views began to shift. Without reaching any firm conclusions we began to question the Tongan solution. Towards the end of February I had got as far as noting to Frank that 'it might be best to stop agonising over our past decisions and reappraise those about to be taken'.

There were growing doubts whether the Tongan solution, approved in rather different circumstances in 1954, would be durable as worldwide decolonisation gathered pace. Our office in New York was already warning that the Trusteeship Council or more likely the General Assembly itself would be suspicious of arrangements for a protectorate and might be reluctant to end the trusteeship. The old Samoa hands grumbled that we were simply pandering to the newly independent nations of the UN. This was a consideration but Samoa, with a population of just under 100,000 and tucked away in the South Pacific, was unlikely to attract fiery anti-colonialism. New Zealand had a good reputation as an administrator and though we would have had to work harder, trusteeship could probably have been terminated on the basis of the Tongan solution.

Our doubts lay deeper. New Zealand ought to be looking to a *permanent* settlement of its relations with Western Samoa, not one which was based on a snapshot in time and one which was already looking a little faded. As a self-governing Samoa became more confident there were bound to be continuing disputes and frictions over the division of powers. What was needed was a relationship which would evolve with Samoa itself, not one which might have to be redone every decade or so. New Zealand was entitled to form its own view on the nature of the future relationship

4

and not be bound, as our colleagues in Island Territories were inclined to argue, by the decisions of past and present Samoan bodies.

The preparations for self-government had, by later world standards at any rate, been lengthy and careful. There was therefore general agreement in Wellington that the last major step in this process – the inauguration of Cabinet government – could now be brought forward. But this itself would change things. The Samoans had a deep-rooted tradition of representative decision-making. As they adapted this to an elected Cabinet their experience would influence the final shape of the relationship with New Zealand.

All this was being talked back and forth as I began work on the memorandum for the Visiting Mission. My first draft was rather muddled but it was patiently revised by Frank Corner. After one or perhaps two more versions it was ready for interdepartmental discussion early in March, attended also by the High Commissioner, who had been asked to come from Apia for these consultations, Paul Edmonds, our trusteeship specialist from New York, and Colin Aikman, the New Zealand constitutional adviser.

The paper dealt first with the advancement of the date for Cabinet government and thereafter, more vaguely, with the final stages of what I had variously termed 'full self-government', 'autonomy' and even 'independence'. In the course of the meeting, in Frank Corner's room on the top floor of Parliament Buildings, I recall pointing out that these terms were not in fact interchangeable and sought guidance as to which should be used. Frank, who had hurt his back gardening, leant back cautiously in his chair and suggested that complete independence should be one of the options to be offered to the Samoans.

This caused some animation. Island Territories were annoyed at the suggestion from someone who had never seen Samoa and who seemed to them to be more swayed by hopes of praise from the international community than by what the Samoans had said they wanted. Powles was also irritated: five years of work based on the Tongan solution were being questioned almost flippantly by 'one of Frank Corner's pipe dreams', as he put it on another occasion.[*] The meeting broke up for lunch on a rather sour note.

---

[*] Writing to Mac about the proposal to appoint me as External Affairs Officer in Apia.

The Tongan solution, however, was dead. Frank saw the Prime Minister and though there was a slight doubt over whether Walter Nash fully grasped the distinction between self-government and independence, he was a firm supporter of self-determination and endorsed the new course. A Cabinet paper based on the earlier thinking was already in draft and there was just time for me to write a new back half for Cabinet's endorsement on 16 March, before the Visiting Mission arrived two days later. This emphasised that 'we are giving Samoa a genuine and not illusory independence, and the continued association of the two countries will be by the Territory's express desire'. There had however been no time to consult the Samoan leaders and so the references to independence were guarded in discussions with the Mission. So the new policy rather backed out into the full light of day. But it was set: Samoa would be offered unqualified independence and any future relationship with New Zealand would be on this basis. At the end of May McIntosh, after some needling from the Soviet representative, made this plain to the Trusteeship Council.

By then I was seeing Samoa for myself. With the Visiting Mission out of the way it was decided that I should make a two-month visit. My official standing was never made clear, least of all to myself, but it was understood that I should lend a hand where helpful and otherwise travel as widely as possible. The High Commissioner saw me as 'Corner's spy' but nonetheless received me with a kindly caution and I settled down in Central Office, the old German administration block on the waterfront, to prepare briefings for his attendance at the Trusteeship Council session. When he left I was free to roam.

My accommodation was a small flat in the back garden of the Casino, built as a German barracks but now run as a boarding-house by Mary Croudace (Auntie Mary to almost everyone), sister of the more famous Aggie Grey and one source of the character of 'Bloody Mary' in the musical *South Pacific*. Mary was both worldly and sweet-natured, reputed to have been the lover of a Marine general in the war, now a member of the choir at the Catholic Cathedral and chaperone of the Children of Mary. In the slightly raffish atmosphere of a South Pacific port this respectability needed careful guarding which Mary managed by ignoring any untoward event. When a Canadian destroyer visited Apia some enterprising person opened an informal brothel at the back of the Casino but others even more enterprising climbed the fence and stole all the sailors' clothes. We all heard the resulting uproar in the night but no one was ever so insensitive as to refer to it in Mary's hearing.

The inhabitants of the Casino were a strange mix of regulars, seconded government servants on transfer, a few tourists when the flying-boat or steamer arrived, and the occasional eminent guest like the Bishop of Polynesia. Bishop Kempthorne was a saintly old man married to an American divorcee – a lively lady who, when I first helped her ashore from a launch, said, 'I'm pooped to pop'. The bishop told me he had been staying at the Casino at the time of the riot in 1929 when the elder Tamasese was shot. Armed young men were roaming the streets and no European would venture out. He decided that night to walk to the village of Vaimoso where the Mau movement had its headquarters. When he entered the *fale* where the body was lying he was surrounded by the leaders of the Mau and their supporters armed with bush knives, none of whom said a word. He stepped in front of the body and said that as a European he had come to offer his sincerest apologies. When he finished there was still no sound and after waiting for a moment he turned and walked back alone to the Casino. But his gesture was remembered.

Mrs Croudace (the original Mr Croudace, reputed to have been a New Zealand official, was long gone) ran an efficient and within certain limits comfortable hotel. But this did not hold her interest. She was a party girl and evenings at the Casino came to life when Auntie Mary, yipping and hooting in the approved style, swayed on to the floor for a Samoan dance. She had great charm; her gravel voice, speaking a mix of American English and kitchen Samoan, and loud laugh made the Casino a lively place. Though always discreet, she gave good guidance on the intricacies of Apia society.

Her other interest, probably more recent, was the church and I found myself recruited to be organist and choirmaster at the Cathedral. Choirmaster was a sinecure since the choir (mainly the Children of Mary) sang like angels. The organ was another matter. It had been built by a French missionary bishop towards the end of the nineteenth century and the tropics had affected its leather and stops. I was not a skilful organist and on occasions, while making that subdued organ noise appropriate when people are taking their seats, the organ would suddenly roar like a bull in the mating season, startling the congregation and sometimes the priest. The organ was dismantled for overhaul.

My first travels were in the banana trade. Banana exports to New Zealand were in a period of rapid and (as it proved) unsustainable growth. With simple packing in wooden crates the bananas tended to ripen on the voyage and to reach New Zealand markets bruised and spotted. But grown on newly cleared land they produced a quick cash crop. Hands of bananas were packed in their cases but could only be boarded up on the day they were shipped. So on successive banana mornings we bumped over rutted tracks and through half-cleared forest, shouting *naile le pusa* (nail the box) wherever people were waiting by the track with their open boxes.

Kindly Samoan officials took me on more leisurely visits to their districts. On the first occasion we slept on mats on the *fale* floor. In the darkness after the lamp was blown out I heard a persistent rustling in the rafters. I was told that it was only the snake kept by the family to hunt rats and this reassurance kept me awake for some time. At the other extreme, on another occasion a large, curtained double bed was set up for me in the middle of the *fale*, posing a problem I had never thought of – how to undress and go to bed in the middle of someone else's living-room. Most surprising of all was lunching with a hospitable Chinese trader on the south coast of Upolu. After asking whether I was married, he disappeared and returned with a most beautiful girl. He put her hand in mine with an invitation so bald that I still blush. I blush even more at my response – I shook the hand which had been placed in mine and hastily left.

The voyage to the larger island of Savai'i (probably the Hawaiki of Maori tradition) was by wooden boat. You sat on the deck, clutching whatever came to hand as the vessel rolled its way across the strait and surrounded by baskets of taro, pigs, chickens and of course your fellow passengers. The young woman next to me was lying on a white pillow which had the word BLEEDING embroidered diagonally across it in red wool. I wondered about this but all was revealed when she picked up the pillow to disembark and HEART OF JESUS appeared on the reverse side.

The Resident Commissioner for Savai'i, Papali'i Poumau, and I climbed into a Land Rover and travelled the length of the island, stopping at a number of villages to meet the *matai*, or village chiefs. These meetings were leisurely affairs, following the course prescribed by Samoan custom. Everyone took his place in the circular *fono*, or council house, usually in the centre of the village, with each title-holder sitting cross-legged against his accustomed post. After traditional speeches of welcome kava was prepared by a girl chewing bits of the peppery root and straining it through water. It was served in a half coconut shell with ritual flourishes in strict order of precedence. Speeches then began. By this time, unused to sitting cross-legged for long, I was in some discomfort but a tactful convention held that legs stretched out under a mat became socially invisible.

At the end of proceedings I would give a brief account, interpreted by Papali'i, of progress towards self-government, stressing that Samoa's destiny would soon be in her own hands but that New Zealand would stand by the new state as a friend. Thereafter, whatever the hour, a meal was served. This too was unchanging: *pisupo* (which turned out to be tinned corned beef), heavy slices of purplish taro, green bananas and *palusami* (a rich dish of green taro leaves cooked in coconut cream). Then, a little heavier each time, Papali'i and I climbed back into the Land Rover to drive on across a rolling lava field or through dense tropical forest to the next village.

He left me at the end of the road in Falealupo at the far end of Savai'i. There I stayed for a day or two with a New Zealand priest, Father Alan McKay, at the Catholic mission. This was an old building with thick walls of coral cement and an upstairs balcony overlooking the sea. Furnishings were austere, the shower being a four-gallon tin which you tipped over yourself by pulling a string, but the house was comfortable. Meals were cooked and sent over by the Belgian nuns from the nearby convent and once I got used to drinking coffee out of what would have been regarded at home as a soup bowl, the food proved an unexpected attraction of the missionary life.

On the first night we were sitting on the balcony finishing a whisky when a young man arrived to say that his grandfather, a high-ranking chief in the next village, had died suddenly and the family wished to take him home for burial that night. We set off through the forest (there was no road) just before midnight in a procession led by men carrying flaring torches, the dead chief carried on a bier made of freshly cut saplings, and the *patele* and myself. We came to a low ridge or dyke running across the path. The pall-bearers crossed and re-crossed it three times before we went on our way. Father McKay made no comment.

In the village the church was crowded and after the journey through the jungle a blaze of light from pressure lamps and candles. The bier was placed at the altar rails, gently fanned by two young women, and the church was carpeted in fine mats as a tribute to the dead man. I knelt at the back (there were no seats) and listened to the singing, the sound of unfamiliar prayers and the surge of the sea on the reef outside. The grave in the rocky ground was not ready so leaving the committal to the local catechist we walked home.

We came to the low ridge again and I asked about the strange little ceremony there. The ridge was the end of a ghostly road running the length of Samoa and along it the dead travelled as they departed across the sea towards the setting sun. The crossing back and forth was to placate these spirits and Father McKay did not think it sensible to remonstrate. The next morning I walked to the end of the spirit path and the westernmost point of Samoa where a rather sinister lava cave opened and closed in the ocean swell. Like many migrant peoples the Polynesians like to go home after death and, as the Maori go north from the tip of New Zealand, so the Samoans go west whence they came 2000 years ago.

Towards the end of my time I made an overnight sea trip to the island of Tutuila in American Samoa. The journey was made in a converted wooden minesweeper, the *Manu'atele*, remembered less than fondly for its ability to roll in even the most placid sea. The passenger list included the usual travelling families, pigs and piles of taro. The more favoured passengers slept in the chartroom, in my case on top of what had once been the chart table. In the course of the night as the ship rolled a large dollop of water several times shot through the open porthole beside me and down on to a man sleeping on the floor below. Each time he would wake, glare at me suspiciously while I kept my eyes firmly on the ceiling and then return to an increasingly damp sleep.

Although I was in Pago Pago to learn a little about the American territory it was also an opportunity to sound out Governor Coleman, the first Samoan-born governor, on what the prospects might be for reunion with Western Samoa. American Samoa had been through a period of neglect and in the deep harbour the former US naval base now accommodated only a handful of tuna boats and a cannery. Four years earlier the Interior Department in Washington had mused about reunion and now, with Western Samoa approaching independence, seemed a good time to look again at the possibility. The two parts of Samoa, split into German and American colonies in 1900, had been separated after all for less than sixty years.

Governor Coleman, an intelligent and courteous man, was in no doubt that the moment, if it had ever existed, had passed. Washington was about to spend large sums on the territory and the inhabitants would be reluctant to share these, and their right of entry into the United States. In any case there was, as I had heard in Apia, a marked difference in social standing. American Samoa had no royal titles since the oldest of them, the Tuimanu'a, was suppressed in the 1930s. Their *matai* felt inferior and at the annual meetings of the Samoan (Congregational) Church – the only assembly which united the two Samoas – they tended to stand at the back and say little. The Western Samoan leaders, though favouring reunion in principle, were in practice little interested. It seemed strange to an outsider but the two parts were on a diverging course and the opportunity lapsed.

The return trip, on the island cruise ship *Tofua*, was considerably more comfortable. The sea was calm and the moon bright and walking on the deck I met Sir John Collins, a distinguished Australian admiral who was now their High Commissioner in Wellington. He was visiting New Zealand territories in the Pacific, mainly to report what was happening in Samoa. The artless admiral drew a paper from his pocket and said, 'They've sent me all these questions from Canberra. Perhaps you can give me a hand with them.' The paper was a cable reflecting Australia's concerns about the course of New Zealand policy. It wanted to know more about New Zealand's intentions, what the real views of the Samoan leaders were, and what the outlook was if New Zealand went ahead with independence. I relished this chance and gave him an extended briefing, even writing down the more significant bits. My enthusiasm failed to convince: years later I read his despatch which was decidedly pessimistic about the prospects for an independent Samoa.

New Zealand's decision to offer full independence to Samoa did not please our closest friends, though their uneasiness was on the whole confined to raised eyebrows and diplomatic representations. Australia, Britain, and to a lesser extent the United States considered (it was the conventional view of the time) that the Territory was too small and too economically weak to stand alone. Worse than that, we were accused of imperilling the calm of the South Pacific and further complicating the task of the administrators of larger and more difficult territories like Fiji and Papua New Guinea. The British worried that we were setting an awkward precedent and encouraging the United Nations in its growing enthusiasm for interfering in colonial matters. The abandonment of the Tongan solution led them to consider how this might affect their plans for other 'protected states' like Kuwait and the Maldives.

These complaints had some force. It was true that New Zealand had an easier task with stable Samoa than its fellow administering authorities had elsewhere, but it was Samoa we were responsible for and we had to put its interests first. It was also true (though we never admitted it) that we saw Western Samoa as the beginning of decolonisation through the South Pacific. Frank Corner and I had discussed this. New Zealand's front yard had for a century been a colonial lake. This would change; this peaceful backwater would not indefinitely be insulated from the anti-colonial turmoil elsewhere. Better to accept the fact and work to ensure that the changeover in the Pacific was as fast and trouble-free as possible.

On 1 July 1959 I was back in Wellington, smitten with the sights and sounds of Samoa. Beneath the excitement, though, the eight weeks visit had a more lasting effect. My view of that historical process known as colonialism had become clearer. Before I had been a theoretical anti-colonialist, aware that the international climate was changing, the white man's burden was becoming unfashionable and we should not be left behind. Experience had filled this out. Now that intellectual inclination had been, to borrow a phrase from Keats, proved upon my pulses.

Tupua Tamasese, one of the two *Fautua* or advisers to the High Commissioner and leader of the movement for self-determination, had a favourite saying that 'good government was no substitute for self-government'. At first I was unconvinced – what after all could be preferable to good government, and certainly there are some states so anarchic that almost anything would be preferable to self-government. But Samoa had a long tradition of representative politics, if not of the Westminster kind, and a settled social structure. It seemed at first incongruous and then wrong for a 23-year-old in white shorts to be telling grave old men what they should be doing in their own country.

For the moment, though, love claimed the right of way. Three days later I became engaged to Juliet Young. I had been proposing marriage so often that it had become almost a social routine, and each time Julie equably declined without ever intimating that I should stop. Whether or not it was my absence this time the routine was interrupted forever when she said yes. The engagement was not universally welcomed by our families, especially by my future mother-in-law, who was public in her disapproval. This, however, was not of immediate concern to the lovers. I had a red MG sports car which, with my father acting as banker, I was able to exchange for a diamond solitaire ring. The exchange was heavily in my favour in every way except financially. Many years later, when having the ring revalued I found that MGs of the same model had appreciated in value twice as fast.

In Samoa the next big constitutional change – the introduction of Cabinet government – was looming. The High Commissioner found himself riding two increasingly divergent horses, as New Zealand representative and head of the Samoan Government. He cabled asking if I could return to help with the representative side of things. So we were hardly engaged before we were separated and by the end of August I was back in my flat in the Casino, now on a posting as Third Secretary and External Affairs Officer. The evening before I left, McIntosh, who could be disconcertingly frank, sent for me. 'Dick Powles is a funny bugger,' he said. 'You never know whether you are dealing with Colonel Powles the military man or Mr Powles the progressive and reader of the *Manchester Guardian*.' He suggested that if I bore this in mind I would get on well with him. While I was still digesting this, he enquired about the effect of a tropical climate on my asthma. 'Try it anyhow,' he said, 'and if you don't like it come home.' With this, perhaps the most surprising brief ever given to a Third Secretary, he waved me out.

In Apia the High Commissioner was moving out of Central Office to make way for the forthcoming prime minister and the old Executive Council room where he had presided for a decade was being redecorated as a Cabinet room. He and his small staff moved up the hill to Government House, Vailima. This was the handsome house built by Stevenson, extended by a subsequent German owner and confiscated by New Zealand in 1914. It sat at the foot of Mount Vaea, below Stevenson's famous grave, and was high enough above Apia to be noticeably cooler. I started work here at the end of August.

The office was on the verandah and I was never again to be so charmingly housed. The verandah, overhung with crimson bougainvillea, looked across the gardens down to Apia and the white line of the reef beyond. Morning and afternoon tea was served on monogrammed china by uniformed houseboys and over all these arrangements presided the butler, Amanono. He had the calm of his profession and walked

through the house with the gravity of one pacing in the funeral procession of a respected colleague. Order broke down occasionally. The
chickens or other livestock would get out and have to be chased from
the front lawn; rain squalls would sweep up the hill and force us to
retreat into the dining-room; or more entertainingly one of the Samoan
Women's Committees would have a *fiafia* or festival outside and substantial middle-aged ladies would dance with a merry bawdiness which
was irresistible.

After discussion earlier between New Zealand and the Samoan leaders
it had been decided to advance the date of Cabinet government by a
full year. The Executive Council had some elected members but these
ministers tended to be silent in the presence of the High Commissioner
and *Fautua*. If ministers were to acquire the habit of making decisions
on their own these three would have to withdraw. There was a snag
however. The *Fautua* were reluctant to move away from the political
centre and to leave matters to an as yet unnamed prime minister. This
was especially true of Tamasese, who was as interested in the practical
business of government as the High Commissioner.

The difficulty was overcome when Professor Aikman, an expert in
constitutional law, devised an ingenious compromise. The Executive
Council would separate into its two parts, the Cabinet chaired by a prime
minister and the Council of State comprising the High Commissioner
and *Fautua*. The Council of State would receive all Cabinet decisions
and would have seven days in which to request a meeting of the full
Executive Council on any decision and if necessary to request Cabinet to
revisit that decision. Thereafter Cabinet's view would be final.

This was stretching the Westminster conventions a bit but it greased
the wheels of constitutional progress. The Council of State was sworn
in and I was appointed Secretary and entrusted with the Seal of the
Territory of Western Samoa. This I preserved respectfully in the safe,
unlike a Lord Chancellor, Lord Brougham, who was reputed to have
made omelettes in the Great Seal at weekend parties. Meetings, presided
over by the High Commissioner, were held in the dining-room at
Vailima, with the four of us sitting rather cosily around one end of the
table. When formal business was over things became more relaxed; on
occasions Tamasese would instruct me on aspects of Samoan custom or
Malietoa, the other *Fautua*, on the proper use of Samoan words. The
compromise worked well – in the first few months only three decisions

were sought to be reviewed – and ministers were so reassured by this backstop that what had been intended as a temporary measure ended up in the constitution of independent Samoa.

Cabinet government was inaugurated with some ceremony on 1 October. On a brilliant morning everyone assembled at the traditional site of Mulinu'u, where the Legislative Assembly sat. A brass band played and hymns were sung. Then the Chief Judge in red robes swore in the Council of State and the Council swore in the new Cabinet. The previous day the Assembly had chosen as Prime Minister, Mata'afa, who held the third of the four Samoan royal titles. Like all the best Samoan ceremonies this one produced an omen: the rain which had fallen intermittently on the proceeding ceased when the Prime Minister began to speak. Mata'afa was both a shy and a proud man whose refusal to lobby for the position had pushed the selection to two ballots. But even before the omen we had reported to Wellington that 'because of his diffidence he seems likely, more than most others, to bloom in the sunshine of power and grow into the office as he becomes more self-confident'.

In the style understood in Samoan politics but less so by outsiders he started in a relaxed and unassertive way. He came to Vailima to meet the Council of State and as I held the Bible for another swearing-in his nervous giggle sounded unstatesmanlike. New Zealand officials, who had worried that ministers would never have the confidence to speak up, now worried that they had begun to take matters into their own hands while the Prime Minister looked on. In the first few Cabinets the Prime Minister's views were regularly disregarded or overridden as ministers enjoyed their new freedom. But this was deceptive. Mata'afa took a little time to play himself in and then quietly began to assert his authority until his dominance of the Cabinet was unquestioned. He was a speaker who could move listeners as diverse as the spectators at Mulinu'u or the United Nations General Assembly and his high rank and easy manners proved to be the right blend to lead Samoa out of trusteeship into independence.

The High Commissioner now had a different role, symbolised by his withdrawal up the hill to Vailima. Instead of the daily drive to Central Office, flags flying and on formal occasions a motor-cycle escort, there was the simple office on the verandah. After ten years of governing, this withdrawal, though planned and worked for by himself, meant a large adjustment and he occasionally liked to refer to himself as 'the prisoner of Vailima'. New Zealand's rule had from the beginning been an uneasy marriage of liberal attitudes and colonial stuffiness. The Mau opposition to New Zealand rule had been provoked by too precipitate a pace of innovation but at its height, in 1931, the Administrator still found time to issue a proclamation regulating the size of mess cuffs to be worn at Government House dinner parties. Powles had no time for such absurdities but he shared the mix of progressive thought and imperial instincts, as McIntosh had warned me.

My work at Government House reflected the same dualism. The work for which I had been sent as External Affairs Officer was that of a New Zealand diplomat, monitoring the final stages of constitutional change and preparing the way for the purely representative New Zealand office which would follow independence in three years' time. Once it was accepted that I was reporting only to the High Commissioner we got on well and not the least of my duties was sitting at Powles's end of the verandah for lengthy periods while we worked over ideas and established a common line. I prepared the High Commissioner's confidential despatches, which became markedly longer as a result, and drafted an increasing flow of cables reporting on events. The office was not equipped for such a flow. After drafting a message I often had to spend an hour ciphering it with the help of a primitive but secure device called the 'one-time pad'. This involved tedious additions and subtractions to convert the text into groups of figures. The resulting message then had to be taken down to the radio station where you handed it through an open window to someone sitting at a Morse key. Garbles were therefore not infrequent but the discipline encouraged me to be as stingy as possible with my words.

Most of our communications went by mail, formerly by the monthly steamer but now by the fortnightly flying-boat from Suva, which stopped for an hour or two on its way to Tahiti. Thick cloud cover sometimes interrupted this in the rainy season. On one occasion the plane was unable to touch down for six weeks. Each time it droned round and round above us looking for a break in the clouds before returning to Suva, with my pay packet as well as all the mail. The Bank of Western Samoa kindly paid my salary anyhow but as the weeks went by I ran out of work as External Affairs Officer. In the end I spent the afternoons playing billiards with the butler, as the showers hammered on the roof and the shirt stuck to my back when I leant to line up a shot.

This was still Government House, however, and there was a certain amount of what might be called 'aide-de-camp' work stemming from age-old practice, ordinances still unrepealed and the fact that there was no one else to do it. I was in no sense a formal aide-de-camp, though Powles had hopefully showed me two dress swords which, since there was no uniform to go with them, I had no difficulty in declining. But I attended the High Commissioner on ceremonial occasions, at meetings of the Council of State and the Executive Council and on his last official visit which was to Savai'i just after the Cabinet had started its work. In form it was to inspect progress in the road being built around the island, in practice it was for Mr and Mrs Powles to have a holiday at Falealupo and they very kindly took me. The High Commissioner and I travelled in the lead Land Rover with flags flying and as we came to each village we would stand up in the back seat and Powles would wave to the people lining both sides of the road. As we resumed our seats each time I remember thinking that my grandchildren will not believe this.

Back at Falealupo in the comfort of the mission house I learnt something else. At night the village gleamed under a full moon which turned the coconut palms silver and the sandy ground white. For much of the night young men strolled about playing guitars and singing softly. Looking down from Father McKay's balcony I thought, the over-worked phrase is right: this is a paradise. But only for a moment. I had been in Samoa long enough to recognise this as a visitor's sentiment. Those young men were bored and longing for the chance to see the lights of Apia, Auckland or any modern city. The enchantments of the age-old way of life, which so delighted the outsider, were no enchantments for them but simply everyday life and one from which many hoped to escape.

This moon, though, marked a great occasion in the Samoan calendar. At the end of the dry season on either the October or November full moon the coral worm released its milt, or tiny eggs, which floated up inside the reef as dark-green strings. These, known as *palolo*, were a great delicacy and eagerly awaited. Only adepts seemed to know which of the two nights the *palolo* would rise, but excited cries from the lagoon told us that this was the night. I stood chest-deep with the *palolo* rising all around me, scooping it up with the only container I had – my hat. The moonlit sea was covered with dark heads bobbing about in pursuit of the drifting eggs and shrieking with the excitement of the chase. Then suddenly it was over: the coral worm had done its reproductive dash for the year. On shore the *palolo* in my hat looked disappointingly like green slime but cooked by the Belgian nuns with a touch of onion and eaten on toast for breakfast it was delicious.

At Vailima the routine of Government House dinners for visiting dignitaries continued – New Zealand ministers, American senators and Cabinet secretaries, Alan Lennox-Boyd, the British Colonial Secretary, and others. My presence at these lunches and dinners was less ornamental than practical. I kept an eye on the dogs. The High Commissioner had two beloved Labradors who were not especially well trained. Ladies who were dressed for the heat at lunches were sometimes startled, while drinking their soup, to feel a cold nose pushed into their thigh. After dinner when the guests sat upstairs in a semi-circle the dogs were prone to add indecent displays to the entertainment. In both cases my unspoken task was to stir them along with a furtive foot.

Then there were the obligatory calls on visiting naval vessels anchored out in Apia Bay. With the New Zealand, Australian and British navies these were hospitable affairs. In the case of one British frigate the call was so sociable that both the captain and I had some difficulty getting down the ship's side and into his launch where we clung to one another as it sped into the wharf. We were on our way to a New Year's Eve ball at Aggie Grey's, a grand affair in the Beach's social calendar. It was the height of the rainy season and a large awning had been put up in the courtyard. The rain poured down and the awning bulged lower and lower. I suggested that it might be prudent to move indoors. Shortly after the awning collapsed, soaking all those guests who had been too tightly packed around the bar to notice.

This proved to be only the beginning of a memorable evening. Aggie had a boarder, Frank Brundle, a remittance man of indeterminate age whom Aggie always referred to respectfully as Major Brundle, although it was never clear in which armed force, if any, he had served. Later opinion was divided as to whether the cause of the trouble was that Frank had not been invited to the ball or that the band had annoyed him. All the same the guests at supper were startled by the appearance of Frank on the landing above them, clad only in brief underpants and shouting, 'Haven't any of you buggers got a home to go to?'

Aggie, who combined raffishness with a strong streak of gentility, immediately expelled Frank and he disappeared from society. Three months later however a hurricane drove some of Aggie's tugs and lighters ashore. Frank Brundle telephoned her, saying that he felt he should say something about her loss. 'That is very kind of you, Major Brundle,' said Aggie warming again. 'Yes, Mrs Grey. What I wanted to say is HA, HA, HA.' After that the Hatfields and McCoys would have sat down together sooner than Aggie Grey and Frank Brundle.

Some visits tested my resources in unexpected ways. The Crown Prince of Tonga, Prince Tungi (later King Taufa'ahau), arrived on the flying-boat and I was despatched to greet and drive with him to Government House. The Prince in his family's tradition was a very substantial young man (his mother the much-loved Queen Salote travelled by sea and had to be lowered from the steamer by crane which, because she was a shy lady, had to be done at night). Although the driver and I wrestled with the seats of the official Oldsmobile it became clear that His Royal Highness could not fit in the back of the car. Protocol had to bow to the facts. We pushed the front seat as far back as it would go and the Prince rode into Apia beside the driver while I crouched in the back with my knees around my ears.

Other occasions were more solemn. In a survival from the pre-war era, the High Commissioner was still the social head of the European community and felt he should be represented at certain funerals. A young man, Shorty Burnett, died from a rugby football injury and the High Commissioner thought I should attend the funeral on his behalf. It was again in the rainy season and a notable feature of the low-lying cemetery at Magiagi was that when the river rose so did some of the departed. When we got to the graveside it proved to be an oblong of muddy yellow water. The vicar peered at it as if uncertain whether or not to read the service for burial at sea. At the moment of committal Shorty's coffin was lowered into the water. We stood mesmerised. The end of the coffin resurfaced. After a pause a respectful foot pushed it back down again. It reappeared. I stood under my umbrella with the rain trickling down my neck, wondering if it were a bad dream. Someone brought a stick and the coffin was submerged for the third time. Back it came. In the end, all propriety abandoned, we were desperately pushing it with sticks and throwing rocks into the water until it disappeared for good.

There were worse moments. The High Commissioner had the power to expel seconded Government officials and those without the right of permanent residence in the Territory for a variety of social or sexual misdemeanours. The practice had its justifications but moral disapproval for 'letting down the side' always lurked in the background. It was an uncomfortable task to call on a broken-down alcoholic or weeping wife to tell them that they should leave on the next steamer. Worst of all was the impending execution of a murderer at Tafaigata prison. As the scaffold was being prepared the High Commissioner decided I should attend as a formal witness. Only the condemned man was more relieved than I when the New Zealand Government commuted his sentence.

Most of these duties centred on that distinctive South Pacific society, the Beach. The Beach was a geological record of all the waves of immigration which had broken on Samoa in European times. There were the descendants of traders and missionaries from the past century who had settled and married Samoan wives. There was still a handful of drifters and remittance men who had followed the earlier beachcombers. There were Chinese and their part-Samoan children, exporters and shopkeepers where, if you ate with the family, you could buy a good Chinese meal. There were two big trading houses, both Australian-owned, and smaller copra exporters. Recurrent booms in cocoa and coffee had built up a community of planters, often New Zealand or German, who had bought or leased land in the interior but who lived in or frequently visited Apia.

Although Germany had governed Western Samoa for only fourteen years until displaced by New Zealand troops in 1914, there was still a sizeable German or part-German community running businesses and plantations. Most of them had long ago accepted the change in their status. One of them, Alfred Jahnke, had as a young man conducted the Kaiser around the Berlin Botanical Gardens. He told me that one night three or so weeks after the New Zealand occupation he was awakened by a thunderous knocking on the door of his plantation house down the coast from Apia. On his verandah stood two German naval officers and eight ratings from the heavy cruisers *Scharnhorst* and *Gneisenau* which were lying out well beyond the reef. In response to their question Alfred confirmed that the New Zealanders had landed and taken control soon after war had broken out. The officers proposed that the cruisers move in and bombard Apia. Alfred said that he argued against: if, as they hoped, Germany won the war Western Samoa would be better restored to it intact; and if Germany did not win the war there would have been no point in destroying Apia anyway. The officers returned to their ship which sailed away towards Chile and the battle of Coronel without, Alfred thought, anyone else having been aware of their visit.*

Others were less reconciled. Some had been Nazi sympathisers in the thirties and when war again broke out in 1939 several were interned in New Zealand. A few young men, whether from conviction or because they were students in Germany, found themselves in the German Army. In my first weeks I sat next to one at dinner and was surprised when he told me where he had been taken prisoner – Stalingrad.

The Beach was an entity distinct from Samoan society proper, though increasingly tied to it by marriage and the taking of titles. It was intimate and gossipy. Even the telephone operator when you gave a number would sometimes say, 'Oh, he's not in. I just saw him going into the Bank.' It was also divided by ancient enmities and new ones created by the rapid change in Samoan politics. Many of the German community had, from resentment of New Zealand rule, identified themselves with the cause of Samoan freedom. The political core of this group was the Nelson family whose patriarch had been O. F. Nelson, champion of Samoan self-determination since the 1920s, and twice exiled to New Zealand. Early in my stay I was invited to tea by his daughter Olive and was shocked by her bitterness towards New Zealand. But her husband, Fred Betham (whose given names, Gustav Frederik Dertag, showed how his parents felt), had moved into mainstream politics, with the encouragement of Tamasese who was himself Nelson's son-in-law. Tamasese had inherited the leadership of Samoan nationalism from his dead brother but his marriage and political skill enlisted this Beach faction in the wider cause.

They were pleased by the accelerating political change, if still not quite convinced of New Zealand's good faith. It was the turn of the other and larger Beach grouping – the businessmen and planters, many of partly Samoan descent – to become alarmed. They were comfortable with the colonial system and saw their economic interests and social position threatened by the changes. So they were critical of New Zealand for, as they saw it, weakly giving in to anti-colonial sentiment and running away from its responsibilities.

This being Samoa their fears were made known in a fairly gentle way, not on the streets but around the bar of the Apia and Returned

---

* The ships caused some consternation by appearing briefly off Apia Bay.

Servicemen's Clubs where much of the Beach gathered in the evenings. The doors of the RSA were hospitably wide, perhaps because members of both wartime sides were admitted, so there was no difficulty in welcoming those like me who had no military service at all.

Liquor had been officially banned since the beginning of the League of Nations mandate in 1919 when the prohibition movement in New Zealand was at its height. Strict observance of the ban, however, would have made Beach life impossible. The fiction grew up that a supply of drink was essential to the health of those who had not been born in the tropics. According to this alleged medical need 'points' were allocated to members of the European and part-Samoan community. The pretence grew increasingly thin as those whose parents and grandparents had been born in the Territory still needed this medical attention and by my time the points were issued, not by a doctor, but by the Commissioner of Police. My ration was twelve points a month, equivalent to a case of beer or a bottle of whisky. If you needed more for any occasion informal access was not difficult to arrange.

Nightly conversation in the RSA was far from being obsessive about politics. But I was the only person from Government House living on the Beach and naturally became the target of occasional arguments. Some of these were schoolboy jokes about the High Commissioner, inevitable in a place which he had governed as a benign headmaster. Some were sharper complaints about New Zealand's motives and competence. With acquaintances around the bar it stayed good-humoured and, aware of how these views were enfolded within a wider Samoa, I was not tempted to over-estimate their importance. Those on brief visits, especially journalists, were more impressed by the pessimistic predictions of corruption and trouble after independence. Newspapers at home, in Australia and as far away as the *Manchester Guardian* began to run stories about Samoa's unreadiness and New Zealand's excessive haste to rid itself of its colonial burden. Wellington fortunately gave no sign of any second thoughts.

I was still living in my flat at the back of the Casino, under a spreading mango tree which in the season kept up an intermittent bombardment on the tin roof above my bed. Our engagement was carried on by mail, unduly preoccupied it seems now by talk of mail dates, missed mails and letters out of sequence. It was clear by now that the wedding would be in Apia. Not only was Julie's mother still opposed but by an unhappy chance our fathers, both Christchurch lawyers, were at slight odds over the

'Mower' case, litigation over some agricultural machinery which achieved modest notoriety as the longest-running case in Commonwealth legal history. The coming months were the wet season but kind Mrs Powles, who took a deep interest, declared that the weather in February would be excellent for a wedding.

There remained the difficulty of finding a house. There was no market in Apia for rental houses. Mrs Powles, Auntie Mary and I all cast about for leads but as the year turned I became increasingly anxious. Inability to provide a house would not be an auspicious start for a new son-in-law. At length the Wesleyan Church came to the rescue. An aged planter had gone back to Sydney to die and had left his house and twenty-acre coconut plantation on the Vailima road to the church.

The house, at Papauta, was a rambling ancient bungalow raised on piles ten feet above the ground and reached by a long, rutted drive through the overgrown plantation. It stood in a little community of its own. At the edge of the lawn, where the coconut palms began, three or four *fales* had been built for Samoan pastors and their families. The cheerful noise of children in the morning and of evening hymns at sundown gave a taste of village life.

Like many of its age the house had grown successive layers of rooms like a nautilus shell. It had started eighty or so years before as a small house but the heat had driven the inhabitants to live on the wide verandahs which over time had become incorporated in the house. In the old style the kitchen was built separate from the house, reached by a gangway. It had no stove or hot water, and the only furniture was a few Edwardian pieces that no one had bothered to take. It had stood empty for two years because, everyone assured me, it was haunted.

I took it – there was no alternative – and no newlyweds ever lived in a more absurd or romantic house. The living-room was fifty feet long and the bedroom was another converted verandah which looked into the palm trees. There were so many rooms that despite such extravagances as having two dressing-rooms there were several rooms that were never entered and another long room down to the kitchen which remained totally bare and was referred to as 'the ballroom'. The bathroom contained just that, a bath, which was rarely used since hot water had to be carried in by the housegirls and once the External Affairs Officer was in the bath only his wife could adjust the temperature. The lavatory was a delight: a trellised outwork at the side, covered with honeysuckle through which the bees and an occasional bird would dart. Some months later the pan, fortunately unoccupied at the time, fell through the floor and for the rest of our time rested placidly on the ground below.

The house had not been painted since Queen Victoria's time and it was clearly necessary to smarten it up. I bought some paint, gathered two young men from Vailima and in a day, though badly bitten by mosquitoes, managed to turn the front of the house and as much of the side as you could see from the drive a gleaming white with pale blue window frames. The rest of the house, unseen by visitors, stayed its ancient colour. That, repairing the mosquito-netting that covered the floor-to-ceiling windows, and buying a primitive kerosene stove completed my wedding preparations.

At the beginning of February 1960 I flew in an Air Force Sunderland flying-boat to the Tokelau Islands, three atolls under the Equator which were administered by the High Commissioner in Apia. We spent the night at the priest's house on Nukunono where he and the Tokelauan nuns hospitably spent all the fresh food we had brought on a feast for us. My contribution was a bottle of Vat 69 and my assurance that it was the Pope's telephone number kept the French priest chuckling at intervals all night. I slept on my back on the floor and whether or not it was generous resort to the papal number I seemed to have no sooner fallen asleep than the priest was shaking me awake to attend Mass. It was 4.30 and totally dark but the whole village was assembled in the church, a special kneeler adorned with fine mats had been placed for me, and I realised what a scandal there would have been if I had yielded to my baser instincts.

Learning that I was about to be married the villagers loaded the plane with the prized Tokelauan mats which would help cover even the broad floors of the Papauta house. Then we took off for Atafu, another of the atolls, where the Air Force wished to make the first landing in the inner lagoon. From the air the atoll looked like a turquoise jewel set in a green and gold ring. It also looked rather small. The plane splashed down without difficulty but getting off was another matter. I was kneeling in the gangway between the two pilots and looking out of the windscreen. The plane set off at a slow walking pace and by the time we were in the middle of the lagoon, with all four engines roaring and straining, we had only been able to reach a shambling trot. The palm trees on the other side became increasingly distinct until I could see the individual fronds. The plane still showed no inclination to leave the water. Just as it seemed inevitable that we would crash across the spit and into the ocean beyond the aircraft lifted off and the trees shot away beneath us. As I was busy reassuring myself that the situation had been in hand all along the co-pilot pushed back his cap and headphones and uttered a single word, 'Christ'. No further efforts were made to land a Sunderland at Atafu.

Two weeks later I met Julie in Pago Pago. Reunited after six months we walked along the waterfront in brilliant moonlight. A coconut fell thirty feet and brushed the back of our heads, the first of two lucky escapes that month. A week later we were married in the Cathedral at Mulivai. Mary Croudace and the Children of Mary (though diminished by pregnancies and other lapses) had decorated the church exuberantly with palm fronds, hangings of *tapa* cloth and fine mats on the floor. There was no music as the former organist waited at the altar while the bride and her father were driven down from Vailima. The bishop had decided against officiating at an inter-denominational marriage but hoped he could come to the reception anyway. Tamasese and Ash Levestam, the Secretary to the Government, were the witnesses and the congregation, apart from my parents and Julie's father and uncle, were from official and Beach society.

We drove back up the hill for the reception, which was held in the Vailima ballroom, the open sides of which were also covered with palm fronds and hibiscus flowers. At one end was a long table graced by an enormous pig (a gift from the butler), as was proper at Samoan weddings. Throughout the day heavy squalls had swept in from the sea and up the hill. Rain was pounding on the roof as the bride and groom welcomed a line of aged chiefs, most of whom congratulated us warmly on choosing such a good day. This was not irony but the widespread Polynesian view that rain is a promise of fertility. Subsequent events did not prove them wrong. After speeches by the High Commissioner and Tamasese, to which I listened and replied in a daze, we opened the Samoan dancing and then, leaving the pig to the guests, departed.

Our honeymoon of a few days was spent in a cottage on the sea past the flying-boat base, lent to us by the Samoan government's Trust Estates Corporation which managed the German government's plantations seized years before. Our first day of married life saw the second lucky escape. We went for a swim in the lagoon which was here very wide and murky with stirred-up sand. Julie called out to me that she had stood on a bicycle tyre earlier and received a cut which was beginning to hurt. A bicycle tyre was about as probable in this distant spot as a ball gown. It was more likely that she had stood on a sea-snake and when we came out of the water there were indeed two toothmarks on her leg. The extent of my knowledge was that there were two types of sea-snake in these waters; one highly venomous but with jaws too narrow to inject the poison easily, and the other not venomous at all. I had not seen the snake and we were an hour from the hospital. We sat on the running-board of the Land Rover while I tried to calculate the chances of getting to the medical kit at the airport. Suddenly I realised that we were still chatting comfortably and, overcome with relief, I told Julie what had happened. A few days later, anxious to start our real life, we moved into the house at Papauta.

By now Cabinet government was well established and though Mata'afa was troubled by a painful arthritic gout his political leadership was much surer. Reviews of Cabinet decisions were less frequent and the two *Fautua* were adjusting to their roles as future Heads of State. The time had come for Powles to move on. He felt himself that he had done all he could and from the constitutional point of view his weight of experience and firmness of character was almost a disadvantage as the new rulers struggled to fill his place. He was appointed as New Zealand's diplomatic representative to India and later knighted. When he and Mrs Powles left the Territory in March his farewell speech on the wharf, warning the new leaders that their personal behaviour must meet the standards of public life, was felt by some to be a little blunt for Samoan practice but the Beach had softened. The *Samoa Bulletin*, not always an admirer, said that he left 'holding the deep respect of the Samoan people and honoured as have been few administrators before him'.

It was difficult to know how to replace him. There was no politician or official in New Zealand who could match his sureness of knowledge in these last delicate years of trusteeship. However, on a coffee plantation in the hills behind Apia there was such a person and Tamasese was the first to suggest him. Jack Wright had been Secretary of Island Territories some years earlier and his wife was the niece of both Mary Croudace and Aggie Grey. Jack had a natural scepticism about everything, including self-government, but he had a shrewd judgement and was respected by everyone in Samoa. That is, by everyone except his aunts. Aggie would sit with a glass in her hand reminiscing about the grandeur of past governors and then her voice would tail off: 'Now it's my nephew Jack'.

At first Jack Wright stayed as much as possible on his plantation – 'the recluse of Potoga', Powles called him. Standing in as Acting High Commissioner in the last few months whenever Powles was away, he would come down in the morning, check that everything was in order at Vailima and then go home. This led to my only term of office. Jack had to go away on a family matter and it was no longer possible for any of the senior officials or judges in the Samoan Government to step in as in the past. After a hurried consultation with the Chief Judge I was given a commission as Acting High Commissioner with instructions to keep it in a drawer of my desk and tell no one unless absolutely necessary.

For ten days I sat on the verandah in executive splendour visible only to myself. There was no crisis, not even a meeting of the Council of State, only a few passports and immigration documents to sign. But I did issue a proclamation. It was in full style: 'To all to whom these presents come, Greeting' and ended with a stirring 'God Save the Queen!' In between, rather disappointingly, it simply fixed the date of the races at Saleloga – a duty which the Attorney-General said could not be delayed.

As the Powles sailed out of the bay Jack Wright was sworn in as the last High Commissioner of Western Samoa and, although everyone including himself regarded it as a stopgap, he was also to become New Zealand's first diplomatic representative to the newly independent state and to take his eye off the coffee for nearly five years. His ironic sense of humour sharpened our reporting, his knowledge of the Pacific going back to the end of the war meant that he had sources of information unavailable to other New Zealanders, and his quiet good sense was perfect for the twilight of New Zealand power.

The Working Committee on Self-Government, which as a matter of principle neither the High Commissioner nor his staff attended, had made good progress over the past year in drafting a constitution. The future relationship with New Zealand had still to be addressed but most other important issues had been dealt with, including the suffrage which, it was decided, should continue to be confined to *matai* or heads of families. The June meeting of the Trusteeship Council in New York had passed a raft of resolutions commending progress towards independence but it was uncomfortable about the restricted suffrage. So were some in Wellington. Others thought it was the business of the Samoans and not of outsiders. Either way the fact was that New Zealand's power to make significant changes had already gone. Although representatives in

New York were questioning whether trusteeship could be ended on the basis of *matai* suffrage it was an issue which would have to be sorted out between the United Nations and the Samoan government.

In the last week of June 1960, as constitution drafting entered its last stages, Frank Corner flew from Wellington to discuss the proposed Treaty of Friendship. At a meeting with Tamasese the night before he made it clear that the independence being offered was no legal fiction and that the form of its future relationship with New Zealand would be of Samoa's own choosing. Tamasese wept and said, 'At last I trust New Zealand'.

Since the abandonment of the Tongan solution the shape of the proposed Treaty of Friendship had evolved considerably. New Zealand had moved from *control* of external affairs to accepting responsibility for the *conduct* of them; now it was offering an *agency*, enabling independent Samoa to use New Zealand services and offices abroad to handle its own international affairs. This would allow Apia to develop overseas relationships at its own pace, and progressively to take over more and more of the administration when it felt ready. At the Working Committee the next day Frank explained the agency concept and suggested that a short and simple Treaty was all that was required. There was some concern about how firmly New Zealand would be locked in by this. He was questioned about rights of immigration, secondments and continued aid but the Committee agreed that goodwill rather than detailed drafting language was the best safeguard of these.

The last major issue was the suffrage. The United Nations had accepted that the Samoan leadership was immovable on *matai* voting. But in turn it was insisting that a plebiscite, based on universal adult suffrage, be held to adopt the constitution. This caused some heartburning in the Working Committee, which accepted it reluctantly as 'the gateway to freedom' through which the country had to pass before returning to the traditional Samoan way. Some of the more far-sighted understood that the gate, once opened, could not be nailed shut again.

In August a Constitutional Convention began consideration of the draft. It was chaired jointly by Tamasese and Malietoa and had 173 members drawn from the Legislative Assembly with three additional members elected by each Samoan constituency. The European voters, some of whom were disgruntled and others indifferent, failed to elect their full number. Its task was not so much to improve upon the Working

Committee's drafting as to win national understanding and acceptance of the text. The timing was tight; the constitution had to be in the hands of the UN General Assembly by the middle of November to enable the necessary decision to be taken for a plebiscite and the end of trusteeship a year later.

The Convention met in the Assembly *fale* at Mulinu'u. It was a round building with a high thatched roof and open sides, cooled by the trade wind blowing in from the glittering sea nearby. As New Zealand Observer I sat at a desk in the outermost ring beside the ancient kava bowl round which members gathered during breaks. There, thumbing through a copy of Pratt's *Dictionary of the Samoan Language*, I listened to the debates each morning, trying to interpret the allusive nature of chiefly oratory. This was a study in itself, with a vocabulary distinct from ordinary Samoan and sequences of ceremonial phrases. The context came to give me the meaning of otherwise impenetrable proverbs: 'the tropic bird exposes his breastbone' (the last speaker is a fool); 'it is near the time when the sun touches the banana leaves' (the deadline is drawing near).

In many ways the Convention proved to be the last grand outing of the traditional Samoan politics. Most members had never sat in a parliamentary assembly before but they had all spent years in village councils where debate continued until a consensus was reached and a day could go placidly by discussing the trespasses of a pig. This, coupled with members' sense of the historic importance of the Convention and their determination to make a contribution, made it difficult for the chairmen to hasten the pace. Samoan custom frowned on going baldly into an issue and some of the older representatives embarked on a full ceremonial introduction, thanking the royal sons of Samoa, the advisers, the Working Committee, the traditional districts, and all the principal titles sitting in the House, until their speaking-time had expired. They then sat down proudly, feeling that they had made a dignified and proper contribution. Others took up their full time to announce, with liberal quotations from Scripture and compliments to the draftsmen, their agreement with the article under discussion.

The High Commissioner in opening the sittings had stressed the need to meet the UN deadline and the chairmen frequently reminded them. 'Let us hasten on,' urged one old chief, 'and finish our journey before we are caught in the rain.' But members were conscious of an even higher duty: to understand every detail before giving their approval. It was their constitution, to be explained, lauded and defended back in their districts, and to do this thoroughly was bound to take time. The only answer was longer sitting hours into the afternoons. The key to this, acknowledged without embarrassment by the founding fathers, was more pay. There were sceptics who argued that most of the elderly members had slept every afternoon for years and would continue to do so in the Convention but be paid for it instead. Others feared that members would use the extra hours to talk more than ever. But longer hours were adopted.

The task of guiding such an inexperienced gathering and coping with the multiple procedural tangles was handled well by the joint Chairmen. Without firm direction the Convention was prone to wallow helplessly in its own oratory. To the surprise of some, Malietoa proved to be the better. Although relying much on the advisers, he handled proceedings with great tact and courtesy. The relaxed way in which he rebuked the verbose and encouraged the diffident kept tempers in check. Tamasese, on the other hand, was familiar with every detail from his work in the Committee but was prone to impatience with some members' doubts and had a tendency to push matters along with un-Samoan bluntness.

Representatives from outlying districts were scrupulous in their examination of every article to ensure that Samoan custom was adequately safeguarded. The most anxious concern was with the rights of village chiefs and orators, the *ali'i* and *faipule*. Like children's conjurors speakers could draw the position of the *ali'i* and *faipule* with equal ingenuity out of the article defining the state and another permitting soil conservation. When considering an article with which it was not especially familiar the Convention tended to talk round it until someone could extract a point on which all had a view – as like as not the *ali'i* and *faipule*. This vigilance about chiefly rights was felt to be essential to ensure the unique Samoanness of the constitution. Such articulate conservatism was in fact a form of nationalism. Members wished to see the *ali'i* and *faipule* recognised, traditional forms honoured, for the same reason that they wept when the royal sons of Samoa spoke – because these things were at the heart of their society, their traditions and their patriotism.

Discussions could veer in unpredictable ways. Capital punishment took up two or three days, with the conservatives tending to oppose it on the grounds that it was unChristian, while progressives like Tamasese and the Prime Minister favoured it as the best protection for life. The article on religious toleration caused another delay. Members, it became apparent, favoured toleration provided no one used it. The entry of foreign missionaries, especially Mormons, became an issue. From the chair Tamasese argued for toleration ('If God has given men freedom of conscience who are we to take it away?') but he was overridden by the dubious argument that preventing the entry of foreign religions did not interfere with anyone's freedom of conscience. In the end both articles were passed as drafted on the understanding that the Legislative Assembly would look into the issues.

The suffrage took more time. An amendment was introduced providing for universal adult suffrage on the ground that it was better to make the concession now than from force later on. Debate was not lively except from one or two of the European members who were regarded (with some justification) as more than a little eccentric. The conservative country gentlemen at Mulinu'u, like their English counterparts in the 1780s, were at first not greatly interested. The franchise had always been restricted and as far as they were concerned it always would be, and talk of revolution seemed meaningless. Now that the issue had been raised, however, they were tempted to settle it once and for all by locking the chiefly franchise into the constitution. In the end the discussion was closed by Malietoa with a memorable analogy which deflected any such wishes. Every season, he said, a fresh stick is cut to knock down the breadfruit. The stick of Samoan custom is too green to be broken, but the next generation may wish to cut a fresh stick and reshape the electoral system to suit themselves. His words were prophetic.

Given the conservative bent of the Convention the most delicate issue of all was the Head of State. As Mata'afa said when introducing the draft, the peace and unity of Samoa depended on it – everyone was aware that the rivalry among the high titles had opened the way for European control at the end of the nineteenth century. Tamasese and Malietoa were to be joint Heads of State for their lifetimes but thereafter there was the position of two other royal titles to consider. Mata'afa underlined this in an indirect but unmistakable way: 'When Ulu is swollen Vaisigano floods'. Ulu is a small tributary of the Vaisigano, the river which flows into Apia Bay. In other words, whatever was decided would affect him also. The Convention was tempted by other possibilities but in the end it endorsed the text providing that after the lifetime of the present *Fautua* the office of Head of State would be held by one of the royal titles every five years.

Towards the end of the Convention Frank Corner arrived as the special envoy of the New Zealand Prime Minister and addressed the gathering on 12 October. He praised the constitution under which Samoa would become the first independent Polynesian state, talked about the responsibilities of independence and outlined thinking on the Treaty of Friendship. The Convention was happy with this. In fact, after all the talk, it made no important changes to the draft text. I produced copies of the completed document for a ceremonial signing by the Council of State and the gathering disbanded.

While all this was going on the household at Papauta had settled into a domestic routine. There was a Labrador, Tasi, who had been bequeathed by the Powles. His fall from office as First Dog did not seem to trouble him but he occasionally returned, on nights when there were important dinners at Government House, to mingle with the guests and put everyone at their ease. There was also a cat, Henry Wendt, called after our plumber who was equally shy about coming when called. Henry had lived wild in the plantation but when he saw that the house was open again he gradually resumed his domestic ways. The henhouse had been repaired by the brother of the Government House driver ('My brother does not accept payment') who also stocked it with seven hens. Of involuntary livestock we had a large number of plantation rats who in the evenings held noisy races up and down the living-room ceiling. They plagued the kitchen where, if you opened a cupboard, there were often one or more rats, not always dead. They besieged the henhouse to the point that if you did not hasten when an egg was signalled you might find it cheerfully being rolled away by two rats.

Despite this the house had a charm. We often dined by candlelight, though less for romantic reasons than that the power had a tendency to fail in the evenings. Wedding presents had leant towards the impractical. We had silver candlesticks, a silver teapot and dozens of silver teaspoons (which were more easily sent by mail), but not much in the way of kitchenware. Furniture was an eclectic mix of cast-offs and occasionally the white ants would cause a chair-leg to vanish in a puff of dust. There was still no hot water supply but after six months External Affairs had sent us an electric stove. Yet it was in fact a prolonged honeymoon, an improvised life. What stayed in the mind were not the shortcomings like the collapse of the lavatory or finding your shoes had turned green with mould overnight but the sound of rain hissing up the hill and then roaring on the tin roof; the palm trees outside the windows giving a dry rattle in the trade wind or glistening silver in the moonlight; the smell of the gardenia hedge under the windows and of the cooking fires from the Samoan houses in the plantation; the prickling taste of a drink straight from a coconut or the sweetness of a ripe, deep-yellow pineapple.

In December our daughter Caroline was born. It was not an easy birth. The doctor had gone to the Tokelaus and the hospital on Boxing Day was virtually deserted as everyone recovered from the parties. The baby was the wrong way round and it was a long labour which Julie and I seemed to be managing more or less on our own. But the doctor arrived at the critical moment and in the middle of the next afternoon I was looking at a child with a purple and yellow complexion and deep violet eyes and thinking, 'This child will see me buried'. Life seemed to have lurched on a generation and at twenty-five years of age this was my first intimation of mortality. There was enough champagne left over from the wedding to fuel some general rejoicing and I set off to acquaint the Council of State. Malietoa said that he would give her a Samoan name, To'oa. I did not grasp the significance of this until reporting it to Chief Judge Marsack who said that this was the senior woman's title in the family, currently held by Malietoa's eminent sister, Salamasina. When I went back to thank Malietoa he said that he had consulted the family who had agreed to split the title. So the birth was registered as To'oa Caroline and the champagne was stretched even further.

Then ghost trouble struck. Ghost stories are a staple of all Polynesian societies. Stevenson who told (or invented) some of the best thought that this fear of the dead came from distant memories of cannibalism: if you could eat the dead they could perhaps eat you. The stories I encountered in Samoa were rather less horrifying. There was even Stevenson's own ghost which could once be heard pacing up and down at Vailima. Regrettably a hard-headed Scot who was living in the house climbed into the ceiling and found a sawhorse left behind by the builders in the late 1880s. A long plank was resting on it and as the rats walked up it produced the tapping sound of footsteps. When the plank was moved the ghost walked no more.

A week after Caroline came home the new housegirl, Leva, said that she had woken in the middle of the night to see a woman leaning over the end of her bed, watching her. We had had a dinner party the previous evening for the new pilot of Polynesian Airlines, an Australian bush pilot who was improbably also an English baronet. I suggested she had seen his wife who may have got lost on the winding way to the lavatory. But Leva insisted that it was a Samoan woman, dressed completely in white and with short hair.

My suspicions were aroused; this sounded like a conventional ghost description. There was a sad story attached to the house. When the old planter had left to go to Sydney the housegirl who had been with them for fifty years was to go too. At the last minute it was decided not to take her and she hanged herself under the house. It was because of this that everyone had tried to convince me that the house was haunted, but ten months' occupancy had not turned up the least evidence. I concluded that people in the plantation had been telling the new girl the story. All the same it seemed worth checking a few details with the granddaughter of the old planter.

When Julie raised the subject cautiously, she said, 'Has Mary come back? I'm not surprised, she was crazy about babies.' Julie dismissed this but enquired about Mary's appearance. It seemed she always wore white. Her hair? Long and worn in a plait in the traditional Samoan way, said Gwen, then corrected herself: it had been cut short when Mary was to go to Sydney. This proved nothing other than the length of people's memories, but it was not helpful, nor was the fact that for the next five nights something unusual happened in the house, at one stage even the dog began to whimper. Household stability was threatened – if we lost our domestic help we would be unlikely to find replacements.

So the next evening for the first time I locked both the front and back doors of the house. The open windows all had metal netting nailed over them. I pointed out to Leva that no one could get in or out. If anyone had been wandering through the house at nights they could no longer do so. Later that night, as I was drafting a report for Wellington Leva passed me with her best red dress which she had ironed and was putting back in her old room, though she refused to sleep there herself.

I went to sleep with the house keys in my hand under the pillow. One or two squalls of rain woke me during the night but otherwise all was peaceful. First thing in the morning I pointed this out to Leva. Wordlessly she pointed to her old room. Outside the window and level with it was the red dress, spread neatly over a tall hibiscus bush. The house was still locked (I had the key in my hand) and I was left wordless myself. The hibiscus was soft and twelve feet high; the dress could only have been spread from a ladder but there were no marks and no footprints in the muddy ground. We sent for the priest who had married us and who had good Samoan. He said the girl was deeply worried and if we had any further trouble he would come and exorcise the house. Thereafter the odd happenings ceased as suddenly as they had started, leaving me only with a nagging bafflement as to how the red dress was moved.

At the beginning of February 1961 elections were held for a new Legislative Assembly. The date itself was a confirmation that the new institutions were working well. A few months earlier Cabinet had been attracted by the thought of prolonging the Assembly's life (and its own) by a year past the due date. This would have set a dubious precedent for the new state and in any case the eve of independence did not seem the best time for elections. The Council of State called for a review and Cabinet, a little abashed, backed down. Otherwise political life after the Convention was smooth. The Prime Minister took a relaxed view of defeats in the House but his authority when he cared to exercise it was unquestioned. Despite earlier fears the move to the sidelines by the future Heads of State was accepted gracefully by them. And by everyone else. When a ceremonial welcome took place on the wharf to greet the returning Prime Minister in January the organisers forgot to invite the Council of State – who came anyway.

The electoral law prescribed the standard Westminster arrangements but these were heavily modified by Samoan custom. The 'European' electorate, now predominantly part-Chinese, stayed with sitting members. A significant number of the Samoan seats were uncontested but this reflected not electoral apathy but the pre-eminent claims of a particular title-holder in those districts. Perhaps because of the interest aroused by the Constitutional Convention there were an unusual number of contests and because of the small number of chiefly voters (typically around eighty) many of them resembled Charles Dickens's account of the Eatanswill election. In Savai'i an able but erratic minister was being challenged by Harry Moors (son of Stevenson's friend of the same name) and it was said that the electors had dined at the expense of both candidates for nearly three months. Moors won and elsewhere there was the traditional high turnover as those who had had their turn gave way to other claimants. My friend Papali'i Poumau, who had been awarded an MBE, advertised that he had the confidence of the Queen but did not win that of the voters.

There was the usual clutter of petitions and irregularities to be cleared up afterwards by the court. One candidate remembered that a valued voter was in prison. A taxi was despatched with a change of clothing to replace the rather distinctive striped *lavalava* worn by the inmates, he was whisked down to vote and replaced without discovery. The vote though was disallowed.

The Assembly which ushered in independence was moderately con-servative. There were few members who did not have some parliamen-tary experience, in the Convention if not in previous Assemblies. The new Cabinet was not greatly changed, with Fred Betham, who had topped the 'European' poll, becoming Minister of Finance. Five of the new ministers were part-Samoans who had taken titles, suggesting that the old prejudices against '*afi-kasi*' were breaking down and integration was proceeding smoothly.

There was, however, a hitch over the position of the Prime Minister. The future constitution laid down that a fresh vote should be held by the Assembly after each election. The current law was silent. The Council of State was divided for the only time in its short history. Tamasese wished a ballot; the High Commissioner encouraged by me thought that the Prime Minister continued in office unless or until the Assembly decided otherwise. Mata'afa then entered the fray by arguing that if he stepped down for a ballot people would think he wanted to retire. Telegraphic consultations with the learned did not help and in the end the Secretary to the Government and I drafted a compromise paper which was read out to the Assembly. There was no ballot.

The way was now clear for the final hurdle on the path to indepen-dence – the plebiscite. In Wellington the government was inconveniently defeated in a general election at the end of the year. However, the new Prime Minister, Sir Keith Holyoake, wrote even before taking office to both Jack Wright and Mata'afa assuring them that there would be no change in New Zealand's Samoa policy. In December, despite arguments by both the New Zealand and Samoan representatives, the UN General Assembly had also reaffirmed its policy: if trusteeship was to be ended there would have to be a plebiscite.

The task of organising publicity, of preparing and delivering infor-mation material to the remotest villages, arranging polling places and returning officers, and even of compiling electoral rolls where universal suffrage had never existed was a formidable one. At the end of January 1961 the Plebiscite Administrator appointed by New Zealand arrived to begin work. He was Cyril McKay, another former Secretary of Island Territories. A hard-working man, he complained in the early weeks that he was finding it hard to stir the interest of either ministers or the Samoan bureaucracy.

Preparations were further set back by a hurricane in March. Samoa was in the hurricane belt and, at a time of international tension over Samoa, there had been a famous hurricane in 1889. British, American and German warships had all been anchored in Apia Bay. None was willing to leave before the others until all were trapped and only HMS *Calliope* (her wheel still preserved in the Apia courthouse) had been able to inch out against the rising wind. The rest were wrecked with considerable loss of life and the remains of the German gunboat *Adler* still rested on the inner reef.

When the storm warning became final we closed the office at Vailima and shifted as much as possible out of the verandah. Down on the Beach a lone New Zealand frigate had put out to sea. The sky had a livid tinge and the sea that peculiar leaden colour which foretells a hurricane. I returned to the house to get it ready. In fact there was not much that could be done about a house that stood on posts with tall windows that could no longer be shut. I walked over to the *fale*s in the plantation to suggest to the pastors that they were welcome to take refuge with us – it was by no means certain that the house would hold up but it was stronger and better enclosed than the flimsy *fale*s. My Samoan was inadequate, I did not know the word for hurricane and was reduced to repeating 'big wind' and making circular motions with my hand. This pantomime was watched with silent bafflement by the two pastors until comprehension dawned and one of them said patiently to me, 'urrigan'.

Everyone then waited quietly for the storm. The Apia radio station added to the jitters by playing mournful and dirge-like music until Julie rang and suggested something more cheerful. For a brief period the radio burst into jaunty song until the power failed and we were into it. The house proved to be protected a little by the plantation and we could keep a dim light with two hurricane lamps. The howl of the wind and din of the rain made conversation impossible unless we shouted in each other's ear. The night was blacker than any I had known but flashes of lightning showed the palms whipping and thrashing, at times bending almost horizontal. It seemed only a matter of time before one or more would come down on the house.

Sometime towards the middle of the night a door in the kitchen began to break loose. I groped along the 'ballroom' to try and secure it and to my dismay stepped on something soft. In the next flash I saw a pair of frightened brown eyes looking up at me – the children from the plantation were lying in two neat rows down the room.

In the morning, though there was still driving rain, the wind began to drop. The full force of the wind had been felt further down the coast and we had escaped fairly well. Trees were down all along the drive and the henhouse had left along with its late inhabitants. But our house and the surrounding *fales* were largely undamaged. So was Vailima though the trees in the teak avenue which had survived an earlier storm were much battered. In the course of the next few days life gradually returned to normal and preparations for the vote resumed.

The UN appointed a Syrian, Najmuddine Rifai, to be Plebiscite Commissioner and he arrived in the middle of April. He complained to me that his first stroll along the Beach road had been an unhappy one. Thinking to take an informal poll he asked a number of passersby for their views on independence and received some strongly worded negatives. He wondered if he had been brought out under false pretences. I explained to him the difference between the Beach and the rest of the Territory, though I felt that even so he had been unlucky in his choice of respondents. Then there was the maverick district of Falealili, which initially refused to enrol on the grounds that they disapproved of the plebiscite and wished to remain with New Zealand. At Lufilufi the people would not enrol because the returning officer had no standing in the village and had been outspoken in his support. These and other local resentments led to some alarmist newspaper reports. Despite them we had no doubt that there would be a substantial 'yes' vote approving both independence and the constitution – even on the Beach. The only doubtful point was the size of this majority.

There was a heavy turnout on 9 May. People flocked to the polls in a festival atmosphere. Tamasese, voting at the Apia Courthouse in an aloha shirt, was embarrassed to find himself in a dignified queue of men and women in their Sunday best. When the poll was counted, 80 per cent of those registered, spread fairly evenly across the Territory, had voted in favour. The vote for the constitution was slightly larger than that for independence, for which the Samoan word *tutoatasi*, or 'standing alone', had lingering connotations of loneliness, but overall the outcome vindicated those who had argued that a plebiscite was hardly necessary.

Just before the vote we had left Samoa. A few weeks earlier the office secretary had handed me a partially decoded telegram, claiming she was needed elsewhere. It said, 'We have it in mind that Hensley should be posted to . . .' In my excitement I subtracted where I should have added on the wretched one-time pad but finally the next words came: New York. I was to go to our UN Mission to help see Samoa through the final formalities of trusteeship and then to work on the colonial issues which were taking up an increasing amount of the General Assembly's time.

We plunged into a round of packing and farewells. The space under the house was littered with packing cases and wood shavings, through which the remaining hens scratched. Weeks later when we unpacked we found they had laid in the cases and two Samoan eggs had travelled all the way to Manhattan. The cat was relocated to Vailima. Years of isolation in the plantation had persuaded Henry that he was the last, or possibly the only, cat in the world. The sight of three others at Government House was a considerable shock. He had to rethink his entire cosmology and retired under the house for three days while he did so.

For Tasi it was the end. The Powles had given him to me with the stipulation that he was to be put down when we left. He was buried under the avocado tree (the oldest in Samoa) beside the house. The funeral was a dignified one: in silent sympathy I was joined at the grave by no less than three pastors and their families who gave a fine mat to wrap the dog in. Immediately after I had to go down to a farewell reception. Tamasese noticed that I was saddened. When I explained he put his hand on my arm and said, 'I had a pig once . . .'

We moved back into the Casino and said good-bye to Mary Croudace and the Beach community in a last fizz of parties. Then the plane lifted off and the peaks of Upolu sank behind us. Upolu in Maori recollection was the fairy land of Kuporu and from then on it was in mine too.

# CHAPTER TWO

# Manhattan and Other Islands

W E ARRIVED IN NEW YORK IN BLAZING MID-SUMMER HEAT.
As we walked along Madison Avenue on our first afternoon
we were accosted in some excitement by people milling about
on the pavement: the power had failed. We were unsurprised – the power
failed every few days in Apia. But in this as in so many other ways New
York turned out to be different and a power failure was an historic event.
The city was as self-absorbed as Samoa but on an incomparably greater
scale. After two years in the South Pacific even crossing the street required thought. Driving seemed unthinkable, but coming back from the
United Nations one afternoon my companion, the redoubtable Quentin
Quentin-Baxter, suddenly remembered an appointment, leapt out of his
Mercedes in the middle of the traffic, and asked me to take it back to the
UN garage. The scars of that (uneventful) trip across town through rush-
hour traffic stayed with me for some time. Even my language sounded
rusty. I had to repeat my words on the simplest requests and a shop assistant in Greenwich Village leant across the counter and said, 'I can't
understand a word but I love to hear ya talk'.

So the shock of change was considerable; New York was dirtier, richer,
more crowded and noisier than anywhere else but once all this was
accepted there was no other city like it. The old adage had it the wrong
way round. New York was a rather disagreeable place to visit but it was a
great place to live. That is, if you were young and poor, as we were, or if
you were old and rich. It was a city where anything seemed possible and
where anything was obtainable if you had the time and the money to seek
it. We were captivated.

We found an apartment in mid-town Manhattan, on East 67th Street between Madison and Park Avenues. Such an impressive address was possible because the apartment had one bedroom and was rent-controlled, an anomalous hangover from wartime price controls. In a tree-lined street of brownstone townhouses and expensive apartment buildings we marked a distinct drop in the economic tone, but the doorman was as happy to help Julie out with her stroller on the way to Central Park as to help older befurred ladies to find a cab. Once we had settled in, the two or three blocks around us took on some of the characteristics of a village. Shops that were part of our regular round would ask after the baby and offer dubious advice on how New Zealand should be voting at the United Nations. One shop sought out Julie in some excitement to advise them on their first case of a strange delicacy – kiwifruit.

More than anything else the noise of Manhattan took some getting used to after the calm of the plantation. Underneath our windows there was a constant honking of horns and shouts of greetings or altercations in the street. There were the police and fire sirens and once a month the ghostly sound of sirens practising their warning of a nuclear attack. It was pointed out to us that one of the advantages of our apartment was its closeness to a fallout shelter but the local cynics noted that it was also close to the Soviet Mission and that by the time we all got there it would be full of Russians. One of the disadvantages was that there was a fire station down the street from us which erupted into loud activity at intervals through the day and night. It had a Dalmatian fire dog which liked to sleep on the pavement outside. When the alarm sounded and the long ladder truck accelerated out of the station the dog remained unmoved. As the engine slowed to turn on to Park Avenue it would canter up and leap aboard and together they would speed down the avenue with klaxon blasting and bell clanging and the dog balanced on top of the cab barking with excitement.

I was posted to New Zealand's Mission to the United Nations. The UN too was a different world. Its handsome buildings on the East River were still fairly new and the organisation, though battered by the Cold War, was still wrapped in remnants of the idealism which had accompanied its founding. This was to change as the West lost control of the General Assembly to the influx of newly independent members, but Americans still felt protective about it. There was an active movement, 'UN – We Believe', which illustrated a persistent and well-meaning view that the UN was a matter of faith not facts, and at a more practical level the ladies of New York society ran a Hospitality Committee which introduced newcomers like ourselves to some of the delights of the city.

The UN, of course, was not a matter of faith. It was a practical and indeed indispensable centre of international diplomacy, with strengths and limits which were both only gradually being discovered. Idealism found a place, an extensive one, in the unstoppable flow of words from the General Assembly building, thoughtfully shaped like a loudspeaker. But the organisation's value lay not in the oratory but in the exploring of positions, testing of responses and bartering of interests for which it provided the framework. For me it was the place where I had my nose rubbed in the future. This was a tedious process as well as sometimes a disagreeable one. There was probably no other institution where the ratio of work put in to results achieved was so unequal. Yet the education it offered could not be acquired anywhere else.

The UN was a kind of terrarium, not so much the hothouse of its critics as a sealed community where the shape of things could be rearranged. In some ways it was a metaphor for life: you arrived on a sunny morning, spent a busy and sometimes exciting day and then, when you emerged on to First Avenue were surprised to find that it was night. It was not a looking-glass world; just that life looked different once you darted in through the revolving doors and up the escalator to the Delegates Lounge. Small wrongs could become magnified; great ones might never surface. My first General Assembly was a special session called to condemn the entry of French paratroopers into a Tunisian base; a year later a regular session found itself unable to say anything about a Chinese–Indian war.

The Bizerta assembly was unmemorable, lasting less than a week, but coming back from the UN the New Zealand Permanent Representative, Foss Shanahan, called me into his office to say that a delegation report would be needed. I assumed that this would be my task but instead Foss called in a secretary and began to dictate, rapidly and with his peculiar machine-gun delivery, the entire report without revision or pause. I understood that I had been called in to be impressed, and I was impressed. Foss's style of dictation was famous. Some time earlier he had swept into the office at night and summoned the young woman on duty. After barking out a lengthy telegram he asked her to read it back. The terrified typist had frozen after the first paragraph and now collapsed onto the floor in a faint. Foss's deputy in the adjoining room heard the thump and opened the connecting door to see the girl lying on the rug. 'I see you've been dictating again Foss,' he said. Happily the young woman recovered to marry a millionaire and live in New Jersey.

My first outing was a gentle one – the final consideration of Samoa in the Trusteeship Council. The Council was a dignified body, established by the UN Charter and with its own dignified chamber, to oversee the administration of those territories under UN trusteeship. It had an equal membership of administering authorities and others, together with the five permanent members of the Security Council, and accumulating success in its mission meant that its agenda was now almost entirely confined to the Pacific. Debate was serious and orderly. The focus of anti-colonial pressure had moved to noisier forums, but as the Council's membership shrank, the propaganda opportunities for the Soviet Union loomed larger. Though the Samoan plebiscite had settled the issue, the formalities could still be tricky and we prepared carefully for the discussion.

The main New Zealand speaker was Quentin Quentin-Baxter, the Deputy Permanent Representative, supported by Jack Wright from Apia and me. Quentin was an able international lawyer with careful and kindly manners. He was also something of an eccentric. In New York he arrived at the office around five in the afternoon and worked through until three or so in the morning. This meant that by evening there was a queue of people waiting anxiously to see him and as the newest arrival I was at the back. We would start on my draft speech for the Council around ten and go on for two or three hours. This extended over three nights as every phrase was cut and polished until it gleamed like a jewel.

This jewel-like speech Quentin then delivered to the Council in a low mutter that would have made the Gettysburg Address sound monotonous. My discomfort was increased when after two or three sessions Quentin turned in his seat and said, 'I suppose we will have to think about a closing speech'. I was speculating with horror on the thought of another three nights when the Soviet representative made a detailed attack on New Zealand's motives. Quentin raised his hand and gave a lengthy speech in which he dealt briefly and cogently with each of the points raised by the Russian and by other speakers, and because he was speaking off the cuff he held his listeners completely. It was our closing statement and the jewel of a speech that we had striven for.

Finding my way around the UN building took some weeks. One day I was hurrying through the Security Council chamber when a man in a dark blue suit stepped back and we collided heavily. We exchanged apologies, more profuse on my part for the man was Dag Hammarskjold, the Secretary-General. Shortly after he was dead, killed in an air crash in the hills around Ndola in what was then Northern Rhodesia. The Congo peacekeeping operation, which had been his most ambitious extension of the UN's authority, had claimed his life. The news came just as the 1961 regular session of the General Assembly opened. The New York Philharmonic gave a memorial concert in the Assembly chamber and the final dissonance in Bach's *Grief for Sin* reflected the sombre mood as everyone filed out.

So the opening General Debate, attended often by heads of government, was more dramatic than usual. The tiny Emperor of Ethiopia, Haile Selassie, peered over the top of the podium to tell delegates that the League of Nations had failed him and that the UN could not be allowed to go the same way. President Kennedy arrived in a gust of charm and energy to tell the Assembly that the 'smouldering coals of war in Southeast Asia' were a threat no less than Berlin. His warning went unnoticed, as did the airy lack of security around him. Through the kindness of Lady Holyoake Julie was able to sit in the distinguished visitors' seats, next to Jacqueline Kennedy and her sister Lee Radziwill. It was very different from the dour atmosphere and heavy-handed security when President Johnson came two years later.

These excitements could not disguise the fact that the UN was in trouble. The strength of character of its moody and introspective Secretary-General had led delegates and governments to become complacent. 'Leave it to Dag' had become the easy answer to any problem. Now there was no Dag to leave it to and the chances of finding and agreeing on another Secretary-General of similar toughness seemed dim. For trouble had been building for at least a year before Hammarskjold's aircraft clipped the trees that night near Ndola. The Congo operation was the UN's first active peacekeeping effort, not policing a ceasefire but trying to restore order and unity in a huge country which had collapsed in chaos after the Belgians left. Like all such military operations it was costly. The UN was in debt and the French and the Russians were declining to pay their share. The Soviet Union was angry at this extension of international authority and angry with the Secretary-General who had led it. A year earlier, in his memorable appearance at the General Assembly, Khrushchev had called for the Secretary-General to be replaced by a 'troika', rule by three persons drawn 'from each of the three blocs' – the West, the Soviet bloc and the non-aligned. Rule by such an unharmonious trio would ensure that the UN Secretariat would do and say little in the future.

Everything depended on the General Assembly which had just gathered. But this in itself was a cause for further apprehension. By now the surge of newly independent countries was in full flow; by this session the membership had doubled. From being something of a Western club the atmosphere and the character of the UN underwent a rapid change. The new members were suspicious of the West, insecure and impatient of procedure. They showed little interest in many subjects of traditional UN concern. Their preoccupation was the struggle against colonialism and racial discrimination and their weapon was publicity. In my first months draft resolutions were still analysed by us point by point to decide whether and what parts we could support. Within a year or so that had gone: you propped your feet on the desk, cast a quick eye over the latest draft and decided on the spot whether it would or would not do. Carefully crafted resolutions based on consultation and compromise were a thing of the past. Debates were viewed more as international protest rallies.

As the session went on the gloom of the older members deepened. The Assembly President was too weak or too frightened to give rulings and parliamentary order at times buckled under the weight of the majority. But the pessimists proved mistaken. Whatever their shortcomings in procedure the new members had no intention of seeing the UN neutered. It was the forum for setting out their foreign policy hopes and it was the only means they had of focusing world opinion on their concerns. They felt that they owed their own independence to it and had no intention of seeing it weakened in the struggle to free the remaining colonial peoples. So they made it clear that the troika had no future and the Burmese Permanent Representative, U Thant, was chosen to succeed Hammarskjold. At first the Soviets insisted that he be only Acting Secretary-General, but within a year he had been confirmed in a full term as his own man and without conditions.

Because of the growing heat of anti-colonialism the 1961 session lasted some weeks into the new year, sitting for a hitherto unprecedented

154 days. Its end was some relief and marked by a memorable party given by a combustible mixture of the Australian, Irish and Finnish delegations in a hotel near the UN building. When I arrived the party was in full throat, with windows open despite the winter chill, and the roar of voices increasingly punctuated by the sound of breaking glass. More strangely, above me the canopy that ran from the hotel to the street now sported a pair of disembodied legs waving wildly. A patrol car summoned by some nervous passerby had drawn up and the Australian Deputy was explaining that the lads were just enjoying a little fun. The legs were still for the moment, having been warned of the danger by urgent whispers from the nearest window, and surprisingly or perhaps diplomatically the patrolman accepted these assurances and drove off. A human chain then retrieved the owner of the legs from the top of the canopy.* The next morning everyone assured their ambassador that the gathering had been one of the highest rectitude and respect for property but a firm UN consensus formed that the Australians, Irish and Finns should never again be allowed to hold a joint party.

In the ensuing calm we made our first visit out of New York, to the South. We had acquired a little Fiat 600 which fitted neatly into small spaces on 67th Street and had other advantages. I parked it on a fire hydrant once to dash into the New York Public Library. Inevitably there was an emergency but the fire crew, finding their spot occupied, good-humouredly lifted the car out of the way, with Julie and the baby still inside.

We wanted to travel because people were always assuring us, no doubt rightly, that New York was not 'the real America'. Neither was the South and I found over the years that wherever you went on the continent 'the real America' was always over the horizon. Driving south we met spring travelling north up the seaboard. Suddenly there was a green mist on the trees, dogwoods and azaleas in bloom. The South we saw from Virginia to Georgia was the dreamy and romantic South of the books – a white Greek Revival plantation house with a pleached walk carpeted in pink camellia petals; black cypress swamps hung with Spanish moss; a forgotten Civil War site at Cape Fear with trenches slowly crumbling

---

* He later became Australia's Secretary of Foreign Affairs.

and a roofless church where the dead and wounded had lain. But even for tourists there was more: service stations had three lavatories, labelled Men, Women and Coloured. The South in 1962 seemed still frozen in the century-long shock of war and emancipation. This was on the brink of change but two visitors returned to New York with some deeper feelings about minority rule.

In May our second child, Gerald, was born. Surroundings in Doctors' Hospital on Manhattan's East Side were rather different from Apia and so was the birth. I went home to get a book for the long haul and when I returned there he was. The hospital was luxurious even for those who had not tried its Samoan counterpart. Marilyn Monroe was there being dried out, though new fathers were understandably kept at a distance. But it was, in my experience at least, the only maternity establishment where fathers were treated not as the source of all the bother but as guests. I could sit talking to my wife as long as I pleased and at mealtimes a table was wheeled in and a menu produced from which to order a meal and bottle of wine.

Our child was a strong little boy but a few months later fell victim to a gastro-enteric virus which was moving through the city. The doctor rang me at the office: 'If your boy does not get to hospital he will be dead within four hours'. We took him straight to Mount Sinai hospital as urged. Then there was a hitch. The receptionist insisted on a deposit of $1500 before he could be admitted. My claims to be able to produce this were unconvincing so I stood there with the child in my arms and the clock ticking while she checked with my bank. The Chase Manhattan to my eternal gratitude said firmly and quite untruthfully that the money was there and little Gerald was admitted. Once in, the care was superb and he made a complete recovery, though his parents took longer.

As the 1962 session started the General Assembly was still struggling to digest its multiplying membership. The attack on colonialism was seen by most as the main function of the UN. Two years earlier the Assembly had passed the landmark Declaration on Colonialism, which defined independence as the goal of all territories and proclaimed the urgency of obtaining it. New Zealand had taken a deep breath and, alone of its administering friends, voted for it on the grounds that its intention if not its detail was right. Now as the new states became more confident about tactics they set about streamlining the UN's colonial machinery. The Declaration was taken, in practice if not in form, as having amended

47

the Charter. Now most of the clutter of ad hoc committees which scrutinised particular territories was progressively swept away, along with equal representation of administering and other states, the notion of careful preparation for independence and other conventions of an earlier day. In their place a Special Committee on Colonialism was set up. Its membership in 1962 was enlarged to twenty-four (it was thereafter usually referred to as the Committee of Twenty-Four) and it was made the instrument of the anti-colonial campaign, of more practical importance even than the General Assembly.

Anti-colonialism had now acquired a revolutionary fervour, that peculiarly revolutionary combination of inevitable victory and desperate struggle which would have been familiar to Lenin, Robespierre or for that matter Calvin. It also at this session found its devil. Central and southern Africa were viewed as the 'bastion of colonialism'. The battlefield stretched from Katanga to Capetown and the attack was the more bitterly pressed because race was involved and not just politics, and because none of the newly independent African states felt secure while the white-ruled territories remained.

Those who complained that as the number of remaining colonies dwindled the anti-colonial fervour seemed to increase missed the point. There was an edge of fear behind the stormy rhetoric. The newly independent states were 'vexed to a nightmare' by what they saw as a threat to themselves. They feared what endless speeches called the 'unholy alliance' of economic, political and military interests stretching back to Europe and the NATO alliance. They worried about the power of the mining companies, the intransigence of the white settlers and most of all the growing military power of South Africa.

So the resolutions became more and more angry and less and less likely to be enforced. No matter, their purpose was not to propose practical steps forward but to keep world opinion focused on the problem. The Western states watched this disconsolately from the sidelines. Efforts to help a friend like Britain sort out the tangle of Southern Rhodesia, still officially self-governing, faltered in the face of Whitehall's refusal to act. Portugal and South Africa were beyond reason. Diplomacy seized up in the heated atmosphere of running protest. The Soviet bloc, though enjoying the discomfiture of the West, could not make much capital out of it. The Afro-Asian majority had no longer any need of their support and made it clear that it would not accept Russian direction.

This was the atmosphere, along with a considerable amount of cigarette smoke, that I breathed in every day in the General Assembly's Fourth or Colonial Committee. There was little that New Zealand could do to mend things; our concern was the prudent one of avoiding damage to our reputation and hence the future of our remaining island territories. We were anxious whenever there was an opportunity to distinguish the smaller territories in the Pacific and elsewhere from the current African focus. This involved a careful judgement on votes. The Western group in the Committee was influenced by an able Swedish woman; on particularly sensitive votes when there was no time to consult Wellington, the Canadian and I concerted our positions. As often as not we ended up, in Arthur Koestler's words, defending the half-truth against the lie.

The seat beside me in the Committee – Nicaragua – was nominally occupied by an elderly First Secretary who may have been installed with the Charter. He was rumoured to be running an export-import business in New York and so was never there. But he had good sources and whenever a vote was to be taken, even late at night, he would slide into his seat and after a minute solemnly listening to the debate would ask me confidentially, 'How you voting, boy?' This caused him a little trouble when I once got him to vote with me against the United States on a minor matter. After that when he asked my intentions he also asked about the Americans'.

When he was not there my right-hand neighbour was Niger, who like most of the French African delegates, wore Parisian silk suits and observed the Committee's proceedings behind inscrutably dark glasses. The lighting in the room hardly required these but they enabled the wearer to doze quietly while appearing to follow the discussion. Sleep, however, could only be intermittent, for this year the Committee was in regular turmoil. Its proceedings opened and closed according to the needs of the Afro-Asian group. Debates would be adjourned while the group worked out a position; when this had been done they would return to the Committee, close further debate and use their majority to force a vote. This was irritating – 'mob rule', said my Ambassador – but Western countries large or small had to put up with it.

The grip of anti-colonialism was so powerful that events in the world outside sometimes passed by the General Assembly in its loudspeaker-shaped hall. In the course of the 1962 session a war between China and India, the continuing mess in the Congo and the Cuban missile crisis were not discussed by the Assembly, though they were on everyone's minds.

The continuing Soviet build-up in Cuba was causing concern as the Assembly opened. The New Zealand Prime Minister, Sir Keith Holyoake, expressed alarm during the opening General Debate at the scale of the build-up and thought that the two super-powers would need to show 'almost super-human responsibility and restraint'. This thought was less evident in the fiery speech of President Dorticos of Cuba. The public gallery was packed with pro- and anti-Castro supporters in equal measure, while the Russians had filled the floor of the Assembly with a claque of clerks, secretaries and telephonists. For the first twenty minutes there was uproar until the anti-Castro hecklers were thrown out and the claques settled down to rhythmic approval. Not for everything. When the President threatened nuclear retaliation if Cuba were touched, there was delirious applause from the gallery but the Russians sat stonily silent.

In October American reconnaissance flights revealed that Soviet nuclear-armed missiles which could reach Washington were being installed in Cuba. Why Khrushchev decided on this challenge will always be speculation. Since the Soviet Union worried about being encircled by American missiles perhaps he felt he could put a similar squeeze on the Americans; perhaps he felt that President Kennedy was inexperienced and could be browbeaten. But the President made a dramatic broadcast and announced a blockade of Cuba which would be enforced by the navy.

Suddenly we seemed close to war and tension was high in New York which assumed it would be an early target. Food disappeared off supermarket shelves and the bridges out of Manhattan were clogged with cars. It was announced that the monthly practice sirens were cancelled; if they sounded again it would be the real thing. Inevitably on the usual practice morning some did. I stood at my office building looking up Third Avenue, listening to the wailing rising and falling, and near-certainty that it was an accident was only near-reassurance.

When the US announced the naval quarantine it notified the Security Council, as it was obliged to do, and the Council session scheduled for the evening of 24 October would be the first public indication of whether the Russians would challenge the blockade by force. On a day tense with expectation it was impossible to get on with normal work. By coincidence it was United Nations Day so I skipped the afternoon concert at the UN and walked home in the warm autumn sun. Julie was in Central Park with the children and at the surprising sight of her husband arriving at the playground in mid-afternoon she said to me, 'Is it all over?', thinking that I might have come home to die with the family.

That evening the Security Council chamber was crowded with observers including members of the New Zealand delegation. There was real suspense as everyone waited for the Soviet response. In a rare burst of extravagance we were holding open the telex line to Wellington to flash the first indication of whether it would be peace or war. There was complete silence as Ambassador Zorin began to speak. Usually a combative and energetic speaker, he began in a curiously low-key and evasive way. After five minutes he had still not said anything definitive. It was clear that they would not fight and I dashed out of the Security Council chamber to battle for a phone (others had reached the same conclusion) to send a first report home.

With the tension eased, the Council meeting the next day was more argumentative. The clash between the Soviet Ambassador Zorin and the American Adlai Stevenson was high drama, reaching a peak when Stevenson challenged his opponent to deny the presence of Soviet missiles in Cuba: 'Yes or no? Don't wait for the translation. Yes or no?' Some weeks after I was told by Harlan Cleveland, the Assistant Secretary of State responsible for UN affairs, that he had been watching the Security Council session when President Kennedy phoned. He too was watching the television and thought that Stevenson could be more aggressive. Cleveland sent the message to New York, watched it being passed to Stevenson at the Council table and then saw his toughened mood. It was, he thought, the first instance of diplomacy by television.

Though the Russian ships turned back the crisis was not over – the missiles, some of which were now operational, were still in Cuba. The first reaction of the non-aligned was to seek to mediate, to find in the jargon of the trade 'a formulation acceptable to both sides'. A group of fifty held a meeting at the UN building to consider this. To the pleasure of other delegates it was inadvertently broadcast, revealing that the Afro-Asians made the same sort of speeches in secret meetings as they did outside. Ghana and the United Arab Republic tried their hand at a Security Council resolution but the two principals would have none of it. The military realities had broken into the closed world of drafting formulations. It became clear to the busiest of bodies that the two super-powers were dancing an intricate and deadly minuet and the best the rest of us could do was to avoid any sudden noise which might cause them to lose their footing.

Yet the UN did play a part which was indispensable if undramatic. It assisted the implementation of the settlement agreed between the two super-powers in ways which gave time for them to arrange the transition from near-war to near-peace. The Security Council sat a dozen times and the Secretary-General, viewed with such suspicion by the Russians a year earlier, played an important part in softening the reality of their retreat by providing verification for each side's concessions.

While the days of 'leave it to Dag' were gone forever, U Thant's realism and good sense were rebuilding the Secretariat's standing. His round and impassive face sometimes left callers uncertain as to which end of him they were addressing but there was courage behind the impassivity. Countries like Australia and New Zealand were heartened by his intervention in the dispute over the future of Dutch New Guinea. The western half of the island of New Guinea had been in contention ever since the founding of the Indonesian Republic. Now President Sukarno had begun a 'confrontation' with the Dutch administration, with naval clashes and threatened military action.

In the middle of 1961 the Dutch told us that in the absence of any international support they would have to withdraw, seeking the best deal they could for the Papuan people. A few months later the Secretary-General appointed the veteran American mediator, Ellsworth Bunker, to broker a settlement. At its 1962 session the General Assembly ratified proposals to transfer the territory to UN administration in October and seven months later to Indonesian rule, with the wishes of the people to be 'ascertained' some time before 1969.

However disguised this was a discreditable retreat from the principle of self-determination whose minutest details were to be so scrutinised by the Assembly in the case of other Pacific territories. U Thant held stoutly to the terms of the agreement in the face of Indonesian pressure and made it clear that he would continue to report to the Assembly on its observance. We were among a handful of countries (Australia and some West Africans) who stressed the importance of a proper act of self-determination but the Assembly as a whole looked the other way. Indonesia was too influential and it was supported by the even more influential India which, having just taken over the Portuguese enclave of Goa, argued that there could be no question of independence for the former Dutch territory. So the West Papuans vanished into the great republic where they lie uneasily to this day.

By this time New Zealand had begun to think about the future of its own Pacific territories, principally the Cook Islands. They were not coveted by any large power, though the United States still had nominal claims on a few atolls. Small size and a large footprint in the sea were hardly less difficult problems. New Zealand's was an empire of the ocean. There were fifteen Cook Islands (thirteen inhabited) scattered over nearly a million square miles of water. The lower or southern group were 'high' islands, volcanic in origin and reasonably fertile, and most of the Polynesian population of 25,000 lived there. Six or seven hundred miles away, with Aitutaki half volcanic and half atoll as the pivot, lay the northern islands, low coral atolls with small settlements and subsistence economies.

The group had been administered by New Zealand since 1901, the only fruit of Prime Minister Seddon's Pacific imperialism. Before that it had been vaguely a British protectorate but governed in practice by the missionaries. Rarotonga, much the largest and most populous of the islands, had first been visited by a British frigate in 1814. Almost certainly the *Bounty* mutineers had called twenty-four years before in their search for a safe refuge. The Rarotongans had stories of a floating island which had arrived from paradise, inhabited by white men who spoke Maori (the language of the Cooks). There were breadfruit trees, sugar cane and taro growing on the island, which had waterfalls flowing down its sides. All this sounded rather fanciful but John Williams, the missionary, guessed that it was the *Bounty*, crewed by the mutineers with their Tahitian women and still with Bligh's overgrown breadfruit in boxes on the deck, with pumps flowing to keep them cool. Tradition says that the first oranges on Rarotonga were stolen from this ship.

As far as UN doctrine was concerned, the independence enjoined by the Declaration on Colonialism applied as much to these islands as to any other territories and it was clear that the Declaration's priesthood, the Committee of Twenty-Four, would before long turn its attention in our direction. Some ingenious thinking was required if the interests of the islanders were to be reconciled with the wider aims of the UN's majority. There was a glimmer of light. A companion resolution to the Declaration on Colonialism in December 1960 had laid down that the aim of self-determination could be met in three ways, by independence, integration or by free association with another country. No one knew what free association meant; it was nowhere defined and had never been tried, but perhaps it offered a way out of the Cooks' increasingly unacceptable colonial status.

In the meantime the Prime Minister, advised by the Foreign Ministry, concluded that New Zealand had as soon as possible to comply with the intention of the Declaration. As he told a somewhat restive Minister of Island Territories some time later, 'I believe, and I have told the British and others, that a small country like New Zealand cannot afford to antagonise the bulk of world opinion'. The first step was to consult the Cook Islands Legislative Assembly. In July 1962 they were asked to choose from four possibilities: independence, integration with New Zealand, a Polynesian federation or full internal self-government. They had little difficulty. Independence was unattractive; they had New Zealand citizenship, New Zealand took all their (subsidised) produce and paid 80 per cent of the budget. Distance made integration equally unattractive. Federation was a dream since there was no one to federate with. The Assembly endorsed self-government.

In December for the first time we used the Fourth Committee's general debate on colonialism to make a statement about the Cooks. We set out a timetable for its constitutional development looking forward to an outcome 'which safeguards their future as a self-governing Polynesian community and conforms to the principles established by this Organisation'. This careful drafting skirted round the uncertainties as to what this future status might be. It was received by the Committee with a complete lack of interest. We were not displeased by this – next year we could claim tacit UN acceptance of the plans.

First, though, we had to sort out our own ambiguities. The struggle between the Foreign Ministry and Island Territories broke out again, more heatedly than ever. The Islands administrators regarded the Cooks' choice of internal self-government as the end of the process. They argued, and the evidence was on their side, that the people of the Cooks were satisfied with that and worried that any further step might imperil their New Zealand citizenship. The diplomats pointed out that a choice made by a colonial Legislative Assembly, chaired by a Resident Commissioner and with nominated members, would never be accepted in New York or anywhere else as an act of self-determination.

There were deeper considerations than fear of the UN. In February 1963 I wrote to Wellington arguing that only free association would work and that we should not from lack of nerve hedge it about with qualifications which would end in making the Cooks an indirect colony. What Islands were saying about the Cooks' reluctance was entirely believable. 'But I do recall that the same was said of Western Samoa early in 1959. They were right then too.' As with Samoa, if we based a settlement on their nervousness at this stage, it might well be too restrictive in later years. 'Having seen the change wrought in the Samoan attitude by only two years, I have little doubt that much the same change will take place in the Cooks.'

The argument – it would be too euphemistic to call it a discussion – went on for some months. It was carried on mainly by Bryce Harland, the head of the South Pacific Division in the Foreign Ministry, with combative and not always tactfully worded support from Frank Corner and me in New York. The upshot was that a team of experienced constitutional advisers – Professors Aikman and Davidson and Jack Wright from Samoa – were despatched to Rarotonga in August to sit with the elected members of the Legislative Assembly and work out what would be acceptable as the next steps. Their report, praised by the Prime Minister and even by the New York Mission, called for full self-government by the Cooks but with a head of state – the Queen – and a citizenship shared with New Zealand and perhaps (they suggested) a seat in the New Zealand Parliament.

Jack Wright thought that this ruled out free association but the cardinals of conscience in our New York office could at last see a clear path ahead. Since we were the pioneers of free association that status would be what we said it was. A common head of state or other links need not matter as long as there was a clear act of self-determination verified by the UN – and the Government had already accepted these requirements. Free association meant 'continuous self-determination', that the Cooks should retain sole control of their future, rather than concerns with specifics like citizenship or immigration.

There was still much to be sorted out, but at the end of 1963 we had a clear message for the Fourth Committee. While Africa was still the emotional centre the debate had become stale and repetitious. Speakers turned with almost noticeable relief to the future of the smaller territories. Liberia even ventured to say that solutions short of independence were not necessarily a betrayal of the sacred cause, provided they met the essentials of self-determination and UN verification. Since our statement on the future of the Cooks was explicit on these essential preconditions it caught the ear of delegates. Rather improbably, we found ourselves being congratulated by Indonesia and hearing countries like Tunisia and Algeria speaking approvingly of New Zealand's readiness to devise new solutions to the problem of small territories.

At home a new approach was also required. Our apartment building on 67th Street had been bought by a Mafia-like firm which set about getting rid of the unprofitable rent-controlled tenants, of which we were a notable example. First, Julie discovered the superintendent lying dead underneath our windows, though this was a heart attack rather than anything sinister. Next, the helpful doorman disappeared and then the hot water followed him, at least at unpredictable times. It was time to move, though not without regrets. We would miss the sight of the Sisters of Charity floating along the street in their wide, winged headdresses; William Greenberg, whose incomparable chocolate brownies had sustained Julie through her pregnancy; the chemist who predicted for us the staff movements in the Soviet Mission because the returning wives bought all his lipsticks; and Gristede's the grocers, where you might on a Saturday morning find yourself rubbing shoulders with the great. Once, in mid-winter when Julie expressed amazement at their peaches costing $40 a case, the assistant leant confidentially across the counter and said, 'The Rockefellers are making jam'.*

It meant giving up a modest toehold on high society. In our case this consisted of passing through the lobby on the way to the laundry in the basement with a bucket of nappies and meeting Adlai Stevenson's son with the beautiful Charlotte Ford. After this had happened more than once his father invited me to breakfast, along with others, at the US Mission. Adlai Stevenson, though an ambassador, was always called Governor Stevenson (he had earlier been Governor of Illinois). At the breakfast someone asked him why. He answered by telling a story. The Perons from Argentina paid a state visit to Franco's Spain. The highlight was a gala night at the opera. As General Franco was escorting Mrs

---

* The Rockefeller apartment on Fifth Avenue was just around the corner.

Peron up the flight of steps, the crowd on either side of the barriers began shouting 'Whore, whore'. 'Pay no attention, my dear,' said Franco patting her hand, 'Why, it is twenty years since I was in the Army and they still call me General.'

We found an apartment which consisted of two back floors in a townhouse on East 78th Street between Park and Lexington Avenues. With high ceilings, parquet floors and a fireplace such elegance was beyond our means, but the previous tenant was impatient to move to Florida and the fact that she kept two pet monkeys may have discouraged others. There was no furniture. The townhouse garden had been left by the monkeys in a ragged condition. No New Zealand male could resist the challenge and so I dug, raked and grew a lawn – probably one of the few since Peter Stuyvesant to lay down a lawn on Manhattan.

Life was slightly less grand – we had swapped Gristede's for a delicatessen called Cheeses of Nazareth – but we could barbecue in the garden in summer and build an enormous snowman there in winter. This was our first Christmas where a tree and decorations were needed. New York took on a Dickensian air then. It snowed a few days before and the brightly lit shops, the Father Christmases ringing their bells for charity on street corners and the good-humoured crowds hurrying along the pavements were as festive as any carols. With the excitement that comes from walking through falling snow we went out to buy a star which, after a battered existence of nearly fifty years, still sits each year on top of the tree.

That Christmas, for New York and the rest of the United States was shadowed by the death of President Kennedy four weeks earlier. On that November day members of the New Zealand delegation were eating their customary pasta lunch at a small restaurant near the office when a man burst in and shouted, 'They just shot the President'. No one quite believed it but gradually we all sidled out to check the television shop windows. Half an hour later I stood looking out the office window as one by one along Third Avenue the flags came down to half-mast.

The death marked a permanent change in the style of the American presidency. Ten days before, I was having my hair cut when the presidential motorcade approached. The barber was unimpressed but I went to the doorway and stood, with a sheet still draped around me, as President Kennedy drove past. He was leaning back in a cream-coloured Lincoln convertible, chatting and laughing in the autumn sunshine. This was the last time I saw him, or indeed saw any President drive in this way. Future presidential motorcades were a fast procession of black limousines with dark windows from which the President could not be glimpsed. At the UN there were no more handshakes with delegates when the President came; instead careful searches were required of all who might come near him.

The shock of loss was felt by everyone. Going home that evening I went into the church of St Vincent Ferrer and found it half full of people sitting or kneeling there. Late that night, unable to sleep I was listening to WQXR when the announcer began to cry in the middle of naming the next record. In the shock of the assassination and the events that followed (when Julie was one of many who saw another first on television – the murder of Lee Harvey Oswald) the strength displayed by Mrs Kennedy played a major part in steadying the nation's nerves. The rituals of a state funeral also helped – the sight of General de Gaulle at the graveside, solemnly removing and replacing his hat at times when everyone else was doing the opposite, or Cardinal Cushing's cracked voice interrupting his flow of Latin to say 'Dear Jack'. But for us the best memory was of passing him off Cape Cod earlier in the year, the President sitting on the side of his boat and waving good-naturedly.

As Frank Corner and I came out of St Patrick's Cathedral, where we had attended a Requiem Mass which had changed little from the time of the Emperor Constantine, America seemed a greyer place. Even those Republicans who had insisted on telling stories about the President's private life (mostly true as it turned out) were stricken. Caroline's nursery school, the Everett Academy, run by traditional Republicans, held a little service. Any Manhattan nursery school was beyond our means – especially Miss Everett's, in a brownstone in the East 70s, which had some of the Rockefeller grandchildren. But the Rockefellers came to our rescue. Miss Everett's, it seemed, wished to expose its pupils to a little diversity and after consideration it was felt that a New Zealand child would be adequately exotic. So Caroline received a 'scholarship' and when the *New York Herald-Tribune* did a story on 'Where the Junior Jet Set Play', its illustration showed Caroline, who as it happened had travelled by jet, pointing rather vaguely to New Zealand on a globe.

As 1964 opened, the Committee of Twenty-Four at last turned its attention to the smaller territories, setting up a Sub-Committee for the Pacific. Work had begun on drafting a constitution for the self-governing

Cooks which would come into force after the next general election in the islands. Discussions with the Sub-Committee revealed a flaw in this. Consultation with the Cook Islands Legislative Assembly had gone ahead on a practical basis but in all the planning there was no occasion when the voters solemnly and formally adopted their new constitution with its new 'freely associated' status. Self-determination had not only to occur; it had to be *seen* to occur. The Sub-Committee was tempted to call for a 'moment of independence'. This had to be headed off – it would frighten those in the Cooks who were already worried about losing their New Zealand citizenship, and it would undercut our efforts to establish free association as an alternative to independence.

We thought about this in the Mission and suggested a different sequence of events. The current Legislative Assembly would endorse the completed draft and ask New Zealand to enact it. But the constitution would come into force only after a general election and when confirmed by the new Legislative Assembly. So an election fought mainly on the proposed new status would be the actual self-determination and the confirmation by the new Assembly would be the formal act. Both events could be verified by the UN. With Wellington's agreement we put this revision to the Sub-Committee and the moment of independence concept died, only to be succeeded by another difficulty.

As winter turned to spring the Sub-Committee began to think of a Visiting Mission to the Cooks. New Zealand had accepted that self-determination had to be internationally verified. Since we had ruled out a plebiscite as unnecessary, some sort of visiting mission might be required to observe the final stages. However, the opening this would give to the Committee of Twenty-Four was anathema to our administering friends. They saw it, no doubt correctly, as an attempt by the Committee to establish the right, previously confined to the Trusteeship Council, to send visiting missions to gather information on any or all non-self-governing territories. If a mission was sent to the Cooks pressure would be brought to have it visit other South Pacific territories such as Fiji. New Zealand had gone too far. In Wellington the British, Australian and American representatives hurried into the Foreign Ministry to express their concerns. In London and Canberra Ministers urged us to reconsider and in Washington Governor Harriman (known to his staff as 'Honest Ave the Hair-Splitter') called in our ambassador to argue against setting an undesirable precedent.

The New Zealand Prime Minister stood firm, even in the face of growing misgivings by his Minister of Island Territories. We were after all setting a desirable precedent if we could gain agreement for solutions short of independence for small territories. Callers were told that New Zealand had accepted the need for UN verification if decolonisation in the Cooks was to win international acceptance. We hoped to concede as little as possible but if necessary we might, as Sir Keith said, have 'to accept some things we and our friends would prefer not to' – such as a visiting mission.

As the Sub-Committee began to prepare its report, Frank Corner told them simply that 'New Zealand stands ready to cooperate with the UN in considering the means which might be most convenient and satisfactory'. This left things comfortably vague but deft diplomacy – long and hard discussion behind the scenes – produced a report we could live with. Its recommendations were by the standards of the time remarkably free from anti-colonial dogma; the Sub-Committee we thought were probably astonished by their own moderation. They referred to UN 'supervision' of the Cooks' self-determination when we would have preferred 'observance' but in the end there was no visiting mission.

At this point, the beginning of July, I was called back to Wellington to work on the Cooks from the other end, as head of the South Pacific and Antarctic Division in the Foreign Ministry. The notice was short and I had not taken delivery of my new car. There was no time to wait for it to be delivered. I would have to drive it myself if it were to catch the only ship that would reach New Zealand within the deadline imposed by Customs. At the plant in Kenosha, Wisconsin, they were sceptical but in a sporting gesture filled the car with petrol and wished me luck. I drove across America through the night, a blur of freeways, neon lights, truckstops and toll booths. These last were a problem as the car was right-hand drive and I was always on the wrong side to hand over my coins. But then I was a problem to other cars whose passengers would turn round at the sight of a car with no one in the driver's seat. After twenty-four hours I drove on to the wharf at Elizabeth in New Jersey to see the ship some way out from the wharf and hooting mournfully. It turned out, though, that the ship was arriving not leaving and the car had made it after all.

The journey home was not without incident. Caroline, at three years old, was thrown out of Quinn's Bar in Papeete for being under age and

Gerald cut his upper lip open by falling on a bottle. A phlegmatic French Army surgeon, with a cigarette in the corner of his mouth, stitched things together again. Back in Wellington we bought, with help from my father, a house on the hills overlooking the harbour. The view was impressive but the steep hillside meant that access was on foot, down that Wellington institution known as the zig-zag. But it was home, even if we were down to one bottle of beer a week, drunk on Saturday nights watching the inter-island ferry sailing down the harbour. We painted and curtained with all the enthusiasm of first house-owners. The garden would never have illustrated a magazine but at the end there was a large kowhai tree. In spring its drooping yellow flowers brought tuis. As the nectar fermented in the afternoon sun the birds staggered around the tree, uttering hoarse croaks and snatches of tipsy song.

Through the southern spring drafting work on the Cooks constitution and the companion bill which would enact it was making steady progress. As the UN difficulties receded political obstacles kept arising in New Zealand. That was to be expected, but it was a surprise that the first was the Governor-General, Sir Bernard Fergusson. McIntosh said to me, 'You have infringed the Royal Prerogative'. Nothing so treasonable-sounding had been in my mind but it turned out that in specifying that the future New Zealand High Commissioner in Rarotonga should also double as Queen's Representative – an economical arrangement in such a small place – we had overlooked the courtesy of consulting Her Majesty first. Sir Bernard, who privately disapproved of the draft constitution and the full self-government it would confer, triumphantly produced a letter from the Queen's Private Secretary to confirm it. He went on writing regularly to Ministers about other defects he spotted, such as the ambiguity in his own position when he next visited the islands. The Prime Minister stepped in to say that there was no clear answer to his concerns (a frank acknowledgement that we could think of none), but he was sure that the Governor-General would be treated with deference and respect whenever he was there.

Then it was the turn of some Government backbenchers. Daniel Riddiford, the chairman of the Select Committee which was about to consider the Constitution Bill, paid a visit to the Cooks in August. He returned with the conviction that the Government was on the wrong track, that federation was the answer and that communists in the Cooks and (more darkly) in Wellington were pushing for a self-government which was not wanted. When he began hearings over the next two months the petitioners were, as one observer had predicted, eccentrics and political bluebottles from the territory and Cook Islanders resident in New Zealand. All were uniformly opposed to the new constitution. Four members of the Legislative Assembly came down to give more informed evidence but the Government was under some pressure.

Sir Keith Holyoake managed all this with his accustomed calm and with an unexpected firmness. Some of his colleagues could not overcome nagging worries about handing over complete autonomy; his reply was that the Government was taking a calculated risk. His liberal Minister of Island Territories, Ralph Hanan, thought we were going too far too fast: there should be a delay of two or three years. Holyoake replied that from an economic as well as a political point of view it was in everyone's interests to have self-government as soon as possible. When Riddiford argued for some reserve powers Holyoake replied curtly that reserve powers were like thermonuclear weapons, they destroyed much more than their target, and so like thermonuclear weapons in practice they could never be used.

A press campaign began in Auckland, ridiculing the notion of self-government and playing up the objections of those residents in New Zealand who feared that the land they had left behind might be taken from them. At its height I was with the Prime Minister one morning clearing up some details and we talked about these protesters, every one of them, Sir Keith said philosophically, in a swinging seat. I expressed an awkward regret for the row our plans had created for him. He laid a ponderous hand on my shoulder, 'Don't you worry about that, my boy, it's my job to handle that'. And he did handle it, using his unchallenged political dominance, but even then the constitution bill passed its third and final reading only after an unprecedented three-hour debate.

Then it was back to the UN to work out what those words 'UN supervision' meant in practice. Our friends were still worried about the term, as with less justification was the Governor-General, and were thinking of entering a reservation. We dissuaded them – it might reopen up the whole question of a visiting mission. Our own interpretation was that the words meant supervision by the Secretary-General rather than the Committee and at the beginning of February 1965 Frank Corner wrote to the Secretary-General inviting him to appoint 'an observer or observers' for the Cooks' elections. There were the customary back-door pressures – some of the observers should come from the Committee of Twenty-Four, or they should at least be appointed in consultation with the Committee – but U Thant stood firm. He chose as his representative Omar Adeel who had just retired as Sudanese Permanent Representative and whose name had been talked of for the presidency of the previous General Assembly. Our Mission thought him 'honest enough' and that his report would carry sufficient weight in the UN.

The general election, at which the draft constitution was expected to be the main issue, was called for 20 April. Although the administration in Rarotonga was comfortably used to running elections this one was different in its significance and the fact that, if not the eyes of the world, at least the eyes of Omar Adeel would be on it. New York reported worries that the voters might not know what they were about. We drafted a leaflet which was translated into Maori and airdropped on the islands by the RNZAF. The Resident Commissioner made a series of broadcasts explaining the issues, though these became so faint by the time they reached the northern atolls that some thought they were on a different subject. Meanwhile local notabilities were campaigning in the time-honoured way, but for the first time a recognisable political party had appeared – the Cook Islands Party led by Albert Henry, a charismatic politician, whose venture in a failed cooperative had led to his withdrawal to New Zealand for some years.

On 8 April Adeel and most of his team arrived on the weekly flight from Samoa. I met him at the airport and we drove to the island's only accommodation, the Hotel Rarotonga. Despite the impressive name it was in fact an overgrown boarding house. My recollection, which cannot be true, is that it served only cold mutton. Adeel was stoical about this but he had fortunately brought with him a bag of chilli powder which, spread liberally over the food, made it reasonably palatable. When that ran out he found a chilli bush in the garden and made a rough sauce which carried us through.

The first night, though, did not go well. I was awakened in the small hours by an uproar coming from Adeel's room, which was close to the street. A group of young ladies had burst in and pulled off his bedclothes. Since he must have been one of the few Africans to stay in Avarua, it may have been anatomical curiosity or perhaps simply youthful high spirits. But my attempts to pass it off as Polynesian jollity failed. The situation was more serious than that. Some months earlier Omar had been sued for paternity by a night-club singer in New York and had had to invoke diplomatic immunity where the reproductive kind had failed. The New York tabloids made much of it and though these were unlikely to have reached Rarotonga Omar was furious. He suspected that New Zealand had laid a plot to entrap and discredit him.

He was in an intransigent mood the next morning when we met in the office of the Resident Commissioner, Ollie Dare, to map out an itinerary of visits to the outlying islands. It was, he said, essential that he visit every one. When we explained that this was physically impossible, that the round trip to some of the northern atolls would take three weeks, his suspicion of the administering authority's motives was redoubled. The discussion became excited and was resolved only by a compromise. He would visit five islands over the next five days; these, together with Rarotonga, would cover three-quarters of the population. If he were still dissatisfied we would see what else could be arranged.

The Cook Islands administration had chartered the newest of the little motor schooners which traded among the islands, the *Akatere*, and Omar and I set off in this the next day. Unfortunately we struck the tail end of a tropical storm. We had two tiny cabins over the stern where the ship's pitching was magnified and the noise of the straining propeller made sleep difficult. The crew accommodation was in the well of the ship, where we ate our meals surrounded by curtained bunks from which bleary, unshaven faces would peer if the conversation rose above a murmur.

Omar had experienced nothing like this in the Sudan but he gamely came down to dinner the first night. We were crammed round a small table in which there were two metal sinks. A character in dirty singlet and shorts, who turned out to be the cook, carried in a bucket of stew which he tipped into one of the sinks. This proved too much for Omar who shot up the vertical steel ladder to the deck above. When I got there he was hanging over the rail, bemoaning the loss of a cufflink as well as his previous meal.

The sea was calmer and everyone was happier the next morning when we got to Mangaia, a rolling green island famous for its pineapples. Omar met the island council and the local dignitaries, explaining who he was and why he had come. Here and at the other islands he tended to mistake Polynesian courtesies for literal truth. When welcoming speakers said things like 'We thank God that you have come from afar to enlighten our darkness and ignorance', he began to wonder about how much the people knew about their constitutional development. It took oblique questioning from me, eliciting that they had read the leaflets, heard the broadcasts and were following the campaigning on their island to reassure him.

At the next island, Atiu, there was no harbour, only a narrow passage through the shelf reef. The ship lay offshore, gently rocking in the swell, and a whaleboat came out to collect us. Once in the whaleboat, though, we had to wait for the right roller to carry us in. On a headland above us sat the old man who called the waves. Sitting cross-legged with the afternoon sun turning him to gold he looked like some ancient sage as he stared unmovingly at the sea. I saw a thousand years of Polynesian seafaring tradition at work. Suddenly he raised a hand, the oars dug in and we shot towards the reef passage. The sage, however, had got it wrong. The whaler slewed round and we were tipped out on to the reef. There was little damage apart from a few cuts and bruises from the coral but Omar's temper and his Italian suit were both impaired.

There was general relief when at dawn the next day we sailed into Aitutaki, the most beautiful island in the South Pacific. Omar had adopted my custom of spending time in the wheelhouse, drinking coffee and listening to the captain's strange tales of the Pacific, which would have been stranger still had they been true. The sea and sky merged into a pearly silver-blue and sitting in the lagoon was the Sunderland flying-boat which was to take us north.

The Sunderland was a staid aircraft whose speed through age and successive refits had been reduced to a pace so comfortable that you could put your hand out the window. It was noisy and you tended to vibrate in sympathy with the aircraft for an hour or so after you had disembarked. However it did not pitch or roll and Omar was delighted with the change as we reclined in what was still called the wardroom and droned northward.

We landed first in the lagoon at Penrhyn where Spanish ships are thought to have called three or four centuries earlier. The island was distinguished from others by having a wartime airstrip, though too cracked and weed-grown to be easily useable, and large red landcrabs scuttled everywhere. The hospitable islanders had prepared a meal which may or may not have included landcrabs. I advised Omar against the suspiciously elongated drumsticks, which looked more like frigate bird than chicken.

Then, flying low over Rakahanga to give Omar at least a view of another atoll, we landed at the nearby Manihiki. The Resident Agent there seemed to be behaving strangely. In the midst of the welcoming songs and dances I noticed that he was wearing a pistol. I took him aside and he explained that the people were of very uncertain temper and he was in fear of his life. I looked back at the people laughing and draping Omar with flowers and back to the tight-lipped Agent, thinking of the paragraph this would make in Omar's report. Back at his bungalow I persuaded him to put the gun in his desk drawer on the grounds that the (unarmed) Air Force crew would be sufficient protection while we were on the island.

Since we were staying the night, the festivities went on for some time, with drumming and dancing – Omar had recovered his confidence enough to allow himself to be called out by some of the girls – and the customary feast (frigate bird again). The moon rose on a strange scene on the bungalow's wide verandah. The air crew sat in a tight circle on the floor surrounded by half of the young men of the island, bargaining for the apricot-coloured pearls for which Manihiki was well known. Clothes not cash was the medium of exchange and the glow of the kerosene lamp shone on the intent faces of the bargainers. Every so often someone would stand up to remove a shirt, belt or even trousers and hand them over for the agreed number of pearls. When we walked towards the plane next morning, to return to Aitutaki, the co-pilot was wearing only his flying overalls – everything else, even his underpants, had been traded the night before.

We got back to Rarotonga five days before polling day, but Omar declared that he had seen enough. The hasty trip had done more than demonstrate the realities of geography; he commented to me in the plane, 'Independence makes no sense for these people'. But we had to start all over again, with less success, when Godfrey Amachree, the UN Under-Secretary responsible for non-self-governing territories, paid a visit. He was lazy (had not even read his Committee's own material) and bored. He grumbled about the hotel, about the weather (unusually rainy) and about the Constitution, which he felt as a lawyer he could have drafted much more simply. Worst of all, he had a bad effect on Omar, who hoped to get a Secretariat job from him, and as long as he was in Rarotonga Omar became more doctrinaire and prickly. I sought an Air Force plane to get him out but this time the RNZAF had had enough and the discontented Amachree had to wait for the weekly plane to go on to Wellington, where he told Ministers that the elections looked fine but the hotel was unclean and had slap-dash service.

A damp election day did not discourage the voters I watched going to the polls around Rarotonga. In the evening a crowd gathered in the open space outside the Government offices to hear the results. As the first returns came and it became clear that Albert Henry and the Cook Islands Party had won, there was a roar of delight and Radio Cook Islands burst into 'Happy Days Are Here Again'. As the night wore on and the magnitude of the victory became clearer the excitement gave way to a slightly awed silence. The CIP won all the seats on Rarotonga and every outer island except Mangaia and Aitutaki.

From New Zealand's point of view it was an unarguable endorsement of the new Constitution. Around 94 per cent of the electorate voted, 52 per cent of them for the Cook Islands Party, and for the first time ever it was a nationwide vote on national issues. Those, including most of the outgoing Legislative Assembly, who had continued to campaign on what they had done or could do for their districts were rejected. The downside was that the Leader of Government Business, much of his Cabinet and those politicians who had any experience of administration were lost to the new Assembly. Most of Albert Henry's new colleagues were political unknowns; the greater number of votes had been cast for Henry rather than for the candidate.

Although the magic of his name was a potent vote-winner there would have been no magic if the name had not stood for a fresh start. Opinions on Henry were still sharply divided; he could inspire distrust as easily as uncritical adulation. But he had proved himself a remarkable political organiser and a genuine leader. In all this he was not untypical of charismatic leaders who emerged in other colonies on the verge of self-government, even down to the shaky background. At last we had someone with political authority we could talk to. In the end, as I said in my cabled report to Wellington, it hinged on this man: 'The people have spoken and in due course Albert Henry will tell us what they have said'.

First, however, there was the complication that Albert Henry did not have a seat. The residential qualification would have to be amended to allow him to win a by-election and come in as Premier. I went to see him the day after the election and found the shrewd old charmer holding court at his house. Our conversation made it clear that the plan for the UN team to observe both the election and the adoption of the Constitution had come apart. The Cook Islands Party was in favour of the Constitution but along with the residential qualification, they wanted minor amendments to abolish the Council of State (which itself had been an afterthought), establish a House of Ariki, the traditional chiefs, and enlarge the Cabinet by one. For the New Zealand Parliament to make these changes and for Albert Henry to be elected meant that the Constitution could not be adopted by the Assembly until 26 July.

We had so far won over Adeel that he did not see this as a problem but to make things as tidy as possible we suggested, and Albert Henry agreed, that the opening session of the new Legislative Assembly might in the presence of the UN observers adopt a resolution stating that subject to the enactment of the proposed amendments the new Constitution embodied the wishes of the Cook Islands people. Adeel paid a week's visit to New Zealand, to meet Ministers and do a little sight-seeing and then retired to Geneva to write his report.

My own journey home was less routine than the Air Force had managed. The Polynesian Airlines DC3 needed to stop at Aitutaki, which had a large wartime airstrip built by the Americans, to top up its fuel for the long journey to Samoa. Landing at Aitutaki the plane hit heavily, bounced ten feet into the air, came down heavily again and slid crabwise towards the palm trees. When it came to a halt just short of the trees there was a profound silence in the cabin. All eyes were on the door to the cockpit. It finally opened and the pilot stood there in shorts and an ancient peaked cap. He surveyed his shaken passengers, said jauntily, 'First landing of the day is always the worst' and marched down the aisle. When we arrived in Samoa the aircraft was found to have a cracked main spar and Civil Aviation in New Zealand later closed the route as being too far over blue water for two-engined planes.

My return had been hastened by the threatened early arrival of our third child, Sarah, who then dallied until the middle of June. She was born, for mysterious reasons, in the Alexandra Home for Unmarried Mothers. Sarah thus became the only one of our children who managed to start life in New Zealand and the fifth generation in a line of matriarchs to do so. Facilities were less luxurious than at Doctors' Hospital. The presence of a father-to-be seemed to be a surprise. The doctor had briefly been a member of the Foreign Ministry; McIntosh on hearing of this exclaimed, 'I wouldn't have a cat delivered by him'. But the nurses were kind, the baby throve and the only casualty was my hat, which I sat on in my excitement.

The following month Adeel produced his report. It was wordy and nervous of his more radical colleagues. We commented to New York that 'From its erratic and egocentric progress one pattern emerges. Consciously or not almost every major affirmative is balanced somewhere in the text by its opposite.' There was a critical analysis of the Constitution as being too elaborate and it erroneously cited some provisions which it believed gave New Zealand power to interfere. But we were philosophical. The important thing was that Adeel had no doubts that the election was fair, that the voters had freedom of choice and that the Constitution reflected the wishes of the majority. The rest were debating points.

The Committee of Twenty-Four, though there were many complimentary speeches, could not bring itself to make a recommendation, and neither could the Fourth Committee. For the purists (and not only the anti-colonial radicals) the Cooks Islands' new status, neither sovereign independence nor colonial dependence, was not easy to accept. But in December 1965 the General Assembly, despite determined opposition by a few delegations like Ghana, endorsed by a large majority the attainment by the Cooks of self-government in free association with New Zealand. It was a practical answer to the peculiar situation of the islands. It was also true that New Zealand had succeeded in the teeth of the anti-colonial gale in establishing a new status for small territories. Ironically both Britain and the United States, which had been so alarmed by this pioneering, were later to use the precedent for island territories of their own in the Caribbean and Micronesia.

# CHAPTER THREE

# The Commonwealth Divided

I N THE MIDDLE OF 1965, WHILE THE LEGAL STANDING OF THE Cook Islands was being tidied away, the Commonwealth was undergoing its biggest change since the independence of India in 1947. It was about to pass into common ownership. By one of those happy historical accidents beloved of British constitutional practice, the Commonwealth had evolved over the years from an empire into an association of over twenty independent countries. But, as Milton Obote of Uganda said, whatever the theory it was still an Englishmen's club, presided over by the British prime minister and run from the Commonwealth Relations Office. Now it was to become as independent as its members, under a Secretariat with staff drawn from across the Commonwealth. By the kindness of the Queen the Commonwealth Secretariat would be housed at Marlborough House in London, a royal palace vacant since the death of Queen Mary in 1953; and a meeting of Commonwealth senior officials had worked out a staff structure, budget and other practical details. All that remained was to choose a Secretary-General.

There was nothing so bald as candidates campaigning. Soundings were taken and views canvassed with all the discretion of an Englishmen's club but it became apparent that Alister McIntosh of New Zealand had wide support for the position. Then the British surprised everyone by suddenly proposing a candidate of their own, a hitherto obscure Governor of British Honduras. The effect of this, as intended, was to veto McIntosh. No one knew why at the time. McIntosh's style of quiet diplomacy seemed perfect from the British point of view, but his homosexuality (not suspected by any of us) may have been seen by Whitehall as a security risk.

This produced a second surprise. Mac went to the London hotel of Arnold Smith, a Canadian diplomat also in the running, and told him that he was withdrawing because of increasing deafness and that he had asked his backers to support Smith instead. This put Arnold Smith over the top and Whitehall found itself with a very different Secretary-General. Arnold, a former Rhodes Scholar, who had spent most of his life in the Canadian foreign service, was a skilful and vigorous operator, a sunny extrovert who was blind to racial differences and who had firm views on putting the Commonwealth into multiple ownership. By a strange turn the 'usual processes' had thrown up the ideal candidate. The newly born Secretariat owed its shape and indeed its survival to Arnold Smith's creative instincts.

As a response to Mac's gesture, Arnold asked if he could have a young New Zealand foreign service officer as his Special Assistant and on his return Mac offered the job to me. I abandoned stripping the fireplace in our new home (years later it was still as it had been left that evening when I threw away the brush to pack) and in mid-October found myself walking across St James's Park to Marlborough House – the first of the diplomatic staff to join after the Secretary-General.

The house, built in 1709 on a site given by Queen Anne, was one of the fruits of the Duke of Marlborough's commanding political and military position. It had been designed by Sir Christopher Wren, though he had then been sacked by the formidably bossy Sarah, Duchess of Marlborough (whose portrait still hangs in the house). There was a pleasing worldliness about the house's origins to offset the idealism of its new tenant – the Duke had brought the bricks back from the Low Countries free of charge, on returning military transports. The evidence of his military triumphs was all over the house, and in rather gory murals up the staircases. After a time there I could understand why the widowed Queen Adelaide had them all whitewashed. After his marriage Edward VII, when Prince of Wales, had lived there for nearly forty years. The Prince, clearly no reader, papered the 'library' with shelves of fake book spines with jokey Victorian titles and filled the house with clocks, set half an hour fast for his chronically unpunctual wife. In the garden was Queen Alexandra's pet cemetery: a semicircle of little tombstones with the names of dogs, cats and even a parrot. There was still a sense of the severe presence of the last royal occupant, Queen Mary, as you ascended slowly in her little lift and entered her bedroom, which had become Arnold Smith's office.

I was along the corridor in the dark-panelled billiard room which still had a faint atmosphere of cigars and bawdy Edwardian jokes. This became more pronounced when I was joined there as co-Special Assistant by a congenial Australian, Michael Wilson. Sir Robert Menzies, the Australian Prime Minister, had been opposed to the establishment of the Secretariat and had insisted on an Australian sharing the position. Michael's irreverence, however, was unlikely to be what Sir Robert had in mind and the Antipodean partnership worked well – dags were rattled, crows stoned, and raw prawns come, to the bafflement of other Commonwealth colleagues.

On the walls hung portraits from the royal collection. Periodically a little man came round and asked us if we would like a change. When queried as to what was on offer he would consult a list and say, 'I can do you William Pitt, Hearl of Chatham, Lady Harabella Churchill or' (with a glance at me) 'the Pink and White Terraces hof New Zealand'. Attempts at bargaining (what about one of Her Majesty's Vermeers?) were sternly rebuffed and we had to settle for a rotating series of Queen Anne's children.

While the process of recruiting two Deputies and other senior staff got under way, Arnold had borrowed two Canadian diplomats and the Foreign Office had lent us the endearingly eccentric Bill Cranston. Bill was gentle and shy, from an ancient Catholic family, with courtly manners that were already old-fashioned. In the billiard room, inevitably, he became known as 'Wild Bill' Cranston but he took an unwitting revenge. I was working there alone late one night, with only one light, when a noise caused me to look up. Standing in the gloom was a tall figure with a cadaverous white face, clothed in a black coat from neck to ankles. I wondered for a second which of the house's earlier inhabitants had come back to register disapproval but it turned out to be Bill on his way home. Home was a flat he shared with his sister, matron of St George's Hospital at Hyde Park Corner. Neither of them had married; in a prominent place on the piano was a silver-framed photo of Daddy, a bull-chested major-general in a Guards regiment.

By the end of October we had found a home; with three children under five years of age life in the St Ermin's Hotel was not enticing. After a quick search we took the first place we had looked at, a neat house of three floors, one of a row built in 1810 allegedly for the mistresses of the officers in the nearby Knightsbridge Barracks. No trace remained of such licence but it had a townhouse garden and was close to Hyde Park for the children. I could walk to work each morning through Green Park. Because I would have to travel frequently we added a nanny to the household – previously the under-nanny in a grander establishment. Then, since the house was furnished in the traditional British style, we had only to learn which chairs not to sit on and how to master the heating and plumbing (which may have been bought for the first mistress) and we were settled.

Commonwealth affairs were far from calm at this time. Two members, India and Pakistan, fought a war and Malaysia and Singapore were divorced. This last was the first test of the new arrangements. The two governments asked the Secretary-General to handle the necessary consultations for Singapore's admission as a separate Commonwealth member, but some in Whitehall felt threatened by what they saw as Arnold Smith's presumption. Sir Robert Menzies was annoyed enough to write a letter of complaint. More delicate, though, was the fact that Prime Minister Bhutto of Pakistan declined to agree to Singapore's admission. This was unprecedented but after several phone calls Arnold secured agreement to a formula whereby he would announce a consensus for Singapore while privately noting Pakistan's reservation. Then the fact that he and not the British Prime Minister made the announcement irritated his critics all over again. In retaliation it was proposed that we move into the servants' wing at Marlborough House. However a tactful compromise was reached and we moved up one floor in the main house, Michael Wilson and I occupying the royal nursery, where there were still discreet iron bars over the windows to prevent the royal infants from falling out.*

These irritants were inevitable as the new Secretariat eased into its role, but a much greater challenge was looming. The politics of the European minority in Rhodesia had moved steadily to the right as resistance to the thought of eventual majority rule hardened. Intermittent negotiations between London and Salisbury had deadlocked and neither side dared compromise further – Ian Smith for fear of being outflanked on the right, as had happened to his two predecessors. Support for secession, for a

---

* The future George V was one.

73

unilateral declaration of independence (UDI), was growing in the colony. It was clear that a crisis was not far off. It was also clear that the crisis would threaten the Commonwealth's own future.

A somewhat doubtful character operating under Zambian diplomatic cover warned us that a UDI was less than four weeks away (our suspicion that he might also have been a Rhodesian agent was not diminished when his information proved to be correct almost to the day). Arnold had been planning a visit to East and Central Africa for the end of November, but in the light of this and the fact that the head of the Commonwealth Relations Office, Sir Savile Garner, and the Foreign Minister of Zambia – who agreed on little else – both urged haste, Arnold decided to bring forward the visit.

We left London on 7 November, landing at Entebbe at dawn the following morning to be met by Yaw Adu who had arranged the details of the visit. Yaw (pronounced Yao), who was about to join the Secretariat as Deputy Secretary-General (Political), was a Ghanaian who had been Secretary of External Affairs and of the Cabinet under President Nkrumah. Then he had discreetly withdrawn to run the East African Common Services Organisation in Nairobi. Before that he had long service in the Gold Coast Colonial Service, becoming the first African District Officer in 1942. He was sent up-country to relieve his predecessor who was going home on leave. The Englishman was in a hurry and dashed out of the office, saying only that there was a bit of trouble in town. When Yaw got there a full-scale riot was in progress. As the handbook required, his sergeant carried a table outside and he climbed on to it to read the 1714 Riot Act, in English. Surveying the angry crowd he quickly grasped the pointlessness of this and instead spoke in the local language, 'Look, I'm the first District Officer from our own country. If I make a mess of this it will be years before we have another. Don't let me down.' The rioters went home. That kind of sense and the wide respect in which he was held throughout Africa made Yaw Arnold's key lieutenant.

We drove up the road to Kampala to meet the Prime Minister in his office on top of the National Assembly building. Dr Obote was welcoming: 'The Commonwealth has gained its independence from the CRO'. But the discussion was dominated by Rhodesia. He was quiet but vehement: if there were a UDI Uganda could not stand by and see South Africa come up to the Zambesi. Its influence was already creeping northwards. Malawi was gradually being eaten away – 'It is still there but its soul has gone'. Uganda itself had received a shock the previous year to find that South African mercenaries in the Congo had come up to its own border. Everyone had sympathised but no one had given any help.

He was suspicious of Britain. He feared that it would become trapped by the tricky game of offer and counter-offer it was playing with Ian Smith. He had asked the Secretary of State for Commonwealth Relations, Arthur Bottomley, a few days earlier whether Britain still stood by its policy of no independence before majority rule and he could not answer. (This was true. We had called on him – known with some justification as 'the topless Bottomley'– just before leaving and apart from wondering if a visit were wise at this time, he had refused to be drawn on majority rule.)

The Secretary-General waded in robustly with an argument that was to be worked hard over the hectic months that lay ahead. The Commonwealth was an international association, not an arm of the British Government. Members who had worries over British policy should use the channels offered by the Commonwealth to influence that policy, and also that of Canada, Australia, New Zealand and the other members, rather than tearing up those channels in a fit of pique. Obote did not respond for a time, thinking this over, and then said merely that he did not think a Commonwealth Conference would be sensible at this time. The last had been heated enough on Rhodesia and another might only lead to angry scenes and the breakup of the association. Arnold had made his point about withdrawal.

It had been arranged for us to visit Murchison Falls, on the Nile. I drove up separately. The dirt road ran straight for miles between high walls of jungle on either side. The monotony was broken when I saw ahead a greyish-white snake (it proved to be an Egyptian cobra) begin to cross the road. It was long, stretching almost the width of the road, and sensing the Mercedes thundering down it had to make an undignified wriggle to get to safety. I was leaning out the window fascinated when the snake, by now in a filthy temper, reared up and struck. I jerked my head back and the snake hit the car door, losing (I hoped) a fang or two, and vanished.

I had scarcely finished winding up the window when the driver, who spoke no English, stopped, indicating that there was something the matter with the back wheels. Boyhood stories of people bitten by snakes wrapped around axles came instantly to mind. I got out carefully and made the driver, who must have thought he had a lunatic as passenger, walk some distance back before we bent down and peered cautiously underneath. There was no snake or anything else on the axle. While the driver slid under for a closer look I walked about, becoming aware that the afternoon was waning, that there had been no traffic in either direction for the past two hours, and finally that vultures were quietly drifting in. In the end there were about fifteen of them, sitting on dead branches above us with the benign detachment of a Samoan host contemplating his pigs. By signs I persuaded the driver that if the car would move we should too and an hour later we bumped into Paraa Lodge.

This was a simple establishment, a dining block surrounded by African-style rondavels as bedrooms. Arnold and a handful of other guests were sitting on the terrace enjoying a sundowner. He and I were deep in conversation when it struck us that everyone else had quietly disappeared. In fact the only other occupant of the terrace was a large bull elephant, flapping its ears slowly and watching us with small bright eyes. It was not easy to read his thoughts. Arnold and I sidled carefully around two walls and stepped into the dining-room, to be greeted with unsympathetic mirth by the others.

Even the night's sleep was haunted by wildlife. A stern notice on the bedroom door warned the guest to lock the door and not stir out before dawn because of roaming lions, and being woken by grunts and roars during the night did not encourage anyone to ignore this advice. In the morning we saw the East African jungle at its most beautiful, cruising slowly along the young Nile between sandbanks with large crocodiles (I discovered how bad their breath is), while black and white colobus monkeys and bright parrots darted and screamed in the branches which almost closed above us. Then a government Caribou aircraft flew us back to Entebbe for the flight to Nairobi and wild scenes of a different kind.

As we stepped from the plane in the late afternoon of 11 November the welcoming group was swept aside by twenty or so journalists and cameramen who surged across the tarmac to get the Secretary-General's comments on the news that UDI had been declared in Salisbury. We were caught by surprise but it was not difficult to know what to say. Then we were swept off to Parliament Buildings to meet Ministers and members in the bar. An impromptu debate on the news had just finished and excitement was running high. A kind of informal seminar developed, with Ministers and ourselves sitting around a table and an ever-widening circle behind. For two hours the discussion was hot and fast.

Then a complete change of atmosphere. We went to dinner at the home of the British High Commissioner, Malcolm Macdonald. He was away and his rather chilly Canadian wife, Audrey, presided. The guests were all European and as the courses followed one another no one seemed greatly disturbed by the news. The air was a little tense, however, as a mob demonstrated noisily at the front of the house and tried with partial success to break the windows.

Nairobi seemed to be marked by these contrasts. Two days later we went to Nairobi University College, where the questioning at a meeting of over two hundred students was pointed, one speaker accusing the Secretary-General of being a British stooge sent out to 'weaken the resolve of our African leaders'. The meeting was impatient of sanctions and unanimously in favour of using force to end the rebellion. Just before that we had been given lunch by the Council of Commonwealth Societies (mainly European in membership) in the leather-and-panelled elegance of the Nairobi Club. Rather naively I asked Yaw if he was a member. He shook his head and showed me the rule book on the selection of new members: 'Two black balls shall disqualify'.

The Kenyan Cabinet was still divided over how to respond to the UDI. As we walked into State House to call on the President, his External Affairs Minister commented that sanctions would not work and that force was the only way. Kenya, however, was still Jomo Kenyatta and he set the course. Now an old man, but still with a powerful frame and an even more powerful presence, he said (as his Minister sat silent) that economic measures were the only ones to take, though they would have to be tough and strictly applied. Military force would lead to bloodshed, the danger of race war, and a legacy of bitterness which would take years to eradicate. The races would still have to co-exist even in a ruined country. He spoke deliberately, obviously thinking of Kenya's own history; nothing should be done in the urgency of the moment which would hinder longer-term racial harmony. Afterwards we went out into the garden for photographs and to admire the bright flower-beds which gave the President great pleasure. While the cameras were clicking, whether in a kindly gesture or to steady himself, Kenyatta put his hand on my shoulder and I felt the pressure of that heavy hand for a long time.

The President had it in mind to call a meeting of his fellow East African heads of government to concert a response to UDI and, though he did not say so, perhaps to exert a restraining influence on what the others might do. The uses of the new Commonwealth Secretariat had sunk in quickly and as we left State House the External Affairs Minister suggested that Arnold might stay on and attend some of the discussions. However, whether or not the other heads of government were wary of the proposal, a day convenient for all could not be found and we held to our schedule, leaving for Zambia on 14 November.

When we arrived in Lusaka, the parties to celebrate UDI were just winding down. The main hotel, the Ridgway, was also a favourite expatriate haunt and as we walked in there were still glasses being banged on the bar and rather fuddled shouts of 'Good old Smitty'. It was a graphic reminder of Zambia's exposed position, with its only industry – mining – and much of its administration dependent on Europeans, many of whom were not especially well-affected, and its economy and communications tied to its old federation partner, Southern Rhodesia. Most of its power came from the Kariba Dam on the Zambesi, now under the control of a hostile regime. All of its exports of copper, all of its oil and petrol supplies and most of its other imports came up the railway line from the south. Even my telephone calls to London went through Salisbury. Lying in bed in the Ridgway, I could hear the lonely calls of the whistles as the copper trains, pulled by huge steam locomotives coupled together, set off across the high veldt on the long journey down the continent to South Africa. The opening up of Central Africa by British energy and technology was turning sour as Britain was blamed for the racial mess which had followed.

Zambia was therefore the awkward corner to be turned in mapping out any response to UDI. Indeed the British Government said that its reluctance to impose a ban on oil supplies for Rhodesia was out of concern for Zambia. Without oil the mines of the Copper Belt would close and flood, some perhaps never to be reopened.

When we saw President Kaunda the next day, however, he was firm that the fullest international pressure should be exerted on Rhodesia, and that Zambia should not be used as the excuse for half-hearted measures. Kenneth Kaunda, whom I had known slightly from his appearances before the Fourth Committee in New York, was an appealing man, eloquent and emotional sometimes to the point of tears. (Much later, sitting beside him at another Commonwealth meeting, Mrs Thatcher said, 'Oh Kenneth, you're not going to cry again!') Over time it became apparent that, like another East African charmer, Julius Nyerere, he lacked a steely realism in guiding the destinies of his new country. He was moderate in talking to us, disclaiming any intention of hasty or unwise actions, but behind him we sensed the strain and the passions of his fire-eating Foreign Minister, Simon Kapwepwe, and others around him.

His reasoning was plausible. Zambia was very vulnerable but with outside support could ride out the term of the illegal regime which he thought like many others would not last long, perhaps six months. That was why Britain had to be tough and use force (which he thought only it could do without bloodshed) or support total sanctions. Otherwise his great fear was that the Smith regime could establish itself, settle in and become accepted. What he wanted from the Commonwealth was short-term help in getting oil in and his copper out, but he also wanted it to band together in defence of its principles. Much would hang on whether Canada, Australia and New Zealand were willing to show that 'kith and kin' did not override race justice.

The talks continued over the dinner he gave at State House, a large columned house where the grass came up to the windows and there were no flowers or shrubbery. Inside, though, it was still the Government House it had been. We were seated around a small table in the middle of a cavernous dining-room. Courses of the standard Government House dinner (laid down perhaps in some ancient ruling from Whitehall) came and went, and then suddenly the lights went out. In the darkness a voice bellowed 'The Queen'. A single light illuminated a full-length portrait of Her Majesty at the end of the room as we stood to face it and raised our glasses. Then the lights came on, the President of the Republic set down his glass and dinner was over.*

In Malawi the following evening we actually *were* back in Government House. Formerly Nyasaland and like Zambia part of the short-lived Central African Federation, its independence was recent and the Governor-General, Sir Glyn Jones, had stayed on. He had hospitably

---

* Another republican, General George Washington, was said to propose and drink the King's health at his headquarters in Harvard Yard every night.

invited us to stay with him in Zomba. It was a splendid old house with highly polished furniture and noiseless white-robed servants who did the polishing. A leopard had been cornered and killed under the billiard table and every evening a bugler played while a guard of three lowered the Union flag.

Naturally you dressed for dinner. Arnold and I had come doubly prepared for this. Apparently at the change of season from summer to winter in East Africa white dinner jackets were exchanged for black. Inconveniently we had arrived just at the change. Both sorts were required, compelling me in haste to have a white jacket made in which I looked like an ill-nourished jazz drummer. Before dinner we conferred and, deciding that it was still summer, came downstairs in white only to find the Governor-General and his aides in black. The next night, therefore, we appeared in black only to find that the tactful Sir Glyn and his party had put on white. It took a quick conference between me and the Private Secretary to ensure that, on the third night, everyone appeared in the same shade.

After some of the earlier accommodation Government House was luxurious. Every morning three gentlemen in long white robes appeared in my bedroom. One swept back the mosquito netting; one placed a silver tea tray beside the bed; and the third disappeared briefly into the stone-floored bathroom. Then all three lined up at the foot of the bed, bowed and left. Curious about the man who went into the bathroom, I asked the butler. 'He is looking out for snakes, sah.' After that I found it a ticklish business stepping into the darkened bathroom at night.

We called on the Prime Minister, Dr Hastings Banda, at his house in Blantyre, an unpretentious bungalow encircled by a high brick wall. We were shown into a darkened sun-porch, with heavy curtains drawn against the African sun. The Prime Minister, we understood, was fearful of assassination. It was stiflingly hot and we sat in silence with the sweat trickling down our backs. Then a side door opened and Dr Banda slipped in, dressed in a thick black suit and waistcoat, both buttoned up. The impression he gave was more that of someone who practised traditional magic with bones than the doctor trained in Edinburgh that he actually was.

He was a loner, shunned by his neighbouring heads of government, and had not been invited to President Kenyatta's proposed gathering. He seemed indifferent to this isolation and to rather enjoy the role of provocative outsider. He had a clear mind and could do this well. At home, though, he seemed to be patterning himself on the African rulers of an earlier age; like them he had a rather sinister manner accompanied by a marked detachment from the affairs of other people. Some of his arguments came to look wiser with the passing of time but in the aftermath of UDI his views on Rhodesia were as deeply unfashionable as his clothes.

Pointing out that he had known Rhodesia since before self-government in 1923, he thought that Britain should be supported because she would handle it best. Majority rule would come in time but it should do so in an orderly way, without economic ruin or embittered race relations. He was cool where his colleagues were agitated and dismissed the Secretary-General's fears. The Commonwealth would not disintegrate over this issue; 'public opinion' would not force any withdrawals unless politicians chose to use it as an excuse.

He laid out his thoughts in a calm way, seemingly little concerned whether we agreed or not. At intervals a little white foam appeared at the corners of his mouth which he dabbed at with a handkerchief. He enquired when we were leaving, saying that he intended to hang a convicted rebel in public and hoped that we could attend. He was mildly disappointed to hear that we were leaving early – indeed with that prospect before us if we had missed the plane we would have bicycled out of Malawi to Tanzania.

In Dar-es-Salaam, where we stayed with the Canadian High Commissioner, the atmosphere was more cheerful and better lit. We went the next morning to see Julius Nyerere in a simple office with the breeze blowing in from the Indian Ocean. He was a small, intense man with bright eyes and an effortless charm, but he was blunt: 'I am going to make a lot of noise about Rhodesia'. It was, he thought, *the* issue for the Commonwealth and if it could not act others would step in and supplant it. He was critical of Britain, which was trying to duck its Commonwealth responsibilities (though he continued to keep up a correspondence with Harold Wilson). Pressure would have to be kept up on British Ministers. Then, despite the vigour of this reasoning, when the Secretary-General raised the issue of possible withdrawals from the Commonwealth he stayed silent.

That afternoon we were flown over the Ngorongoro crater along one of the world's great animal migration routes to the game reserve at Lake

Manyara. The lodge was literally on the edge of the Rift Valley. A large window had been provided beside the bath so that as you lay there you had a dramatic view down into the blue-shrouded depths of this huge tear in the earth's crust. Lake Manyara's other distinction was that lions climbed trees there. We had not grasped this until Arnold stood up in the open Land Rover to take photographs and found himself face to face with a lioness dozing in the fork of a tree.

We left the next morning for Zanzibar, the plane becoming airborne by simply running off the end of the runway over the Rift and then sagging down until height was gradually regained. Zanzibar, a clove-rich island off the coast, had recently overthrown its Arab rulers with some bloodshed, and had hastily been merged with Tanganyika – hence Tanzania. The new rulers seemed a tough group on whom the implications of the merger still rested lightly. We were put up for the day in a wealthy merchant's house which had been taken over from its murdered owners. For sale along some of the streets stood ancient Arab chests and ornate beds looted in the killings, though who the buyers were we could not see. It was a dreamily beautiful place but with chilling undertones.

Back in London at the end of November we took stock. Arnold's forthright talk had headed off any impulsive responses. But the visit had bought only a little time. Early in December the Organisation for African Unity called on its members to 'break links' with Britain if the UDI had not been ended by 15 December. The Secretary-General immediately wrote to all African Commonwealth heads of government to restate his points and undertook some energetic telephone diplomacy. When the deadline expired only Ghana and Tanzania broke relations with Britain. No one withdrew from the Commonwealth, though both these countries stayed away from meetings for some months.

Amid this diplomatic manoeuvring, the practical problem was Zambia, economically isolated and with its fuel stocks sinking week by week. It had established a Contingency Planning Organisation to work out ways of getting the necessary minimum of supplies flowing again. They asked for someone from the Secretariat to review the situation with them. They were looking for Commonwealth help but were anxious that Zambia should not be used as the excuse for not tightening sanctions against Rhodesia.

So in the middle of December I hitched a lift down with a British delegation led by the Minister of State for Commonwealth Relations,

Cledwyn Hughes. He was a Welshman with a fund of cheerful political stories which lasted even through several hours' delay when the chartered Britannia landed heavily at Benghazi. British–Zambian relations were strained, though, and it was two days before he was able to meet President Kaunda.

In Lusaka the first effects of sanctions were unexpected to a visitor: small consumer goods like soft drinks, soap and toothpaste which had previously come from Rhodesia now came from South Africa. I sat down with the CPO, going through a lengthy shopping list of Zambia's needs. There were working parties on oil, on staffing requirements, on the economy; we looked in detail at airlift capacity and how over time to upgrade the available surface routes. The information suitably digested was then circulated to Commonwealth countries for each to volunteer what help it could. Things began to move. Within four days Britain and the United States began an oil airlift, to be joined by Canada and later by New Zealand and others.* I did not see the need for a permanent attachment to the CPO but, at the President's request, the Secretariat found a senior officer from India to head up rehabilitation and resettlement measures. When I returned home a few days before Christmas Zambia's fuel stocks had ceased to fall.

In the meantime the diplomatic activity had not slackened. On 10 December the Nigerian Prime Minister, Sir Abubakar Tafawa Balewa, proposed an urgent Commonwealth meeting in Lagos, to be devoted solely to Rhodesia. Whether or not Harold Wilson was willing to attend would be decisive, but he told Abubakar that he welcomed it to help hold the Commonwealth together. When Tanzania and Ghana broke relations and some Africans made an ill-judged walkout during his address to the United Nations, he began to have second thoughts about Britain 'not being put in the dock'. However, when we saw him in Downing Street on 4 January, sitting in his customary seat in the Cabinet Room, lighting and relighting his pipe as he talked, he had recovered his natural optimism.

This would be the first Commonwealth heads of government meeting held away from London, and the first to be run by the Commonwealth

---

* Flying out, the aircraft carried copper.

Secretariat. Both were daunting prospects – the infant organisation had not yet held a conference in Marlborough House let alone in another country. We had less than three weeks to do so. Sir Burke Trend, the British Cabinet Secretary, lent us some of the expertise from his office and we hastily improvised seating plans, relays of minute takers, arrangements for briefing the large numbers of the press who were likely to arrive, and all the details of an international gathering that were later to become routine. There were no frills, no monogrammed pens or briefcases; all the distinguished delegates had in front of them were a simple blotter and pad. In an effort to simplify matters still further I had even drafted the conference communiqué on our dining-table the weekend before leaving for Lagos.

On 9 January 1966, we moved into the Federal Palace Hotel where the meeting was to begin two days later. The Nigerians were helpful hosts, finding telephones, typewriters, document reproduction equipment, and good liaison officers to smooth out the rough spots. Haste produced the usual oddities. A telephone had been installed in Arnold's bathroom which (he claimed) rang whenever he sat on the lavatory. Michael and I had been assigned a car but here I first learned a truth about international conferences – that being assigned a car is like being assigned a cat. We saw it from time to time sitting in the sun or parked in the shrubbery but it was never there when we called.

Given the short notice there was a good turnout of prime ministers or senior ministers. Ghana and Tanzania were absent, and Sir Robert Menzies, who disliked the innovation, sent his man in Lagos as an 'observer', a position unknown to the Commonwealth before or since. It was Sir Keith Holyoake's haymaking time at home and so New Zealand was represented by Sir Thomas Macdonald, the High Commissioner in London and a former External Affairs Minister. The gathering met in the Independence Hall of the hotel, with senior officials meeting in separate rooms to consider details of sanctions, cooperation with Zambia, (a proposal from the Secretary-General) the creation of a programme for training Rhodesian Africans against the day when they would be needed – and of course the draft communiqué.

The conference took only two days, 11–12 January, though this must have seemed long enough for Sir Abubakar, who presided with a soft-spoken dignity. It was Ramadan and his fast did not allow him even to sip water as he managed each day's discussions. He opened the meeting with a temperate speech, politely doubting that sanctions would work but arguing that the key thing was for Britain to affirm clearly that the objective was majority rule. The African case was opened by Vice-President Kamanga of Zambia. Rhodesia was a threat to its neighbours and time was not on their side. He and most of those who followed favoured the use of force and complained that Wilson's ruling it out publicly had been a serious tactical error. Obote said presciently that sanctions might dislocate the Rhodesian economy but they would not bring down the regime.

Others took a different line. Lee Kuan Yew of Singapore, attending his first Commonwealth conference, held the Africans' attention by stating that the difficulties were not confined to Africa. If Britain was branded as condoning the illegal regime the position of those, like him, who were closely associated would be made much more difficult. Harold Wilson had his own political difficulties, but that did not mean that he was making only a show of resistance to the Smith regime – there was too much at stake for Britain and the West. Like him, most other speakers were cautious about the use of force, urging that peaceful methods should be tried first. Sir Tom Macdonald put it more plainly than he perhaps intended: a balance had to be struck 'between what should be done and what could realistically be achieved'.

Harold Wilson was in confident mood, giving the impression as he spoke that he was increasingly being persuaded by his own arguments. 'Sanctions are biting and they are biting effectively.' Ninety-five per cent of Rhodesia's exports were embargoed. For the first time in history oil sanctions were being applied. It could be a new weapon to replace the use of force. No country could survive without oil; Ian Smith was already feeling the pinch and in desperation proposing that the oil pipeline from Beira should be flushed with salt water to glean an extra 17,000 tons, whereas the airlift for Zambia had been astonishingly successful, already shifting 14,000 tons of fuel a month. All the information available to the British Government suggested that the nerves of the regime had broken.

The debate was frank but not bad-tempered. Whatever their private doubts, Wilson's Commonwealth colleagues were willing in these early days to give him the benefit of their uncertainty. He proposed that they should meet again in July if the rebellion had not been ended by then and Lester Pearson of Canada suggested that in the meantime a Sanctions

Committee serviced by the Secretariat should keep sanctions and aid to Zambia under review. When I took him a copy of the draft communiqué, Wilson thought it was too cautious and at his dictation I amended the text to state that the cumulative effects of sanctions might well bring the rebellion to an end 'within a matter of weeks' rather than months. Sir Savile Garner, who was there, later said he was aghast at the recklessness of this prediction but the Wilsonian optimism gave it plausibility. In the end it was all anyone remembered of the proceedings.

The evening before we were to leave Arnold and I went to Sir Abubakar's house to say goodbye. He was standing in the courtyard outside with Chief Festus, his jolly but notably corrupt Finance Minister. As the four of us stood talking one of the press people who were milling about pushed a powerful torch past our knees, lighting the faces from below. It produced an eerie photograph, made more eerie by the fact that next morning only two of us were alive.

That night a group of army officers carried out a coup in which Abubakar and Festus were murdered, along with several senior officers. Secretariat staff staying at the Ikoyi Hotel were awakened by a burst of gunfire when a brigadier who was a fellow guest was gunned down, and they walked to breakfast carefully avoiding the long trickle of blood that ran from the brigadier's room. Our first indication at the Federal Palace was when a nervous young lieutenant arrived saying he had orders to take us to the airport immediately.

We left in an Army Land Rover, the young officer sitting beside the driver with an automatic weapon on his knees. People were milling about in some excitement as we sped through the slums of Lagos in the early morning. At one point someone sluiced a can of petrol across the road in front of us and then set fire to it, so that we drove through a wall of flame. At another a policeman signalled to us to stop but saw the weapons and thought better of it. When we drew near to the airport terminal the crackle of rifle fire revealed that a fight was going on around it. We veered away to one end of the runway to a small house that had been vacated perhaps by an expatriate family on leave.

There, like a scene from a Hollywood movie, a haphazard group was assembled, ranging from David Astor, editor of the *Observer*, to a young woman with a toddler and a baby. As the heat increased we moved restlessly around the modestly furnished sitting-room. No one quite knew what was going on; the supply of cold drink in the fridge ran out;

and conversation became desultory. Periodically the rattle of small arms fire would draw closer, the talk would become strained as people tried silently to gauge how much closer, and the Nigerian soldiers there to protect (or guard) us would pick up their rifles. Then the noise would die away and disconnected talk would resume.

The day wore on and the heat became oppressive as the breeze died. Mysterious rumours began to circulate, no one knew where from, of which the most encouraging was that a Royal Air Force plane coming to rescue us was stuck in Kano. Around four o'clock we heard the clatter of a helicopter approaching. The soldiers looked apprehensive and everyone crowded to the door. A large French helicopter belonging to the President's flight landed just outside the small front garden. It sat there while we waited, then the door opened and there stood Archbishop Makarios of Cyprus in his clerical robes. He surveyed the motley band below, raised a hand in benediction and said, 'Ah, there you are', as if he and his pilot had been searching all over Nigeria for us. A few minutes' conversation, though, convinced him that ours was a dead end. He withdrew and the helicopter with its consecrated cargo took off again.

Night fell and several were dozing in the darkened house when there was a sudden roar of engines and brilliant light flooded the room. A British vc10 had arrived. An officer urged us, needlessly, to be quick, two burly loadmasters picked up the toddler and the baby and everyone sprinted for the aircraft. The steps they had brought stopped a little way below the door of the plane but hands from inside heaved everyone on board, the door closed and we were away within minutes. By breakfast next morning we were back in London.

The Commonwealth Sanctions Committee, consisting of High Commissioners and a British Minister meeting under the chairmanship of the Canadian, Lionel Chevrier, got down to work at the end of the month. It met roughly every three weeks to review the working of the embargo on trade with Rhodesia. What it saw was not encouraging: the measures, selective and not binding on all countries, were as leaky as the supposedly secret proceedings of the Committee itself. In April, at the Committee's urging, Britain obtained a mandatory Security Council resolution on oil and mounted a naval blockade on the oil terminal at Beira. This however only shifted the flow to South Africa's roads and Rhodesia continued to receive almost three-quarters of its normal needs.

By then British Ministers had come to accept that ending the rebellion was likely to take much longer than Wilson's confident optimism had declared, and that the effect of the imposition of partial sanctions had only been to unite the white community. Nonetheless they continued to be evasive over majority rule, holding on to hopes that negotiations might yet persuade the Smith regime to back down. They were also uneasy about seeking United Nations authority to make sanctions comprehensive and binding on all countries, fearing the uncomfortable precedent this would set for their future relationship with South Africa.

The commitment for the Commonwealth to meet again in July began to seem decidedly risky. In the middle of May the Secretary-General discussed this with the British Prime Minister. Wilson preferred a postponement to September and wondered whether it might be better to meet in Ottawa where he would not be in the chair and so freer to make his points. On our way to the independence celebrations in Guyana we stopped in Ottawa for Arnold to discuss this with Lester Pearson. He was reluctant. Like others he could see a real risk of presiding over the disintegration of the Commonwealth – hardly good politics for a Canadian prime minister.

We travelled down to Kingston on Lake Ontario, where Arnold received an honorary degree from Queen's University. That evening we dined with family friends of his in a house whose style and furnishings were exactly those of my childhood home in Christchurch. We were drinking coffee after dinner when I noticed that everyone else was standing up: *God Save the Queen* was playing on the radio. I scrambled guiltily to my feet hoping that no one had noticed, but my hostess said reproachfully, 'We thought you were all so *loyal* in New Zealand'.

In the Caribbean we stopped at Trinidad and Tobago, where the Prime Minister, Dr Eric Williams, lectured us on the slave trade, and Barbados where we stayed at Government House. Built in the seventeenth century, it boasted a mahogany staircase lined with the portraits of early governors. In that more broad-minded age two had been pirates as well as governors and a third pulled off the trifecta, becoming Archbishop of York as well.

Guyana was one of those colonies (like Fiji and Mauritius) where British commercial policy, by importing Indian labour for the sugar plantations, had created two separate and mutually distrustful communities. The difficulties of forging a stable nation from these communities meant that

Guyana had lagged behind the other West Indian states. Independence now marked the belief that a political settlement had at last been reached which might (and did) prove durable.

The Prime Minister, Forbes Burnham, was a genial but quick-witted barrister of African descent. There was a touch of flamboyance about his clothes and his manner as we sat having a drink in his sitting-room and admiring his new hi-fi equipment. His easy-going approach to ideology and much else contrasted with that of the Leader of the Opposition, Cheddi Jagan. He was a Marxist intellectual of Indian descent who took the simple view that people's troubles were largely caused by the United States and big business.

We were taken in hand by the Attorney-General, Sir Shridath Ramphal, known to all as Sonny and destined nine years later to be Arnold's successor. After the now traditional ceremonies as Guyana became independent and the twenty-third member of the Commonwealth, a picnic was arranged in the backblocks of Rupununi, rolling savannah country where the raising of cattle and hell were said to be the main pursuits (indeed there was an abortive revolt a few years later). We left in an ancient DC-3 with ammunition boxes welded down the sides serving for seats and the missing door-lock supplied by a piece of wire. After landing we bypassed the races and rodeo contests to travel to a branch of the Amazon which formed the border with Brazil. A dugout canoe paddled by Indians appeared through the overhanging greenery and they agreed to take us across.

Brazil turned out to be a thatched shed mounted on a raft. It served as a bar and simple store, though in the half-light of the surrounding jungle there was no sign of who the customers might be. As we waited out a heavy downpour conversation languished since the storekeeper spoke no English. Politeness compelled us to drink a glass of a murky liquor and we were paddled back, little schools of piranhas beneath us ensuring that the passengers sat very still. The little excursion remained memorable: not many people have been to Brazil by canoe.

When we returned agreement had been reached that the next Commonwealth conference should be in September and in London. Tensions, though, began to rise as the time drew near and the Secretary-General found himself battling on two fronts. The strain on Zambia was beginning to show. Simon Kapwepwe came to the Sanctions Committee to complain that Britain was not doing enough to support them and to say that his country was thinking of leaving the Commonwealth. Wilson was bothered and grumbled to us that he could hardly be expected to write a blank cheque. Arnold wrote a firmly worded letter to Kaunda saying that withdrawal would be 'a slap in the face' for all those who had been trying to help Zambia.

The bigger problem was the growing distrust of Britain's motives. As 'talks about talks' and other contacts with the Salisbury regime continued, it became clear that the Wilson government would agree to independence under white rule provided there was a guaranteed path to a universal franchise. This and British hesitation over full sanctions persuaded many African (and other) leaders that Wilson was contemplating a sell-out. The events of the past six months had ended the presumption of goodwill by many and the storm clouds were clearly gathering over the September conference. Arnold, who never lacked nerve, went to see Wilson at the end of August and told him that there was a crisis of confidence over Britain's intentions. If Britain could give a firm assurance that there would be no transfer of sovereignty before majority rule was achieved, it would be doing no more than recognising the future course of events but would make a great difference to confidence now.

Wilson dismissed this. If he thought it would have been useful he would have done it at Lagos 'and saved a considerable amount of argument'. When Arnold, recounting this to the Canadian Prime Minister later, said that in his job you had to be prepared to stick your neck out occasionally, Pearson (who had been talking to Wilson) said, 'You stuck it out all right'. Wilson's anger was increased by my first draft of a communiqué. We left it with him on this visit and, according to one of his staff, Wilson threw it across the room after reading it. There was little more that could be done to head off trouble: the future of the Commonwealth would depend on the meeting finding more good sense than several of its members had so far shown.

When the meeting began in the main drawing-room of Marlborough House on 6 September Rhodesia was firmly placed first on the agenda (only incurable optimists had ever thought otherwise). More than that, the African leaders had enrolled their Asian and Caribbean colleagues in a bloc to make a concerted challenge to British policy. The 'caucus' was borrowed from Afro-Asian procedures at the United Nations, the only international assembly with which many were familiar. It was an unhappy experiment. The tactics of a voting bloc made less sense in a gathering where there were no votes and separate, ethnically based groupings ran counter to the individual nature of Commonwealth discussions. As the timetable was interrupted for successive caucus meetings Pearson and other prime ministers began to complain. Holyoake wondered why he had bothered to come; the Commonwealth was not an association of racial groupings.

The discussion opened with a lengthy statement by Wilson, defending his preference for staying with selective sanctions (though he hinted he was willing to discuss going further), and the need to hold on to the possibility of a negotiated settlement, going into considerable if optimistic detail about Rhodesia's economic difficulties. It boiled down to his asking the question, will sanctions work? 'My answer to this remains "Yes, undoubtedly"', but he acknowledged that things were moving more slowly than they had thought. When he finished, Obote, in a prepared move, said that a handful of people should not divide twenty-three countries and bring to an end one of the most promising organisations in the world, and proposed an adjournment to allow the British Prime Minister's statement to be studied.

The debate went on over the next three days, with heads of government outlining positions which by now were becoming familiar. There was a rather listless air about the proceedings, though, as everyone waited for battle to be joined. At one point speakers ran short and the Secretary-General proposed moving on to other business in the meantime. When Obote opposed, saying that Rhodesia must be dealt with first, Arnold became angry and said that Rhodesia was not the only problem in the world and the Africans were damaging their case by this single-mindedness. He spoke for a number in the meeting who, as Holyoake said, had prepared thoughts on other issues, such as Vietnam, and wondered if they would ever get to speak.

Over the weekend Wilson entertained his colleagues in three relays at Chequers in the country (only Kapwepwe and Hastings Banda declined). Thereafter the meeting diverged into two tracks. Speeches on the world political and economic situations rolled along uncontroversially in the regular sessions, while the real struggle over Rhodesia began in a series of restricted sessions, with only one adviser to each delegation and no minutes being taken.

Lee Kuan Yew introduced the views of 'those who had been consulting together', set out in a paper which asserted that force was the only sure method of bringing down the regime; that comprehensive mandatory sanctions should be applied; and that Britain should firmly endorse the principle of no independence before majority rule (increasingly referred to as NIBMAR). He offered Wilson an adjournment but the British Prime Minister, digging in his toes, said they should talk it through but if that was the Afro-Asian-Caribbean group's final position then the communiqué would simply have to set out each side's point of view. The Secretary-General's reception, in a marquee in the garden, was arranged for the evening but the ensuing argument ran over time. Julie was left to entertain the British Leader of the Opposition, Edward Heath, in the empty tent for twenty minutes, until the meeting broke up. It was not an easy task: he was uncomfortable with ladies and in a bad mood at being kept waiting.

When the argument resumed after dinner no one was in the best of tempers. At the end of the evening an exasperated Wilson said, 'we are being treated as if we were a bloody colony'. There were indignant protests and he said, 'All right, I withdraw the "bloody"'. Of the three points in the caucus paper no one took the assertion about force very seriously. On comprehensive mandatory sanctions, Wilson did not agree but as the argument went on he progressively widened the list he was prepared to support and even our British colleagues privately accepted that a full list was inevitable in time.

The sticking point was NIBMAR. Wilson argued that to proclaim that independence could be granted only to a majority government would drive Rhodesia into a union with South Africa. He was determined to keep open the possibility of a negotiated end to UDI, a deal in which the white minority government would be given independence in return for guarantees of progress to 'one man, one vote'. This, however, was to go back to the 1961 constitution, which had seemed to guarantee unimpeded progress to majority rule only to be overturned by Ian Smith. Wilson's ongoing contacts with Salisbury were widely known (he was in fact preparing to make yet another 'final offer' to the Smith regime the following month) and most of his Commonwealth colleagues were understandably wary. If they endorsed his aims they might find they had endorsed a continuance of white rule and their positions at home would be untenable.

Five restricted sessions did not change this. Wilson elaborated in ever-greater detail the safeguards around his position. Any deal would have to be seen to be acceptable to the people of Rhodesia as a whole and the Commonwealth could be associated with this, but he ruled out a referendum and Royal Commissions for consulting the chiefs and 'ascertaining the opinion of the people' were unconvincing. The caucus group could not be shifted and the argument turned to how to word the communiqué.

Drafting this had become a task of Byzantine complexity. After my first effort had been rejected by Downing Street, I tried my hand at a set of paragraphs on Rhodesia designed to nudge the British more gently in the desired direction. The British themselves circulated a set of 'proposals'. Then Lester Pearson was commissioned to prepare a fusion draft. He recruited me to work on this and when we had finished I asked him about restricting the circulation of the text to avoid leaks. He grinned at me and said, 'The ship of state is a curious vessel, it leaks from the top'. All my subsequent experience in government confirmed the truth of this.

However, the fusion draft did not work either. Wilson said he had gone as far as he could. Rigid processes like the caucus did not allow any give and take. It might be better, he suggested, to adjourn and meet in three months' time in another Commonwealth capital, perhaps Nairobi. The prospect of no communiqué at all frightened everyone. The attempt to find common ground was abandoned – trying to marry the remaining drafts would by now have amounted to incest – and a small committee was established which produced an antiphonal communiqué, with alternating paragraphs on Rhodesia in which 'most heads of Government' declared their wishes on NIBMAR and 'the British Government' set out its position. But it did note that if the current offer was rejected the British Government would not accept any settlement involving independence before majority rule, and that with Commonwealth support on the Security Council (New Zealand, Nigeria and Uganda were members) it would seek selective mandatory sanctions. On 15 September everyone went home, cross with one another and with the course of the meeting.

Further British proposals were put to Salisbury in October. Sir Morrice James, who took them, doubted that they would be accepted. 'The white laager is tightening,' he told us, and he thought it would be a fight to the finish. At the beginning of December, Harold Wilson flew to Gibraltar for talks on HMS *Tiger* with Ian Smith. Fortunately for the Commonwealth Wilson's offer was rejected. The next day, at a meeting of the Sanctions Committee, the Secretary-General said the consequences envisaged in the September communiqué must now follow: no further offers of independence before majority rule and the adoption of selective mandatory sanctions by the Security Council. A sanctions resolution went to the Council and four days later we drove to a packed House of Commons to hear the British Prime Minister confirm that majority rule would henceforth be a precondition for Rhodesian independence. It was a near thing. Arnold told the Pakistani Foreign Minister two months later that there would have been 'hell to pay', including withdrawals from the Commonwealth if the *Tiger* proposals had been accepted.

A comparative calm descended and the Secretary-General resumed his visits to member countries, going in February 1967 to Pakistan (whose President, Ayub Khan, had like the Prime Ministers of India and Ceylon missed the last conference) and to Nepal, whose Foreign Secretary had indicated an interest in possible association with the Commonwealth. We flew to East Pakistan (now Bangladesh), stopping off in Cairo where we shared Shepheard's Hotel with King Ibn Saud who had taken over the whole floor above us. In Dhaka we stayed in the government guest house, a comfortable old house where an elderly gentleman lived outside my bedroom door and every time I moved around the room opened the door to ask if I had any laundry. We visited jute mills, high schools and art institutes, travelled to Chittagong and up the lovely Karnaphuli River, whose name, 'Jewel within the Ear', was even lovelier. It was plain that this part of Bengal was only artificially joined to its distant co-religionists, though there was no hint of the bloody war of separation that was to occur four years later.

We flew from there to Nepal, passing Everest with a plume of snow-smoke streaming from its peak. We were the only passengers on the little plane. As we contemplated cold chicken in cardboard boxes, a delicious-smelling curry was carried past us to the flight crew. Arnold called for a share and the result was the best airline meal I have ever had. In Katmandu the Prime Minister pointed out the help the Gurkhas had given in Malaysia and thought that the Commonwealth could do more to help Nepal. 'When you are struggling for survival between two giants, a little aid goes a long way.' China and India had just fought a war and there was some apprehension in Nepal about the possible military uses of a splendid new road which Chinese aid had built down from the Tibetan border.

There was, though, no serious thought about the Commonwealth – joining it might have disturbed the precarious balance between the two giants – and our days in Katmandu were largely a holiday. Even so it was wise to remember your brief. In a note Antony Duff (later head of MI5) had warned against critical remarks about the Rana family – 'they are everywhere in Katmandu'. (The Ranas, who had ruled Nepal for a long period as hereditary prime ministers, had been overthrown only a few years earlier.) One afternoon we sat on the ground in the bazaar as jewellers unwrapped paper twists of stones and poured a little shining stream into your hand or weighed out white diamonds on tiny balances. One opened a dirty piece of rag to show a necklace of cabochon emeralds and baroque pearls which I thought Julie might like. At dinner that evening, sitting beside the lively wife of the Foreign Secretary, I was moved to take it from my pocket and ask her advice. She said rather sharply, 'Those emeralds came from my grandfather's head-dress', but brushed away my apology to urge me to buy the necklace at once.

We looked at the curiously indecent Tantric carvings on the temples and visited the 'living goddess' Kumari, a richly robed child who regarded us gravely from a grated window high up in her temple courtyard. We drove through terraced valleys past monasteries where monks in rust-coloured robes stood on the roof and acquired merit by playing ten-foot long alphorns, their booming notes reverberating around the hills. We were taken to Pokhara to see Tibetan refugees, passing on the way a column or two of Gurkhas, marching along in what looked like a version of the scouting or New Zealand army 'lemon-squeezer' hat.

And best of all we spent a night at the British ambassador's rest-house, Kahana, high in the mountains. This was a hundred years old. An earlier ambassador, tiring of diplomatic life, had moved up here, signalling his needs by flags to distant Katmandu. One colour meant 'Send bread' and the other 'Send gin', which between them covered the essential requirements. We drove up a hill road through valleys terraced with narrow green paddy fields, their dark edges forming a pattern of wavering isobars. The house, a wooden bungalow with imposing pillars, was at 8000 feet altitude, and we arrived at sunset, with a cold mountain wind blowing. The valleys below us were already veiled in a blue dusk when even higher above us Mount Dhaulagiri caught the last of the sun and flamed out as a pure gold pyramid against the deep blue of the darkening sky. Despite the wind and the gathering night I watched as the gold retreated up the mountain and was snuffed out, and then went inside to a blazing log fire, a gin and the company of more rats than I had known since Samoa.

Flying to Karachi was a change of civilisations, from Buddhist to Middle Eastern Islam, emphasised at the government guesthouse by the sight of Arab fellow-guests descending from large limousines with hooded hawks on their wrists. We called on President Ayub Khan at Government House in Lahore. The President, very Sandhurst in tweed jacket and chestnut-brown shoes which had the appearance of having been polished by two generations of batmen, had a military bluntness in his speech. The future of the Commonwealth depended on finding a substitute for Britain; Canada, Australia and New Zealand are 'damn rich' and should put back more into the association – 'Tell them this from me'. Then we went in to lunch. A tray of orange juice arrived but as I went to take a glass a firm hand closed over mine. 'I think that one is for me,' the President said, and I learnt afterwards that he liked a little gin with his juice.

That evening the Governor of the Punjab entertained us to dinner in the Shalimar gardens, a legacy from the Mughal emperors which reflected their Persian taste and love of water. We sat on a kind of marble raft in the midst of a lake while beside us there were waterfalls behind which were set dozens of twinkling oil lamps. On a nearby raft a Pakistani army band dressed in kilts played 'Will ye no come back again' on the bagpipes.

From Peshawar we drove through the Khyber Pass to the Afghan border, past mud forts, the carved badges of British regiments once stationed there, and villages with open shops which seemed mainly devoted to the repair or manufacture of guns. Almost every man seemed to go about armed, even on the ancient buses which swayed up the road. The tribes were 'fairly quiet', our escort reported, but smuggling was rife. The guard of five or six cheerful villains, festooned with belts of ammunition, who rode in a truck in front of us were thus more for honour than security, though I felt sure that their absence would have made a temporary dent in the smuggling. We stopped at the mud-walled house of a tribal chief in Landi Kotal for a rooftop lunch of shashlik and other skewered meats, followed by blood oranges and green tea.

Within a few weeks Arnold was on the road again, to pay his first visits to New Zealand and Australia but also to lobby for support for a new Commonwealth aid concept which was to be considered at a Senior Officials Meeting in Nairobi towards the end of May. I was to combine the visit with home leave, for which Julie and the children went on ahead. I was left to a bachelor existence, the house being cared for by a gay footman moonlighting from Buckingham Palace.

Seeing your own country as a visitor is a slightly dislocating experience. In Auckland Arnold and I called on the Governor-General, Sir Bernard Fergusson, with whom I had had difficulties over the Cook Islands. All was forgiven and Sir. Bernard, though it was early in the afternoon, suggested a drink. When they came these proved to be brandy balloons half-filled with brandy. Even drinking snake wine in China did not demand the heroic effort required to empty these.

Recovered by next morning we drove down the North Island, stopping for lunch in Taihape, the Gumboot Capital of the World. I wanted Arnold to see the bar of a country hotel and took him in. A row of farm workers in black singlets, shorts and boots were propping up the bar with dogs and rifles propping up the wall behind them. A startled silence fell as Arnold, in flowing black overcoat, broad-brimmed hat and large walking-stick, appeared in the doorway. From the back an awed word floated up, 'Jesus!'

Michael Wilson took over for the Australian leg and the family and I returned to London through Mauritius and Nairobi where Bernard Chidzero, an exiled Rhodesian working for the UN, took everyone to see lions and giraffes in the Kenya Game Park. Then we set to work to prepare for the aid meeting. The idea behind the Secretary-General's thinking was simple. With a common working language, a network of public and private contacts and many common institutions, the Commonwealth was less subject to the difficulties of the unfamiliar which often hampered international technical assistance. The catch was an imbalance in the geographical distribution of experts and the money to fund them. Countries like Canada and Australia were stretched to provide ever-increasing numbers of experts; other countries like India, Ceylon or Jamaica had experts in a number of fields but no money to pay for them. The answer was to link them and for the Secretariat to arrange, for example, for a Pakistani hydrologist to go to Botswana with funding supplied by Canada.

Such a straightforward idea was bound to arouse misgivings. Harold Wilson was wary of an increasing drain on British aid money, and

Australia was also cautious. But the heads of government had blessed the proposals the previous September and referred the details to a meeting of senior aid experts in Kenya. In Nairobi we went to lunch with President Kenyatta, looking older and frailer with his young Ministers solicitous as well as respectful. But his talk was as vigorous as ever, discussing the weakness of the Rhodesian African movements and his concern about the developing crisis in Nigeria. After the meeting we also travelled to the other East African capitals, where we had become a familiar sight, to touch base with Obote, Kaunda and Nyerere.

The main business, though, was to establish the Commonwealth Fund for Technical Cooperation. The experts were lukewarm about proposals for trade promotion and market development which had been tacked on to our paper, and referred them 'for further study'. However, they liked the concept of a distinctive Commonwealth-wide aid programme. I sat up all night pulling the discussions together into a conference report in plain language, finishing it as the sun rose over Nairobi. I fell asleep in my seat behind the Secretary-General as it was being discussed and when I woke up the scheme had been approved.

From a modest start it grew to make a major contribution in the succeeding decades. Even in the first six months, there were technical advisory missions to eight countries, short-term consultancies in seven; and third-party finance had been arranged for two. Experts had been drawn from Britain, Canada, Ceylon, Jamaica, Pakistan and Uganda.

In August we were awaiting the birth of another baby. It was a busy time as Nigeria descended into civil war and I was drafting and redrafting proposals to put to both sides. Arnold confided to his diary on 8 August, 'I hope Juliet does not have her baby so soon that Gerald cannot get this done'. Six days later our fourth child, Sophie, was born at King's College Hospital in Dulwich. By now I was becoming something of a judge of maternity establishments. King's was spartan but snooty – Sophie was delivered by the Queen's obstetrician and an even grander figure, Sir John Peel, made visits like a general inspecting his troops. My uneasy relationship with matrons continued. I managed to smuggle a bottle of champagne into Julie's room to celebrate. The cork had just been removed with a carefully muffled pop when the door opened and there stood matron flanked by her entourage. I was caught wet-handed, so to speak, with a tooth-glass in my hand. Then I had one of those inspirations which sometimes come in life's darker moments and said to her, 'Would you like a drink?' She looked appalled, her younger acolytes looked as if they were trying not to laugh and they withdrew.

The Sanctions Committee worked on through the year, patiently tracking bogus companies, unregistered tankers, false manifests and all the now familiar detail of sanctions busting. It was, however, unable to unravel let alone disrupt the complicated arrangements that saw oil being trucked over the Beit Bridge from South Africa. It came to be a lonely vigil. The Americans were leaving the matter to Britain and when Arnold talked to the UN Secretary-General, U Thant, he seemed happy to leave both Rhodesia and the civil war in Nigeria to the Commonwealth. The Committee managed to get another slice of mandatory sanctions adopted in May 1968 but otherwise there were few high spots.

One was the decision by the British Foreign Secretary, George Brown, to address the High Commissioners in Marlborough House. He came late from lunch and as we got him into a chair it was clear that he had lunched rather well. When he was handed the statement that had been prepared for him he sent it spinning down the polished table saying, 'They've written this for me but I want to speak to you from the heart'. Beside me his Permanent Under-Secretary stiffened with disapproval. When Brown did speak it became apparent that it was not only his heart that was full. He seemed to have forgotten not just what he was supposed to say but even what the meeting was about. Long parliamentary practice enabled him to speak for half an hour about nothing in particular and withdraw to his car with a rigid-faced departmental head.

George Brown's appearance at Marlborough House marked another stage in the Secretariat's acceptance in Whitehall. The permanent heads and other senior officials were large-minded in their approach but the middle levels, especially of the Commonwealth Relations Office, felt threatened. Their days as a separate department were numbered and they tended to take a conservative and often negative view of the Secretariat's work, its budget and even its social standing. For some years the Foreign Office refused (much to Arnold's irritation) to invite him to the Queen's annual diplomatic reception at Buckingham Palace. In 1968 the Queen herself overrode this and Arnold was kind enough to include us in the party. Julie rented a long white silk dress from Moss Bros, so slim-fitting that it showed her underwear. So she dispensed with this, observing that it was unlikely to be the first time that ladies had been in this situation in the palace.

In the Throne Room ambassadors and high commissioners were lined up in order of precedence, with the Secretariat at the end. After their dinner the Royal Family moved around the room with each little national group being presented to the Queen. When she had finished speaking to Arnold, and the Duke of Edinburgh had finished his conversation with Julie, the formal part of the proceedings was over and everyone turned with relief to champagne at the bar. When I got there, though, it was sealed off by a solid wall of red backs. The gentlemen of the Queen's Household, elderly generals in full-dress uniform, were seasoned campaigners at this sort of thing and a flying column had taken possession of the bar before anyone else had thought of moving. So when a band struck up there was nothing to do but dance. We had both been taught by the same dancing teacher in Christchurch, with the result that we could only dance comfortably with each other. As we waltzed slowly around the Throne Room it seemed that the labours of Miss E Comyns Thomas on my behalf, not much enjoyed by either of us at the time, had at last been rewarded.*

Early in 1968 the discomfort about the last Commonwealth conference had begun to fade and there was a general feeling that too long should not pass before another. Wilson agreed but thought it should be in Ottawa. Pearson, who was about to step down, was unwilling to commit his successor. Since no one was eager for an early meeting the issue drifted down the months until Pierre Trudeau, the new Canadian Prime Minister, ruled out Ottawa, Wilson rejected October for parliamentary reasons and it was agreed to meet in London in early January 1969.

October instead was used by Wilson for yet another attempt to reach a deal with Ian Smith at a meeting held this time on HMS *Fearless*. Told in confidence before it had gone to the British Cabinet, Arnold said that 'this kind of annual autumn exploratory exercise' would merely renew suspicions of a British sell-out. In fact Wilson's regular 'final offers' had come to have almost a ritual air, enhanced by Ian Smith's equally regular rejection of them. So despite the fact that the British again went back on their NIBMAR commitment and offered independence provided

---

* Miss Thomas had taught both our fathers and was rumoured to have begun when the minuet was fashionable.

there were guarantees of *progress* towards majority rule the damage to Commonwealth confidence was less than we feared.

By this time the Secretariat had established a specialised Conference Division and preparations for a Commonwealth conference had become routine. There was still the odd surprise. A man arrived to repair the telephone exchange in the basement. When I told him that there was nothing the matter with the exchange he, apparently taking me for a British official, tapped the side of his nose and smiled at me. Arnold laughed when I recounted this. We had always assumed that his office was bugged. A portrait of the Earl of Sandwich (he who famously called for 'a slice of beef between two slabs of bread' and was the patron of Captain Cook) had been hung over the fireplace. Since he looked a little shifty the fancy was that his picture concealed the bug. This did not bother Arnold. I can recall only two or three occasions when we walked in the garden to be certain of having a private conversation. Otherwise he took the sturdy view that a bug gave a better chance of getting your views across – that a frank statement directed towards the noble earl and laboriously transcribed from a tape was likely to have more impact on the recipients than the polite phrases of a formal call.

The Commonwealth now had twenty-eight members and a tight squeeze was required to fit everyone into the usual room when the meeting opened on 7 January. There were complaints about the crush and the stuffiness as the windows were kept closed against the chill of early January and this was the last time the drawing-room was used for such a gathering. Among the twenty-four heads of government who attended were some new faces: Indira Gandhi of India; John Gorton of Australia, who caused some protocol difficulties by wanting equal treatment for his wife and his mistress; and Pierre Trudeau of Canada. A self-consciously dashing bachelor, he kept the London papers in copy with photographs of him taking a different beauty each evening to the nightclub Annabel's. Towards the close of the conference, at a reception upstairs in Lancaster House he was urging Julie to accompany him that evening when I appeared. Discovering that she was married he took his leave by sliding down the banisters, wobbling a little as he gave us a jaunty wave.

The aged Prime Minister of Ceylon, Dudley Senanayake, who attended his first Commonwealth conference in 1953, was asked to open the proceedings. In a sign of the new moderation the first agenda item was the World Political Situation. The usual sentiments were expressed about the usual subjects – the rivalry between the two super-powers, the need for nuclear disarmament and a better deal for the developing countries. An act restricting immigration into Britain had aroused the concern of West Indian and East African countries but the Secretary-General, arguing that this was a bilateral and not a Commonwealth issue, managed to shift the topic to an informal meeting. Vietnam was the subject of some discussion. Harold Wilson had private hopes of reviving the idea of a Commonwealth mediation mission, and several of us were asked to renew our shots against this possibility. Whatever hope there was, though, languished as the countries nearest Vietnam gave more realistic assessments of what was happening.

The mood on Rhodesia was calm or at least resigned. No one wished a repeat of the near-disaster of September 1966; and whatever the misgivings about the *Fearless* proposals, the truth was (as the Minister of State, George Thomson, pointed out) that Britain could have sold out at any time over the past three years. Beneath it all was an acceptance that the original fears of President Kaunda and others had come true – without more decisive action the illegal regime had been able to settle in. We had all, as Thomson also noted, learnt a hard lesson in the limitations of economic sanctions. The Sanctions Committee agreed that they were insufficient to achieve their political aim, because South Africa and Portugal were frustrating them. Comprehensive mandatory sanctions would still leak, they acknowledged gloomily, but at least they would show greater determination by the international community.

In the course of the discussion Julius Nyerere (back again) and several others twitted Wilson for going back on his NIBMAR pledge – an undeniable fact that in no way disturbed Wilson's geniality in the chair – but reiterating the point was the best many speakers could do. Trudeau and Holyoake supported the principle too, but thought the British Government had to be left to use its discretion in getting an acceptable settlement. As Trudeau put it, in politics it was sometimes wise to take the second best if it was a step in the right direction. Lee Kuan Yew summed up the position with bleak realism: the Africans had either to be prepared to fight a guerrilla war like the Vietcong or they had to accept the best the British could provide. This proved sadly true. In the seventies the dull edge of sanctions began to give way to the sharper pressure of warfare inside Rhodesia and this by 1979 brought about the collapse of the minority regime.

In the calmer atmosphere the communiqué was no longer an incendiary document and drafting it reverted to senior officials. They in turn reverted to their old habit of sitting till the small hours of the morning, with those of a pedantic disposition enjoying the almost limitless possibilities for re-wording sentences. As we prepared paragraphs and fed them to the group, the Australian, Sir Lennox Hewitt, would tilt his glasses and scrutinise each as if it were the balance sheet of a failing company, before asking the Secretariat whether he could dissociate himself from it. By now the struggle for unity of view had been abandoned and the antiphonal formula, using terms like 'most' or 'several' or even naming an individual head of government, had greatly eased the task.

The meeting broke up on 15 January in a hum of self-congratulation. Kaunda and Nyerere were impressed with it; Canada talked of a new maturity and realism; and Harold Wilson wrote to the Secretary-General to say that the conference 'was the most soberly constructive and positive of any in recent years'. That was a piece of Wilsonian exuberance. The relief was more that the Commonwealth had survived and had perhaps got to know itself better. The problem of Rhodesia remained and was to worsen, but the crisis for the Commonwealth association that began as we flew from Entebbe to Nairobi in November 1965 was over.

# CHAPTER FOUR

# *War in Nigeria*

T HE OVERTHROW OF THE NIGERIAN GOVERNMENT JUST AFTER
the Commonwealth meeting in Lagos was the culmination of
growing tensions in the country. The coup by army officers was
ostensibly a response to the widespread corruption which disfigured the
country's politics. In fact it reflected the disintegration of the already
delicate balance of regions and ethnic groupings which Britain had
bequeathed to the independent state earlier in the decade. Nigeria was
divided into four regions (each larger than many independent African
states): the Moslem North, the Ibo East and the Yoruba West, with the
mixed Mid-West between these two. The North had been traditionally
dominant in Nigerian politics, its political strength based on weight of
numbers. Brisk population growth in the South was eroding this to the
point where the next census was expected to tilt the balance. Publication
of the census results was suppressed, and unrest broke out in the West
over dubious elections. His critics charged that the Prime Minister, Sir
Abubakar Tafawa Balewa (who was from the North), had offered to host
the Commonwealth conference in an effort to provide a distraction.

The coup was carefully organised. Even in the North it was initially
welcomed as a chance to end the corruption. Only eleven were killed;
most of them senior army officers who had clearly been targeted.
Months later Major-General Gowon claimed he owed his life to the
Commonwealth Secretariat. Returning from leave he had planned to
stay at the Ikoyi Hotel but because of the Secretariat numbers he could
not get a room. A senior colleague who was staying there was sought out
and killed.

As time went on the mood changed. It was noted that none of the officers killed had been Ibos from the Eastern Region and that the new military government under General Ironsi was Ibo-dominated. Inter-ethnic jealousies, never far below the surface, began to ferment. The Ibos, sometimes called the Chinese of West Africa, were the traders and businessmen of Nigeria. Their energy and respect for education led inevitably to others complaining that they were 'arrogant' and 'scheming'. The political ineptness of the Ironsi government heightened these resentments. When in May 1966 a Unification Decree abolished the separate regions fears of an Ibo 'plot' to take control of the whole country seemed more plausible.

In July a counter-coup, this time more bloody, brought the then Lieutenant-Colonel Gowon to power. Over 200, including General Ironsi, were killed by Northern troops and Gowon told us that he had great difficulty in reining in the soldiers. The damage was done. Anti-Ibo riots and killings had broken out in the North at the time of the Unification Decree but in September-October these erupted again in a massacre of unprecedented fury in the North. At least 30,000 Ibos there – businessmen, school teachers, civil servants – were slaughtered and over a million refugees streamed out to seek shelter in their homeland in the East. Nigeria, it seemed, did not want the Ibos. As with the American South a century earlier, an aggrieved population concentrated in a geographically compact region raised the risk of secession.

The march of events confirmed this. The Military Governor of the Eastern Region, Colonel Ojukwu, would not recognise his colleague General Gowon as head of the central government. A meeting of Gowon with all the military governors of the regions at Aburi in January 1967 led only to confused recriminations about what had been decided. Discussions about revenue-sharing had been regarded as informal and tentative but Ojukwu then moved to withhold funds from the central government, on the grounds that they were needed to care for the refugees. In retaliation Lagos suspended Nigerian Airways flights to the East and week by week the institutional links between the East and the rest of the country began to snap.

In March a disaster was looming. My family was in New Zealand and on Saturdays I lunched on my own at the Travellers' Club. Every Saturday I was teased by the head steward – 'You're not going down to the country this weekend?' – but this condescension was banished forever when one day he approached my table to murmur respectfully, 'The Secretary of State would like a word with you on the telephone'. Patrick Gordon Walker wished to urge the Secretary-General to try some private and highly circumspect diplomacy to see if Nigeria could be held together. The idea was that an independent Commonwealth mission might take a discreet look at the situation and report back to the Secretary-General on what might be done to help.

Yaw Adu was just the man to take some preliminary soundings and towards the end of the month he visited Lagos and all the regions. He went first to Accra to talk to Ghana's new head of state, General Ankrah (it was the decade of generals in West Africa). Ankrah had been trying to pin down the difficulties between Lagos and Enugu, the capital of the Eastern Region. He had managed to get all the military governors and General Gowon together to try and clear up the Aburi misunderstandings but had been unable to get any agreement. His impression was that it was going to be 'extremely difficult to hold Nigeria together in one piece'.

In Lagos there was no interest in any Commonwealth initiative, at least not for the present. They preferred to rely on General Ankrah's efforts, though these were upset in mid-April when he himself was the target of an abortive coup in Accra. After talking to Ojukwu and the other military governors Yaw's view was even more sombre. He saw the situation developing 'on a tragic course'. There was a complete breakdown of trust and confidence between the East and the rest of the country, and no leader with sufficient stature to bridge this. On the one hand he noted a general belief that the crisis stemmed from the excessive ambitions of the Eastern Ibos. On the other in Enugu he noted an intense emotion, excitement and tension after the trauma of the earlier massacres and the influx of refugees.

This last was born out by another report to Arnold. Emeka Anyaoku, a rising star in the Nigerian Foreign Service, had joined the Secretariat a year earlier. He came from a chiefly Ibo family and had been home that month. He confirmed that Ibos felt they could no longer live safely in Nigeria, and added that they had become deeply distrustful of the British and their motives.

Matters came to a head in May. Conscious that the old political framework had become unworkable, and that fear of Northern domination was not confined to Ibos, General Gowon issued a decree establishing twelve states in place of the unwieldy four regions. This was followed three days later by a declaration of independence by the old Eastern Region under the name of Biafra. There was some doubt as to which was the trigger and which the shot in these two events. It is possible that Gowon made his constitutional changes knowing that Biafran secession was near. Certainly, small signs like the immediate appearance of Biafran flags and badges suggested that the secession had been planned for some months.

Historical experience again suggested that a civil war would follow. Both sides stepped up their preparations. The Biafrans bought a B26 bomber in Luxembourg and tried to recruit mercenaries in Lisbon. A senior Nigerian politician went to Moscow to check the arms market. Arnold was keen to visit Lagos and urge restraint. Yaw and I were cautious, arguing that we should wait until the confusion cleared and there were clearer signs of what could be achieved. In the end we waited until it was too late.

On 6 July the three of us flew to Lagos. We drove straight to the Dodan Barracks where Gowon had prudently remained when he took over as head of government. His bungalow in the grounds was a standard one for a middle-ranking officer, typical of army houses the world over. Its modest furnishings seemed to reflect the personality of the man who greeted us. The immediate impression was of a decent and conscientious man, and although there were many of a contrary view, our later experience did not alter this. After a year in power he was still rather shy. Although on this occasion he was in uniform there was an unmilitary hesitancy about his manner, the hesitancy of an intelligent man who found himself working outside the limits of his training.

When we paused for morning tea in the general's small sitting-room he asked me if I was a New Zealander, saying that his room-mate at Staff College in England had been a New Zealander whom he had greatly liked. He was Chairman of the Federal Military Government but his power was still provisional, and for all he or anyone else knew, as temporary as his predecessor's.

We sat around the homely dining-room table and Arnold made an eloquent plea for one last effort, suggesting that the Commonwealth might help in the search for some common ground; it would be much more difficult if not impossible to do this once fighting had started. He was heard patiently but then Gowon said that months of attempts at reconciliation had failed and now there was no course but 'police action'. Federal troops, he told us, had crossed into Biafra that morning.

On that note the meeting broke up in the early afternoon with the agreement that we would meet again. We were staying at the government guest house and after dinner that night we gathered to discuss the next steps. Yaw warned that the British had earlier arranged for the house to be bugged as an independence present for the Nigerian Government. We therefore moved outside into the garden. It was a humid night with the moon slipping in and out of the clouds as we huddled together on the rough grass of the unmowed lawn. Yaw mentioned in passing that we should take care not to step on a snake, after which the details of our discussion were rather lost to me as every rustle started a speculation as to how many might be at large in the guest-house garden.

At Gowon's suggestion we drove the next day to Ibadan, hurtling along in an ancient government Cadillac past numerous wrecks of crashed or burnt-out cars. The Yoruba capital was the power-base of the country's leading civilian politician, Chief Awolowo, who was also Vice-Chairman of the Federal Executive Council. He too had led a conciliation mission to the East just before the secession. He had been well received, only to be publicly repudiated by Ojukwu after his return. 'I have written him off,' he said. Ojukwu was blinded by ambition and by a five-year projection of the likely oil revenues. Talks would get nowhere while he was there. As Awolowo's grandchildren ran in and out of the room he ended on a reflective note: much of the present difficulty was because the army was in control – politicians might talk and manoeuvre but they would have avoided these confrontations.

Back in Lagos we went to the Dodan Barracks for a second meeting. Gowon said the Federal troops were fighting on foot in the winter rains, a slow method but the way they knew best. He was hoping for a result in a few weeks, though 'in war you can never be certain'. There was no opening for Commonwealth mediation at this stage, but he acknowledged that the time might come when he would welcome help in bringing the two sides together or in organising the economic recovery of the East. That was the best we could do. At least the thought had been planted in Gowon's mind and its time might come in a struggle which the experts told us was likely to be long and messy.

We flew to Accra to brief General Ankrah. We talked in his office high in Christiansborg Castle, the hospitable general refilling our glasses with champagne at intervals. He too complained of having been deceived by Ojukwu, who he now thought had been preparing for secession for months – everything else, including Ankrah's own mission, had been delaying tactics. As a soldier he was not happy about Gowon's campaign plans – the troops should have gone in at divisional strength – but he was no longer willing to mediate or to have anything to do with Biafra. Then he took us on a tour of the castle dungeons.

At Accra airport Arnold met the Nigerian Secretary of External Affairs, who asked when Emeka Anyaoku could take the oath of allegiance. We talked this over when we returned to Marlborough House. With mediation a prospect it was best to avoid the question as long as possible. Arnold sent Emeka on a month's leave and then appointed him Secretary of the Commonwealth team observing the Gibraltar elections. It was important to protect him, an Ibo married to a Yoruba wife, though we carefully never asked his views. If the issue came to a head Arnold would take his stand on principle: as the servant of the Commonwealth Emeka was not at the command of any individual government.

Whitehall expected a military stalemate; the Federal troops might be able to advance along the coast and seal off Biafra but an advance into the heartland would be difficult. With General Ankrah's mission at an end British Ministers made it clear they would welcome a move by the Secretary-General to get talks started on a ceasefire and settlement. After talking to the Nigerian High Commissioner and a prominent Biafran academic Arnold decided to try. In August I drafted messages to both Gowon and Ojukwu urging the value of a temporary ceasefire to allow peace talks without preconditions and offering his help in organising them.

Neither side, however, was ready at this early stage and both replied setting out preconditions, Ojukwu demanding recognition of Biafra's sovereignty and Lagos its renunciation. Their willingness to consider talks was always geared directly to the military situation, waxing and waning with the fluctuations on the ground. At the beginning of August there were some early Federal successes which encouraged Ojukwu to refer to this 'wasteful conflict'. Later in the month, in a surprising coup, Biafran forces seized control of Benin in the Mid-West. They held it for only a few weeks but in the face of this embarrassing loss General Gowon did not feel he could start talks or agree that the Secretary-General should visit Biafra.

The effort, though, was far from wasted. In this first round of consultations the cast of characters were introduced to one another, the concept of mediation became more firmly established, as well as some confidence, if still shaky, in the Commonwealth Secretary-General as a go-between. The price of this from our point of view was an inexhaustible patience as listeners. Getting the confidence of each side meant listening at length to their arguments, often angry and emotional, without endorsing any of them. For weeks through September and beyond the representatives of both sides called at Marlborough House or less public locations to elaborate their views.

The Biafrans had the sharpest grievances and we spent long hours with them until we could recite their views from memory. We even took it in turns. On one occasion Arnold was at his cottage in France when the Biafran Minister of Home Affairs, Christopher Mojekwu, arrived and wanted to talk. In his room at the White House, a hotel favoured by his side, I sat on the bed for well over an hour while he denounced Britain for its perfidy, its cynical concern with oil not peoples, and its willingness to arm the Nigerians and thus to support genocide. When he calmed down I promised to relay this carefully to the Secretary-General and then asked conversationally what had brought him to Britain. 'Oh,' he said, 'I am putting my daughter into school.'

By the end of September Arnold was ready with a new proposal, suggesting that the two sides open a channel for secret exploratory discussions even while the fighting was going on, citing the precedent of the Allies' talks with the Italian Government in 1943. The Nigerian Commissioner for External Affairs said he was willing if the Biafrans were. When the Biafran representative in Washington telephoned in mid-October to relay their consent it looked like a breakthrough. Then the niggles started. The Biafrans were worried about meeting in London and unhappy with the level of representation proposed. They complained that they would be fielding 'ministers' as against the permanent secretaries Lagos was proposing to send.

Their unease persisted for months. It may have been political, for there was no doubt of the popular resentment against Britain in Biafra, and any disclosure that peace talks had begun there might not have been well received. It was unlikely to be safety, for Biafran representatives moved freely around London, even holding press conferences at Westminster. We looked for other venues outside the city, such as Wilton or Ditchley, and were offered Cliveden and even Windsor Castle. None, however, promised to be more private or comfortable than the

Secretary-General's flat in Carlton Gardens, a short step from a door into the Marlborough House garden.

When the first meeting was ready to start in late October, Mojekwu, the head of the Biafran delegation and reputed to be closest to his leader, stayed behind in Paris, stating that he would meet only with his ministerial counterparts. The Nigerian delegation thereupon declined to meet with the 'incomplete' Biafran team. It began to look as if protocol delicacies, which of course were a reflection of the underlying uneasiness, might prevent any talks at all. Arnold cut through this by proposing that Dr Kenneth Dike and a Nigerian Permanent Secretary, Allison Ayida, come to his flat on the following morning (Saturday, 20 October) for coffee. The atmosphere was tense at first. We stood about in Arnold's sitting-room, admiring his collection of Kandinskys and other early Russian abstract art at rather unnecessary length. In time, though, they began to relax. They knew and respected one another, and the talk loosened to the point where a fuller meeting could be arranged for that evening and for six hours on the next day. At the end the Nigerians left for home but said they would return as soon as the Biafrans were ready.

A few days later Mojekwu turned up but said he was nervous about his own security in London. He wanted us to provide a bodyguard but could not accept a British one. His sensible colleague told us to make the best arrangement we could and say nothing. So a silent shadow was arranged with Special Branch. He would follow Mojekwu rather than accompany him and since they could not meet I undertook to point out his charge to him. When I arrived at the Secretary-General's flat it was not difficult to identify the Special Branch man – someone sitting in the deserted downstairs lobby reading *The Times* was obvious enough, added to which he was wearing a trench coat with his hat pulled over his eyes. When we emerged from the lift, I walked as arranged behind Mojekwu, pointing him out with my finger in an elaborate pantomime. After I had seen Christopher into his car and watched it drive away, I turned to find the Special Branch man still there. 'Aren't you supposed to follow him?' 'Yes,' he said, 'but all the office cars are out this morning.'

Now that we had the full Biafran delegation in London there were signs of misgivings in Lagos. An odd message came from Gowon asking for a reaffirmation in writing of the basis of the proposed talks – something that had been fully discussed with him two weeks earlier. In the Nigerian High Commissioner's study in Kensington Palace Gardens we put together a response to go back that night. It was no use. The hawks counter-attacked at an all-day Cabinet meeting in Lagos, and their delegation failed to return on the date they had promised. The Biafrans went home, Mojekwu claiming that he was disobeying instructions by even being in London. Nervousness and ambivalence on both sides had ended a second and more promising start.

The war went into one of its quiescent periods throughout most of November. Cables were exchanged and conversations continued at Marlborough House. Cordial messages came from Ojukwu, hopeful signs were relayed to us, but nothing happened. The strain of waiting, all the draftings and re-draftings in the search for an opening, began to be felt by us all. Yaw Adu commented to Julie that I was looking tired; he thought I should take a second wife. When this suggestion was received with considerable frostiness he hastened to explain: the custom in his country was that a second wife had to be approved if not selected by the first. Julie's outrage softened but by then I in turn had lost interest.

In any case Yaw's stories of life in a polygamous household were not such as to cause any rush into that institution. His chiefly father had four wives, contriving at the same time to serve as a respected elder of the Presbyterian Church (doctrine seemed to become milder as the distance from the mother church increased). Each wife occupied a house of her own in one of the four corners of the compound and according to Yaw fought continuously. When his father became exasperated with the quarrelling he lined wives and children up and dosed them all with castor oil, which he had sent out from England by the case. After this it was understandable that Yaw had never taken his own advice and instead stayed happily married to the one wife.

By the end of the month, when Mojekwu arrived with yet another promise of willingness to resume talks, the Secretary-General lost patience. The stalling, he said, raised doubts about Biafran sincerity and weakened the moderates in Lagos who had been made to look foolish. When hostilities resumed negotiations were hardly going to be easier.

The time had come to press harder. Months of listening had made clear what was negotiable and what was not on each side; to an outsider the outlines of a compromise were plain. The bottom line for Lagos was Nigeria's territorial integrity and the twelve-state structure which had removed for everyone the fear of Northern domination. For the Ibo leaders it was the physical and economic security of Biafra's people.

Human passions had made the other issues formidably difficult but they were soluble. So, Arnold said bluntly, was there any chance of reaching agreement along these lines? Mojekwu not surprisingly hedged but then dropped a broad hint. It would be easier, he said, if each side met separately with the Secretary-General; then each would be free to confide in him how far they were prepared to go 'in certain matters'.

Hitherto Arnold had been reluctant to contemplate separate talks. At best this was a cumbersome and much slower method with more chances of misunderstandings. As policemen and marriage counsellors know, intervening in a quarrel can be a thankless task. There was a significant danger that any probing of the position of each side would be taken as advocating the other's and it would be fatally easy for both to lose faith in the Secretary-General's impartiality. Now the risk had to be accepted – there was no other way forward.

For three days after Christmas we sat down with the Biafran delegation. Things were still sticky; the first full day went by in a restatement of the familiar concerns. By the second day we began to bite into the substance. Their primary concern was to secure a ceasefire but the price for this was obviously acceptance of one Nigeria in some form, otherwise Lagos would be accepting defeat. With some reservations they acknowledged that this could be discussed. They were nervous, though, that any undertakings could be used to discredit them at home and pressed the Secretary-General to put forward his own proposals. We prepared a paper setting out 'hypothetical' possibilities on issues like security, territorial viability, economic opportunities, transitional arrangements and a constitutional settlement. They took this home with them saying that the consultations were making progress.

We were encouraged and asked for the Nigerian delegation to return a week later. When they came, early in January 1968, we explained that, though the Biafrans had been deliberately vague to protect themselves, they had hinted very strongly that there was room for compromise. The Nigerians began to show interest. The pre-requisite for a ceasefire, they said, was acceptance of one Nigeria and its new state structure. Provided this was unambiguous the constitutional details could be settled later.

Common ground was now emerging. I was able to draft a paper setting out the Secretary-General's proposals with some confidence that they were at least broadly acceptable to both sides. The breakthrough came at Heathrow Airport where we met with a Biafran delegation now led by Michael Okpara, a former Premier of the Eastern Region, who had political standing of his own. He and his colleagues were reluctant to come through British immigration so we arranged a meeting-room on the other side of the barrier. This turned out to be a glass-walled office in the middle of the concourse with two policemen outside to ensure that we were even more conspicuous. We found an empty office upstairs and there Arnold was frank: they would have to accept a Nigerian entity in return for safeguards for a constituent state of Biafra. If they could do this he would have enough leverage, with help from Britain and the United States, to get suitable guarantees on internal security and economic recovery from Lagos. There could then be a ceasefire and a temporary Commonwealth force to ensure its effectiveness.

The Biafrans gulped; it was a great sacrifice. The war, however, was not going well and Okpara, a broader and more experienced negotiator than his colleagues, said that the package was worth 'very careful consideration'. Was the heart of the proposal that if Biafra agreed to a central Nigerian authority it would retain control of internal security? Assured on both points, he returned with an acceptance in eight days. On 2 February with some sense of ceremony we all initialled a document setting out the 'package proposals' for an end to the war. It was agreed that the Secretary-General would discuss these with the Federal Government on the basis that if they could accept the package 'he had reason to believe that the Biafran Government could do likewise'. We went home and had a celebratory drink; it looked as if the most difficult and delicate part was behind us.

A week later the three of us were in Lagos where, in a pattern that was becoming familiar, the package was coolly received. For two days of meetings we were back at General Gowon's dining-table. On the other side this time were fourteen members of the Supreme Military Council, including an admiral, and one civilian, the Commissioner for External Affairs. The air was heavy with suspicion as Arnold set out his proposals. Even the Commissioner, with whom they had been earlier discussed, was determinedly critical, perhaps to cover himself in this company. Gowon noted that it was a significant change if the Biafrans were no longer insisting on sovereignty but the rest suggested not a federation but a loose association of states. His colleagues weighed in with suitably sceptical comments. After nearly four hours of talk, however, Gowon surprised us (and perhaps some of his colleagues) by saying that a meeting between the two sides was needed. The Federal Government was ready and the next step was to draw up a neutral agenda. Everyone stood up, the talk in the crowded room became lively from relief, and we stayed to eat a belated curry lunch.

Early next morning we were back, waiting for half an hour in the sun-porch while the Supreme Military Council worked out its position in the dining-room. When we sat down at the table a draft agenda and set of annotations were distributed. The five-point agenda which covered one Nigeria, a constitutional review, ceasefire arrangements, amnesty and economic matters such as property rights and employment opportunities was straightforward. The annotations were another matter. If they were intended as preconditions it would make a meeting difficult if not impossible. There was a silence. Gowon broke it by saying that he had gone against the advice of many of his colleagues in agreeing to the earlier talks in October. Were the Biafrans more serious now? Arnold pointed out that one Nigeria was part of his proposals, adding that a deal was possible but would require some give-and-take on both sides. Gowon then said that the important thing was to start talking and the meeting agreed that the annotations were simply explanations of the Federal position.

Two days later we relayed this response to Ojukwu, asking him to send properly accredited representatives to start talks. Then silence fell and a month went by (which Biafra could ill afford militarily). We never knew why. The leadership may have become fearful that they had conceded too much in advance and that direct talks would be used to push them into a surrender. They were still worried about talks in London and were aggrieved that the Secretary-General, who had been in and out of Lagos, had never been to Biafra. This was indeed a serious weakness in our mediation efforts. Without a visit we could not make our own appraisal of the balance of views there. Nor could we make our points directly and instead had to rely on envoys who were fearful of offending Ojukwu. It was a weakness we were never able to overcome for we could not go without clearance from Lagos and this they would never give, thinking a visit would be a form of international recognition.

In the meantime Arnold had written to Commonwealth heads telling them in broad terms the position that had been reached. In the raft of replies received Lee Kuan Yew welcomed the cheerful note and added, 'It takes a lot of optimism, stamina and faith to do the things you are doing' – which pretty much summed up Arnold's best qualities. Yaw went to Accra to brief General Ankrah and fuller messages went to those countries which might later be asked for a peacekeeping contribution. It was prudent to do some planning for the quick deployment of a force might be crucial to getting a ceasefire. We went to see Harold Wilson, sitting in his usual seat half way down the long table in the downstairs Cabinet room. He was initially cautious: Cabinet 'was in a fairly general withdraw-into-Europe mood'. However, he agreed to look into it, saying that his military advisers, who had told him four battalions would be needed, tended to be over-cautious. Lester Pearson from Canada also agreed that some contribution would have to be considered.

The Secretariat's efforts had now become widely known, and as we waited for the Biafran reply a number of church representatives, earnest humanitarians, liberal peers and plain cranks flocked to Marlborough House with suggestions. The Emir of Kano, resplendent in gold-embroidered robes and accompanied by a white-garbed attendant with a dagger, called to wish us well – he was a friend of Col. Ojukwu. Lord Fenner Brockway urged us to make greater efforts. Major 'Mad Mike' Hoare, who had led a mercenary group in the Congo, made several visits to explain his plan for ending the war and why he would not work for Ojukwu. He left his wife, a faded blonde in a black mink coat, downstairs with the porter. She seemed terrified of him. I had to repress the temptation each time he came to say, 'Good morning Major Hoare, and how is Mrs W?'

As the weeks went by and their troops made more progress the Federal Government's position began to harden again. A message arrived from Gowon saying that they now wanted convincing evidence – a signed note from Ojukwu no less – accepting one Nigeria. By a helpful coincidence the Commonwealth Education Conference was about to meet in Lagos, giving Arnold and me good cover for another visit in late February. We had come to another break-point and it was again time for some blunt talking, this time to the Federal side. At the Dodan Barracks Arnold put it plainly: was it worth continuing his efforts? Gowon was silent for a time and then suggested waiting for the Biafran reply. His private secretary took us aside some days later to say that they were having serious difficulties with their hawks, particularly the field commanders who were concerned that a ceasefire might prevent them from finishing the job.

We stayed on for the Education Ministers conference. At the beginning of March we flew north to see the Military Governor, Col. Katsina, at Kaduna. As we gathered in the pre-dawn darkness our pilot, an elderly New Zealander, reached with shaking hands for his second cup, saying that it took strong coffee to get him going. With that encouragement we got to Kaduna, where the Governor said that Gowon had kept him informed, that he liked Michael Okpara, and that he favoured a negotiated settlement.

From there we flew further north over increasingly arid country to Zaria, to call on the Emir. The emirate was not a major player in any peace process unless you were thinking of the Crusades but that did not detract from its interest. Zaria was an ancient Moslem town with mud walls which shone russet-pink in the strong sun. The palace was a desert fort of the same colour. The dress and everything else about the Emir and his court breathed a conviction that there was no century like the twelfth. He wore flowing robes with shoes whose points curled up in Arabian Nights fashion and an attendant similarly dressed stood behind his chair with a broad-bladed sword. In these surroundings conversation paled into bland niceties as coffee was served in tiny cups and the Emir surveyed the two infidels before him.

In his waiting-room the walls were decorated with curling photographs of earlier British Residents. A succession of these young men had lived in a bungalow outside the town and, it appeared, rode a bicycle to call on the Emir. The bicycle had in no way diminished the authority of the Empire; indeed it was a mark of imperial confidence. Although there were normally no troops much closer than Lagos, 800 kilometres away, the instructions of each young man seemed to have been accepted without complaint. When the Emir was told to stop beheading evildoers in the marketplace on Fridays he did so, returning to the practice as soon as the British had gone.

While we were away the peace party in Lagos had regrouped and Chief Anthony Enahoro, an able politician who was now Commissioner of Labour, took over the negotiations. He listened carefully to the Secretary-General's account and then came back the next day to say that he had 'consulted' and now wished to put the outcome in a brief communicable form. He proposed what he called a two-stage approach: talks to establish the basis for a permanent ceasefire, including the acceptance of one Nigeria and guarantees of security for Biafrans. After a cooling-off period there would then be a constitutional conference of all the states, to discuss boundaries, control of resources and other matters of common concern. He was clearly looking for a way to get the contacts back on track and equally clearly was acting on Gowon's behalf. Arnold said he was willing to explore this with the other side. Enahoro then revealed the divisions on his own side by asking that we not telephone him or use the normal channel of the Nigerian High Commission; it would be best to communicate through the Canadian office in Lagos.

The Biafrans, though, remained elusive. The war was intensifying, with Federal troops making significant advances. Biafra was now sealed off from the sea with communications increasingly reduced to night flights from São Tomé and elsewhere in old Constellation aircraft. Towards the end of March Mojekwu reappeared but still without any response. He complained that the Biafrans had 'stuck their neck out' with the package proposals and the Federal Government would not even look at them. When Arnold corrected him, saying that Lagos had proposed a meeting without preconditions Mojekwu dismissed the so-called neutral agenda as containing implied preconditions.

Another three weeks drifted by with successive Biafran representatives preferring to argue about Lagos's motives than to try to move things forward. Arnold told them they had made a serious tactical error in not accepting the earlier offer of talks – it had strengthened the hand of the war party in Lagos. He then put Enahoro's plan to them saying that Gowon was aware of it but had not put it through the Federal Executive Council. There was still no reaction until late April when Arnold relayed a message saying that Gowon was prepared to begin unconditional talks to see whether a settlement could be reached.

Three days later Ojukwu accepted this and said that his delegation was ready to leave – for Dakar. We put our heads in our hands – was this another precondition? We hastily got hold of Ignatius Kogbara, a sensible younger Biafran with whom I was on sociable terms, and he obliged by stating (on what grounds was never clear) that this was a suggestion not a precondition and that the talks could start in London and then move to Africa if desired. That was good enough and Arnold was able to telephone Lagos to say that secret talks to settle the procedures for a peace conference – venue, chairmanship and agenda – would start in London the following week.

Life, as Malcolm Fraser famously observed, was not meant to be easy and there were times at these talks when we looked back on the simple days of trying to arrange them. The Nigerian delegation consisted of Enahoro and Ayida; the Biafran of Sir Louis Mbanefo, the Chief Justice (perhaps significantly we did not see Okpara again) and Kogbara. Together with Arnold and me the two sides met at the Secretary-General's flat. The six of us grouped ourselves around a small coffee table on which stood a microphone and tape-recorder – the Biafrans had initially insisted on a verbatim record. About the only speedy agreement reached was to abandon this. My secretary rebelled at the confusion of disembodied voices and accents which the tape-recorder produced, and instead I dictated a summary record between sessions.

We met on 6 May, the two delegations arriving at different times, partly to preserve secrecy and partly to spare the opposing sides having to jam into the building's small lift which opened directly into Arnold's hallway. Even before this it had taken two three-hour sessions with Sir Louis at the White House hotel to get over his insistence on Dakar. A distinguished lawyer and most upright man, he seemed to regard this and all subsequent differences as judicial issues to be settled by a decision rather than by negotiation. On the site for the peace talks it became clear that whatever was suggested by one side would be opposed by the other. The Nigerians preferred London, the Biafrans somewhere in Africa. Sir Louis, with an impatience which was to become familiar, wondered if it was worth pressing on with these meetings. It was agreed to exchange letters overnight with fresh suggestions, and mercifully both letters named Kampala.

The next day, though Sir Louis worried about what was meant by 'servicing', it was agreed that the Commonwealth Secretariat should service the meetings. After two days of discussions we had managed to clear just two hurdles. On chairmanship, the Biafrans would not accept the Secretary-General (insufficiently impartial) and the Nigerians would not accept an African head of state (implied recognition). After a week's wrangling a compromise was reached – there would be no chairman – after Arnold pointed out that the forthcoming Paris peace talks on Vietnam would not have one (we had checked with the American Embassy). Agreement was reached fairly quickly that Milton Obote, now President of Uganda, would be invited to open the conference and to name an observer.

The stumbling-block was the agenda. Things started badly on 8 May when Enahoro (perhaps to satisfy requirements at home) tabled a highly tendentious seven-point agenda specifying agreement on one Nigeria and the twelve states structure in return for an immediate ceasefire. Sir Louis naturally rejected this and Arnold urged everyone to keep in mind that the talks should start without preconditions. The atmosphere was soured, though, and a two-day adjournment was agreed to allow the Secretary-General to talk privately with each.

In the course of these consultations Enahoro came up with a better idea – just two broad agenda headings: 'conditions for ending the hostilities' and 'arrangements for a permanent settlement' – though he had to clear it with Lagos first. He suggested that under these headings each side could give notice of the topics it intended to raise; the Federal list would be the seven points he had tabled earlier. Sir Louis was indignant, scenting an attempt to smuggle in preconditions. What, he said, if he were to propose the 'sovereignty of Biafra' as one of their topics? Fine, said Enahoro, that was the point: each side was free to raise what it wished. But Sir Louis, stiff and legalistic, was unmollified. The argument dragged on for three days, broken only when for variety we turned back to disagreeing over the chairmanship or whether the OAU rather than the Commonwealth Secretariat should service the peace conference. Sir Louis' background made him see compromises as collusion between two opposing litigants; even when he accepted a point the best he could sometimes manage was 'no comment'. Periodically we had to call half-hour pauses while Arnold and I ducked into the kitchen to devise a way through.

Finally the two-point agenda was agreed and with the other issues out of the way I could draft a communiqué announcing agreement on a peace conference. Then, unbelievably, a dispute broke out over the starting date for the Kampala conference. Sir Louis pressed for the following week; Enahoro said that he needed ten days to return home and get his instructions before flying to Kampala. Sir Louis was unyielding but he had used up his credit by days of obdurate bargaining over minor points and now Enahoro too became bloody-minded. It began to look as if the conference might collapse over a difference which had been narrowed to twenty-four hours.

We broke up in the middle of the afternoon, hungry and despondent. Then Kogbara and I had a chat and he suggested quietly that, though Sir

Louis could never propose it himself, the Secretary-General might offer a face-saving compromise. When Arnold split the difference Enahoro was willing but Sir Louis said he had decided to withdraw – he had 'stuck his neck out several times' already. Arnold relieved his feelings by commenting under his breath that it was a mark of the puritan mind to do stupid things as a matter of principle. Then a timely telephone call (which we pretended not to hear) from the Biafran office in Lisbon brought final acceptance by Sir Louis. A tray of glasses and champagne was set down on the coffee table, now overflowing with papers, and everyone (except Sir Louis) raised a glass. After eleven meetings the communiqué was released the next morning, 15 May. Substantive peace talks would begin in Kampala on 23 May with Dr Obote to address the opening session.

The Kampala conference was inevitably in the public eye. Sixty correspondents and television crews descended on the Ugandan capital, along with churchmen, lobbyists and the shadowy people who haunt the fringes of international occasions. The Secretariat and the Nigerians were accommodated at the Apolo Hotel (known to the press but not the President's countrymen as the Milton Hilton) and the Biafrans at the Grand. Each delegation consisted of half a dozen principals, headed still by Anthony Enahoro and Sir Louis Mbanefo.

The meetings were to be held in Parliament Buildings. The size of the chamber rather dwarfed the handful of delegates and the Secretariat conference team which assembled there on the opening day. The leaders addressed one another across a distance which only emphasised the gap between their views. Confidence was unlikely to blossom or quiet deals to be done in this high hall where microphones were needed to be heard. The earlier discussions around dining- or coffee tables had at least encouraged quiet conversational tones. However proceedings got under way with an opening address by the President who appointed his Foreign Minister, Sam Odaka, to sit in on the discussions and made it clear that he was ready to play a helpful part in the process.

This helpfulness made itself immediately apparent when the President invited Arnold and me on two successive nights to the strange late-night sessions he liked to hold with his Ministers and friends in his spacious office on the top of Parliament Buildings. Everyone sat in armchairs while drinks were served by the President's mistress, the beautiful Helen from Toro. As the night wore on there would be heavy-handed jokes about how many cows she was worth, as the tall girl drifted around with a smile refilling the glasses.

The proceedings were jocular but they were not jolly. It was not just tiredness and an increasing desire to be elsewhere that affected the two of us. There were uncomfortable, even sinister, undertones: I wondered if Stalin's parties had been like this. Obote's comments invariably drew appreciative laughter but it was an artificial hilarity. There was some edgy teasing, much of it directed at Obote's Chief of Staff, a Colonel Amin. If we were looking for gold dust or ivory, we were told, Idi would be happy to get us some (we learnt that he had acquired a reputation for smuggling these from the Congo). The colonel would giggle while his eyes darted around the room to see how serious the President was. Then Helen would silently fill all the glasses again.

The need to settle housekeeping matters meant that serious discussions at the conference did not get under way until two days later, on Saturday, 25 May. As lengthy speeches were made, taken down verbatim with the help of technicians from Radio Uganda, it became clear that no deal-making was likely in this forum. The Biafrans perhaps made a tactical error in opening with a long recital of their grievances, which gave Enahoro the opportunity to seek an adjournment until the following day, so that he could prepare a suitable reply. Sir Louis, always on a hair trigger, saw this as stalling and a ruse to prolong the proceedings.

Then a tragedy disrupted everything. A confidential clerk in the Nigerian delegation, who occupied a room in the corridor down from me, disappeared. Hotels, brothels, hospitals and mortuaries were searched without success. Whether he had been kidnapped or lured away it seemed likely that he was dead, and indeed his body was found in a swamp near Kampala three weeks later. Since he knew no one in Kampala his murder must have been connected with the talks, and Nigerian suspicions were heightened by the fact that he was from the old Eastern Region. It gave the hawks in Lagos their opportunity and Enahoro was instructed to attend no more meetings until the Ugandan police had completed their enquiries.

I hastened down to see the Police Commissioner, a corpulent Ugandan Asian, whose face glistened with sweat and goodwill as he assured me that everything possible was being done. I doubted that but clearly there was little to be hoped for from him, unless perhaps we were willing to offer a financial incentive.* When I returned, though, worse had happened. A letter had arrived from Sir Louis saying that there was no point in continuing and his delegation was leaving the following day. The only consolation was that there was time for an effort at reconsideration. One of the unforeseen advantages of meeting in a place like Kampala was that plane schedules did not permit anyone to flounce out and slam the door.

The signs were not promising. A meeting of senior members of the two delegations was arranged that evening (Sunday, 26 May) in the Secretary-General's office. Enahoro appealed to the Biafrans to accept his desire to overcome this difficulty and get the talks restarted. He thought his instructions misguided and was confident of getting them reversed – he even read out his message home, saying that he was satisfied the security arrangements were adequate. He told Sir Louis that he had not come to Kampala to see the talks fail if that could possibly be averted. The old judge was unmoved; he told Enahoro that he accepted his sincerity but was not confident of his government's.

The next morning Arnold tried again, at a meeting with the Biafran delegation. Lagos had lifted its ban and the talks could continue. Sir Louis was haughty: he was not, he said, to be thought of as a supplicant seeking the prerogative of mercy. He resented a news report that the Secretary-General was 'appealing' to him to return to the talks. Then the President intervened, summoning Sir Louis to his office. The Biafran leader agreed to think it over, but it was unlikely that he would wish to offend the Ugandan head of state, and so there was little surprise when that afternoon he signified he was willing to meet the next day.

This roller-coaster ride did not promise well. That evening the President and Sam Odaka came for a drink and a discussion on strategy. We had no brandy and had to send over to his office for a bottle of the President's Cordon Bleu. Obote confirmed that the Biafrans had taken the decision to leave in all seriousness (Sir Louis' two deputies had in fact gone, it was thought temporarily) and that Sir Louis was convinced that the Federal delegation would find excuses for further delays. The President thought as much as possible of the discussions should be off

---

* The killers were never caught.

the record, in the Secretary-General's room. We needed to work out 'some behind-the-scenes activities' to lower the risk of further explosions. Could we think of a gesture that would sweeten the atmosphere? Arnold said we had considered seeking a voluntary pause in hostilities or at least in the bombing while the talks went on, but had concluded that Enahoro would have trouble getting this accepted at home. Perhaps the Red Cross might provide an opening.

The day before the talks opened the International Committee of the Red Cross had appealed to both sides to agree to urgently needed humanitarian measures. It proposed agreements on allowing food supplies into Biafra, on the protection of civilians, refugees and prisoners of war. That day Dr George Hoffman, Delegate-General of the Red Cross, had called on the Secretary-General to seek his help in meeting the two delegation leaders. Both agreed. He saw Sir Louis who asked Arnold to be present also. His meeting with the Federal leader had to be postponed for a day and in that time the Voice of America carried a report that Enahoro had rejected his appeal to allow Red Cross supplies into rebel-held areas. Enahoro, offended when he had not even met the man, wrote to Arnold saying curtly that Hoffman should put his proposals to the Nigerian Government through the normal channels. Someone had made trouble for the innocent Dr Hoffman but he had dipped his rounded pink form into alligator-infested waters and he disappeared.

When the plenary sessions resumed the next morning (Tuesday, 28 May) the outlook remained unsettled. As accusations were traded back and forth there were angry skirmishes on issues that were beside the point. Tempers became inflamed and the mood more intransigent. The peace process was not merely stalled, it was going backwards. Enahoro agreed that private talks offered the only hope and when the President put this to Sir Louis he said that he was 'not necessarily averse'.

In the early evening the two delegation leaders together with Odaka and Arnold gathered in the Secretary-General's office. Enahoro welcomed the chance to say what would be difficult elsewhere. He understood the Biafran insistence on a ceasefire first but the fact was that the war was about secession and he could not accept a ceasefire without knowing what was going to follow. The ultimate goal must be a reunited Nigeria but if this was accepted, he could discuss a sequence of steps to bring this about, including a ceasefire, without fear of being repudiated.

Sir Louis said that these were 'surrender terms'. The only thing that would convince Biafrans that Lagos was serious would be a halt to the war. After that a closer association could 'maybe' be considered. He simply could not go home and say that they had fought a war in vain. Enahoro conceded the difficulty. He could contemplate a ceasefire as a confidence-building measure as long as everyone could see ahead to a common future, for example to a constitutional conference in six months or a year. As the discussion went on he stretched further: as long as one Nigeria was the goal 'at the back of our minds', even if it took two or three years, almost everything else could be worked out.

Suddenly we were into a real negotiation. Sir Louis' colleague, Eni Njoku (a former Vice-Chancellor of Lagos University), responded saying that reversing the split would take time but he had not lost hope that a united Nigeria would come by mutual consent. If a way could be found to separate the ceasefire from the political questions progress might be possible. Enahoro said that this alone justified the move to private talks. It was what he had been asking for: if they could agree on their *hopes* they could then work on the stages to realise them. The meeting agreed that we would work on some formulations along these lines and put them to each side the next day.

It was by then late at night but Arnold produced a supply of coffee and I set about drafting a paper which went through four versions to become the proposals called 'Basic Understandings'. The gap between the two sides had been narrowed but it was still profound. The Biafrans wanted a ceasefire, arguing that it would take time to reconcile their people to any form of political association. The Federal Government, which had gone to war to keep Nigeria together, would not accept a halt to the fighting without some assurance that they would reach their goal. No amount of ingenious drafting or diplomacy could bridge this gap. One or other side was going to have to make the leap and, given their military situation – driven from their capital and with dwindling supplies – logic suggested that it would have to be the Biafrans. All that drafting could do was to find formulations that might ease their task – if they were willing to face it.

Out of the hot flow of language the two main issues were plain. The headache was how to combine them. It might help if, instead of having to renounce their secession, the Biafrans were invited to join in establishing a new Nigeria. The Basic Understandings paper proposed that 'It is agreed to establish a new Nigerian union, covering the territories controlled at the time of the ceasefire by both parties. The constitutional arrangements for this new union will be worked out at a constitutional conference of all the parties concerned.' In a second part the paper then proposed a standstill ceasefire, to be supervised by an observer force the sources and composition of which was to be agreed, with a limited lifting of the blockade to enable relief supplies to enter and exports to leave.

The next day with Sam Odaka we tried this out on the two parties. The President had made available his lodge at Makindi, on top of a hill looking out over both Kampala and Lake Victoria. There we met first with the Biafrans. Sir Louis liked the part on the standstill ceasefire but repeated that it was not politically possible to sell agreement on one Nigeria at home. Time would be needed, time in which areas could be found where the two sides could work together and move towards a closer association.

We drove down to the Apolo to collect Enahoro who had a painfully infected gum (we lent him a bottle of codeine tablets) and then took him back to Makindi to a delicious lunch of Ugandan dishes which Helen cooked for us. Chewing cautiously, he repeated that he in turn had no chance of selling any compromise to his Cabinet without a clear and irreversible acceptance of one Nigeria.

Back to Sir Louis, who unexpectedly suggested that we try again for a middle course which one of them could take back to Biafra and try to sell. Enahoro was sympathetic. Obote undertook to speak to his fellow presidents from Zambia and Tanzania, who had recently broken the international line by recognising Biafra, to ask them to appeal to Ojukwu. All that remained was to find the elusive middle course.

There were only a few cards left to shuffle. On the morning of Thursday, 30 May, Yaw Adu, the Ugandan Secretary of Foreign Affairs and I tried again. In an effort to make the unpalatable easier to swallow we suggested that the two sides might make their concessions simultaneously. A ceasefire and acceptance of the need to build a new Nigerian union would be announced at the same time. In the course of the day this was tried out on both sides, and both rejected it. We suspected that each had reported back and that positions at home had hardened.

The following day (Friday, 31 May) the plenary session resumed at Sir Louis' request. It went no better than the others. When the Secretary-General tried to get an adjournment of two or three days to allow the delegations to seek fresh guidance, Sir Louis interrupted him, nervous perhaps that Arnold was about to read into the record the proposals discussed the previous day. The tone became emotional, Sir Louis saying that 'If the price of not having a negotiated settlement was extermination, then Biafra was prepared to pay it'. Enahoro was concerned at the 'ominous and retrogressive' sound of this but still thought that progress was possible with new instructions. However Sir Louis said that 'there was now no option but to register disagreement and disperse'. He then launched into a formal valedictory, expressing his appreciation to all concerned, leaving Enahoro to lament that he had not thought to prepare anything. We walked out of the hall and the peace conference was over.

In the heat of the afternoon I went to see the old man at the Grand Hotel. We met on the verandah and, emotional myself, I appealed to him saying, 'Sir Louis, thousands more will die because of this decision'. A shower of rain pattered on the leaves of the frangipani trees beside us. Then he said, 'I and all of us count ourselves as dead men already'. I stared at him wordlessly. Then he gave me a letter for the Secretary-General, thanking him for his efforts and ending, 'Please accept, Mr Secretary-General, the assurances of my highest consideration . . .'.

The talks, officially only suspended, were never resumed. It was hard to see the sense in the Biafran walkout. Sir Louis, humourless and unyielding, was out of his depth as a negotiator. He was pedantic and unwilling to be bold where Enahoro was easy and willing to push on the limits. Enahoro and Okpara might have resolved their differences in a few days and had the standing to get endorsement at home. But then, perhaps significantly, Ojukwu had chosen Sir Louis and not Okpara as his negotiator. Yaw Adu said that Ojukwu looked up to Sir Louis as an uncle but he can hardly have been unaware that the judge's virtues did not include flexibility.

It looked as if Ojukwu had agreed to the talks reluctantly and called them off when they approached the heart of the matter. Months later Sir Louis was reported by a colleague as saying that he knew the walkout was a blunder and that he had done so only after reiterated instructions from his leader. Like some earlier rulers in his position Ojukwu was unable to back down. His gamble had not succeeded and militarily there could now be only one outcome, but it was easier to stay locked on, hoping for a miracle perhaps, than to face the humiliation (conceivably fatal) of changing course.

Tired and numbed by the effort of the past days, Michael Wilson and I took a car and driver and travelled west to the Congo border. As we drove through the rolling green of the Ankole cattle country we came to a yellow stripe painted across the road. It was the line of the Equator made visible and, no doubt like everyone else, we got out and took photos of each other with a foot in the northern and southern hemispheres. We stayed at a simple place near Lake Edward, one of the smaller lakes along the great Rift, sleeping and eating and watching the wildlife. In rainy weather we took a boat out on the lake, down the middle of which ran the border with the Congo. The cloud lifted suddenly to reveal a breathtaking wall of black buttresses rising steeply from the other side of the lake, the Ruwenzori mountains. Their remote and snow-streaked summits, over 16,000 feet high, seemed unapproachable, from another world, and the ancient Greeks were right to call them the Mountains of the Moon.

Down to earth we bumped back along a narrow grassy track and inadvertently came between a herd of elephants crossing the path. Two took exception to us and advanced on the car trumpeting and flapping their ears, neither striking us as welcoming signs. There was no room to turn the car. We faced a choice of abandoning it to be turned into scrap by the elephants or allowing it to be turned into scrap while we were still in it. We told the driver to back while we held the doors half-open in order to be able to dive out if we lost the race. As the car reversed slowly the elephants advanced slowly; as our speed increased so did theirs. The contest went on for several hundred yards until the elephants lost interest and the car reached a place wide enough to turn.

In London we picked up the pieces, resuming contacts with Enahoro and Sir Louis to discuss the composition of a possible peacekeeping force. A compromise, though, was going to need more open international pressure than the discreet backing we had earlier from Britain, Canada and the United States. The British took over the running in the form of a genial junior Minister, Lord Shepherd, who flew to Lagos in June with a personal message from the British Prime Minister. He stressed that international concern over the war was growing; the Federal Government would look bad if it resisted peace overtures. He returned, elated that he had secured its agreement to informal talks in London as a prelude to a return to the Kampala conference.

Sir Louis, though, had declined to commit himself over the Shepherd mission. We too were doubtful that the Biafran authorities were interested in anything other than a ceasefire but Arnold agreed to try. I drafted yet another message to Ojukwu asking him to send a representative for fresh talks – even the phrases had come to sound routine. Two weeks later a message came back saying that, in the absence of an immediate and unconditional ceasefire, 'we cannot agree that a basis now exists for a resumption of meaningful negotiations'.

The only hope of getting negotiations back on track was for the Secretary-General to go to Biafra and put the case himself. He tried without success to seek clearance from Gowon but was unable to reach him. Meanwhile I looked at transport possibilities. The Red Cross was willing to take us in on one of their relief flights, darkened aircraft weaving through the clouds at night to avoid Federal fire. A more attractive option was the offer of a Canadian plane. Nothing came of either for the Nigerians restated their firm opposition to any visit.

Their irritation led them to renew their campaign for the recall of Emeka Anyaoku. Over the previous months there had been occasional attempts to reopen his future with the Secretariat. Late in the previous year a letter had arrived saying that the Nigerian Government had been anxious for some time about Emeka's loyalty 'to the country of his birth'. Now they wished to withdraw him from the Secretariat on the grounds that he was no longer a suitable Nigerian nominee. Emeka, however, had resigned from the Nigerian Foreign Service and Arnold had no difficulty in turning aside the demand. His stand was a wise investment for Emeka not only later became Nigeria's Foreign Minister for a brief period but went on to become the third Commonwealth Secretary-General.

In September, after President Obote had commented to us that the Biafrans had missed their chance and their situation was now desperate, a strange episode suggested that this desperation was having its effect. At midnight I received a telephone call from Kogbara to say that all the senior Biafrans, including Okpara, were in Paris and intended to fly home to urge the abandonment of secession, acceptance of one Nigeria and immediate negotiations. He asked that the United States, Britain and Canada be informed at once and we did.

Kogbara came to Marlborough House the next morning and Arnold told him plainly that they would be seeking surrender terms and should not try to quibble. Physical security could be safeguarded and we talked about how soon an expanded observer force could be got into place once arms were laid down. Lord Shepherd, who happened to be chairing a

Bahamas Constitutional Conference downstairs, ducked in and out of these discussions growing increasingly excited by the prospect. With Wilson's agreement he flew down to Lagos to be on the spot to influence the Federal Government when the Biafran call came. Then Ojukwu disowned the whole thing, talked of falling back on guerrilla resistance, and called the 'Paris group' home. The fiasco effectively put an end to any further attempts at a settlement.

The Biafrans had increasingly turned their attention to the public relations war at which they were considerably better than their opponents. They perhaps calculated that their aim of an unconditional ceasefire might have a better chance with public opinion than with governments. The trickle of recognitions (two francophone West African states had now joined Zambia and Tanzania) might be augmented by popular pressure on Western governments. This was not entirely fanciful – the North Vietnamese were pursuing the same strategy with some success – and as the underdogs in the war they had an innate appeal to the media.

Even this could hardly explain the intensity of the campaign which now swept the British media and to a lesser extent that of other English-speaking countries. British support for Nigerian unity was fiercely denounced by leader-writers in both the tabloid and quality dailies. Nigeria, they claimed, was pursuing a policy of extermination through war and starvation and Britain by supplying arms was morally responsible for this. Reputable journalists visited Biafra and saw the evidence, mass starvation and death, all around them. The number of the dying rose with every reiteration until it reached millions. The literary world joined in with harrowing tales repeated by people who had never been there and Auberon Waugh announced that he was adding Biafra to the names of his new child.

It was hard to get reliable information about the state of life within the shrinking Biafran enclave. Deprivation and malnutrition certainly existed and an exasperated fondness prompted me to send bottles of multivitamins and brandy through the blockade to Sir Louis. Those who followed the slow advance of the Federal troops, though, reported no signs of extensive food shortages, neglected crops or the kwashkiorkor (a protein deficiency disease) which was seasonally endemic in the region. This was not necessarily true of the unknowable number who had fled from their homes into the bush. No civil war is ever kind to civilians but individual horrors however true did not add up to a Federal policy. The clearest rebuttal of the wilder claims came when peace was restored. No country torn by war can have come back together with less reluctance and resentment than Nigeria did.

The emotional press campaign, though well meant, probably prolonged the war by encouraging Biafran hopes. Journalists who abandoned investigation for agitation turned out to be no wiser than other lobbyists. Governments remained unswayed – though even New Zealand felt compelled in mid-1969 to send a sheaf of messages expressing its concern. There were no further recognitions of Biafra and the Federal Army continued its slow but inevitable progress. The end came in January 1970 when Ojukwu fled and Major-General Philip Effiong ordered the remaining Biafran troops to lay down their arms. The general did his countrymen one last service: he said there would be no government-in-exile and no guerrilla warfare, it was the end. Sir Louis Mbanefo carried the surrender documents to Lagos.

By then my four years in the Commonwealth Secretariat had come to an end. Living in London in the sixties had been enjoyable despite the run-down state of the British economy and the efforts of Harold Wilson to try everything that rhetoric could do to revive it. To live and walk in London in the age of the mini-skirt was itself a daily blessing.

A few months earlier a division of the *Economist* group had prepared a commodities study for the Secretariat. They approached me in a rather embarrassed fashion. While they had no wish to be thought to be 'blackbirding' they wondered if I would like to join the Economist Intelligence Unit at the end of my time in Marlborough House. When I mentioned the offer to Sir Bernard Fergusson at a party, saying I was not interested, his response was vigorous: 'If you go home, dear boy, believe me you won't be able to do anything'. In the future, he argued, New Zealand would increasingly come to focus on its economic vulnerability. I turned down the offer anyway. It had illuminated a fact never much thought about before: the choice was not mine to make. I was a New Zealander and a permanent departure meant giving up too much. I had joined the Department of External Affairs to enter a wider world – but at the end of a long rope anchored at home. The tug of this rope took me back to the foreign service.

CHAPTER FIVE

# A Washington Spectator

THE HEAVING GREEN SWELLS ROLLED OUT BEHIND THE SHIP as it skirted the fringes of a tropical storm. The liner *France* was crossing from Southampton to New York. The mostly elderly passengers lay wrapped in rugs behind the glass of the sundeck, though the servings of bouillon had been halted until the deck was more stable. My family were sheltering in two cabins on the main deck. The children, excited by the storm, had devised a cure for seasickness which involved drawing all the curtains and then ringing for the steward to bring bananas. Whether this would have been helpful was never proved because after two calls the stewards ceased answering the bell. Julie, exhausted by farewells and cleaning the house before we left London, was asleep. I wandered unsteadily about the ship, clutching the occasional handhold and wondering if this was in fact the best way of travelling to the United States.

It was August 1969 and I was on my way to Washington to be counsellor and head of the political section in the embassy there. The administrative discontinuity between the Commonwealth Secretariat and my own service offered the chance to make a transatlantic crossing on one of the last of the grand liners. Apart from the rigours of French cooking – being served poached eggs in a glass was a horrified memory for years after – the children enjoyed life on the ship. It turned out that while I was preoccupied with the toddler, Sophie, and Julie's worsening condition, they had commandeered the ship's central lifts for an afternoon.

Julie was in pain and unable to get up. The ship's doctor was an ageing Frenchman whose kindly greeting – 'I knew your Kiwi soldiers during the war' – did not inspire confidence. He had no difficulty diagnosing acute appendicitis but then lit a cigarette and stood silent. At length he said that the rolling of the ship ruled out operating. Looking at his shaking hands I could only agree. Instead he treated Julie with generous amounts of antibiotics and morphine which eased the pain and for the rest of the voyage she awoke only occasionally to enquire drowsily after the children.

After the lift episode, when some passengers had been unable to move between decks, my immediate task was to keep the children entertained in a more socially acceptable way. One of the much-advertised features of the ship was a large nursery and playroom where children could be left happily for hours while their parents swam, played deck golf or sampled the bars. I made for this haven. The children, however, took an instant dislike to it. The supervisor was a grim-faced lady built on the lines of a prison warder, a resemblance which was increased when she locked the children in with a flourish. Three tearful faces were pressed to the glass walls as I walked away with Sophie riding on my shoulder – another durable memory to go with the unnatural state of French food. After that the five of us walked the decks together and when the weather improved we sat in sheltered corners on the upper deck watching the ship's wake while I improvised a serial story which could be cut and shaped to fit the hours to be filled.

Julie was awake to look out with me at the Statue of Liberty and the Manhattan skyline as we steamed into New York on a hot morning in early August – in fact the day of the Woodstock festival. She was now very ill but was adamant that she would not be left behind in hospital and we travelled straight to Washington by rail. When we arrived in the late afternoon she was taken immediately to Washington Hospital Centre while I took the family to the Alban Towers, a slightly depressing set of apartments for short-term occupants. In the early evening, as I was feeding the children and putting them to bed (another instalment of the serial on which invention was flagging), the telephone rang. The surgeon said that Julie's appendix had burst during the voyage and she now had acute peritonitis. He proposed to operate at once but needed my consent: 'I cannot guarantee that the operation will be successful'. I made him promise to ring me as soon the operation was over.

The longest night of my life began. A noisy summer thunderstorm broke out, flashing and banging around us while I sipped whisky from a bottle which the embassy had left and looked in on the children to reassure them. As the clock drifted past eleven and on towards midnight I began to lose hope – surely the removal of a burst appendix could not take more than four hours. At one the phone rang: 'Mr Hensley', said the surgeon's voice, 'you are a very lucky man'. Perhaps because of the French doctor's antibiotics the infection had not spread as far as had been expected and, while there were still difficulties, he was now confident that Julie would recover. In my relief the questions tumbled out of me until he said gently that he was still in his blood-covered apron, having stepped straight out of the theatre to ring me, and that he would like to go and wash.

On the night of the operation, having been warned about her chances of not surviving, Julie had sent for the Catholic chaplain and, as the surgeon waited, asked if she could be buried as a Catholic so that her children would be spared a funeral in unfamiliar surroundings. The next day, when she was in the recovery room, the priest returned to tell her cheerfully that her conversion had lacked conviction and, while he would never want to turn away a prospective member of the flock, he thought the Anglican Church was where she should remain. After that her recovery made slow but uninterrupted progress.

Fate had one last flick. Between visits to the hospital I was trying to come to grips with my new duties at the embassy. An agency found a woman to look after the children while we were still in the Alban Towers. She went mad – not as anyone looking after four children might, but seriously unbalanced. I returned one afternoon to find her talking of throwing the children over the third-floor balcony. In the struggle that followed I was finally able to push her out of the door and out of our lives. Thereafter kind members of the embassy staff took turns with the children until a suitable nanny could be found.

When Julie was well enough we moved to the house in the Maryland suburbs near Potomac which I had (rather daringly) taken a few months earlier when on a visit with Arnold Smith to the Caribbean. It was a comfortable five-bedroom house in a quiet neighbourhood. The astronaut, Neil Armstrong, lived around the corner, so that when walking the dog you could look at the moon then at the man who walked on it as he sat watching television in his living-room. The house backed on to half an acre of woods which allowed the children to stretch out after living in inner London. Indeed, the only drawback was that what had been an attractive leafy drive in summer turned into a lengthy ski-run when it had to be cleared of snow in winter.

The embassy occupied a neo-Georgian townhouse in the centre of Washington's diplomatic district, with the British embassy on one side and the Naval Observatory, which had become the Vice-President's residence, across the road on the other. It had been acquired at the time of the Pacific war when New Zealand was anxious to strengthen relations with the Roosevelt Administration. The buyer was a maverick Cabinet Minister, the Hon. Frank Langstone, whose government had sent him abroad for its own good. We owed him a debt for providing us with a chancery which was a house not an institution. We were also grateful to him for one of the more memorable moments in the New Zealand foreign service. He had moved on to be first High Commissioner in Ottawa where Princess Juliana of the Netherlands had taken wartime shelter. Her husband, Prince Bernhardt, was flown over for rest and recreation and the occasion was marked by a diplomatic reception. When he came to the head of the receiving line Frank Langstone grasped the princess warmly and said, 'Orrrrrr, Princess, it must be good to have him back, eh?' The awkward silence that followed this was relieved by Mrs Langstone, who laid her hand on the princess's arm and said, 'Don't you listen to him, dear, he hasn't done it for ten years'.*

In the office a marble staircase swept grandly up to the ambassador's room and then less confidently up to the second floor where I occupied a former bedroom. It had its own strong room where any satisfaction over a good week's work would be deflated by the dusty shelves of already forgotten reports. It also had a white-tiled bathroom from which projected the embassy's flagpole. On solemn occasions I would step in there to raise or lower the flag to mark the passing of the great, tying the halyards round the knob of the bathroom radiator.

The aim was to spend as little time as possible in the office. The federal bureaucracy was enormous; even the departments and agencies devoted to foreign policy numbered over a dozen. Then there were numerous task forces and working groups working on particular issues, with no less than five offices, for example, devoted to divining the thoughts of

---

* Told to Frank Corner by R. M. Firth who was there.

Chairman Mao. The differences in outlook among departments working on the same topic – the State Department, National Security Council and the intelligence agencies – meant that clues from one could be discreetly used to elicit more from another until a pattern formed. Washington's sprawl was such that getting round these agencies in the embassy's Volkswagen took a large part of the day and grappling with the traffic jams caused by the street layout often caused me to suspect that supplying the city's designer had been the last revenge of the departing British.

Knocking on doors was standard diplomatic practice made especially important here because the Americans were not good at keeping their friends informed. The effort of clearing a decision through all the interested groups in Washington meant that the State Department or White House often had little energy or little time to consult its allies about some impending decision. On the other hand the town was a bottomless well of information and we enjoyed a privileged access. Our standing as an ally and a troop contributor to the war in Vietnam meant that at the working level very few doors were closed to us. Like cut-price barbers appointments were not always necessary. Walking the corridors of State or the CIA you could look in on anyone you knew and discuss what was going on. Since analysts, however discreet, love talking about their subject this kept us as well informed as any embassy in town. The work was similar to journalism and it paid to cultivate and read those who worked for newspapers like the *New York Times* or *Washington Post*. Sometimes there was a bonus. The children of Neil Sheehan who broke the story of the Pentagon Papers were in Julie's school carpool.

The State Department, its building occupying a depression unhappily known as Foggy Bottom, was the formal link for diplomats. We shared some friendships from other places and a certain trade-union fellow feeling. But State was losing influence. The new President, with clear ideas on foreign policy, preferred to work through the National Security Council (and its Secretary, Henry Kissinger) which he controlled much more directly. So it was necessary to make friends of the NSC staff as well and add to the itinerary the grey Executive Building beside the White House which President Grant had built a century earlier to house the entire Federal Government. The NSC were more wary of diplomats than State; on the other hand they were better informed and their closeness to the President meant that even a cryptic comment could confirm or open up a line of enquiry.

I was also Intelligence Liaison Officer and accredited to the CIA. Though this was not declared there was nothing cloak and dagger about it. My work was not with the undercover agents in the agency's operations directorate – 'the other side of the house' – but with its research and analysis. The Intelligence Directorate drew on information which came from all sources – newspapers, broadcasts, diplomatic reporting, agents, signals intelligence and satellites – to prepare daily briefings for the President and other senior officials, weekly bulletins and longer-term 'estimates' on major issues. After some editing much of this was available to us. The staff of the directorate were in many cases drawn from the academic world. They were clever, sceptical, irreverent and funny. Their professional (and sometimes political) detachment from the Administration meant that anything important that was edited out was often supplied by a middle-level analyst irritated by the mangling of his conclusions. The country analysts might spend years on their specialty, with the result that their instincts were sometimes better than the intelligence they were scrutinising. It is, said my predecessor, driving me over the Chain Bridge to the CIA headquarters at Langley in Virginia, the best postgraduate school in international affairs.

This seemed an odd thing to say but my experience confirmed it. The value of intelligence lay not so much in dramatic revelations – rare in my experience and even more rarely able to be acted upon – as in the compost of information built up in the listener's mind by regular briefings. Out of this compost as it deepened over the months grew a sense of patterns and underlying trends; these in turn enabled a more confident interpretation of events yet to come. A good example of this patient accumulation of facts was the CIA's conclusion, eighteen months before the oil shock of 1973, that market power had moved to the oil producers and a sharp price rise was likely. I reported their reasoning at some length but there was not much that could be done about it: in public policy to be forewarned does not necessarily mean to be forearmed.

The only regular class was on Wednesday mornings when a small group of old Commonwealth allies were given a briefing on current issues, a cut-down version of that prepared for senior officials. It was sometimes necessary to speed down the George Washington Parkway to get to Langley on time. After one or two tickets had been received we received a gentle warning: the agency had first become suspicious of one of our British predecessors when he began collecting speeding tickets.

His name was Donald McLean. Everyone's driving became a model of decorum.

Apart from this weekly event there were regular briefings for Australia and New Zealand on Vietnam, on which the agency was becoming progressively more sceptical. At longer intervals we would file into a darkened room to see the startling results of the new satellite imagery, scanning grainy pictures of Soviet missile silos, submarines under construction and on one occasion my car parked in an almost empty lot at Langley on Christmas Eve. Otherwise I was free to pursue whatever interested Wellington. Being a specialist can be lonely. If not busy they liked getting into an argument and trying alternative explanations, politely overlooking your own lack of knowledge in the interests, as they would say, of getting a non-American point of view. For the same reason they valued the selected diplomatic reporting we released to them in return for the huge volume of analysis they volunteered. But when I offered to supply more on the South Pacific the analyst said warily that she already knew more than she felt was necessary.

The best way of getting on easy terms with your counterparts was by entertaining, the oldest (or perhaps second oldest) diplomatic device. People in State were well used to this, if a little jaded by the diplomatic round. CIA officials were less accustomed to being dined and enjoyed the experience. Perhaps because of unfamiliarity there was a certain military precision about their arrival. As the clock was half way through striking the hour the doorbell would ring and all the guests would be standing on the doorstep. The house itself was a source of hilarity – it turned out that I was leasing it from an agency man who would shortly become station chief in Saigon. The dinners were lively for agency members liked for a change to talk about books, music and Washington gossip.

As acquaintance ripened hospitality would be returned. Standing in his farmhouse kitchen as we were making a salad, one analyst gave me a disconcertingly frank briefing on the American incursion into Cambodia and its likely effects, and I hoped that our cypher system gave him adequate protection. Another occasion was stranger. We were at dinner in an old house in Virginia where there was a screened porch with two grand pianos back to back. This was a rare opportunity and my hostess and I sat down to try the slow movement of a Mozart sonata for two pianos. The sonorities of the pianos blended with the sounds of cicadas in the midsummer heat. Leaning on the piano half-enjoying and half-laughing at my efforts was a bearded expert on Soviet missiles who was later found floating in Chesapeake Bay with his hands tied – whether a suicide or not was never settled.

More elaborate entertainment was occasionally provided by the CIA Deputy Director, General Walters. The general, as he would quickly explain, had fought only bureaucratic battles. He was a clever man who had been educated in France and England and who had the President's ear. He once took the small Commonwealth liaison group to see the Washington Redskins play, picking us up in a stretched airport limousine with about four doors down each side. It was snowing at the stadium but the general produced rugs and then, when interest in the snow-obscured football was flagging, long sticks of French bread and sherry. The merry ride home was not in the least disturbed when someone dropped a large rock on the limousine as we drove through an underpass.

Once or twice I lunched with Walters at his quarters, a late-eighteenth-century house in Fort McNair on the Potomac River. He had been at staff college in England with Sir Bernard Fergusson. When he was American Military Attaché in Paris Sir Bernard had rung him to renew acquaintance and asked him what he was doing. Walters gave an account, confided proudly that he was about to be promoted major-general, and said, 'What about you, Bernard?' 'Dear boy,' the voice boomed down the line, 'I'm a *Governor*-general.' After lunch Walters liked to play 'God Defend New Zealand' on an electronic organ and demonstrate the abilities of his cat Snowball, certainly the only cat I have ever known amenable to military or any other sort of discipline. Snowball would leap on and off a silver tray then at the stern command of 'Snowball, snuggle!' would rub itself against the general's closed fist.

After Soviet intentions and Vietnam the CIA's main preoccupation was China, and on the principle that competition is as good in analysis as in business there was a luxuriant growth of 'offices' dealing with aspects of that mysterious empire. When I arrived they were trying to make sense of a baffling orgy of destruction in China, known rather lamely as the Cultural Revolution. Debate over different explanations became heated and one expert would warn me against listening to the credulous and uninformed views of another. The truth that emerged was more surprising than any of the theories. Mao Tse-tung had started a rebellion against his own government and its institutions to the point where, like more than one earlier emperor, he was leaving his northern borders defenceless. As I arrived in August news was coming in of armed clashes with Soviet troops in Sinkiang and along the Ussuri River. The danger to a country that knew its history was clear and the Chinese government struggled to contain the disorder and get back in the bottle the genie it had loosed. The answers the CIA and other agencies gradually pieced together were to underpin the great diplomatic surprise of the Nixon Administration.

The Administration was seven months old when we arrived. The turbulence of the sixties was ending in domestic upheaval over the country's entanglement in Vietnam and racial tensions had sent parts of Washington up in flames the previous year. Richard Nixon had been elected on a promise to extricate America from its war, though the voters had not trusted him enough to elect a Republican Congress as well. The months after his inauguration were less the traditional honeymoon – the President lacked that sort of charm – as an expectant pause while people waited to find out what he proposed to do.

All administrations have their own flavour, decided by the tastes and character of that elected monarch, the president. This administration was marked by a dour reserve. The delicacy of President Nixon's task in ending the war called for some secrecy but it quickly became apparent that this was a habit, his preferred way of working. He was by no means the first chief executive to arrive in Washington with a distrust of the capital and its institutions but his solitary ways and determination to work through a small circle of his own advisers if anything grew stronger with time. His two closest assistants, the Californians Haldeman and Ehrlichman, were known as the Berlin Wall. On foreign policy, his deepest interest, he bypassed his own Secretary of State and worked with Henry Kissinger at the National Security Council. For most others he was a remote figure, sitting somewhere in a line of black armoured cars speeding through the city or seen on television where his jowly, dark-shadowed face belied his awkward attempts at affability.

Washington has always taken its social tone from each administration. In the early months some traces of the hospitality of the Kennedy and Johnson years still lingered. When Keith Holyoake and his wife arrived in September the Nixons gave a dinner and a dance for them at the White House. The social pages were excited over the fact that Dom Perignon champagne and not 'plain old Californian' was served and by the strange appearance of the 'chinese gooseberry' (renamed the kiwifruit). The guest list was described by one newspaper as a 'mixed bag ranging from Senator Thomas Dodd of Connecticut to a prophetess'. These dissipations soon faded, however, and a workaholic administration soon became a disappointment to would-be hostesses and the gossip columnists.

Almost the only newsworthy couple was the Attorney-General, John Mitchell, and his wife Martha. It says much about the Nixon years that she was the social star – lively, silly and indiscreet, she revelled in her sudden celebrity. At an embassy dinner she put her hand on my chair when leaning across to make a point and then said archly, 'I hope you don't think I'm being fresh'. Dressed in pink tulle and pink, diamante-encrusted shoes she giggled with excitement as Ambassador Frank Corner flirted with her in the hall of the residence. Her husband went along with this but four years later when there was talk that the Senate Committee investigating Watergate might summon Martha, he said, 'I doubt it. The Committee has enough troubles of its own.' So did he; he went to jail.

Policy not popularity was the President's passion. Whatever his other faults, he was a brilliant strategist and some justification for the secrecy was that he was preparing a diplomatic revolution in America's Asian policy – the most dramatic leap since President Wilson's on the League of Nations. The starting point was the increasingly evident fact that the American public would not support 'foreign policy wars', sustained commitments to struggles which were remote from the voters' concerns. 'No More Vietnams' was a political necessity; America was over-stretched and the Kennedy readiness to bear any burdens had wilted. Yet Asia was still unstable and it was difficult to see how the United States could disengage.

The heart of the Nixon strategy was a reappraisal of China. The established view, in the United States and elsewhere, was of an aggressive Communist state which had fought the United Nations in Korea and fomented subversion in Thailand, Malaysia and Singapore. Its current domestic upheavals were just another sign of its inherently violent and unpredictable nature. Every visitor to CINCPAC's headquarters at Pearl Harbor was familiar with briefings by the redoubtable Admiral McCain, illustrated with alarming charts showing enormous arrows snaking out of China to point directly at Australia and New Zealand. The admiral himself was not easily frightened. His wife was a beautiful identical twin whose sister also lived with them. One day, as we were going down in a

State Department lift, someone said boldly, 'Admiral, how do you tell them apart?' The stocky little admiral shifted his cigar to the other side of his mouth and said, 'I can't. They can', and stepped out of the lift.

Nixon and Kissinger grasped how much had changed over the past decade. They concluded that China, weakened by internal factionalism, posed no direct threat to the region. Instead they saw a country frightened by the threat on its northern borders and suddenly conscious of its diplomatic isolation. China, like the United States, needed a friend rather than a propaganda demon. If an understanding could be reached between them it might be possible to assure the stability of Asia without the need for American forces.

The first step was to signal that the outlook and therefore the approach had changed in America. The Nixon Doctrine, first rolled out in July 1969 as an anonymous briefing, was a signal to America's clients as well as its opponents. American forces, the President made clear, would in general be withdrawn from the Asian mainland and regional countries would be expected to carry the main burden of their own security, with support from the United States. However encouraging this was to Hanoi and Beijing, the shock rattled the windows of all other government round the rim of the Western Pacific. Diplomats gathered in huddles to try and interpret what it meant for all our countries. How serious was this 'backgrounder'? Was it political soothing syrup for home consumption or did it mean that the United States was withdrawing from Asia, abandoning its trade and security interests in a huge slice of the world? Argument in my second-floor office became so steamy that it was some time before we noticed that the air-conditioner had broken down.

The Nixon Doctrine gave an important hint about future directions but it did not spell out how the President was going to handle his immediate problem: the ticklish matter of ending the fighting in Vietnam and bringing home the half-million American forces based there. Nixon had spoken in the election campaign of having a plan to end the war. Although there had been some cynicism about whether this really existed, it turned out to be a two-pronged approach; continuing efforts to reach a negotiated settlement with Hanoi, while at the same time initiating a policy of 'Vietnamisation' – the progressive replacement of the departing American forces with newly trained and equipped South Vietnamese troops. The peace talks in Paris were dormant. Hanoi was well aware that it was winning the war on American soil, and neither side saw any real prospect of a negotiated settlement. So instead the President concentrated on Vietnamisation. The second round of troop withdrawals, running at 12,500 a month, was announced the day of Holyoake's call at the White House.

New Zealand had a small infantry and artillery force joined with the Australian troops in Phuoc Tuy province. It had for some time been concerned about the stability of South East Asia, its nearest landmass after Australia, and a battalion and an air transport squadron had been based in Malaysia for nearly fifteen years. Worries over South Vietnam's future were an extension of this outlook, underlined by the fact that the deployment was largely drawn from the forces in Malaysia. The Prime Minister (who five years earlier had made the smallest contribution to Vietnam that would be acceptable) made it delicately clear that the major part of New Zealand's contribution to the regional security burden lay in its commitment to the security of Malaysia and Singapore. Nonetheless he assured the President that 'we are your sort of people' and could always be counted on to help within the limits of our size. The President said that New Zealand's contribution was 'just right'. Then they went on to talk about beef quotas.

Vietnamisation was a race against the rising tide of domestic impatience. The difficulty was that it set no timeframe. The withdrawals were gradual, tailored to the progress the South Vietnamese forces were thought to be making. The Tet offensive in early 1968 may have heavily damaged the Vietcong's infrastructure and opened the way for Vietnamisation, but more immediately it had destroyed the confidence of Americans in what their government was saying. A new phrase became current – the 'credibility gap' – and many of the official announcements about pacification and military progress were lost in it. The growing number of opponents of the war, predominantly young people subject to the draft, were suspicious of the President's policy and impatient with its pace.

The President faced his first test in mid-October with the organisation of the Vietnam Moratorium. Students and anti-war groups held local demonstrations, ranging from hourly masses in the chapel of Georgetown University, a noontime funeral procession through the streets of Milwaukee to the tolling of a bell every four seconds at Bethel College in Kansas. All this, though attacked by Vice-President Agnew as the work of an 'effete corps of repellent snobs who characterise themselves as intellectuals', was rather gentle. The mood grew sharper four weeks later with the Vietnam Mobilisation. The 'Mobe' was more radical and it focused on Washington. Around a quarter of a million people, young, white and middle class, walked to the Washington Monument in the warm autumn sunshine chanting 'Peace Now'. My impression was less of an organised movement than a sort of political Woodstock, the excitement of taking part in a great emotional event, as the calling of the names of the dead in front of the White House certainly was.

The Vice-President, who never laboured under the imputation of being an intellectual, must have taken some satisfaction from the outcome. Support for the President in fact rose after the demonstrations and a new phrase, 'the silent majority', joined 'light at the end of the tunnel' on the lengthening list of familiar phrases. Nevertheless the tangle of public feelings about the war had shaken down to an argument over two alternatives: the Nixon policy of gradual withdrawals, or a complete American withdrawal by a publicly stated date. That in itself showed how narrow the President's room for manoeuvre had become.

The withdrawals proceeded regularly over the next two years although the announcements tended to cover larger numbers and to look increasingly further ahead. The President's reiterated claims that this was a cautious policy of 'cut and try' and that the withdrawals could be halted or delayed at any time became less and less convincing. By the end of 1971 most American combat troops had left. New Zealand's small combat force had also gone, leaving only a troop training group as a gesture towards Vietnamisation. This orderliness, though, was bought at a growing price in public support, a price which became so high that we began to wonder in the embassy whether even a non-Communist Indochina was worth the cost of our great ally tearing itself apart.

President Nixon held to his course, acknowledging more frankly his belief that American interests in Asia would be severely damaged by a precipitate withdrawal. His difficulty was a mismatch of timing: the now inflexible timetable of withdrawals (announced as much as a year ahead) did not fit easily with the less predictable progress of Vietnamisation. Since he could not halt the withdrawals he turned to buying time by a series of intimidatory strikes at North Vietnam. As a columnist noted drily, 'the purpose of widening the war is to shorten it'. In April 1970 there was a three-month incursion into Cambodia to damage North Vietnamese supply bases there; periodic bombing campaigns were mounted against the Ho Chi Minh trail through southern Laos and

Hanoi itself; and early in the following year there were further raids into Laos and again into Cambodia.

Militarily these eased the pressure, helping to cover the vulnerable interval when departing US forces were leaving the fighting more and more to newly raised South Vietnamese regiments. The gain, though, was at a large cost in public support for Vietnamisation. The argument that the operations were belligerent camouflage for the gathering pace of withdrawals was unpersuasive. As new fronts seemed to be opening up every few months, the suspicion grew that the President was seeking a decisive victory in Indochina and that the war, far from winding down, was likely to be prolonged indefinitely. The first Cambodian incursion coincided with the spring protest season on university campuses and the shooting of four protesters at Kent State University shocked the nation.

Congress, controlled by the Democrats, became more and more restless. The desire to reassert a constitutional standing which had been lost to a decidedly imperial presidency led to a struggle between the two ends of Pennsylvania Avenue for control of Vietnam policy. Efforts were made to ban incursions into Laos and Cambodia and to set deadlines for a complete withdrawal from Vietnam. A number of broader attempts were made to limit the President's war-making powers and to define in a workable way the Congress's constitutional monopoly on the declaration of war. These if they had succeeded might have had unpredictable consequences. George Ball, a former Deputy Secretary of State and one of the wise men of the foreign policy establishment, told us gloomily that periods of congressional domination of foreign policy were always bad, instancing the 1920s and withdrawal from the League. None of these congressional efforts, however, had much lasting effect. Both houses were wary of using their ultimate power of the purse for fear of being tagged with responsibility for any debacle in South Vietnam.

The hope in the White House was that the fears of the public would diminish as more and more US divisions were removed from the fighting and came home. The 1971 spring protest season seemed to bear this out. Nationwide demonstrations were more moderate in tone, though the efforts of groups like the Mayday Tribe to interfere with the citizens' right to assemble peaceably in traffic jams around Washington led to fist fights and some, like me, found ourselves tear-gassed in trying to navigate through a student riot at Washington Circle. Two hundred thousand gathered at the Capitol saying simply, 'We've come to be counted' and young amputees in wheelchairs led a silent march of hundreds of returned soldiers past the White House. It became clear that the majority of Americans now wanted the earliest possible end to their involvement in Indochina.

Pessimism about the likely end of Vietnamisation was also growing within the Administration. The President had never been over-ambitious in his claims: the Pentagon told us that his aim was to give South Vietnam 'a reasonable fighting chance' since it was not possible to guarantee the country's security. At the end of 1970 we were shown an inter-agency report which concluded that the US could not achieve a military victory in Vietnam and that the North had the means and the will to carry on for some time. So the question of how long was a reasonable fighting chance became important to those concerned with the future of South East Asia. Wellington made a surprising request. It was, the cable said, receiving a huge quantity of intelligence from us on the North Vietnamese and Vietcong efforts but much less on the doings of the other side. The paradoxical result was that it knew more about the enemy's tactics and dispositions than those of its friends.

I went to see a senior official in the Defence Department who agreed to give a regular briefing. He had been a political appointment of President Johnson's. In the interregnum before the Nixon inauguration he received a standard circular by accident from the Republican transition team asking him what sort of position he would like in the new administration. He suggested his old job and got it back. So his ability was combined with a certain detachment from the party political scene. We hit it off and meetings were signalled by an exchange of names from the Washington phone book. I would leave a message saying 'Pocahontas C Outlaw' and he would riposte with 'Immaculata Concepcion' – bonus points for this one because unbelievably she worked in the State Department's population control section. From his own Defence Department directory, though, I found Gunga L Din.

Although these briefings centred on how the Americans saw South Vietnamese affairs they revealed a pessimism about Saigon's future. Patient probing among CIA and other intelligence experts strengthened this. There was a growing scepticism that South Vietnam could hold off attacks from the North without substantial American support, support that was steadily drying up under congressional and public pressure. In August 1971, in one of the oddest arrangements ever made for a foreign diplomat, a friend in State's Intelligence and Research Department organised an inter-agency seminar for me on the future of South Vietnam. Analysts from the CIA and State and some of the university experts contracted to them sat around a table for the length of an afternoon while I listened to them combing through the various scenarios. No one thought the present political balance could last much longer. Arguments were advanced for neutralist governments, different kinds of coalitions embodying the Communists, or a full takeover by the North. The different analytical tracks all led in one direction. Whichever way you held the picture it was hard not to see Hanoi dominant in Saigon by 1975 and I told Wellington so.

Next month into this hardening consensus dropped the Pentagon Papers. In President Johnson's time the Secretary of Defence had commissioned a highly classified history of American involvement in Indochina up to 1968. Most if not all of the forty-seven volumes had been purloined by a former Defence Department official, Daniel Ellsberg, though the first anyone knew of this was when Neil Sheehan began publishing a series of stories in the *New York Times*. The uproar was great. The Administration immediately sought an injunction preventing further publication of the 3000 pages and 4000 documents. The case rose at once to the Supreme Court which by a majority authorised printing to resume, an interesting step towards building a public 'right to know' into the Constitution's protection for a free press.

The embarrassment was also great. Washington's discussions with a number of Asian and other governments were laid bare. The five or so references to New Zealand were enough to start an argument at home over the way the Holyoake Government had been brought to commit troops in 1965. The Nixon Administration's own doings were not an issue, since the papers stopped almost a year before the inauguration. In the way that public issues ricochet, though, it confirmed the feelings of many Americans that their government was systematically deceiving them. The credibility gap yawned wider than ever and into it disappeared the Administration's hopes of getting sustained congressional support for South Vietnam once the US troops had gone. Neither of the President's two options for ending the war now looked promising. He had earlier made one or two desultory efforts to revive the peace talks but no one had expected any results; for lack of political support in the Congress Vietnamisation did not look much better. Hanoi had only to be patient.

Instead it over-played its hand. In the spring of 1972 a major offensive was launched across the demilitarised zone into South Vietnam. It assumed perhaps that President Nixon's hands were tied and that it was better to act before the South Vietnamese forces grew in strength. In any case the loss of the Vietcong's once pervasive presence in the provinces meant that guerrilla warfare was no longer a serious choice. The only way to overthrow the Saigon authorities was to defeat them by massed divisions in conventional warfare.

The thrust made early progress. Two of the four regiments in a southern division broke and ran and for a time Hue in central South Vietnam was threatened. Faced with the first serious test of his Vietnamisation policy there was not much the President could do. All but a handful of US combat troops were gone. He turned to bombing as his only way of upping the ante for Hanoi. The big B52 bombers and other aircraft were flying up to a thousand sorties a day in the hope of cutting northern supply routes and blockading the port of Haiphong. In the meantime the South Vietnamese army had time to pull itself together and fight back. The North Vietnamese offensive became bogged down and by September the last of its forces was pushed back over the border. Hanoi, said the military experts, would not be able to mount another offensive for two years. The bombing, though, had triggered another round of protest in the US. With sporadic violence and only two thousand arrests the reaction was low-key on the relative scale of American restlessness. What was more significant was a widespread war-weariness. People were sick of the war and sick of the protesters. If Hanoi chose to return to the attack in two years' time there would be little on the American side to oppose it.

For the moment, though, Hanoi had also run out of options. With prodding from China and the Soviet Union, who had business of their own with the United States and were irritated at Hanoi's refreshing of a war which had seemed to be quietly winding down, the North Vietnamese negotiators signalled a new flexibility in Paris and peace negotiations started in earnest. Henry Kissinger and Le Duc Tho began 'private talks', an understatement for such tight secrecy that only my Defence Department colleague would drop the occasional hint. The most that John Holdridge, Kissinger's Director of Asian Affairs, would say to me was that 'Henry is not wasting his time'. By late October both sides were ready to agree on a ceasefire and fresh elections in South

Vietnam supervised by a Council for National Reconciliation composed of government supporters, neutralists and Communists.

Then Hanoi went cold and began to drag its feet, going back over old issues. Amid much speculation over what had gone wrong, the President resorted to his old persuader and resumed the bombing of North Vietnam over Christmas. The need for such a drastic measure at this late stage was widely questioned even within the Administration. At our government's urgent request the ambassador and I called on Marshall Green, the Assistant Secretary of State, who could be reached at short notice, to deliver a letter. Green listened to our representations in a correct and non-committal way, then walked with us to the lift. When he was alone he thanked us warmly, saying that the points we had made, coming from a close ally, gave State another chance to urge the same views on the President.

The bombing ended and a month later peace was signed amid great fanfare in Paris. Kissinger and Le Duc Tho received the Nobel Peace Prize. Two years later North Vietnam launched a second offensive, which in the absence of any American stiffening decisively defeated the South. My landlord, now station chief in Saigon, was still urging the possibility of a neutralist government as he climbed on to the roof of the American embassy and flew away. The New Zealand embassy looked ruefully at the new black Mercedes that had just been delivered and also flew away. Vietnam was at last reunited and the exodus of boat people began.

Vietnam was a current which ran below the surface of daily life in Washington. Parents of college-age boys kept their worries about the draft to themselves, though occasionally someone's son would be reported to have gone off to Canada. The issue was never far beneath the surface – convivial gatherings could be soured or broken up by a tactless voicing of opinion – but suburban life was placid. Life in Bethesda, like most other American suburbs then, revolved around children and schools. It was lived largely in the car. We had two of these, a stationwagon and a little MG bought with a timely legacy from a great-aunt, but even so the demands on them required the scheduling skills of a motor-pool manager. There were school runs, after-school ballet, swimming or music lessons, Campfire Girls and Boy Scouts, coffee mornings and committee meetings, not to mention sports matches, shopping (the nearest shops were several miles away) and my own commute to the embassy. Whatever the growing body of literature said, the suburbs seemed not boring but busy. The intensity of American life was domestic here. Neighbourhood gatherings, barbecues and coffee mornings, took in new arrivals with an easy hospitality. The seasonal round of blossoming dogwoods and bicycles; summer cicadas and swimming; falling leaves and walks in the Virginia woods; the clank of the snow-plough at night promising winter-blue days with the sleds – all this gave a recurring rhythm to everyday life.

Caroline and Gerald, our two elder children, started at the local elementary school, a few blocks down the road. The school was funded by the county and since Montgomery County was one of the wealthiest it was well resourced and well run. Nonetheless it was very much under the parents' eye. Mothers were expected to help in the library or lunchroom, and in this way the neighbourhood kept itself informed about the school's performance. While supervising lunch Julie discovered that our Labrador, Toby, had been relieving Neil Armstrong's two little boys of their lunch boxes as they waited for the school bus. A stoical pair, they had said nothing and gone without. At the first parent–teacher meeting I attended we fired the principal. Even he could hardly have been more dazed than I was by the insouciant way a show of hands ended his work at the school.

Sarah started at Sidwell Friends' School, to be joined a year later by her sister Sophie. Founded in the early nineteenth century, this Quaker school was the oldest in Washington. It had been recommended to us in London where I applied for a place. The entry procedures were elaborate, requiring a four-year-old to supply references and be interviewed by a psychologist. It was only when Sarah had been accepted that the school thought to mention its level of fees. An embarrassed letter from me then explained that she would not be attending after all. I received a reply stating rather haughtily that children accepted by Sidwell went there and then less haughtily asking how much I thought I could afford. I sucked my pen and put down a figure and a 'scholarship' was awarded to cover the difference. Sidwell's scholarships were on a sliding scale based on ability to pay. There were no full scholarships; the parents of black children from the inner city had to pay at least 5 per cent, and so everyone was a fee-paying pupil.

This combination of kindliness and practicality summed up the school's approach. I drove Sarah there each morning on my way to the office. On occasions we became a carpool and our arrival would look (but not sound) like a scene from a silent film as seven or eight children unfurled themselves from the recesses of the little MG. Learning to read was more fun than I remembered: Miss Anne would ask, 'Ch – is for?' and when someone answered 'chocolate' little pieces were distributed to everyone. I wondered what would have happened if some craftier child had called out 'champagne'.

Out of school the unfenced neighbourhood offered plenty of excitement, not all of it intended. Gerald and a friend started a small fire in the woods behind us to which no less than seven fire engines were summoned. I was called home urgently ('Children can't do anything these days,' said the ambassador) but the fire chief, no mean child psychologist, managed everything. In his full regalia of yellow slicker and high helmet he tramped up the stairs to where the boys were hiding under the bed, hauled them out to discuss the menace of forest fires, and left behind as determined a pair of ex-arsonists as could be desired.

Gerald was interested in politics. When the Leader of the Opposition, Norman Kirk, came to dinner one evening he was cornered while still taking off his coat in the hall while Gerald sought his advice on whether it was better to stand for President or Prime Minister (born in New York he was qualified, at least legally, for either). Kirk, who had lost his first election, said, 'Don't ask me; I can't even become Prime Minister of New Zealand'. He advised against political ambition, but ignored this himself and was successful at his second attempt.

Gerald's first elective office was in fact chairman of the class Reptile Committee, a body whose main business appeared to be to bounce in the piles of autumn leaves around the house. We had one official reptile, a Maryland box turtle – Ivan the Terrapin – for which a supply of worms had to be dug and which plodded off from the house each morning, managing fifteen feet or so before being brought back later in the day. Unofficially, though, Gerald, who did not share his father's view of snakes, had smuggled two into a packing case behind the house in the hope that they would breed and the reptile committee's frequent visits were to see if they had got started.

The family's principal pet was Toby, the larcenous Labrador, acquired in memory of his Samoan predecessor. An inspector from Wellington, doing the rounds to check conditions at each embassy, contemplated the dog gloomily while looking at the house and said, 'A very expensive dog that', as if there were a scale of fiscal prudence even in dogs. And as far as cost went his words were almost prophetic. One morning Julie, alerted by the frantic blowing of a horn, found a police car parked at the top of the drive. Two Maryland state troopers were sitting nervously inside while Toby on his hind legs was peering suspiciously at them through the windscreen. With notable presence of mind Julie berated the young men for upsetting the dog, to such effect that they apologised. They had come to deal with a reportedly rabid raccoon in the woods and they relieved their feelings with a burst of gunfire shortly after. Whether they got the raccoon was unclear but a large pileated woodpecker which lived there became even more pileated at the disturbance and was not seen again.

There was little time for travel outside Washington – the cable line to Wellington like a nest of squawking birds required feeding every day. Occasionally I would go on a speaking trip to places like Nebraska, North Carolina and South Dakota and once even to Los Angeles where, inching along a freeway past trees and scattered houses I was naive enough to ask when we were coming to the city. To believe that these talks raised New Zealand's image required a considerable act of faith. Away from either coast the magnitude and the isolation of inland America was striking. In some of the places I visited Washington was the limit of the known world and a pretty dubious one at that. Some newspapers covered events in the capital under a general international page. People would listen to my talk or watch the film as if they were stories of Cathay and sometimes compliment me on my grasp of English. They were kind, homely and hospitable but I learnt that their view did not extend much beyond their continent, round which other countries were ranged like exotic cardboard cut-outs.

One longer journey was to Samoa. Returning from home leave we stopped in Apia to celebrate our tenth wedding anniversary. The Casino hotel was gone, along with the forlorn wreck of the *Adler*, when the inner harbour was filled in, but Auntie Mary and the other wedding survivors who came for dinner on the night seemed unchanged by the years. I was the only exception for Apia's steamy warmth brought another (and blessedly final) recurrence of the malaria I had caught in East Africa. Some sort of speech was uttered through increasingly chattering teeth but my hands were shaking too much to cut the cake. The reminiscing went on while I retired to bed to ponder why, in a place under the doorsill of the equator, a pile of hastily assembled blankets topped by my winter coat from Washington was not enough to keep me warm.

Earlier we had taken the nine-year-old Caroline Toʻoa to call on the

ABOVE: *The Masiofo Lili Malietoa, Julie, author and the Masiofo Noe Tamasese at Vailima after the wedding. Government House staff had provided a roast pig as the traditional centrepiece for the celebration.*

BELOW LEFT: *Leva with Caroline To'oa. The ghostly manifestations which marked the baby's arrival disrupted life in the old plantation house.*

BELOW RIGHT: *Julie with Mrs Mary Croudace. Popularly known as Auntie Mary, she was a good guide to the intricacies of Samoan life.*

LEFT: *A small New Zealand family in the Commonwealth's new headquarters, Marlborough House. From left: Caroline, author holding Sophie, Gerald and Sarah.*

ABOVE LEFT: *The increasingly reclusive President and Mrs Nixon were generous in their hospitality to the children of diplomats. Their parents were restricted to glimpses of the president in his motorcades. Here Caroline (front) sits beside the First Lady's chair.*

ABOVE RIGHT: *The Commonwealth Secretary General, Arnold Smith, and the author at the Nairobi meeting which established the Commonwealth Fund for Technical Cooperation.*

THERE WILL BE A HOMELAND
FOR ALL OR A HOMELAND
FOR NONE!

DEATH TO ZIONISTS, AND THE

FUNCTIONNKIES.

ABOVE LEFT: *Leonard Hensley, the author's father, framed by glass broken by the bullets which narrowly missed him. 'Had I', he said, 'been an upright lawyer I would have been dead.'* Washington Post, *April 1973.*

ABOVE RIGHT: *Sir Robert Muldoon was a regular visitor to Singapore. Here he is seen with Lady Muldoon, the Prime Minister of Singapore, Lee Kuan Yew, Julie and the author.*

BELOW: *Shopping in Singapore: Lady Muldoon, Sophie and Julie.* Straits Times

The Democratic Socialist Republic of Sri Lanka required morning dress to be worn for the presentation of credentials. Appropriately attired, the author meets President William Gopallawa in the Queen's House, Colombo.

The NZ Defence Force helicopters were an asset to life in Singapore. Here on board, from left, are: Mrs Pauline Smith, Brigadier Lin Smith, Sir Keith Holyoake, author and Julie.

Dr Goh Keng Swee (centre) taking the salute as the New Zealand Forces march past on the Padang in Singapore.

ABOVE: *Pointing out the pitfalls. Newly appointed Secretary to the Treasury, Bernard Galvin, going through the papers with the author, his successor as Head of the Prime Minister's Department. 'The life of a permanent head', Bernard once observed, 'is one of rejection and dejection.'*
Dominion Post

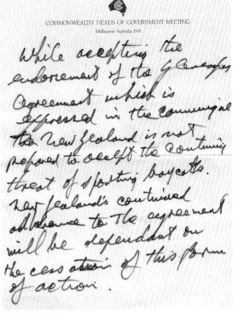

ABOVE: *Sir Robert Muldoon's handwritten note for the 1981 Commonwealth Heads of Government Meeting in Melbourne. He said that New Zealand would continue to carry out its obligations under the reaffirmed Gleneagles Agreement but would withdraw if there were any more boycotts of its sportsmen.*

ABOVE: *The Advisory Group in 1981. Clockwise from the top are: Graham Tuohy, Brian Lockstone, author, Colleen Pilgrim, Simon Murdoch, George Green, Murray Sherwin and Denys Crengle.* New Zealand Herald

BELOW: *Cartoon by Bill Leak.* The Bulletin

ABOVE RIGHT: *Sir Robert Muldoon in battle order at the Fourteenth South Pacific Forum in Canberra, 1983.* Canberra Times

BELOW: *Cartoon by Nevile Lodge, 1983.* Dominion Post

*Cartoon by Nevile Lodge, 1982.* Dominion Post

*Cartoon by Eric Heath, 1982.* Dominion Post

*Christmas at Vogel House before David Lange abandoned the residence for a flat in central Wellington. Author, Caroline and Julie.*

ABOVE LEFT: *Prime Minister David Lange carving the pig which was the centrepiece of our silver wedding celebrations.*

ABOVE RIGHT: *Wedding party twenty-five years on. Front from left: Lady Powles, Mrs Tui Hensley and Sir Guy Powles. Back: Mr Len Hensley, author, Julie and her father Mr Austen Young.*

BELOW: *A ninety-year span. Mrs Tui Hensley with her great-grandson Peter, front centre. Behind her from left: Sophie, Gerald and Audrey Hensley, author, Julie, Sarah with Jonathan Gould, Caroline, Nicholas and Geoffrey Peren (with his back to the camera).*

Head of State who had given her one of his family's titles. His Highness received her at his own house, a stately *fale* with modern additions, with the affability and courtesy natural to the ancient Malietoa line. After we had sipped drinks and chatted for half an hour he said, 'Now, To'oa, we don't see you very often and we should mark the occasion. Tell me what you would most like and I will give it to you'. To'oa's parents leant forward in anticipation. Caroline said, 'I would like my brother to be here', and they leant back again. The royal limousine was despatched to find young Gerald on the Beach Road and fetch him to join us all at the house. So the call ended fittingly in a little contest of royal good manners, where the generosity of Malietoa's offer was met by To'oa with the tact that became her high title.

Back in Washington there were other diversions. Friends from New York, who had shared our brownstone with us, had in the intervening years risen to fortune and if not fame at least to an appointment in the Nixon Administration. Living in a desirable street in the heart of Georgetown they introduced us to the Washington establishment, that circle of political notables, lawyers and media figures who reigned whatever administration was in power. The surviving members of the Kennedy family were part of this and every year Ethel Kennedy organised a charitable event, the Pet Show, at her home, Hickory Hill, which had originally been bought for Jack and Jackie. It was an elaborate affair, and the preparations were overseen by a committee of Washington ladies (to which Julie was co-opted) who in the East Coast tradition of fund-raising were both fashionable and efficient.

On the day itself Washington's leading satirical columnist, Art Buchwald, ran the show dressed in full circus ringmaster gear. Scattered around the grounds were stalls, prizes and excitements that children could only dream about. The Green Berets, the commando force set up by President Kennedy, rigged a rope adventure trail high up through the Hickory Hill trees. Uniformed members of the special forces ran the attraction. Five-year-old Sophie, sliding down a rope between two trees, slipped from her minder's grasp and fell, breaking her collar-bone. We drove her to Georgetown Hospital where, after advance warning from the family at Hickory Hill, the five-person trauma team was waiting at the hospital entrance. The speed with which she was admitted and strapped up was a glimpse of what imperial power was like, and perhaps the effect it had on those who enjoyed it.

In the meantime his critics accused the current President of becoming more imperial, designing rather implausible uniforms for the presidential guard and retiring further from the public view as the protests mounted. Only our children met Mr and Mrs Nixon, at the annual White House Christmas party. However congenial to his personality, though, there was also a reason for some of this secrecy. He was laying the groundwork for a dramatic flourish, ending nearly a generation of American hostility towards China.

By calling for the withdrawal of substantial numbers of American troops from Asia, the Nixon Doctrine accepted that China was not a threat and quietly ended the policy of 'containment'. This opened the enticing prospect of a much better relationship between the two countries but few in Washington in 1969 could see how this could be achieved without abandoning Taiwan. It was a modern version of the question which had vexed and defeated the earliest embassies to China: how low should the kowtow be; how far would it be necessary to go to meet China's terms. Or to put it the other way: how far might China be willing to compromise on its hitherto inflexible position that Taiwan was no one's concern but its own.

At the end of the year an inter-agency group was set up in tight secrecy to consider the way through. 'We are beginning to think the unthinkable,' one of them told me. The signals of a change in the American attitude were already accumulating. There was a gradual easing of trade and travel restrictions in a series of small but definite signals to Beijing. Naval patrolling in the Taiwan Straits was cut back and it was announced that American troops stationed on Taiwan would be brought down to their low, pre-Vietnam levels. These steps were taken without any expectation of early reciprocation by China. In a subtle and unhurried way, more reminiscent of Chinese than American diplomacy, Beijing was being given time to consider its response; the signals were spaced 'not to overload the circuits'.

In the year that followed China was left to reflect on these moves, reinforced by further gestures such as the President for the first time referring to the country as the 'People's Republic of China'. As the American withdrawal from Vietnam advanced it became clear to Beijing that the Nixon Doctrine had to be taken seriously. As so often happens in life, what China had ardently called for began to look less attractive. The departure of the Americans would be less agreeable if their place were to be taken by the Russians, whose growing role as North Vietnam's supplier might give them a privileged position in Indochina. Then China could be squeezed on both its northern and southern borders. So it was time for Beijing to reconsider its view of the 'white-boned demons'. 'Yankee go home – slowly' was how someone summed it up.

In the meantime continued secrecy was essential, not just to give the Chinese space to think, but also to avoid alerting the China lobby at home. The China lobby was actually the Taiwan lobby, descended from the wartime alliance with Chiang Kai-shek and still led by formidable Sino-American widows like Anna Chenault. It had been a maxim of American politics for decades that this group, which comprised all those conservatives who felt that President Truman's weakness or worse had 'lost' China, had an effective lock on any changes in the country's China policy. I had a small taste of their zeal. On a speaking trip to Atlanta in April 1970 I had addressed the English-Speaking Union (in the South the Episcopalian Church at rest) on the harmless topic of 'English in Common Ownership'. When I returned the ambassador asked what I had said to upset Wellington. The morning newspapers had carried a story 'No threat from Red China says diplomat' and a cable sought urgent clarification. In response to a question I had said that China was preoccupied with problems of its own and posed no threat to New Zealand, and this mild comment had been immediately telephoned through to the press. The Ministry accepted this, adding somewhat unconvincingly that they had 'assumed that whatever Hensley said was balanced and reflected Government policy'.

As early as September 1969, just after the clashes with Soviet border troops, four marshals urged Chairman Mao to work for better relations with the US, and President Nixon opened a covert channel of communication through President Yahya of Pakistan. It was not until early in 1971, though, that the Chinese began to respond to Washington's overtures, first in small signs, then in a rash of ping-pong diplomacy when the American and other table tennis teams were invited to China to be trounced. Fears of the domestic reaction proved misplaced. Congress and the public were delighted and the President's popularity surged. Long-suppressed feelings welled up with a force which drowned the misgivings of the China lobby. As with the British and India, many Americans had maintained a continuing attachment to things Chinese; a country could hardly be 'lost' unless you had felt close to it in the first place. Many families had members who had worked in China as missionaries, doctors or social reformers – several of the Administration's top advisers were the children of missionaries. Commerce had brought others to Shanghai or other cities and the export ware displayed in New England cabinets went all the way back to the fur trade with Canton. These sentimental links became respectable again.

Excitement was already bubbling when Henry Kissinger made his secret dash to Beijing in July of that year and returned with the electrifying news that President Nixon had been invited to visit China. The Kissinger flight had been arranged through President Yahya. Under cover of a weekend in Pakistan's hill country he left from Islamabad on a Pakistan International Airlines plane. Secrecy held, even though a stringer for the *Daily Telegraph* managed to be on the tarmac in the pre-dawn darkness as the plane took off. To maintain the cover story the Kissinger party had to leave their laundry behind. Kissinger discovered he had no clean shirt for the momentous meeting and John Holdridge lent him a new one his wife had bought from a supermarket at the last minute. They had hardly got to the resthouse in Beijing before they were told of the first meeting with Premier Chou En-lai. The shirt was then revealed to be too large and to have extravagantly long collar points and the historic meeting began with an apologetic explanation by Dr Kissinger for his appearance.

Everything else went smoothly. The path of compromise had been opened up by the Administration declaring that the best way to resolve the Taiwan issue was for the rival authorities to settle it between themselves. The US would stand aside, requiring only that the settlement be peaceful. China now had urgent reasons to accept the compromise and to resume its place among the great powers. The outlines of what was to be settled in the President's visit were quickly agreed, Kissinger saying afterwards that once broad agreement was reached on principles the Chinese showed an 'aristocratic generosity' over the details – quite unlike the Russians who never knew when to stop. On his return he and the President retired to a Californian restaurant to drink a bottle of very expensive claret in celebration of their triumph.

In September there was a backlash, all the more unexpected for being on the Chinese side. I arrived at the CIA one morning to find the place buzzing. All Chinese aircraft were grounded for several days and military communications shut down. Even observance of the forthcoming

National Day was cancelled 'for economy reasons'. Theories abounded – that war was about the break out with the Soviet Union, or more persuasively that Mao had died – but the Chinese Government, which could teach President Nixon a thing or two about secrecy, said nothing. Days and then weeks went by before enough fragments of information could be pieced together to make a pattern.

It seemed that a pro-Russian party in the Politburo led by Lin Biao, Mao's designated successor and Defence Minister, opposed any warming of relations with the US and the Nixon visit. The differences widened and over several months some of Lin's clients and supporters began to be removed from their posts. Matters came to a head at a meeting of the Politburo on 12 September, when Lin was decisively defeated, possibly having attempted a coup against Mao. He fled that night with several senior generals on a commandeered Trident jet. It was presumably making for the Soviet Union when it ran out of fuel and crashed in Mongolia, killing all on board.

After that the remaining diplomatic obstacles did not seem too difficult. The main one was the question of who should sit in China's seat at the United Nations. A nineteenth-century French statesman, contemplating a number of royal claimants, observed that 'the throne is not a settee'. Neither was a UN seat. Only one China could hold it – the possibility of two seats, floated by the hopeful, was scouted angrily by both sides – and voting for one meant accepting its claim to be the only China. For more than a decade Western diplomats, including New Zealand, had fought a rearguard action and every year the cables flew round the world as tactics were concerted for the next General Assembly. As the numbers voting for the Republic of China (the island of Taiwan) diminished, ever more ingenious ideas were tabled to delay the inevitable.

It was declared an 'important question' requiring a two-thirds majority but even that had become imperilled. In 1971 the State Department joined in the usual tactical discussions, partly because it could hardly stand aside and partly because it was not fully in the President's confidence (the department had not been aware of Kissinger's visit to Beijing) but the US, which had once orchestrated the annual battle, was now on the sidelines. With its eyes on North Asia rather than the General Assembly the Administration was content to let the game be played out to the end, knowing that its public opinion like ours would accept the result. In October the seat changed hands.

The Nixon visit in the following February attracted huge interest in the United States and around the world. An opera was even composed about it. This was encouraged by the two governments: both wanted the clearest possible demonstration, to Moscow and Hanoi especially, of the change in Asia and of China's part in it. So Beijing was happy to accept the enormous press corps which trailed after the President. Every step of the visit and its attendant sightseeing was chronicled in media releases. Nixon's less than original comment stepping on to the Great Wall ('It certainly is a great wall') was immediately distributed to waiting reporters as was the mishap shortly afterwards when the battery-warmed presidential socks blew a fuse. It had to be managed as a piece of ceremonial theatre – that was its purpose – and no one had a longer tradition of the meticulous conduct of state ceremonies than China. So Chou En-lai also supervised every detail, having drafts of Chinese newspaper stories for the following day brought to him at the theatre for approval, and getting up at three in the morning to check weather reports for the visit to the Wall.

The effort was worthwhile; it was one of those moments usually more trumpeted about than genuine – a turning point in history. Washington may have had the better of the gift exchange (like thousands of others we went to see the pandas at the zoo) but China got what it wanted, acceptance as one of the four great powers and an end to American hostility. 'The era of containment, collective security and alliance diplomacy is over,' said the President, causing a slight raising of eyebrows by his allies including us. In return China had agreed to shelve the Taiwan issue for the time being, in the expectation that time was on its side. It was the high point of the Nixon diplomacy and in election year too.

The Greeks had a word for what followed but the tragedy was not so much the price of pride or overweening confidence as of faults in the character of the President and his Administration. The secrecy which had its diplomatic justification and which enabled results to be announced with a dramatic flourish grew into a habit. The President retreated behind the Berlin Wall of his circle of trusted advisers; senior and experienced members of the State Department would admit to us their ignorance of what was going on. It is always a sign of trouble when heads of government begin to narrow the scope of their consultations. Distrust of the press, natural to any government past its honeymoon, hardened into almost a paranoia about the East Coast papers and the liberal establishment behind them. As the pressure mounted over Vietnam and the leaks multiplied the President became increasingly suspicious of his own departments.

This siege mentality was abetted by a more humble cause: weariness. Governments become progressively more tired as the years in office accumulate but in the case of the Nixon administration this was reinforced by its worship of the work ethic. It was a mark if not a boast of the President's circle that everyone worked long hours throughout the week, pausing only to go to church on Sundays. Anyone who had gone home when you telephoned was clearly not influential and therefore not worth talking to anyway. This dedication must have got through a lot of work but at a cost; after three years the judgement of the President and his White House group started to fail. Even the paranoid may have real enemies, as Kissinger observed, but resentment and failing energy magnified them to the point where the Nixon Administration like an ill-tempered child destroyed its own political triumphs.

In June 1972 we sat having dinner at a restaurant in the Watergate complex. A kind friend in the Agency had arranged a dinner with Richard Helms, Director of the CIA. As the four of us sat out on the terrace on a pleasant summer evening we looked across at the windows of the Democratic National Headquarters, which had been broken into two nights earlier. We talked about the oddity of the bungled operation which seemed more of a prank than anything else. Dick Helms, a smooth and charming professional, joined in the speculation and seemed as baffled as the rest of us. Perhaps he did not know or had forgotten that the Agency had supplied some of the conspirators with red beards and 'voice alterators'.

If so the press began to supply the details. The burglars, part of a covert group set up a year before and soon known as the 'White House plumbers', had intended to replace a radio transmitter in the ceiling of the Democratic National Chairman's office and a phone bug as well as to photograph files. They were led by the security coordinator of the gloriously named CREEP, the Committee for the Re-Election of the President. It turned out that the Republican campaign was funding no less than three intelligence operations including the plumbers. This was embarrassing and the White House moved to cover things over, with the White House legal counsel investigating and reporting that no one 'presently employed' by the White House had any connection with the affair. Even so the Attorney-General resigned shortly after, the first of the President's dominoes to fall.

The comic-opera overtones of the affair still evoked more laughter than outrage. For all the denials few doubted that the President was involved and had at least acquiesced in the burglary. His popularity, never high, fell. Strangely, though, his election prospects were unaffected; he would have had a comfortable majority without the risks of making covert war on the Democrats. For the Democratic Party had turned to their left wing to choose Senator George McGovern, whose platform of immediately withdrawing from Vietnam and abandoning the South Vietnamese to their fate was too extreme for most voters. The choice, it was said, was between a crook and a fool and, as usual in politics, people preferred the crook. Only Massachusetts and the District of Columbia went against the Nixon tide and, as the President's downfall unfolded, bumper stickers appeared saying 'Don't blame me, I'm from Massachusetts'.

In these circumstances it was hardly an exciting campaign. The Democrats who always had the best lines turned to jokes to make their points about the President. A less humourless man than Nixon might have chosen different campaign slogans. 'Nixon – Now More Than Ever' did not sound reassuring to those who distrusted him in the first place. But it was 'Nixon's The One' that brought out the creative in his opponents. There were several variants, the best being a photograph of heavily pregnant teenagers grouped under a large banner with this message. I went to a political rally in Philadelphia which was addressed by Vice-President Agnew. As he began to speak under a huge sign reading 'Nixon's The One', another descended jerkily from the flies to read 'And Agnew's Another'. It was not only the despised 'nattering nabobs of negativism' who were helpless with laughter.

Agnew was the rough-tongued bouncer of the Administration (most have one). A small-minded Maryland politician, already under investigation for the corruption which was later to force his resignation, he was out of his depth in national politics. Some time later, after his disgrace, I was sitting opposite him in a mobile lounge at Dulles Airport when it caught fire. The lounge filled with smoke and when flames leapt from the rear compartment there was an incipient panic. The fire was quickly put out and when the smoke cleared Agnew was still sitting motionless, staring ahead unseeing as if still unable to understand what had gone wrong for him.

The President must have expected that his landslide victory at the polls in November would bury the Watergate scandal but a persistent Chief Judge thought otherwise. The Justice Department was unenthusiastic about prosecuting the burglars but the judge's questioning led to hearings by a Senate Committee and the knot of obstruction began to unravel. The legal counsel changed his story, saying characteristically that 'the truth was the only thing that would sell', and contradicted large parts of his colleagues' evidence. He gave graphic accounts of the running of the Nixon White House and the heavy cloud of political paranoia that hung over it. An 'enemies list' came to light, along with plans to use Federal agencies to harass those on it. There were some 200 names – newspaper and television commentators, actors, columnists, distinguished academics, women's page reporters, all twelve black Congressmen and some so obscure they could not themselves explain how they got there.

One by one a sad procession of the President's closest associates went off to jail. His own complicity in the cover-up and subsequent obstruction of justice was clear to most but the evidence was still circumstantial. Until there was a direct linkage (that came later with the Oval Office tapes) talk of impeachment was premature. Nonetheless Nixon, one of the great foreign policy presidents, was a political cripple while barely into his second term.

In the embassy chronicling this dispiriting decline was offset by more domestic events. The frigate *Canterbury* on its delivery voyage sailed up the Potomac River to Washington, said to be the first foreign warship to do so since the British raid in 1814. Memories were long. A barbecue was held on the ship to promote New Zealand lamb and as I came away a man said to me, 'What are those guys doing in this town? Last time they were here they burnt the place down'.

There was an even more novel activity – buying houses. The New Zealand economy had reached the pinnacle of its performance as an exporter of agricultural commodities to Britain. The dollar was worth $US1.15 and the country was running a healthy trade surplus. The Secretary to the Treasury arrived to say that this situation would not recur in either of our lifetimes (he has yet to be proved wrong) and that some of the overflow should be invested in houses for the foreign service. Being now deputy to the ambassador the task of house-hunting fell to me.

With cash in hand we could get good prices and when I cabled to say that we had run through the sum first allotted, Wellington sent more; an experience harder to credit than any other in a foreign service career. In all nine houses were added to Frank Langstone's original purchase. The Trade Commissioner had a house excellently placed for entertaining; the Defence Attaché had one next door to the chairman of the Senate Armed Services Committee; and we moved to a house on the edge of Georgetown. Shifting the household, now including a Peruvian guinea-pig and three Mexican fighting fish (our children never settled for the quieter option), across town was straightforward. The only unexpected moment came when four of us shuffled out the front door carrying my square piano, an oblong box of polished mahogany, and two passers-by paused and respectfully removed their hats.

The house (since sold with all but one of the others – Treasury changed its mind) occupied a small back section on a bluff and was reached by two narrow drives between the neighbouring houses. Two months after the move my elderly parents came to stay and were placed in the downstairs study, converted into a bedroom for the occasion. In the small hours of the next morning I was suddenly awake, with an indefinable feeling that something had just happened. My father appeared in the doorway to say politely, 'Someone has fired a gun into our room', perhaps assuming as a recently arrived Christchurch lawyer that this might not be unusual in gun-carrying America.

When I hurried downstairs, the wind was blowing the curtains through the shattered window and a thin cloud of blue gunsmoke was drifting around the room. My first thought was that a deranged gunman was loose in the garden. I slipped out the front door to find out. It was a cool spring night with a moon behind fleeting clouds. Black shadows came and went as I groped my way around the house and I regretted embarking on the search. By the time I was back in the house the police and Diplomatic Protection Squad were arriving and they ended thoughts of a deranged gunman. On the brick wall below the study window they found a message painted in black: 'There will be a homeland for all or a homeland for none! Death to the Zionists and their functionaries!!' and it was signed 'Black September' within a five-pointed star. It looked as if the intruders had painted this and then fired two or three shots into the house to draw attention. The bullets passed across my father's bed (he said, 'If I had been an upright lawyer I would have been dead') and into the wall above my mother.

The police traced the getaway car as far as the Chain Bridge and then lost it. Questions of the houses around us brought a little more information. Our Texan neighbours heard the shots but assumed that Julie and I were settling a domestic difference and with southern courtliness felt they should not interfere. Others had noticed a car with Virginia licence plates parked on two occasions at the end of our drive which appeared to be keeping the house under surveillance. Why was unclear. New Zealand's new Deputy Prime Minister, Hugh Watt, had been visiting Israel but his reported statements contained nothing new. The house had been let to the Jordanian ambassador two years earlier and it looked more plausible that the attack would have been aimed to frighten him. I was chargé d'affaires at the time and the sight of the embassy Cadillac parked in the drive must have convinced the surveillance men that they had the right place. They corrected their error. A few weeks later the Israeli Air Attaché was murdered as he returned home late at night, with what the FBI decided was the same pistol.

The attack, described by *Time* magazine as 'the first suspected act of violence by Black September terrorists within the US', caused a passing stir. The *Washington Post* headline talked of 'Arab terror'; other newspapers relished the mild oddity of an elderly New Zealand lawyer having a 'spot of tea' and then going back to bed after the broken glass had been swept up. I lost no opportunity of emphasising that the whole thing must have been a mistake and that New Zealand had a very low profile in the Middle East. It seemed more likely that the attackers had been the victims of an old diplomatic directory and papers like the *Wall Street Journal* concluded that 'the gunmen apparently thought they were shooting at the previous owner'.

For the following six weeks we lived under an armed guard. It was a mixed blessing. By day we shared the house with two large policemen. All night long the radio in the patrol car beneath our bedroom window crackled with vague messages and periodically the engine was gunned to keep the heater going. In the morning the parking place was marked by two piles of cigarette butts on either side of the car doors. There was only one alarm. I was called home to examine a suspicious parcel which had come from Beirut. The guards had laid it cautiously on the lawn where I bent to look at it. It was addressed to me but I knew no one in the Lebanon and it was left in the gently falling rain for the explosives experts to deal with. In the meantime Sophie, coming home from school, opened it, removed a learned quarterly from the American

University in Beirut and brought it into the house saying, 'Look what's come for Dad'.

A few months later we moved again, this time back to New Zealand. The usual round of farewells began. On a Sunday morning we held the traditional gathering to drink up the remains of the cellar. There was an overflow attendance, partly to see the now famous wall with the slogans and partly to find out the meaning of the word 'elevenses' which we had unwisely used on the invitations. The CIA had a more decorous party at Langley and a medal was presented – not a decoration but a large bronze medallion like those worn around their necks by wine waiters. A medal from the Agency was an ambiguous distinction; I assumed it was for attendance. Then it was time to catch the flight from Washington, always described as the Nation's Capital but now becoming the world's too.

CHAPTER SIX

# New Zealand Adrift

THE KOWLOON TO CANTON RAILWAY DID NOT LIVE UP TO THE promise of its name. It stopped in fact at Lowu, on the border of Hong Kong's New Territories. The atmosphere was that of the Cold War as I lugged my suitcase across a shabby iron-girdered bridge to the Chinese border post at the other end. The atmosphere became more pronounced as an unsmiling guard studied my passport, shining a torch on it for added visibility, and then disappeared into a shed where I could see a telephone call being made. I waited rather apprehensively, but the guard emerged with a newly arranged smile, handed back my passport and directed me to the train for Canton (Guangzhou).

It was October 1973 and, newly installed in Wellington as head of the Foreign Ministry's Asian Division, I was on my way to gain some first-hand impressions of North Asia. It was much needed – I had never visited any part of it before. The visit started in Tokyo, where New Zealand (and Australia) had just been admitted to a regional conference sponsored by the Japanese. MEDSEA was a development gathering which the Japanese had some hopes might expand into a widely accepted regional organisation. So the Deputy Prime Minister and I took our seats, listened to two days of worthy speeches and went our separate ways. The conference was well-meaning and indeed useful in encouraging several regional aid initiatives but it was an artificial construct, held together by Japanese money. It was unlikely to grow into the kind of Asia–Pacific organisation we were looking for.

From there I went to Seoul. The underlying edginess of life in a divided Korea became more understandable as you moved around a

165

busy capital which was within range of artillery massed on the other side of the ceasefire line. This understanding was reinforced by the standard itinerary laid out for the visitor. A trip to Panmunjom was obligatory (over the years I was to make it four times) but observing the peculiar and carefully choreographed rituals of the truce village was never dull. On this first occasion a North Korean officer spat on the door on my car, reminding me involuntarily of the Egyptian cobra in Uganda except that there was something both practised and detached about the gesture. For all I knew he had been selected for his ready saliva and performed the feat for all cars entering the zone.

The same scripted air hung over a tour of the truce negotiations hut, occupied by an unimpressive conference table with a line down the middle which marked the actual border. While we inspected the American side, North Korean soldiers jostled to watch us through the windows, hoping perhaps that we might walk around to their side of the table and create a welcome provocation. This constant surveillance became surreal when we drove to an observation point looking over the no-man's-land to the North Korean positions on the other side of a shallow valley. I was handed a huge pair of binoculars but when they were focused, all I could see was a close-up of a North Korean officer peering through an equally large pair at me.

At Kap'yong, two withered bunches of late-summer flowers had been laid on the steps of the modest war memorial. This narrow valley had been the scene of one of the most desperate battles of the Korean War. As part of a general spring offensive by Chinese and North Korean forces in 1951 the Commonwealth Brigade, of Australian and Canadian battalions with artillery support from a New Zealand regiment, found itself isolated and under attack by a Chinese division, which flooded down the valley in overwhelming numbers. The New Zealand guns fired continuously for thirty-six hours; when they ceased on Anzac Day, they were worn out. At one stage, when radio contact was lost with the Australians, an Auckland lieutenant perched on a conspicuous crag to try and direct the fire but was killed himself. At another, the Canadians were so overrun by Chinese troops that they called down the New Zealand fire on their own positions. In the end the guns were firing over open sights at the tide of attackers. But the Commonwealth line held and the Chinese lost heart. It proved to be a decisive battle; some weeks later the two sides agreed to open truce talks. I looked around the steep little valley, where the hillside trees were already growing back over the scars and laid my formal wreath. It seemed to lack feeling lying beside the faded blue and red wildflowers left by unknown hands.

Now after a short stay in Hong Kong I was on my way to Peking (Beijing). The train to Guangzhou was crowded but this did not prepare me for the crowd when I stepped off the train. Wondering how to get to the airport, I stood like a rock in a Zen garden as a mass of people in blue Mao suits swirled around me. I need not have worried; a solitary European rising high above the blue-clad crowd was nothing if not conspicuous. A perspiring lady followed by two young men pushed her way through the crowd to ask 'Mr Hansley?' and her relief at our meeting was even greater than mine.

We flew to Beijing on a Russian Ilyushin aircraft. China had not then entered the age of air travel and the only other passengers seemed to be officials or members of the People's Liberation Army. Most smoked the pungent local cigarettes – the rules were more informal then – and tucked into the rather good food provided. Curious about the tobacco I bought a tin of Pansy brand pipe tobacco when I got to Beijing but it appeared to be made from the fossilised droppings of Genghis Khan's cavalry and I did not persevere.

Our embassy in Beijing was only a few months older than my appointment to the Asian Division. After President Nixon's visit the way was open for countries like New Zealand to recognise the People's Republic. In its last year in office the outgoing conservative government baulked at withdrawing recognition from Taiwan but the Labour Party's victory in the polls at the end of 1972 removed this constraint. Then surprisingly the new Prime Minister, Norman Kirk, hesitated. After barely two weeks in office he suggested that it might be better to delay recognition until his second term. However he was talked out of this by the Foreign Ministry (now under Frank Corner) and the recognition formalities were completed just before Christmas.

An embassy was opened in Beijing the following year and the first ambassador, Bryce Harland, took up his position just over a month before my visit. It was dark by the time my plane landed, to be met by Bryce and his newly acquired driver, a large, gap-toothed Mongolian called Shang. We then drove into Beijing at high speed down a wide boulevard with our lights off. Periodically, obeying perhaps some herder's instinct, Mr Shang would switch on his lights just in time to illuminate a wobbling line of blue-suited cyclists riding eight or more abreast across the road in front of us. We would swerve around this line and the lights would be immediately switched off again until he sensed the next group. This was a little exciting and I enquired through Bryce why he turned off the lights. The driver turned to face the back seat (adding to the excitement) and said, 'Chairman Mao bids us save power'. Then he grinned. I began to suspect Mr Shang of comic if not ironical tendencies. At the Great Wall, seeing him locking all the car doors, I quoted back his own assertion that there were no thieves in China. 'That is true,' said Mr Shang, more than equal to this challenge, 'but there are a lot of foreigners about' – though the ambassador and I were the only ones in sight.

The ambassador had a temporary apartment in the San Li Tun diplomatic compound where the newly arrived New Zealand furniture and paintings lightened the somewhat heavy Soviet style of the building. The Chinese Foreign Ministry, however, had just revealed a surprise. Unknown to us they had built a whole new embassy for New Zealand, at the memorable address of No 1, Street No 2, East Temple of the Sun. Since they had not consulted us about the plans, or even mentioned them, I was curious to see their concept of how New Zealanders lived. The building, a combination of office and residence, was only half built and Bryce and I wandered through the construction site trying to work out the purpose of rooms still windowless and littered with rubbish. The office layout was plain enough; as was the slightly eccentric arrangement of the bedrooms upstairs, but we were baffled by an enormous room downstairs, more suited to indoor basketball than diplomatic parties. It was strongly reminiscent of the Great Hall of the People and we speculated whether this was now obligatory; it proved a headache to make liveable.

For dinner that first night Bryce had assembled some Western ambassadors and my sparse acquaintance in Beijing, including John Holdridge from the United States Liaison Office (an embassy in all but name), which had opened a few months earlier. The cook like all local staff was supplied by the Diplomatic Service Bureau, whose shortcomings were a feature of embassy conversations, much as the servant problem was in earlier times. Members of the staff were required to report all conversations and events of interest; in return the Bureau skimmed off a third of their pay – a requirement which in time caused some interesting conflicts of loyalty. The cook, though, was superb and topped the meal with a confection of sweet chestnut over which he had built a temple of spun sugar. It was very Chinese in its playful fantasy and bluntly Chinese in the name he gave it: Peking Mud.

When the conversation was not about the latest vexation of the Diplomatic Service Bureau, it was trying to divine the intentions of the secretive Chinese government. The diplomatic community felt beleaguered. The upheavals of the Cultural Revolution had died down but China was still far from open to the world. Chairman Mao's restless spirit had begun a new campaign, *Pi Lin Pi Kung*, a struggle against the odd couple of Lin Biao, who had died in an air crash fleeing from China, and Confucius, who had died 2500 years earlier.

In the long-standing Chinese tradition this struggle was carried on through historical allusions readily decipherable by the educated. Newspapers and official speeches were full of references to events in the remote Warring States period, treacherous ministers, corrupt and self-serving elites and intellectuals, and in shining contrast the righteous first Chin Emperor, who had unified China and burnt books and scholars alike. The tone of these denunciations had chilling resemblances to events in the mid-sixties and the Americans were already calling it the neo-Cultural Revolution. In this closed society where truth was a state secret and all facts were ambiguous, normal embassy practice gave way to a cooperative effort in puzzle-solving. Groups of Western diplomats would gather around the dinner or coffee table to pool scraps of the jigsaw and then try fitting them together. Someone had seen a poster on a wall in a working-class district; a provincial newspaper had run an unusual story; a junior minister had dropped a mysterious hint. Out of all this a plausible explanation would gradually emerge. The tentative view, as I listened silently at the tables, was that this was not a lapse back into the past disorders but a movement against any revolutionary backsliding, an effort to tighten discipline as the Mao years drew to a close, and time proved it correct.

The cordial welcome I received at the Foreign Ministry bore this out. Lin Ping, Director of the Americas and Oceania Division, made it clear that this was a domestic campaign and that China's post-Nixon stance would not change. He then gave me a dinner at the city's famous duck restaurant where all the dishes from duck nibbles to duck dessert were based on that bird, ending with a clear soup in which rested the last bits – two yellow feet. More difficult though was the snake wine brought out as a special treat. It was a bottle of yellow liquid the bottom third of which looked like a grey sediment, presumably the remains of the late snake. 'Makes you strong,' someone whispered to me with a wink. Later experience taught me that the Chinese are prone to make this hopeful claim about any exotic food, and in Singapore I endeavoured to spread the same story about kiwifruit. I closed my eyes and swallowed: it was awful.

As the toasts circulated the party atmosphere became more and more convivial. My host asked courteously about the New Zealand Communist Party, then in fraternal association with the Chinese Party. Perhaps made strong by the snake wine I replied merrily that it was doing well: 'They need two taxis to go to a Party Congress'. In the silence that fell as this was being translated the rashness of the remark came home to me and the moisture broke out on my brow. Then the silence was broken by a shout of laughter and the atmosphere became even more convivial. In the end the eight of us went off unsteadily into the night, like the eight Immortal Sages who were the legendary patrons of insobriety.

In the course of a round of calls we met David Bruce, the recently arrived American representative. An able man who had been American ambassador in London and Paris, he had considerable experience and even more considerable wealth. I admired a ceramic T'ang horse and rider on his table. He agreed and then, with the magnificence of a man with the Mellon money behind him, said, 'It's a cheap reproduction from the market here, but I like it better than the genuine ones I have at home'. For his part he confided to his diary that two pleasant young New Zealanders had come to see him but he wondered how much they knew about Asia.

We also went to see Rewi Alley, the New Zealander who had become the most eminent of China's 'foreign friends'. He had lived and worked in a remote province of China for half a century and maintained good links with the Communist leadership. He now lived in the old Italian Legation, a handsome late nineteenth-century building which had been converted into flats for the leading foreign friends. The flats were allocated on the bleak basis of seniority. On the death of the previous occupant, Anna Louise Strong, Rewi had moved downstairs into the best front apartment, and everyone else had moved on one place. One wall of his spacious high-ceilinged sitting-room contained a huge and ornate cupboard from the Imperial Palace, looted by the Italians at the time of the Boxer uprising, and two others held shelves of his books. The windows looked out on a most un-Peking view of lawns and trees.

He was in his seventies, a bald, pink-faced man with bright blue eyes, and an inexhaustible flow of conversation. We sat and talked for most of an afternoon, with Rewi occasionally jumping up to fetch a book or check a point. He had, he said, lost the best of two libraries, once to the Japanese and again to the Red Guards, who had thrown out his collections and torn up his pictures in front of him. He was still bitter over their behaviour. As he poured tea I admired the plain lines of the creamy-white teapot and asked if it was modern. 'No,' he said, 'it is Ming and I should not be using it but it is one of my luxuries.' This led the talk to porcelain. He opened the black-lacquered cupboard to show examples from different imperial kilns, modestly offering what became an extended tutorial on shapes and glazes. When the dark began to descend and I got up to leave he gave me a little vase decorated with blue-and-white plum blossoms.

We drove to the Ming tombs in the Western Hills, the scattered tiled buildings and avenues of stone beasts a reminder of the continuity of China. Another dynasty had come and gone since the Ming but now a ruthless soldier had like the first Ming Emperor succeeded in founding a new one. The place was deserted; we picnicked on ground strewn with fragments of yellow imperial roof tiles as the autumn wind sighed in the pines above us. On the way home we saw another fragment of the past – an old woman with a stick hobbling along on bound feet.

The imperial buildings in the Forbidden City were also largely empty – there were few foreigners and given the political uncertainties most Chinese might have felt it safer to stay away from these feudal relics. So we wandered untroubled through the Great Within, examining the surprisingly modest Dragon Throne in the Hall of Heavenly Purity, on which the emperors held audience and on which the officials of the last Ming emperor arriving in the pre-dawn darkness had seen the horrific vision of a black dragon curled in the wide chair and had concluded that Heaven had abandoned the dynasty. By chance walking through the sequence of courtyards behind the official halls we ended up in the Chien Lung emperor's library, a comfortable and scholarly room. In one corner, ticking sleepily in the mellow October sun, was a huge standing clock with a wooden ladder at the back – if not the clock built by the sixteenth-century Jesuit missionary, Father Ricci, then at least its lineal descendant. Perhaps because of the incongruity, perhaps because it symbolised the tangled history of China's relationship with the West, this is one of the pictures that hang permanently in the living-room of my mind.

That evening I caught the train for Guangzhou. Abandoning air travel meant a journey of two nights and days across the length of China. The country was still in the Railway Age. The large Beijing Railway Station was crowded with travellers and those farewelling them and it took Mr Shang with my suitcase to make a path to our carriage. This was near the end of a long train headed by two steam locomotives gleaming in black paint with red trim and a huge red star. The impression they gave, of stepping back into the 1920s, was reinforced by my compartment in the carriage which though seemingly new was furnished from the same period, with lace curtains, cut-glass flower holders, swan-necked lamps and two upholstered benches which turned into beds at night.

The arrangements had the confidence as well as the air of the golden age of rail travel, for rail was how most Chinese travelled over any distance. The Guangzhou express carried the population of a small New Zealand town and on even gentle curves it was difficult to see the front. It would pull into stations which at all hours of the night would still be brightly lit and crowded, like airports in the West, coasting slowly past a long line of glass-topped food carts piled with noodles, dumplings and cakes. People would stream off the train to throng round them, arms waving through the press to take the food and hand over the price. After ten minutes the train would pull out past the food hawkers standing beside carts, now completely emptied.

We could contemplate this recurrent scene with detachment for, as first-class travellers (the Chairman had to make some concessions), we had a restaurant car which served the best food I have ever eaten on a train or in many other places. It was always crowded with the usual officials and PLA members. Since badges of rank had been abolished positions in the hierarchy had to be deduced from the quality of the uniform but the eye quickly became adjusted to judging grades of fabric and therefore the wearer's seniority. Most on this occasion appeared to be middle-grade officers who noticeably deferred to a lady with straight iron-grey hair and a stern appearance. She had the air of a fairly senior Party member and whenever she was eating at her customary centre table there was a feeling of constraint in the carriage. At breakfast and other times we had to endure a loudspeaker which shrilled propaganda exhortations. When she left, after a respectful pause a hand would reach up and turn down the sound.

My experience at dinner on the first night was an embarrassment. I was handed a large menu card which was liberally stained with practical examples of the dishes on offer. The problem was that it was entirely in Chinese and posed a dilemma for an illiterate Westerner. Haunted by the thought that if I simply pointed to something at random it would turn out to be a bottle of snake wine, or the Chairman's thought for the day, I looked around. Across the aisle a man had just been served a dish of noodles which looked to be (and was) delicious. I pointed to it but the waiter shook his head. The kitchen, though, could hardly have run out of something it had just served so I pointed again, more emphatically. The waiter looked more and more alarmed but at length with a shrug went over, lifted the plate of noodles from under the startled traveller's chopsticks and banged it down in front of me. After the tangle had been sorted out, with the help of someone with a little English, it was accepted thereafter that at each meal I walked along the aisle inspecting the offerings and indicating what I would like – unobtrusively since some of the diners were still apprehensive about the foreigner's urge to steal their food.

Life in the compartment settled into a routine, reading, looking out the window, waiting for the next meal. In the evening bedding was brought round and you stretched out comfortably where you had sat, though sleep was punctuated by stops and the noisy bustle of life in provincial stations. Beneath the table was a jar of green tea and a large thermos flask which the attendant filled with boiling water several times a day enabling everyone to enjoy the Chinese pleasure of sipping tea throughout the day. Just beyond our compartment was the carriage lavatory which for some reason was kept locked. The whole carriage was therefore alert for the unpredictable times it would be opened and as soon as the rattle of the attendant's keys was heard the corridor outside my compartment would fill with a small queue. Inside the furnishings were a bit stark. Apart from a tiny handbasin there were two footprints in white porcelain bolted on either side of a hole through which two feet below you saw the rail-bed flashing by.

As the train went south the seasons wound backwards like a film. The morning after our departure the fields of the northern plain were closed down for the onset of winter, an austere landscape of browns and greys with little sign of life. As time went by the picture softened; the trees began to recover their leaves and people reappeared in the fields. After the train clanked over the long bridge across the Yangtze River at Wuhan the scenery changed dramatically. We were into the greens and yellows of southern China. Rice was being harvested and planted; water buffaloes appeared and men perched on stopbanks pedalled waterwheels for irrigation.

Hour on hour the train ran on through tumble-down brick villages, the backyards of farmhouses, past peeling temples, patches of dusty ground where boys were playing soccer, duck ponds of a sinister green, teahouses of a faded red. The journey was a two-day documentary on life in rural China watched through the square carriage window, with only the visits of the lavatory attendant to provide a rival attraction. In the pre-dawn darkness of the second morning the meaning of all this came upon me. I woke to see a misty procession of figures in conical hats with hoes over their shoulders, walking along a path parallel with the railway. Well before sunrise they were off to work in the fields, an emblem of the hard life of the peasant.

What struck me, though, was the antiquity of the scene. What I saw could equally have been seen by Lord Macartney in the eighteenth century or for that matter by Father Ricci. For a week I had heard everything about China interpreted and explained from a Marxist angle. Now I saw the sheer *Chineseness* of China, overwhelmingly more Chinese than Communist, whatever standing this Western faith might have as the currently established religion. It was impossible not to feel a momentary sympathy for Chairman Mao's exasperation with the past: the weight of over 4000 years of tradition was going to sink his hopes of a radically new social order. Communism lay as deep as a thin dusting of snow on the Chinese countryside and would evaporate as surely. I sank back on my bunk and never forgot the lesson.

Back home New Zealand's foreign policy was undergoing a reappraisal. As with our neighbours, the American pull-back from Asia and its new emphasis on regional self-help lowered the significance of the alliance network and required a search for a new balance. For us, though, this also coincided with Britain's entry into Europe, taking with her a large slice of our export markets. New Zealand was left rocking on the wide waters of the Pacific, looking round at a world grown less familiar.

In a favoured phrase of the new government of Norman Kirk, New Zealand was 'at last coming to terms with its geography' but we were still uncertain about the shape of this geography. It was not the South Pacific, now increasingly referred to as 'New Zealand's backyard', since like most backyards it provided no economic future. Our instinctive response was to look to the wider Asia–Pacific region. The idea that there even *was* such a region was novel, but three wars and the expansion of trade, travel and investment had created a shadowy sense of neighbourhood following the curve of the Western Pacific from Hokkaido to Invercargill.

The trouble was that a vague sense of common interests was not easily convertible into politically workable arrangements. That the urge was widely felt did not guarantee success. The regional landscape was littered with the rusting wrecks of earlier efforts – ASPAC, SEATO, and now the Japanese effort MEDSEA whose latest meeting I had just attended. All of these had fallen victim to the political divisions of the Cold War. With China being welcomed back into the international community now was perhaps a promising time to try again. Kirk proposed a new organisation which would be open to everyone in the region (except North Korea when he thought about it a bit more), and my colleagues and I tried this out in our Asian travels. Everyone was invariably in favour of it – but not yet. The Japanese were wary while the deadlock on the Korean Peninsula was unresolved; the South East Asians were still unhappy about China; and no one could make up their minds about North Vietnam. It was not difficult to predict that all these impediments would disappear in time, but the awkward fact was that here and now they were insuperable. Though no one put it that way, we were caught, in Matthew Arnold's phrase, between a world that was dying and a world that was unable to be born.

There was one regional organisation that already was universal – the UN agency then called ECAFE (the Economic Commission for Asia and the Far East). It had a modest profile and equally modest achievements but it brought together thirty-six countries in Asia and the Pacific and although principally a development organisation it might provide a foundation on which to build. It met in March 1974 in Colombo, assembling in the Bandaranaike Memorial International Conference Hall, newly built by the Chinese and as grandiose as its name. Sitting in our midst like some elephantine presence was the first major oil shock which had occurred during my stay in China. Some $10 billion had been skimmed from the developing countries, more than the entire amount of aid they received in 1973. Perhaps it might be possible to use this meeting to concert a regional approach to this economic crisis and to give a lead to the special session of the UN General Assembly which was about to meet.

It was a lively meeting and with the Sri Lankans we sponsored a proposal for an emergency World Fertiliser Fund to tide over food production in the poorest countries. But of any sense of regional solidarity or common purpose there was no sign. The Americans, sitting glumly under their post-Vietnam cloud, had no new ideas. The Japanese took the ballroom of the Intercontinental Hotel for their delegation of thirty, where they sat locked in the search for consensus for so long that as often as not when they arrived to deliver the results the conference had moved on to the next item. The Chinese, courteous and well liked, attributed every problem to 'imperialism, colonialism and plunder' and throughout the meeting went on doggedly firing their shots well to the left of where everyone else was aiming. There was inevitably a Colombo Declaration* but the rambling and talkative structure of the Commission was plainly too weak to carry the weight of serious political cooperation.

Still Colombo had a great if shabby charm. I walked on the Galle Face Green, looking at the kites flying in the brisk trade wind. The two that I bought proved unequal to the more rigorous Wellington wind but the sales patter alone was worth it: 'In England, sir, all the people are saying "Oh my Jesus, these are the best kites in the world"'. In a little South Pacific togetherness the Tongan Director of the South Pacific Forum, Mahe Tupouniua, and I spent a day in Kandy, where we rode bareback on an elephant, an experience like sitting on an undulating tennis court with the added anxiety that you might be wobbled off.

We gave up on the Prime Minister's desire for a universal regional organisation, leaving it on the table to await a more encouraging time (it lay there for a decade and a half until APEC filled the gap). Instead we turned to the second part of the Kirk vision, closer links with ASEAN and with individual East Asian states. ASEAN too had followed a number of earlier attempts to bring the countries of South East Asia

---

* The first draft, I reported to Wellington, was 'dreadful even by the usual standards of these things'.

together. It had been formed in 1967, a bare year after the end of Indonesian confrontation with neighbouring Malaysia and Singapore, and was tactfully promoted as an economic association. The threat from Indochina, though, ensured that its importance was primarily political. By 1973 it was clear that the infant organisation was going to play a major role in shaping post-war South East Asia. When Norman Kirk left for a tour of the area at the end of the year his brief told him that 'as far as we are concerned, ASEAN is the key grouping'. Kirk made it clear, to the relief of his hearers, that New Zealand was not seeking membership of the group but would welcome some form of closer cooperation. The following year New Zealand with Australia became the first 'dialogue partners' of the association. Our regional diplomacy was no longer tethered solely to security.

Kirk and Lee Kuan Yew of Singapore got on well – Lee circulated the transcript of their conversations to all his Ministers and still liked to talk about the visit years later. They swapped ideas of how to strengthen the Singapore–New Zealand links after the departure of the British forces, as security concerns were overtaken by trade. More broadly Kirk was assured that New Zealand had no need to apologise for being an outsider. Geography had, in a witty Australian phrase, ensured that we were 'odd men in'. A region fissured by ethnic, cultural and linguistic differences should have no trouble accommodating two rich and white countries within its diversity (a point neatly illustrated when Kirk went to church on Christmas Day with the Christian Batak people in the interior of Sumatra). What mattered was not who we were but what we did to help stabilise South East Asia, and Kirk was prepared to make this a focus of his foreign policy.

However the over-lengthy Asian tour that saw this plan take shape was also the beginning of its decline. In New Delhi Kirk had a heart attack and though this was kept a closely guarded secret, his health began to fail and the creative period of his prime-ministership was over. After taking over at the end of 1972 he had established himself effortlessly: instinctive, vengeful, intelligent, suspicious and perceptive – a natural leader. That he lacked formal education and was a poor administrator hardly mattered. 'Big Norm' was an overweight man with a powerful personality to match his size. What caught those who met him was an impression of decency and of strong if fitful gleams of a wider human vision. He had a Churchillian grasp of what needed to be done, and a

Churchillian vagueness about the detail. He looked as if in the New Zealand tradition he would hold power for some years to come but after barely a year he was a sick man.

His refusal to seek proper medical help reflected in part his distrust of doctors but much more his distrust of his colleagues in the parliamentary Labour Party who he was convinced would plot to overthrow him if they suspected his condition. As his strength ebbed the burdens of office became harder to bear and he began to spend increasing time away from the office, the Chatham Islands being a favourite retreat. Then in April 1974 in an act of fatalistic recklessness he had the varicose veins stripped in both his legs. My father-in-law, Austen Young, who was his lawyer and trustee, felt he lost his friend at this point. Two or so weeks later Austen took me with him down to the railway station (a rather anomalous situation for a middle-ranking Foreign Ministry official) to see Kirk off on the overnight sleeper to Auckland. He was travelling in great secrecy to consult a doctor and could not face the flight. We were the only others there which was just as well; the Prime Minister climbed slowly into the carriage and then sat down heavily on the bed, breathless and sweating.

In August a fresh medical examination revealed a gravely weakened heart. He went into the Home of Compassion for a 'rest', knowing that he had only days to live. They were spent in concealing his illness and worrying that the Labour Party might find out and replace him. He died three nights later, sitting up in bed watching a police drama on television.

Julie and I found a half-empty bottle of Valium tablets and left for the Kirk home in the suburb of Seatoun. A disparate group gradually assembled in the living-room: the Governor-General and his wife (who thoughtfully brought a large cake), the Minister of Internal Affairs, who was responsible for the funeral arrangements, and Frank Corner as Head of the Prime Minister's Department. There were only a couple of Kirk's other colleagues – politics is a chilly business – Joe Walding, the Minister of Overseas Trade and Matt Rata, Minister of Maori Affairs.

Upstairs Julie and Nellie Rata were trying to calm a distraught Ruth Kirk. When the phone call came from the hospital she had been unable to tug open the garage door and though a neighbour provided a lift she arrived too late. The Valium was of some help but in the end kind Nellie simply got into bed and held her in her arms until she fell asleep.

Downstairs we talked in low murmurs. The success of Kirk's concealment showed in the shock in everyone's eyes. Periodically someone would voice a reminiscence and then fall silent. 'He used to say, "Joe, you're a peasant but you're a *cunning* peasant",' said Walding (who had some of Kirk's qualities) and then stared wordlessly at me. The fire sank unattended in the grate and the Kirk cat slept undisturbed in the best chair; no one wished to sit down. As we waited for the sons to arrive from out of town the little group gradually dwindled and the talk became even more sporadic. Someone voiced a desire for fish and chips, agreeing that in the early hours of a Sunday morning this was not very practicable. Matt Rata offered to see what he could do and disappeared into the night. Half an hour later he was back clutching a fan of hot newspaper parcels in his arms – a miraculous manifestation never afterwards explained. Then the first of the boys arrived and we went home.

The next morning, after we had delivered Julie's father to the house, Ruth asked us to go to the Home of Compassion 'to make sure that Norm is not on his own'. I assumed that this meant a visit to the chapel but instead the sister led us down the wide polished corridors of the convent hospital until we came unexpectedly into a small sunlit room largely filled by the bed. Lying on it in his pyjamas, Norm looked like the effigy of some Roman senator carved in marble. From the large and untidily dressed politician of his early days he had progressed by stages to this final magnificence. I knelt beside the bed. Keeping vigil on the other side of the bed was a nun whose brother, Bernard Galvin, was a good friend. In the peaceful silence the soft spring wind blew the curtains in and out. A paper bag stood in a corner holding the Prime Minister's last possessions.

The pomp of a state funeral took over, with mourners arriving from all over the world. I looked after the American representatives, the Secretary of Labour on behalf of the President and Senator Vance Hartke from Indiana, whose conviction that New Zealand had been set back on its feet after the war by American aid left us both a little irritated. The nation though was still shocked. When the flag-draped coffin left Wellington Cathedral on its gun carriage the rain-swept streets were lined with people all the way to the airport where an Air Force Hercules carrying the coffin and funeral party took off into a darkened sky.

The burial was arranged for the following day in the small country town of Waimate. There was one last irony which would have been enjoyed by a man who never greatly liked order and ceremony. Weather prevented the Hercules from getting into the nearest airport and instead the cortege went by road from Christchurch. The delay and consequent rearrangements meant that the afternoon was slipping away. Burials could only take place in daylight, Austen pointed out, and the journey would have to be speeded up. So those on the Canterbury plains who stood by the roadside for a last respectful glimpse of their dead leader found the glimpse short indeed, as the procession flashed by in a hectic ride to get to the cemetery before dusk.

Norm's last months were sad ones. Ill health and distrust were made worse by increasing differences with his wife. In Ruth he had married his equal in strength of will and political passion, though Ruth's unremitting dislike of 'Tories' was more vocal. Such a spirited partnership brought friction. Ruth felt that success had encouraged Norm to neglect her: 'Look at the bastard,' she whispered to Julie one evening at Government House, 'he's going to walk right past me.'

Resentment could break into open warfare. On one occasion, when a television team were to make a documentary on the Kirks' home life, my father-in-law arrived to find a major row in progress, with Ruth throwing china plates. While dodging them Austen looked out the window and saw the camera team coming up the front path. There was just time to impose a truce and tidy up before they were admitted to film a more peaceful side of the Kirks' marriage.

In many ways Norman Kirk was an old-fashioned figure, a former 'stationary engine driver' representing a working-man's Labour Party which growing incomes were changing. He was a feelings man, but about practical issues rather than ideology, and socially his instincts were on the right. An increasingly university-educated and ideological party found little to admire in his leadership. When on the tenth anniversary of his death I asked David Lange (travelling in New Guinea) whether he would like to send home a commemorative message he looked at me in astonishment. And yet New Zealand has had few leaders of such unchallenged standing. I once walked with him into the lobby of the House of Representatives. As he opened the door to the chamber he surveyed his own side of the House and said, more to himself than to me, 'I don't see my successor there'. This may have been a reflection of his persistent suspicions but it was also a frank acknowledgement of his pre-eminence.

By the time of his death New Zealand's comfortable economic surplus was also gone. President Nixon's devaluation of the American dollar and the international inflation which was partly a malign legacy of the Vietnam War had already signalled that the world had outgrown the post-war Bretton Woods settlement. Now the oil shock seemed to foreshadow an even more radical reshaping. The oil-importing countries faced a bill of $60 billion, the most swingeing tax rise in history. Trade stagnated for two years in a row and inflation roared away like a chimney fire as the world grappled with the most severe recession since the 1930s. New Zealand safeguarded its employment levels and avoided any protectionist tightening of import controls (one of the first battles of my new appointment as head of the Economic Division). It could not however cope with a 63 per cent rise in import prices over two years and one of Kirk's last official acts was to announce a devaluation and a resort to borrowing, both of which became a habit over the next decade.

There was a significant risk that devaluations might become a competitive weapon and that lessons learnt in the 1930s would be forgotten in the rush by each country to find shelter and reliable supplies of oil. In mid-June Frank Corner and I went to Tokyo for talks with the Japanese and found that the embargo, coming on top of earlier shocks from Washington, had reinforced their feelings of isolation. They were scouring the world for oil and paying large premiums when they found it. Their sense of vulnerability seemed excessive – after all unlike many countries (including our own) they had plenty of cash to pay for their needs – but the national self-image was still of a country with few advantages other than skills and hard work. Resources diplomacy concerned them much more than a coordinated international response. Their list of 'most seriously affected countries' (an aid initiative) looked to us 'extraordinarily like a list of those countries from which the Japanese would like to gain raw materials'.

As far as Frank and I were concerned, these shortcomings were more than compensated for by a tour arranged for us by the hospitable Gaimusho. We bathed in the hot springs of Hakone and visited temples in the old capital of Kamakura but nothing prepared me for the strange and imaginative palaces and gardens of Kyoto and Nara. In early summer the carefully laid out gardens of the Katsura imperial villa were as beautiful as any in the West but the rigour of concept behind gardens of silvery moss or the gravelled one at Ryoanji monastery was as unfamiliar as the meditative calm they induced.

We drove to a lonely valley in the nearby hills, to an ancient Buddhist nunnery perched on a slope amid pine trees. It had been built by an unfortunate lady whose imperial husband had been murdered in front of her only for his successor, her young son, to suffer the same fate. She retired to this simple retreat, a set of wooden rooms linked by covered pathways, to pray and perform good works. We stood on her moon-viewing platform where she perhaps composed the poem which summed up her life better than any biography: 'How strange that I should sit here, watching the moon slip in and out between the clouds'.

That evening dinner was arranged for the two of us at a traditional house in Kyoto. We knelt on the *tatami* matting in front of small trays as a series of dishes were brought in through the sliding door by a kimono-clad girl. The food, the lacquerware and the bare room all had the elegant austerity that marked the best of Japanese style. Frank was emboldened to ask whether our host had any of the special cedar-barrel *sake*. Face was at stake and through a small open window I saw a man despatched on a bicycle and return with a barrel of *sake* strapped to the back. It then appeared that having ordered the barrel we had to finish it. Our face was now at stake and we applied ourselves, no great effort being required since it was delicious. But when the time came to leave the effect of the *sake* combined with the hours spent kneeling made it impossible to get up. It was necessary to roll over on the floor and crawl out the door before rising on stiffened knees to attempt a dignified farewell to our host.

Caught by the oil embargo the instinct of other rich countries was to work together. To the cartel of oil producers the best answer might be a cartel of oil consumers. In the excitement the sorrowful fact known to all exporters of commodities, that over time market forces always defeat attempts to rig prices, tended to be overlooked by governments. Instead the big importers took comfort from pronouncements like Henry Kissinger's, that if an act of political will could raise oil prices, another could lower them. Spurred on by the United States, the OECD in Paris produced plans for an international energy agency whose members would share their oil in a crisis and provide a platform for dialogue with OPEC.

New Zealand was dependent on imports for two-thirds of its oil and was at the end of the oil companies' supply lines. Any disruption in the

Middle East's production might see nothing reaching us at all. Some oil producers were offering to sell us crude directly in 'special deals' but the price of these would be to pawn our foreign policy. Bill Rowling, the gentle and quietly spoken man who had succeeded Kirk, agonised over whether joining what could bluntly be called a counter-cartel would be pawning our foreign policy in another direction, to the rich European countries. We argued that joining did not mean choosing between the rich and the poor but taking out insurance against future lurches in oil supplies. To do nothing was to gamble. Early in 1975 New Zealand signed up to the OECD's energy insurance programme. Four months later, as the recession in world trade deepened, we detected the first signs of a softening in oil prices.

Meanwhile the international community was trying to decide what could be done about the situation. A New International Economic Order was proclaimed at a special session of the UN General Assembly in 1974 and under this bold banner the developing countries were looking to push for all the aims – better access to industrialised markets, better and more stable commodity prices, and help with their up-ended payments deficits – for which they had been lobbying for years. Led by the United States, the developed world was more cautious about the radical change implied in this 'integrated approach'. But even the rich had been shaken by the upheavals in the world economy. There was a pervasive feeling that the world might be testing the limits of growth and a more immediate concern about the sharpening tensions between rich and poor.

The situation though worrying could have been worse. Trade was stagnant but at least it was not being depressed by any wave of protectionism. While there were huge imbalances in the world's finances the international banking system was functioning. There was another major difference from the crisis forty years earlier: the world had acquired the habit of consultation and after the first shocks there was a flurry of international meetings. To those who sat for days listening to impassioned rhetoric, pious twaddle and lengthy accounts of countries' woes this sometimes seemed a meagre advantage. All the talk however did narrow the differences and ease the frustrations. Large untidy meetings were unlikely to produce neat solutions but they could begin to define the most pressing problems and to form a consensus for dealing with them.

The Commonwealth heads of government met in April 1975 in Kingston, Jamaica. Their need to talk brought a record attendance. One of the few absent was Idi Amin, who sent a message offering instead to relieve the Queen of her position as head of the Commonwealth. It was also Arnold Smith's last meeting. He was given a farewell dinner and afterwards came up in the lift with us, flushed and understandably a little emotional. My temperate Prime Minister, Bill Rowling, was disapproving but I thought back ten years: without Arnold it was doubtful whether we would still have had this opportunity to come together.

Security was tight and the guiding hand of Jamaica's Prime Minister, Michael Manley, was amiably lax. We spent the days and nights in endless meetings, confined inside a compound of three large hotels. Apart from the customary drinks on the Royal Yacht the only excursion I made was across the harbour to Port Royal, where I bribed a verger to show me the silver Communion vessels Captain Henry Morgan had stolen from the cathedral in Panama – one of the few relics to survive the earthquake which sank that noisy pirate town not long afterwards, to the satisfaction of all believers.

We hoped that this franker and more intimate meeting might ease the increasingly rigid confrontation with the developing world and perhaps sort out the more practicable possibilities in advance of the next special session of the General Assembly. On the whole, to no little surprise, these hopes proved justified. The sessions might be long and disorganised but they made headway. The developed members accepted the broad aim of putting the world economy on a more stable and equitable footing and the radicals (Guyana and Jamaica) pulled back from their more sweeping demands. Lee Kuan Yew, somewhere between the two, saw the drawbacks of unrestrained growth, citing the rather improbable example of my home town of Christchurch. A decade ago, he said, it had been one of the most beautiful towns he could remember – 'more beautiful even than Cambridge' – but two weeks earlier he had not been able to sleep for the noise of the traffic.

Rowling, much more of an economist than Kirk, supported the need for freer access to economic opportunity. He argued that international cooperation imperfect though it was had stopped the present crisis becoming one of survival for the system; we should use it intelligently to look for practical remedies. We had planned to suggest a Committee of Experts (title inflation had not yet made these Eminent Persons' Groups) to give a better focus to the next stages, but it said something of the level of consensus that Guyana did so first. Rowling instead made amends to my home town by appointing an able Christchurch economist as a member, joining Alister McIntyre, Secretary General of the Caribbean Community, who chaired it.

Even more surprisingly (given the reputation of such committees), it was a success. There was the usual wrangle over its terms of reference with everyone adding bright ideas until it was being directed to enquire into everything short of the riddle of the Sphinx and what songs the Sirens sang. This was sidestepped by asking the committee to make an 'interim' report on the most pressing matters for Commonwealth Finance Ministers who would be meeting just before the next UN special session, and the rest could safely be forgotten.

So four months later I was back in the Caribbean, this time with Bob Tizard, the Minister of Finance, in Guyana. These meetings were traditionally a prelude to the ministers going on to the annual IMF-World Bank meetings in Washington but this time they were to discuss the interim McIntyre report and then, it was hoped, carry its conclusions on to Washington, New York and the raft of population, food and trade conferences meeting elsewhere. The report was unanimous and it was practical, quietly deflating the dreamier ideas. On commodities, for example, it discounted the value of commodity agreements in sustaining prices artificially (almost all of them had collapsed over the previous few years), suggesting that it might be better to stabilise total earnings rather individual commodity prices. The Finance Ministers had no difficulty endorsing any of this, then with wives, girlfriends and hangers-on they all went by riverboat up the Demerara River. Encouraged by rum and two steel bands, we danced on the deck under an enormous moon and a Canadian slid quietly overboard.

In September we moved on to New York, where the speeches were more fiery and went on considerably longer. Yet at this second Special Session there was already less talk of a radical transformation of the existing economic order and more of remedies for particular concerns. A year and a half of debate had not only spread ideas, it had weeded them out. With time the early anxieties were fading. There were signs that world trade was beginning to revive. With help from the IMF the banking system was recycling petrodollars and compensatory finance was found for those who had trouble paying their quadrupled oil bills. The plight of the poorer countries remained as did seemingly intractable problems like inflation, low commodity prices and trade access. All the same, when the Special Session broke up after thirteen days, the issues of the new international economic order looked increasingly like those with which the old economic order had struggled for years.

We turned to more parochial concerns. The New Zealand economy still rested on agriculture and so matters like beef quotas, bananas and phosphate fertiliser were frequently on the Cabinet table. Bananas were in fact an aid issue. They had been a worthwhile cash crop for South Pacific countries like Samoa, Tonga and the Cooks. Now their small family plots found it increasingly difficult to compete with the highly organised plantations of Ecuador and the Philippines. Quantity dropped from soil exhaustion and the arrival of new diseases. Poor packing and erratic shipping meant that quality suffered as well – to the point where only a fifth of shipments were saleable in shops, the rest having to be auctioned off for what they could get. The trade was dying but New Zealand's responsibilities to the South Pacific meant that an effort had to be made to revive it.

Kirk had announced a hastily arranged subsidy for island bananas but this bought time not better bananas. Some incentive had to be found and at the end of 1974 we set up a working party to look for it. An improved return for growers was clearly needed, so that they could afford fertilisers and disease control. The other side of the bargain, though, required that more cash should only be paid out for better quality. This was politically delicate. The scheme we devised therefore laid down that no one would get a lower payment; those who met a higher level of quality (actually the standard which had existed in name for some time) would get a premium of a dollar a case extra. The unstated aim was to hold the lower payment level unchanged over time, gradually putting the sub-standard growers out of business, while adjusting the premium to maintain the incentive for good fruit.

After the Kingston Commonwealth meeting I tried out this scheme on the three South Pacific governments at a meeting of agriculture officials in Apia. It was received by them with considerably more enthusiasm than it was by New Zealand's monopoly importers, Fruit Distributors, and New Zealand ministers agreed to give it a try. In the first year only 3 per cent of cases attracted the premium, and none from Samoa, but over the next few years both quantity and quality gradually increased to the point where shipments from the Cooks and Tonga were regularly getting the bonus. Timely shipping, though, became more of an obstacle, the New Zealand housewife continued to prefer Ecuador bananas and the South Pacific trade died out.

The phosphate business was by contrast a vital link in the chain of New Zealand's own agricultural efficiency. Both Australian and New Zealand soils were deficient in this mineral which was vital for pastoral farming. Several Pacific islands, most notably Nauru, had deposits of high-grade phosphate rock formed from the dung of untold generations of seabirds. The British Phosphate Commission (BPC), a partnership of the two consumer countries and Britain, was set up at the end of the First World War to mine and ship this phosphate at the least possible cost. For sixty years this arrangement worked well and Australian and New Zealand farming prospered on other people's phosphate. Now, with Nauru independent and Ocean Island almost worked out, the BPC was to be dissolved and new arrangements would have to be put in place.

We met in London at the end of January 1975 to carve up the BPC's assets and to agree on some compensation for the people of Ocean Island (Banaba), who had been resettled on an island in Fiji. The occasion was unexpectedly lively. On my first night in the Hotel Meurice I was roused in the small hours by a rapid knocking on the door. Outside stood a porter who said, 'I'm sorry to disturb you, sir, but there seems to be a possibility of fire'. This rather understated the situation: as he spoke a cloud of smoke coming up the stairs almost obscured him. I hurriedly pulled on my tweed suit, thinking that the cemeteries are said to be full of people who went back to pull on their suit, and then groped my way down the staircase to join the other guests who had taken shelter across the street under the overhang of the *Economist* building. The suit proved a wise move in the freezing winter drizzle. In due course we were moved around the corner and given coffee and brandy. By breakfast the fire was over and we made our way back to retrieve our luggage. People in overcoats and bowlers on their way to work betrayed not a flicker of surprise as a ragged line of guests in nightgowns and pyjamas passed them on Jermyn Street.

I took my suitcase to Brown's on the other side of Piccadilly* and then went to a first meeting at the Australian High Commission. There

---

* The Meurice could not be reoccupied.

was an IRA bomb scare and we were forced to work in an inner corridor away from the windows. When I got back to the hotel in the evening a bomb *had* gone off in a tailor's across the road and the police would not allow us in for two hours while they checked for more bombs. After this first day the talks seemed tame though heated at times. Simply put we wanted more money. New Zealand's original contribution to the BPC had been modest but the nearly $50 million of assets had been built up partly from sales in New Zealand (Britain bought nothing) and it seemed only equitable that we should receive a larger share of the payout. This argument had understandably less appeal to our partners and I had to sit on over the weekend to secure a further $3 million which at least compensated for the excitements of the visit.

Eighteen months later we met again in Tarawa, in what was then the Gilbert and Ellice Islands. On the way I stopped in Nauru to see how the island republic was managing its phosphate business. The Secretary to the Government was an old acquaintance from the Cooks. He lent me a large car, saying only that a petrol strike meant that it could not be refilled. I drove around the narrow belt of fertile land that formed the island's perimeter (the interior was a moonscape of tall coral pinnacles left after the phosphate was mined). Forty-five minutes later I was back where I started, with no discernible fall in the petrol gauge. There was only one hotel, its woodwork and windows already peeling in the salt mid-Pacific wind. It was run entirely for the benefit of its staff whose families occupied most of the rooms. Family preoccupations made it hard to get a meal, even within the advertised times; I sympathised with a group of Japanese businessmen who were being ejected dinnerless from the hotel's Japanese restaurant. Families who owned phosphate land did well on the royalties. The island's liquor store displayed large bins of the most expensive first-growth French clarets which, the manager claimed, those who could afford to liked to drink with their tinned beef and rice.

With only two or three years of mining left on Ocean Island the Banaban people were suing the BPC for a greater sum in royalties. They were also suing the British colonial government for misdirecting their money. Whatever the rights about royalties it did seem hard that 85 per cent of them had gone to the Gilbert and Ellice government and only 15 per cent to the Banabans. Tarawa was an atoll so low that you had to time your bath by the tides, otherwise the bath slowly filled with seawater. It was the scene of bitter fighting in the Second World War and the seaward lagoon of Betio was still littered with the remains of half-tracks and trucks from the American assault. The coastal guns of Singapore had ended up there, shipped in by the Japanese and to no more useful effect: their broken barrels pointed drunkenly at the sky. As you flew in there was the sobering sight, perfectly outlined in the clear waters of the lagoon, of a Liberator bomber which had come down short of the runway.

Australia and New Zealand were willing to contribute to a trust fund for the Banabans but stayed carefully away from the issue of revenue distribution. I did, however, indicate a willingness to put New Zealand's whole share of the BPC surplus into a trust fund for the two successor countries, Kiribati and Tuvalu, who were about to become independent and who would have few other sources of regular income. I suffered a sunstroke urging this in the course of a lunchtime walk around an islet in the lagoon, and thereafter spent some time in bed watching two huge and menacing black shadows on the wall discussing my character and efforts with a painful frankness, a point of view which reflected that of Treasury and the Ministry of Agriculture back home.

The other possible use for our surplus windfall was to invest in a new phosphate business. The only place with a mining future was Christmas Island in the Indian Ocean, whose phosphate was owned jointly by Australia and New Zealand. It had been the biggest bargain of all: in 1946 the two countries had bought it from Britain for $3 million each and had since received $80 million a year from it. Now Australia wished to incorporate it fully into its territory and laws. The Foreign Ministry was concerned about challenges to Australian sovereignty; the island's contract labour system was in possible conflict with the Whitlam Government's new human rights legislation; and environmentalists were worried about the future of the aptly named Abbott's booby, whose ecological niche had become so straitened that it could no longer take off from the ground to fish in the surrounding sea but had to launch itself from the tops of an endangered stand of tall trees.

In theory New Zealand had a veto on any changes which might threaten low-cost access to the phosphate. In practice this was not realistic. It might be preferable to trade our notional rights on Christmas Island for access to the lower-grade deposits being opened up in Queensland. Perhaps an Australia–New Zealand Phosphate Commission could be established to develop these. I went to Canberra to try it out. Senator Reg

Withers, the minister who was apparently responsible for phosphates, invited me to have a drink with him in his office. He asked me where I worked and seemed surprised to hear that it was the Foreign Ministry. 'Do you know', he said, 'that they are all fairies in our Foreign Affairs Department?' I expressed a doubt. He looked at me more closely and said, 'Well, they are'. The Fraser Government, of which he was a member, decided not to support the idea of a joint venture in Queensland.

In the end time solved our problem. It was claimed by unsympathetic persons that General Franco had only two boxes on his desk labelled respectively 'Problems Time Will Solve' and 'Problems Time Has Solved' and that administration consisted in transferring files from the first to the second. In public business activity is reassuring but not always more productive. We had worked hard on phosphate but our anxieties about a secure supply were exaggerated and our thinking too bound by the past. A state monopoly was not the only way to serve the farming economy. As with bananas, importers could be left to make their own arrangements on world markets and the fertiliser companies did so. The problem faded away, like the phosphate surplus and indeed the Ministry's Economic Division, which was broken up on my departure as having become too large and too busy.

# CHAPTER SEVEN

# Tropical Asia

I STOOD ON THE TERRACE IN THE SOFT DARKNESS, LOOKING ACROSS to the tall trees at the edge of the lawn and listening to the croak of toads, the rustlings of a tropical evening and the irregular clicks of the *tuk-tuk* bird.* It was my first evening in Singapore; I had just arrived to take up the post of New Zealand High Commissioner, to which a liberal hand had added the positions of High Commissioner to Sri Lanka and Ambassador to the Maldives. It was September 1976. The appointment had hung fire for two months, partly to accommodate an ex-Minister elsewhere and partly, a senior colleague had told me, because the new government had doubts about my Labour connections. These had been happily resolved (though the Prime Minister, Mr Muldoon, retained the abiding belief that I was a Labour supporter for the rest of my association with him) and with cat and corgi and the two younger children we had made the ten-hour flight from Auckland and were ready to explore our new home.

The house in Queen Astrid Park was a rambling colonial bungalow, completed in 1941 just in time to be seized (along with the whole street) by the Japanese as officers' quarters. Fifteen years of New Zealand ownership had enlarged it for entertaining without destroying an endearing homely character. Everyone who lived there loved it. Downstairs there

---

* This bird spoke only in the minutes after darkness fell and the number of clicks was a popular gamble, even our children at school in New Zealand would occasionally mail a bet.

was a long reception room with couches, Persian rugs and slowly revolving ceiling fans. A range of doors along its length opened on to a large terrace, shaded by flame trees with hanging pots of orchids, which looked across a lawn and garden cleverly planted to look larger than it was.

Upstairs the diplomatic dignity declined into a family muddle with a sitting-room for the children which could never be kept tidy and several bedrooms. Apart from the dining-room and study, only the bedrooms were air-conditioned and sleep was punctuated by the reassuring rattle and wheeze of the machines. We awoke to the sound of Burel the gardener sweeping the leaves and watering the flower-pots which surrounded the house (a strange survival from British India where people often carried their gardens around with them). Then Ah Lung the maid brought in the tray with morning tea and opened the windows along one side of the room, so that the cat Arthur could jump in from the tiles for a saucer of milk and we drank our tea looking out on a wall of greenery made bright by the sun and listening to the early morning calls of the yellow orioles.

For all the changes that had come in Singapore this house, and others like it, still ran on lines laid down by many decades of colonial custom. The household staff were Chinese: a housekeeper, cook and the two maids; the outside staff were Malay, the gardener and the driver, who lived with his family in a house at the gate. The Singapore authorities were sternly colour-blind in their efforts to build a Singaporean nationality but their efforts had so far succeeded only in maintaining lane discipline among the three main ethnic groups of Chinese, Malay and Indian. In the house working relations between inside and outside were correct but neither group would miss an opportunity to quietly draw attention to the shortcomings of the other.

An incoming New Zealand family had therefore to learn to navigate some rather choppy cross-cultural currents. Out of doors it might have been straightforward but Burel had made advances to the young second wife of Kamari, the elderly driver, (how successful I never dared enquire) and so a careful separation had to be maintained between the two. And when the dignified and devoutly Muslim Kamari spent the better part of a morning cleaning every vestige of fur after the corgi had been driven to the vet we learnt never to take the dog in the car again.

Inside there were the complexities of Chinese custom to learn. At one of our first lunches Julie's arrangement of white flowers was removed by the housekeeper with horrified exclamations – because white is the colour of mourning. For some time I was puzzled every morning when I came down to breakfast to find the pictures askew on the walls. When I straightened them they were tilted again next morning – moved by the ancient 'black and white' amah, who was anxious to ensure that evil spirits did not perch on the frames. She also liked whenever possible to close the front door because the house lacked the traditional screen just inside to deflect evil influences.

There was another little clash of cultures when I lay in bed upstairs with asthma, listening to the rising screams of the aptly named brainfever bird as the mid-morning heat increased. The kitchen, anxious to help, sent word that I should swallow seven live baby mice. When I declined, Julie returned with the offer that as a second-best they would grill eight cockroaches for me. When I continued to prefer asthma the kitchen gave me up as an incurable hypochondriac. Singapore must indeed have been an asthma-free nation because almost everyone I met had an infallible cure, of which the least unpalatable was flying-fox stew.

Then there was the matter of the Chinese bed. On a visit to Melaka we acquired an old marriage bed, over a century old and brought out from China by an immigrant family. Such beds were rare because they were made for a marriage and custom required them to be burnt when the couple died. After export permits were arranged and an ancient truck had brought it to Singapore the bed was reassembled in our bedroom, amid the unspoken disapproval of the household. It was a glorious thing of red and gold with a canopy of intricately carved coiling dragons and side panels of peonies, plum blossom and what were tactfully referred to as scenes of love and harmony. It was like sleeping in a throne room, except that I experienced the most vivid dreams – not nightmares but so intensely coloured as to be exhausting. Julie reported the same thing and we moved back into our old bed, passing the Melaka bed to Caroline who in turn passed it on to her brother and sisters, everyone experiencing the same uncomfortably vivid sleep. It was finally standing in an empty bedroom when a Chinese friend caught sight of it and said, 'I hope no one sleeps in that bed – they will have the most painful dreams'.

There were also the delicacies of another system of etiquette to consider – that care not to openly diminish someone else's dignity and self-worth which is translated into English as 'face'. On Sunday evenings I had traditionally cooked a spaghetti meal for the family and since that was Cookie's day off it seemed simple to keep up the custom in Singapore.

Even so Cookie was unhappy; he would not dream of coming to my office so why should I step into his kitchen. Every Sunday more and more of the ingredients would be silently got ready for me. At the point when even the pot of water was placed ready on the stove I gave up and good will was restored.

Cookie had in earlier years cooked for the political adviser to the commander of the British forces and he was good with standard English food. He resisted preparing any Chinese food for us until, after sustained pressure from the family, he produced a 'Chinese' meal for us that would have disgraced a takeaway bar in Eketahuna, let alone a country where delicious food could be bought at any roadside stall. His mind was certainly not on cookbooks. His reading matter, occasionally left on the kitchen bench, was graphic picture-books from China. I hoped that they were on subjects like '101 Revolutionary Things to do with Noodles' but their propagandistic appearance did not encourage this conclusion. Their presence made me thoughtful.

Cookie though had a bourgeois side which was unsurprising in a commercially minded culture. He had a pet sulphur-crested cockatoo on which he lavished much affection, hanging the bird's cage in the courtyard of the servants' quarters and moving it carefully around with the sun. One day a wild cockatoo arrived in the garden from Johore and with saucers of sunflower seeds and much patience Cookie managed to entice it to join his. The cage was too small for two so one Saturday morning Cookie set off on his bicycle to nearby Holland Village to buy a larger one. He returned without either bird. Someone had made him such a good offer for them that he had sold his pet of several years along with the wild bird and was more than satisfied with the exchange.

When he retired he was succeeded by Ah Yong, a Hainanese, who had been a ship's cook, and who, speaking some English, was more sociable and more deft with either school of cuisine. He was loved by everyone in the house and especially by Rusty, the German shepherd guard dog who had been given to us by the Singapore Army – the late afternoon calm was punctuated by cries of 'Lusty, dlop' as he tirelessly threw a ball for the dog. Sadly he became ill with stomach pains and went to hospital for observation. He telephoned Julie from there to say, 'Mem, you need to find new cook'. When Julie protested that she had no such desire he said, 'I die soon – you advertise now'. He had inoperable stomach cancer and died two days later, the bleak nature of his announcement being somehow heightened by the fact that when he died his wife, who also worked for us, was not with him but going through the mattress in his room to see whether he had hidden any money there.

Young Gerald and I hurried back from Malaysia for the funeral, marching uncomfortably hot in dark suits at the head of the little funeral procession which made its way to a tent on a housing estate, where Buddhist prayers were said to help dear Ah Yong through the nine hells, one freezing cold, through which (as I understood it) he was now travelling. As the round-topped coffin was carried out I turned respectfully to face it, only to be seized by the shoulders from behind and firmly turned away. I had committed a breach of etiquette: to look at the coffin was to imply that you were pleased. But there was another less traditional side to Ah Yong's death. He and his wife had worked as cook and maid in the time-honoured way, but the children when they came to the house were from the new Singapore – a daughter who worked for a bank, one who was a psychologist and a son who was a police inspector.

The island Republic of Singapore, barely eleven years old, had by then solved the first generation of problems – security and survival – and the building blocks of a prosperous society were firmly in place. The appeal of the 'new China' to many of the Chinese-speaking young had faded as China sank into turmoil and Singapore's growth sprinted ahead. The pace was almost dislocating: income per head had tripled in eight years. Like so much else of Singapore its government, energetic and incorrupt, was unlike any other in the region – 'a bureaucracy of experts' in the telling phrase of an opposition manifesto. It was also as preachy as an assembly of kirk elders. There was no sense of triumph, only a focus on the next set of problems for this was a society which not only thought and planned ahead, it worried ahead, about the young, about the old, about the social laxity wealth might bring. Singaporeans always seemed able to see the lead lining in any silver cloud they had created.

A general election was called shortly after I arrived and the issue, the government said, was 'the problem of the next generation'. It understandably worried about how the values of an immigrant society which it had championed – thrift, hard work and an unsentimental realism – could be passed on to a new generation of political leaders which had had no experience of the poverty and risks which underpinned these values.

There was indeed a deeper generation gap than any Western society could know. Anyone much over fifty had seen the British Empire in its confident heyday and then its collapse; lived through the Japanese occupation, the return of the British, the communist Emergency and civil disorders. They had gone into Malaysia and out of Malaysia, warded off the confrontation threat from Indonesia and faced independence and the need to restructure Singapore's economy. It was not surprising that they had a sense of vulnerability however high the achievements were piled; for them Singapore was like one of its own orchids, a fragile flower clinging to the South East Asian peninsula and dependent on its surroundings.

Those under thirty, though, had known only steadily expanding prosperity and opportunities and a rapid move away from the very lifestyle which their elders applauded. There were no rights and wrongs in this; simply that the experience of the two generations had been very different. Time had turned around the truth.

The election, though, like its predecessors, was more a referendum on the performance of the government in creating jobs, housing and educational opportunities. I travelled around a number of polling booths where the procedures and the atmosphere seemed exactly like those at home, though the campaign itself was very short. The result was never in doubt. The opposition candidates secured 25 per cent of the vote, largely a protest vote over local grievances, but no seats. While the government was delivering such spectacular results there was no inclination to risk a change. An aged lady at one booth said to me, 'This is a good government despite its shortcomings', and that seemed to express the mood.

There was a certain deadness about the resulting Parliament, even though government members were told to move across to the opposition side to fill up the empty spaces. The President, a softly spoken Eurasian gynaecologist, delivered what might have better been called the sermon from the throne, making no reference to impending legislation but ex-horting everyone to try harder. There was an obvious difficulty in adher-ing to Westminster forms without that basic Westminster assumption, an opposition. The government was authoritarian in the Chinese tradi-tion of 'virtuous governments' (when our Leader of the Opposition came to lunch the housekeeper was shocked to learn that our government actually paid him to make trouble), but it was no dictatorship whatever its critics might allege. It was an electorate rather than a parliamentary democracy – something new to constitutional theory which seemed to work well enough in practice. In this crowded city electorates might comprise half a street or a handful of high-rise flats. The government kept an ear continuously cocked to hear the hubbub of opinion in these places; members of parliament spent more time sitting at tables in the lobbies of these buildings than in the debating chamber and they understood very well that their future careers depended on doing so.

Despite the government's worries the change of leadership was some time distant. The leadership was well into middle age; the fiery young orators of the fifties were now greying and in glasses when they sat in line at the National Day parades but they were still vigorous and confident. They were led by a triumvirate of exceptional ability, demonstrating once again the historical good fortune that bestows this on the founding fathers of some new nations. They were all of high intelligence and education, to which Goh Keng Swee added a common-sense ability to get to the heart of a problem and Rajaratnam a clear grip on world affairs and a sharp tongue which could needle everyone from the British to the Non-Aligned.

To this intelligence, though, Lee Kuan Yew added a charm and a breadth of mind which made him indisputably the leader. My first encounter with him was rather challenging. On that occasion I joined a group he was talking to. He turned and said, 'Ah, High Commissioner, I was just saying that the difference between New Zealanders and Australians is that New Zealand was settled by the younger sons of gentlemen. Is that so?' My diplomatic experience had not prepared me for this. I thought hastily and said, 'Some New Zealanders would like to think so, Prime Minister' and hoped this had got me off the hook.

After that calls on him at his office required some preliminary mental bracing. He used to say that because of his northern Chinese ancestry he could only work in the cool ('otherwise I feel loose and can't think') and so I normally put on a woollen suit before a visit. On the way down in the car I would go over my points and vow that I would not be diverted by the charm. Once there all that would be forgotten in conversations that would range over the importance of the four-character poster in Chinese propaganda, Malay customs, the spirit world, how airlines should be run, the risks to the world's financial structure and whether asthma could be cured (he offered no remedy). Driving home, the influence of that powerful mind would start new lines of thought bouncing around in my head.

He sometimes revealed a lingering anglophilia. At the fall of Singapore he had watched the surrendered troops march off into captivity, the

Australian and Indian forces demoralised and shambling. Then round the corner towards his father's house came the British forces. They were filthy, unshaven and had been without sleep or food 'but their heads were high, they swung their arms and marched in perfect step and I said to myself, "Now there's a people"'.

Unfortunately the British had not lived up to Lee's high standards and he was disillusioned with the decline of Britain in the sixties. The Americans were the hope of East Asia but he was not entirely comfortable with them either. I came into his office once to find him with his head in his hands, giving a groan. This seemed alarming but when I asked if anything was the matter he raised his head and said that he did not know how long he could stand calls from American Assistant Secretaries of State who would hold office on average for eighteen months but who were confident that within that time 'they would find the answers to problems which have defeated the rest of us for forty years'. The caller before me had been Richard Holbrooke, newly appointed by President Carter.

The atmosphere was rather different when I made my first visit to Sri Lanka. It was somehow characteristic of the confusion between rhetoric and practice that the Democratic Socialist Republic of Sri Lanka asked me to present my credentials in morning dress. This proved no problem to the resourceful Peter Tan, the tailor at Robinsons ('High Commissioner, the last morning coat I made was for a member of Lord Mountbatten's suite in 1946') and so attired I called on the President (previously Governor-General) at the Queen's House in Colombo.

Before seeing the Prime Minister, Mrs Bandaranaike, Julie and I lunched with the hospitable American Ambassador, Howard Wriggins, a distinguished professor of political science and a Quaker who knew a great deal about the country. He said 'take flowers' and so on the way to the Prime Minister's house I stopped at a corner florist and bought an armful. It was good advice. The Prime Minister giggled coyly and said, 'Are all these for me?' After that we got on splendidly. Together we discussed how young she was looking despite the strains of office and then we marvelled at her son Anura, then just entering politics, and the way the dear boy had risen by his own efforts to be son of the leader of the country.

The hymn claims that in Sri Lanka 'every prospect pleases and only man is vile'. It is true that the writer, Bishop Heber, had lost his baggage there while on the way to Calcutta and might have had a jaundiced view, but it was a view held by most of the inhabitants. In politics they combined a fondness for extravagant aims with a weary cynicism about the outcome. It was Sri Lanka's misfortune that politics was theatre, calling for sweeping gestures, while reality was protecting the future of your family. Mrs Bandaranaike's government was fervently socialist and even Marxist in its policies but there was no worker in the Cabinet. Making my rounds of the Ministers required some stamina. Courtesy required that tea and fruit juice be served and drunk on each occasion and after eight calls in the course of a day's rounds I felt waterlogged.

There were worse alternatives. I asked a Minister to have dinner with us in the decaying magnificence of the Galle Face Hotel, one of those late nineteenth-century hotels like Raffles which British steamship lines had built along the main routes of Empire. It had declined into the appearance of a slightly seedy gentlemen's club but still had its beautiful position, built at the edge of the sea. We sat looking over the moonlit water while the Minister sank a tumbler of neat brandy and then, without waiting to be pressed by me, waved to the waiter for another. I suggested that we go in and eat, but not before my guest had somehow snaffled a third tumbler.

So the meal was quiet but not restful. There were periods of silence as the Minister's head slowly sank until it was almost in his soup; at other times he became voluble to the point of lecturing the whole dining-room. His Permanent Secretary seemed paralysed. After a time, though, the Minister turned pale and began to sweat. I realised that he might soon be violently sick – a thought so horrendous as to require action. I gestured to his companion and we lifted him from the table. Holding him firmly under the armpits, we walked him out of the room and down to his car, maintaining the dignity (I hoped) of three friends in close conversation. Then I went back inside – and had a brandy.

I found Mrs Bandaranaike's Ministers in general to be charming and articulate, able to talk intelligently about the country's difficulties but not to do much about them. Most were well-educated intellectuals drawn from the upper levels of Sri Lankan society, which had run Sri Lankan politics under a variety of party labels for years. The radical views they expressed in public were less evident in conversation; like Lord Melbourne on religion they seemed to think it a poor thing if politics were allowed to interfere in the realities of private life.

The difficulty was that Sri Lanka's rulers talked and acted as if many of the cheques they cheerfully wrote in the currency of political rhetoric would never be cashed. The regular proclamations of radical change and betterment, set against the reality of stagnation and shrinking opportunities, produced a simmering exasperation. The opposing pull of socialist doctrine and family realities had produced neither equity nor efficiency, but only muddle. Mrs Bandaranaike explained to me that her economic policy was based on Lord Buddha's middle way. Remarkably this had managed to combine the weaknesses of both capitalism *and* socialism, the country suffering simultaneously from profiteering (often by the state corporations) and bureaucratic inertia. Sri Lanka's once-great tea exports were withering as the tea estates were broken up into one-acre plots and a state corporation placed in charge. There was a pervasive network of regulations, protection of favoured interests and wangling permits from Ministers. The characteristic noise in otherwise quiet post offices and banks was the rapid staccato of rubber stamps as bits of paper went from hand to hand in the pyramid of controls.

Inevitably the best brains in Sri Lanka spent their time finding ways to evade these obstructions. Though once-prosperous Colombo houses were leprous with peeling stucco, there were always businessmen in new Mercedes who had good political connections and who spoke openly of their illegal export of sapphires or other commodities that were in theory a state monopoly. Corruption scented the air. Sri Lankans were resigned to what they called 'family-bandyism' because in a society where the family was the focus of loyalty, failure in a Minister to find a job for his wife's second cousin was not simply to admit to a lack of influence but to reveal a shameful indifference to duty. But 'fixing things' had gone beyond this. The Bribery Commissioner, who insured against the varied risks of his position by wearing both a revolver and a crucifix, told me that corruption had greatly increased with the growth of the public sector and the 'rule' that applicants for such positions had to go through their MP. Some indication of how this worked was given by the immigration hopefuls who queued outside my hotel room, each clutching a small present and each upset by my apparent inability to understand the rules of the game. I concluded that there was no point in New Zealand investing more in aid until the policy outlook changed.

Matters were rather different in the tight and impoverished string of atolls that was the Republic of Maldive. We stayed in a ramshackle place on an islet adjoining that of Male, the country's capital. I travelled across the lagoon in a small whaler to present my credentials to President Nasir, arriving with wet trouser cuffs after a flying-fish skimming over the water had splashed into the boat. The President with Maldivian caution read through my letter of credence in which the Queen, rather sportingly in view of our limited acquaintance, referred to me as her 'right trusty and well-beloved cousin'. He asked if I knew the Queen. I said, 'Not really'. Silence fell while I examined my damp trousers, the Queen and I both diminished by this failure to tell the truth.

The President was a nervous and secretive man who perhaps had much to be nervous and secretive about. He had not shown himself to his people for over five years, not even during the Haj festival, when the security forces drew themselves up outside his front gate and played 'Pack up your troubles'. The hundred yards from the house to his boat was covered in a furtive dash in a closed car. During the rest of our interview he stared fixedly at another corner of the room, spoke in a low voice and smiled anxiously from time to time for no obvious reason. Having silenced all overt opposition, exiled his popular Prime Minister to a treeless and sun-struck islet off Male, and built up a guard of unpleasant-looking soldiers armed with rifles and long clubs, he now seemed prey to the multiplying fears and mistrusts of his own success. He had only one kidney but his lively wife, who had been trained in Australia as a nurse, told Julie that he would not let her treat him. The President, it was apparent, trusted nobody.

That evening I gave a reception on our own islet, chartering a large launch to bring the guests from Male where no liquor could be served. As the line of notabilities in long white gowns shuffled past each pressed my hand and murmured what I took to be a courteous welcome in Divehi, the local language. By the sixth, however, it dawned on me that they were saying, 'New Zealand are 278 for 5'. The Maldives, where space for a cricket field was hard to find, were mad about cricket and my guests had been following by radio the test match in progress in India. It turned out that nearly a third of my guests had a New Zealand connection, either personal or through relatives.

The Maldives were a curious mixture of a conservative Islamic state and a modern business enterprise of which the President, his relatives and friends were the principal shareholders. Thirty thousand people lived on Male, a flat islet of half a square mile, only a foot or two above the water and prone to outbreaks of cholera. With only sand and sea to rely on, the Maldivians resembled an atoll version of the Bedouin or Highlanders – poor, half-starved in the remoter islands, self-respecting, hard and thrifty. They were exacting about what was their due and meticulous about meeting their own obligations.

No one made more economical use of aid. When I was shown typewriters given by New Zealand years earlier, the enamel had in places been worn down to the shiny metal with use but they were still in perfect working order. The high-school library was stocked with incongruous English books like *Black Beauty* and novels by Jane Austen, the corners of their pages transparent with grease from being repeatedly thumbed. With no other entertainment reading aloud at night was popular. We arranged for a crate of books to be sent from Singapore and for the Ministry of Education in Wellington to send some of its *School Journals* and stories on the South Pacific which might be more recognisable to these other atoll-dwellers than tales of horses, coaches and country houses.

There was no doubt about people's religious devotion: there was a mosque at the centre of Male and twenty-five years earlier the President of the first Republic had been stoned to death, among other things for trying to abolish the veil. The veil had gone but nonetheless many women held a bit of their scarf between the teeth as a vestige of the practice. When we walked down the white, shadowless roads between high coral walls topped by pink oleanders, Julie although wearing a long dress to her feet was once hissed for having short sleeves.

The business of the President, though, was business and his government was organised like an American corporation, with five Vice-Presidents and three Ministers, of which only one counted – his brother-in-law, the Minister of Public Security, who in Orwellian fashion was mainly concerned with the private security of members of the government. The Maldives Shipping Line, run by an elusive associate who lived in Singapore, was a tramp enterprise which provided useful employment for young seafarers. The shelf around the atolls was also rich in fish and every morning the graceful white-sailed dhows would tack out for a day's fishing, returning in the evening like a flock of sea-birds. Most promising of all in a land of white sand, hot sun and turquoise-blue waters was tourism. Negligible only a few years earlier, visits by mainly German tourists doubled over my term before the floodgates opened with the building of an airport that could take direct flights from Europe.

The atoll geology, unsatisfactory for so many purposes, offered the perfect compromise. Tourist hotels, all the main ones owned by the presidential family and friends, were built on uninhabited islets where dancing, drinks and decadence could flourish while a puritanical Islam continued undisturbed on Male. Only hotel workers lived at the resorts and only small parties of properly dressed tourists visited Male. Julie and I went to lunch at one of these resorts, a dizzying experience after days spent in government offices. Music throbbed, a lavish meal was laid out on tables under the palms while bikini-clad women wandered about sampling food and wine. I went for a swim afterwards and through an error of navigation surfaced between the feet of a large woman reclining nude on a small float. My nearness was such that the traditional excuse of 'I'm very sorry, sir' would have been totally lacking in credibility. I sank in a seethe of bubbles hoping to emerge far enough away to avoid embarrassment.

Returning to Singapore after these excursions was not just to return to a city where the air-conditioning worked and the bath water was not the colour of beer but also to a more anxious intellectual climate. Singapore was worried, not about its buoyant domestic economy but about foreign policy. As a predominantly Chinese city-state in a largely Muslim sea it was always conscious of an underlying vulnerability but the immediate concern was Vietnamese intentions. With the fall of Saigon and Phnom Penh two years earlier Vietnam's forces controlled the whole of Indochina. Pressure would now come on Thailand and with a Communist insurgency already operating in its north-eastern provinces and trouble along the Cambodian border it might begin to crumble. Singapore felt the chill of loneliness, the more so because in the wake of the Vietnam War the American people seemed moodily disinclined to carry foreign burdens and to have lost interest in the future of a South East Asia whose stability and prosperity they had done so much to underwrite. Like many East Asian leaders Lee was doubtful about President Carter's firmness, though he kept his suspicions discreetly to himself, unlike Mr Muldoon whose public reference to the President as 'a peanut farmer' brought a temporary cloud over New Zealand–American relations.

In these circumstances Singapore turned with relief to ASEAN. This regional association with its four neighbours was made for Singapore, giving an isolated city state protection and protective coloration while offering tactful opportunities to influence the policies of its friends, especially Malaysia. ASEAN, however, had been established primarily to promote closer economic ties, and the realistic Singaporeans had only moderate enthusiasm for such a distant goal. With the fall of Saigon it emerged as indisputably a political association, a reassuring enclosure from which its members could face the uncertainties of Vietnamese policy, and Singapore began to emphasise it accordingly.

Indirectly this also increased the importance of Australia and New Zealand. Though not strong militarily they formed a secure southern flank, had been the first to support and encourage the growth of ASEAN, and in the ANZUS treaty they had a tripwire leading back to Washington. (At the time of Confrontation Dean Rusk had told the Indonesian Foreign Minister that any attack on the Australian or New Zealand forces in Malaysia would bring American intervention.) New Zealand had compensated for its lesser significance by its staunch support for Singapore. It was the first country after Britain to recognise the new state after its abrupt expulsion from Malaysia in 1965. When Sir Keith Holyoake passed through on his way to London to become Governor-General, Goh Keng Swee insisted on calling on him, saying to me 'He stood by us at a difficult time and we will never forget that'. New Zealand had also been the only country to leave forces in Singapore at the time of the British withdrawal.

By now Wellington was beginning to wonder about their strategic purpose but there was no doubt that while they stayed they were a major diplomatic asset. While trade links were beginning to grow, the defence forces were still the core of New Zealand's presence in the region. Successive High Commissioners found themselves being treated like the representative of a middle power, with a battalion, transport aircraft and helicopters based on the island and periodic visits by frigates and Skyhawk fighters. In an odd reversal of roles the American ambassador – John Holdridge, a friend from Washington – would ask if I could spare a helicopter to take a visiting senator around the island – a half-hour flight around the perimeter with the door open was still the quickest way to get an impression of the country.

Singapore too was privately weighing up the advantages of having foreign troops based on its soil. Its formal position was that the force was welcome to stay as long as we wished but that no objection would be raised whenever we wished to withdraw it. After the fall of Saigon the small deployment began to be seen as a comforting token of Western support; its departure would hardly send the right signal. Talk about the force staying on became less coy after Vietnam invaded Cambodia and in what was doubtless a deliberate move Singapore invited our soldiers to celebrate Waitangi Day in 1979 by parading on the Padang, the central space in the city overlooked by City Hall. This was the place for National Day parades and no other foreign troops had ever been granted this privilege (if we passed discreetly, as we all did, over the fact that Prime Minister Tojo had reviewed Japanese forces there in 1943). So the New Zealand troops marched past City Hall with band playing and colours flying, with the doughty figure of Goh Keng Swee on the reviewing stand. At a reception in City Hall afterwards we presented him with a *tauihu*, the elaborately carved prow of a war canoe.

Living on each other's doorsteps the Singaporean and New Zealand forces became close, swapping training assistance, kit and even some of our experienced NCOs. Jungle training, though, was carried out across the causeway in south Johore. The battalion would camp out there for weeks on end, learning to live and operate silently in those inhospitable surroundings and to cope with the wildlife which had already done so. A diplomatic incident was caused when a tiger was shot, whether intentionally or not was obscure, but the skin was quickly repatriated to Singapore. The Sultan of Johore was outraged – tigers were his – and senior officers had to make a pilgrimage to return the skin and offer apologies. Mollified the Sultan then presented the battalion with a much better tiger skin of his own.

In general the young soldiers were the best representatives New Zealand could have hoped for. They played football, joined charity drives, bought heavily in the local shops and went home to bed in good time. The one exception was the celebrated 'battle of Orchard Road'. A group of soldiers was drinking in a bar there when in the small hours an altercation developed with some off-duty policemen, one of whom unwisely drew a gun which he should not have been carrying. The Kiwis, trained for this, immediately attacked and disarmed him, kicking the pistol into a monsoon drain. The resulting fuss and newspaper publicity upset Wellington. I was told that there was no question of interfering with Singapore justice; on the other hand a general election was coming up in New Zealand and it would look bad if the soldiers were caned or given a sentence seen as severe.

After careful consideration, and with the support of the Force Commander Brigadier Lin Smith, I decided to interfere anyhow. I went to see the Defence Minister, Dr Goh. He greeted me in his tiny darkened office by solemnly putting on a suit jacket that did not match his trousers. I launched into a rather convoluted preamble, cut short by his leaning on an elbow across the desk and saying, 'What is it you want?' I told him and he expressed relief that I had come. 'When you train young men to fight they are bound sometimes to do so at the wrong time and in the wrong place.' Shortly after I got back to the office he rang to say that the Attorney-General had arranged matters and what we had to do was send the offenders home.

In March 1977 we had the first of four visits by the Prime Minister, Mr Muldoon. He was a demanding presence but not a difficult one in the sense that he liked things to be organised and never deviated from the itinerary planned for him. Knowing his interest in plants Julie thoughtfully wrote on her hand the name of the white orchids on our terrace – *Phalaenopsis amabilis* – and with a quick glance was able to answer the first question he asked on stepping outside.

Driving around with him in the car was the only time he would talk in a relaxed fashion, and not always even then. Passing the National Museum on our way to call on the President, I remarked that it had been built by a New Zealand Prime Minister, Sir Frederick Weld, who had subsequently become Governor of the Straits Colony. Suddenly I had the Prime Minister's full attention. Was he Governor after being Prime Minister? Yes, I said, seeing the point of the question, but of two different places. The interest vanished and silence fell, broken after a minute by the Prime Minister saying, 'You know, they made an awful fuss about Keith'. His interest had been briefly aroused by the thought that here was a precedent for his controversial recommendation of Sir Keith Holyoake as Governor-General in New Zealand.

On this occasion, and on the others where time permitted, he visited the Force and spoke to a New Zealand businessmen's lunch. I would arrange for him to visit the Economic Development Board or one of the other engines of Singapore's extraordinary growth but he showed only a polite lack of interest at my attempts to draw lessons for New Zealand. The centrepiece if Lee was in town was a dinner party beside the pool at the Istana, the ornate building that had once been Government House. A small group of guests sat around a table in the garden and so the talk was easy. Muldoon, who read only official papers and magazines, did not have Lee's range of interests but both were intelligent and tough-minded and so 'Harry' and 'Rob' got on well

An ASEAN summit was being planned. Lee said that New Zealand would be invited along with Australia, the US and Japan but unlike Japan we would not be expected to buy a ticket to the gathering by making trade concessions. He added though that we would be there on a 'fly now, pay later' basis. Commitments as vague as this did not trouble the Prime Minister and so a few months later we found ourselves walking from the plane in Kuala Lumpur, preceded by a bevy of Malaysian beauties strewing red rose petals in our path. It was difficult to savour such a moment as it deserved because every few seconds there was a tremendous BANG from saluting guns sited rather too close to the arriving guests.

The summit was still ostensibly about economic cooperation and about pressing the four developed country guests to be more forthcoming about imports. Underneath it was about political solidarity and adjusting to the post-Vietnam world; for the first time in a generation American policies were peripheral to the discussion. Two days of speeches could be a bit numbing. In the course of a long and rather mystical speech by the President of Indonesia the Prime Minister turned to ask what President Suharto was saying. I had to confess that I had lost the thread. 'Why doesn't he speak English?' Muldoon said irritably, but the President *was* speaking in English.

He in turn might have been bemused by the Prime Minister's own contribution. Stressing that New Zealand would always be a reliable friend to ASEAN, he gave a disquisition on the national bird, noting that it produced the world's largest egg in relation to its size and that the male kiwi sat on it devotedly, losing half its weight in the process. 'Not for nothing is the kiwi our national symbol. It may be small and few in numbers. But the kiwi sticks to its commitments and in the end it produces – a surprisingly large result.'

No such result came from the economic discussions, the pressure on New Zealand to relax its restrictions being held over for a future meeting. I still hoped that we might profit from the opportunities opening up in South East Asia. For eighteen months, enlisting the help of the whole office, I sent back suggestions, arguing that we should not be talking defensively of 'concessions', looking on ASEAN as a problem to be managed. Instead we should be calculating what we wanted from the grouping and what we would be willing to pay to get it. Wellington finally brought me home to help the Officials Economic Committee prepare a paper on this but there was no political impetus and it died in Cabinet.

Domestic life in Singapore ran smoothly along time-honoured lines which included someone keeping chickens in a secluded corner of the garden, which I was assumed not to know about, and the housekeeper, Ah Heng, running a laundry business from the house, which I certainly did not know about. The ten-year-old Sophie did though, and after a business-like negotiation her silence was bought with a weekly case of Fanta added to my provisions bill.

When all four children were home the Queen Astrid Park Croquet Club flourished. A raucous form of croquet first played by Julie's family in Akaroa, it took up most of the lawn in front of the house. Unwary visitors would sometimes be startled by the frankness of the terminology but it was worse if they played. Gamesmanship was ruthlessly employed to cover any lack of skill. One hoop was sited close to a clump of bamboo where a snake had once been seen. When a visitor was bent over lining up a shot it was customary for a member of the home team to say, 'You can take a mallet's length in if you are worried about the snake' and this rarely failed to unsettle the stroke. Official writing paper was printed on behalf of the club, describing it rather airily as 'South East Asia's oldest' since we had never heard of any other, and when we went home on leave at the beginning of 1978 the children had luggage labels which said 'Queen Astrid Park Croquet Club – Tour of New Zealand'. Some months later I received a letter from the West Australian Croquet Association inviting us to play in their Golden West Croquet Carnival. As Club President I had to write a hasty response explaining that the club had that year completed a major tour of New Zealand and was unable to take on any further international commitments for the time being.

We entertained a steady stream of ministers, politicians from all sides of the House, generals, departmental heads and experts, for which the house was superbly equipped. Since politicians speak more frankly when away from home – surprisingly so – I found myself better informed about New Zealand affairs than when I lived in Wellington. There was sometimes a price to be paid. The oddity of Western dining etiquette decreed an even distribution of men and women around the table (a practice not native to Asia). I would look down the table at my wife and the men on either side of her as their laughter and brisk talk drifted towards me while at my end the talk seemed to be becalmed on diets and daughters-in-law.

This division of labour was important however: spouses could reach places inaccessible to the official approach. Julie took lessons in Peranakan cooking, the traditional Straits blend of Chinese and Malay dishes, from Mrs Lee Chin Koon, the Prime Minister's mother, from whom he had perhaps inherited both his charm and strength of purpose. This led, not merely to some delicious dishes when Cookie could be coaxed, but to an invitation to Julie to join a Sewing Club of Singapore ladies who met regularly for lunch and needlework. The sewing description was misleading: in three and a half years Julie completed a small tapestry square of the cat, Arthur. As an informal window into the private side of Singapore life and matters that would never be the subject of ministerial conversations, it was invaluable

Back in Sri Lanka, politics had taken a more lively, and more sinister turn. In mid-1977 there was a general election. Mrs Bandaranaike had remarked to me earlier in the year that many people were urging her to avoid this distraction when there was so much still to do. 'But I say to them, that would not be right,' she said, looking at me as if hoping I might disagree. Parliamentary practice had struck deep roots in the country. The government had changed at almost every election since independence and this was no exception. I went to Colombo to meet J R Jayewardene, the new Prime Minister (later President) – whom rumour asserted had once been a prospect to marry the young Mrs Bandaranaike – and his team of ministers.

As in all countries which enjoy elections hope had burgeoned again in Sri Lanka. 'When you are buying an elephant look at its tail', ran a somewhat surprising Sinhala proverb about marriage, but looked at from any side the new government, whose symbol was an elephant, showed unexpected agility. While the IMF stood helpfully by, Jayewardene and his ministers took to the chilly waters of economic reform. Price control was abolished and a start made in reducing the bloated food subsidies which no government had had the courage to tackle since the war. State monopolies were ended, along with exchange controls and much of the import licensing bureaucracy. Farmers' prices were freed and two years later, with the help of good weather, Sri Lanka found itself again self-sufficient in rice. Paint, house repairs and new cars all reappeared. When I drove in from the airport and looked for the sign of Sonderam's food shop, 'We Make the Famous Balls', it had given way to one which said, 'The Best is Getting Better' and this seemed to sum it up.

Such a promising start, though, was checked and hobbled by the ethnic strife which broke out almost simultaneously. A month after the election there was rioting in Jaffna in the Tamil heartland; it then spread like a plague down the railway line to Colombo. A curfew was imposed which I evaded for an hour or so to form some idea of what was going on, driving in a car with the New Zealand flag and talking my way through police roadblocks. The sights were as shocking as only ethnic violence can be: Tamil passers-by set upon and beaten up, Tamil shops being looted and set on fire while their neighbours looked on, the streets buzzing with young men as out of control as swarming bees. Like the remark a Tamil judge's wife made to us about a Sinhalese friend – 'We went to school together and have been friends for fifty years but she would kill me tomorrow' – these were glimpses into a well of ethnic hatred too deep for any rational soundings.

The rioting died down and the refugee camps slowly emptied. The government began to hope that this was another of the temporary disorders which flared up at intervals, as they did in India. This time, however, there was an ominous sound of ticking. The races began silently to separate. Tamils who had lived in Colombo all their life began to move home or to look for property there; the price of property around Jaffna trebled. The able Minister of Trade (later assassinated) put his finger on the underlying problem. Sri Lanka, he said, had two minorities, the actual minority of two million Tamils and the Sinhala who felt themselves threatened by the huge bulge of forty million Tamils hanging over them in South India. Hemmed in between Tamil aspirations and Sinhalese fears the government had dangerously narrow ground in which to manoeuvre.

Many years earlier the government of Mrs Bandaranaike's husband had made Sinhala the only official language and abolished the teaching of English in schools. It was one of those grand and satisfying nationalist gestures, and the Bandaranaike children like those of several other Cabinet members were safely at schools in England. Tamil children were not. For them English was a passport to a wider world, to jobs in the government and business. Now they found themselves locked into their own dry land with few chances of employment. The resentment which had built up over the years had boiled over.

I decided to visit Jaffna at the end of the year. Opinions in Colombo were divided about the advisability of doing so. 'Why ever are you going to Jaffna?' said the Prime Minister's wife, 'So arid'. Others, noting the slow rise of kidnappings and murders, thought it was no longer safe to go by road. I hoped our new transport – an ancient, sage-green Austin Princess of monarchical splendour but plebeian reliability – would awe troublemakers.

On the way we stopped at the second holiest site in Buddhist Sri Lanka, Anuradhapura, set on the borders of the Tamil lands in flat country irrigated by an ancient but highly sophisticated system of 'tanks'. A temple in the town sheltered the Holy Bo Tree, a child of the very bo tree under which the Lord Buddha had attained enlightenment, brought to the island two and a half millennia ago. As was to be expected the Holy Bo Tree was showing its age, propped up with iron crutches, but there it was, the world's oldest recorded tree. A steady stream of pilgrims thronged through the courtyard and we joined them, walking barefoot on the sandy ground and keeping a wary eye on the small black snakes that abounded in the sacred precincts. The obsequies of the Venerable Incumbent of the Holy Bo Tree had just concluded and we paid our respects. His funeral pyre was still hot, an oblong of fluffy ash in which the Venerable Incumbent's skeleton was outlined in black as it had sunk in the flames.

For all the forebodings the rest of the journey passed without incident. As we passed into the Northern Province the language on the shops changed and the land became flatter, drier and more sparsely dotted with trees until we came through the Elephant Pass into Jaffna, dominated by its harbour and the thick walls of the Dutch-built fort. These walls had reverted to their original purpose – the police had taken refuge inside. The town was faded and rundown, with the curious feature that virtually all the cars were old British Austin A40s – esteemed in thrifty Jaffna as the most reliable ever made and few had felt it necessary to look further.

The walls of the town were splashed with garish political slogans and the rising sun emblem of the Tamil United Liberation Front. Even to someone who could not read them they conveyed a sense of ferment. Those we talked to seemed both frightened and resentful. Their immediate complaints ranged from police extortion to government indifference (no minister had visited for months). Along with the constants of language and religion, the growing secessionist movement was being fed by anxieties about 'colonisation' – the belief that Sinhalese farmers were pushing into the borderlands, especially in the east – and education. Though Jaffna was South Indian in culture, a large minority was Christian and before the decree banning the teaching of English three-quarters of the people had been educated in mission schools. These educational openings had vanished. The Catholic priests at the schools we visited did not trouble to conceal their anger and frustration. The Government Agent said that every household had at least two un-employed young men.

They were beginning to look for trouble. There was a growing number of murders and bank robberies to arm and fund clandestine groups though, the Police Superintendent told us, some of the money was diverted to provide dowries for the insurgents' sisters. The Super-intendent was a Sinhala with a Tamil wife and he was, he said, struggling to persuade his force to move into the community and not behave like a garrison. A brave man, he paid the price for this, being assassinated not long afterwards. We had dinner with him on our last night, a dinner mercifully free of the evil-smelling rice beloved in Jaffna. Sensing that Julie was apprehensive about the drive home he offered to provide an armed escort to travel with us but, with an admirable firmness I knew was assumed, she declined.

We drove home by the inland route through thick jungle. We came round a bend to find a large tree lying across the narrow road and a group of young men standing beside it. Julie's hand tightened in mine and the car came to an uncertain stop. I told the driver to go on, calculating that the absurd car and the New Zealand pennant might improve our chances in negotiation. When we got to the roadblock, however, it appeared that the tree had simply fallen over and the young men were wondering what to do about it. We got out and with some grunting and shoving, oiled with the distribution of rupees, the tree was pushed to the side of the road and we were on our way. I avoided catching my wife's eye, however, until we were nearly in Colombo.

To balance this visit to the Tamil lands we went to Kandy, home of the Holy Tooth Relic and the guardian of traditional Sinhalese culture, the last independent kingdom which had defied Portuguese and Dutch to fall to the British only in 1815. We stayed in a bungalow on the hill looking down on the town as guests of Mr Senanayake, a softly spoken man whose large liquid eyes and silent movement around the darkened house gave him a strong resemblance to a marmoset. Each morning the sounds of religion floated up to us across the lake – a muezzin's cry before dawn, followed by drums and flute-playing from the Temple of the Tooth and then the bells of the Church of the Good Shepherd.

Whatever may have been said about the last King of Kandy (and much was – strangely he was a Tamil from India) he was a landscaper of genius. He flooded the marshy land beside the temple and by setting this jewel of a lake in the centre he made the whole valley a reliquary. Apart from this the king was by no means an ostentatious liver. The Royal Palace was a low, white-plastered building like a farmhouse. He extended the moat to cover both palace and temple (his only political asset), and stocked it with crocodiles: he had lost the confidence of his subjects.

We made a night visit to the Temple of the Tooth. The antechamber to the shrine was adorned with faded but lively frescoes of lions, birds, fish and an elephant which on closer examination turned out to be nine women with linked arms, intended to convey the slightly ungallant message that nine women united could do the work of an elephant. Racks of flickering votive lamps were ranged around and heaped trays of the 'temple flower', frangipani.

Outside the main doors to the shrine drums and a flute began to play. The wailing music, heat and encircling dark evoked memories of Kipling. The musicians fell silent when three priests appeared, each with a key to the triple locks. When they passed inside we were beckoned to follow. The priests moved up a narrow wooden staircase with the briskness common to their profession and we stood in front of small double doors sheathed in beaten silver. Again the triple locks were opened and we stepped into the innermost room. The quiet after the drumming was eerie and the sweet scent of incense, jasmine and frangipani almost overpowering.

The Lord Buddha's tooth rested within seven consecutive caskets made in the bell shape of Buddhist stupas. The outermost stood almost three feet high. It was made of heavy silver chased with gold and festooned with gold chains in which were set large cabochon rubies, sapphires and emeralds. They were the regalia of the ancient Kings of Ceylon and offerings through the centuries from the Kings of Burma and Siam. There was a new gift: a large chain of gold filigree and gems presented by a Colombo businessman.

After a pause for prayerful reflection a silver tray appeared in front of us and I made an offering. The clergy meditated on this for a moment, then the tray was removed and the viewing was over. We came downstairs, crossed the moat, filled now with carp rather than crocodiles, and came to the edge of the lake. As the night breeze ruffled the reflections on its surface the lights went out and the temple closed. The lapping of water was suddenly the only sound to be heard in Kandy.

In South East Asia concerns about Vietnam's intentions continued to mount. As its relations with the Soviet Union grew closer the neighbourly links between it and China – once routinely described as closer than 'lips and teeth' – began to fray. China offered discreet support to Thailand. In itself this was cheering for the members of ASEAN but it raised the alarming prospect that they could be dragged into any intensification of the Sino–Soviet quarrel.

The rivalry first showed itself in diplomacy: in the second half of 1978 ASEAN countries found themselves the target of a charm offensive. The first visitor, who prepared the way, was the Vietnamese Deputy Foreign Minister, Phan Hien, who was coolly described to me by Lee as the 'coffee and cigarettes man', the man in police states who comes in to offer a soothing chat between beatings by the nasties. Phan beamed tirelessly and in all his public comments was agreeability itself. He was followed by his Prime Minister, Pham Van Dong, and then a month later by the Chinese leader, Deng Xiao-ping. In one sense the two rather spoiled each other's act. Pham firmly promised that Vietnam would not engage in subversion but he could not bring himself to endorse ASEAN or even to utter the word. Deng was entirely relaxed about ASEAN but felt unable to discuss subversion which would have meant disavowing the dwindling support China still extended to local Communist parties.

Singapore listened to Pham with a sceptical reserve. With Deng it wished to establish firmly that 'we are we', that its citizens were Singaporeans with their own interests and outlook and not overseas Chinese. Deng for his part wanted some views on what was to be done to check Vietnam's ambitions. Looking round at Singapore's achievement may also have strengthened his conviction that if China were to grow rich a more practical approach was required. Driving to the airport Deng looked intently out the window and then said, almost to himself, 'I could do this if I had only Shanghai'.

The scepticism about Pham turned to alarm when, shortly after he returned home, Vietnam concluded a friendship treaty with the Soviet Union and joined Comecon. Although negotiations must have been well advanced he had given no hint of this in his travels around South East Asia. With material backing assured, Vietnam invaded Cambodia a few weeks later.

China reacted, as Deng had perhaps hinted, by administering what was called, in haughty language that would have been approved by the T'ang emperors, a 'first lesson' to Vietnam. It invaded and occupied for a time part of Vietnam's northern territory. The Chinese forces did not perform flawlessly (they had not fought for a generation and faced some very experienced troops) but their incursion if not welcomed by the ASEAN countries certainly gave some quiet satisfaction. With the United States out of the ring it signalled that at least one powerful state was prepared to put serious pressure on Hanoi. Thailand, now sharing a border with Vietnamese-occupied Cambodia, might breathe a little easier.

Vietnam, however, made an unexpected move. It released a second wave of refugees onto the shores of the ASEAN members. After the fall of Saigon there had been an outpouring of over a million 'boat people'. Now after five years the flow suddenly recommenced. In the first quarter of 1979 about 80,000 Vietnamese landed on the shores of Thailand and Malaysia. They set out in leaky and overcrowded fishing boats with little fuel and unreliable engines. For every one who landed it was estimated that at least one died at sea, drowned in bad weather or the victims of the pirates that preyed ruthlessly on the slow and helpless vessels. The lucky ones drifted ashore at random – there were few navigational aids – and the long white beaches of eastern Malaysia were dotted with them, cranky craft unpainted and patched with warped wood, abandoned by their passengers as soon as they grounded.

They were clearly leaving with at least the tolerance of the Vietnamese government. The great majority were Chinese Vietnamese from places like Cholon. Hanoi may have welcomed getting rid of those it thought of suspect loyalty, and at the same time turning a useful profit, for the sad human cargo paid substantial sums to the shadowy people who organised the departures. The ASEAN states saw it as a weapon to destabilise Thailand and others who could not cope with such large numbers.

Those countries which had given homes to the first wave now began to do so again but the bureaucratic processes of interview and selection were inevitably slow and large refugee camps began to build up in Thailand, Malaysia and Indonesia. New Zealand took 1500 in this first year and more in the year following. To speed things up one group of 51 came from a Malaysian camp to Singapore to be flown south on Air New Zealand. The Singaporean authorities were apprehensive about possible disappearances into the city and so for the length of a day until the plane left the refugees were looked after at the battalion's barracks. Soldiers and wives bustled about providing meals and colour TV, with toys and a place to play for the children. The group accepted it all silently, as if they still could not quite believe in the kindness of strangers.

I found an elderly man who spoke better French than I did and enquired about two children, aged perhaps five and eight, who were holding hands and seemed to be on their own. They were brother and sister, he said, but no one knew who they were; no parents had come with them on the boat. Unable to say anything, I stood grinning foolishly at them, orphans now with only each other and bound for a land where voices, customs and attitudes would be incomprehensible. Had their parents been unable to raise the money for their own places on the boat? I could only ponder the desperation which must have led them to say goodbye, probably forever, and to send their children alone on a perilous voyage.

The involuntary hosts in South East Asia were angry and alarmed. They had, however, an effective entity – ASEAN – through which to develop their response. The association had matured over a decade to the point where collective diplomatic action was possible. When I was first in Singapore ASEAN had seemed an affair primarily of meetings. Telephone calls to a minister or departmental head were often met with the answer that he was out of the country, attending an ASEAN committee. The immediate fruit of these meetings was not always apparent but over time the neighbours came to know one another very well. Ethnic differences became less important when personal acquaintance was close; differences of approach were shaved down in repeated discussion.

So when the pressure came on the members found they had built up not just the machinery of consultation but a collective instrument capable of formulating a policy and holding to it. ASEAN, militarily weak, went on the diplomatic offensive. Its aim simply stated was to 'bleed' Vietnam, to keep raising the price of its Cambodian adventure. This had the awkward corollary of defending the UN seat still occupied by the appalling Pol Pot government. ASEAN coordinated the attack in the

Security Council and later on defended Cambodia's representation in the General Assembly, supported a little uncomfortably by its friends. We urged the need to start the search for a political settlement in Cambodia, pointing out that no democratic country could long stomach a Pol Pot ambassador in New York. Singapore did not disagree. Most issues, said Rajaratnam, were a choice between two evils and Cambodia was certainly one of them. After a visit by one of Pol Pot's lieutenants, Ieng Sary, the Secretary of Foreign Affairs said, 'I refused to shake the hand of that bloodstained monster', but he went on to argue that aggression could not be countenanced. ASEAN was not ready to compromise. The immediate task was to apply the strongest practicable penalties to Vietnam. Only when Hanoi had absorbed these would it be time to talk of a settlement.

In the middle of the year the UN Secretary-General called a conference on the refugees in Geneva. The prospect of an international discussion was welcome but also a little worrying. The ASEAN members were aggrieved that they were being placed in the dock, compelled to defend their reluctance to resettle this latest wave of refugees when they felt the blame lay with Vietnam. The ASEAN Foreign Ministers were meeting in Bali and they asked their closest friends – the United States, Japan, Australia and New Zealand – to join them. The aim, Rajaratnam said, was to 'create the right mood' for the Geneva conference, the hope being that ASEAN's friends would help keep the finger of debate pointed at Vietnam. The world should see the crisis for what it was, a mass expulsion for political reasons, and not be side-tracked into compromises about 'orderly departures' or other purely humanitarian measures.

It was a measure of ASEAN's new influence that despite the short notice everyone came, including the American Secretary of State, Cyrus Vance. We all stayed at the Pertamina Cottages, small units scattered over several acres of tropical gardens. It was the change of the monsoon and sleep was interrupted by the tremendous thunderstorms which were known, in Singapore at any rate, as 'Sumatras'. At breakfast, Richard Holbrooke, who shared a cottage with the Australian Foreign Minister Andrew Peacock, said he had not been disturbed by the thunder so much as the way that every time the lightning flashed Peacock leapt out of bed and said, 'I'll take two copies'.

The ASEAN ministers were looking for reassurance. They felt that their own efforts could amount only to 'a poor man's defiance of Vietnam', while hoping that this larger grouping could exert real pressure on Hanoi.

The opening speeches had a desperate ring but the tone became calmer as they got the reassurance they were seeking. Each of their friends endorsed the main points of the ASEAN position, that the refugee problem had to be tackled 'at source' and that more help was urgently needed to help the frontline countries to cope. Brian Talboys, the New Zealand Foreign Minister, kept to the theme of reliability, emphasising his country's record of sticking by its friends. There was applause and Rajaratnam responded by describing New Zealanders as stout-hearted gentlemen – 'when a New Zealander says "I am with you" you don't need to have it in writing'.

By the dinner at the end of the meeting the mood was relaxed and convivial. Then it was the turn of the friends to be apprehensive. Someone came round the tables letting us know that each delegation would be expected to provide a song or other entertainment. This was a feature of ASEAN gatherings, where delegations like the Filipinos were expert singers and dancers and the Malaysian minister might (as he did this time) improvise a series of *pantun*, satirical and slyly improper quatrains on some of the company. English-speaking diplomats were not accustomed to such merriment; the more desperately we tried to think of something, the more elusive inspiration became. Suggestions went back and forth between the American, Australian and New Zealand tables as we gloomily got through our pudding. In the end the three delegations mounted the stage, linked arms and sang 'Home on the Range', 'Waltzing Matilda' and 'Now is the Hour'. As an act it did not set the room alight but some of the audience were struck by the fact that the ANZUS delegates all knew the words of each other's songs.

In offering reassurance the visitors also stressed that sooner or later a negotiated settlement would have to be reached over Cambodia. Vance was so struck by the ASEAN worries that he concluded the search for such a settlement would have to be speeded up. After he and his two counterparts left for an ANZUS Council meeting in Canberra, he sent Holbrooke off to Beijing to seek Chinese support. Both Peacock and Talboys contributed views to his instructions. Talboys then made a round of South East Asian capitals. The ASEANs remained sceptical. Vietnam had twenty divisions in Cambodia trying to impose control; while it could carry the cost Hanoi would be unlikely to compromise.

Geneva at the end of July was in high summer, crowded with holiday-makers around the sparkling lake with its high-jetting fountain. I felt less sparkling as my luggage had gone astray. This was not unprecedented but this time it seemed to have gone on a tour of its own. Along the way I received little encouraging messages like postcards. The suitcase was in Dubai, then it stopped for a time in Zurich, after which it looked in on Copenhagen. I went straight from the plane to the meetings of something called the Like-Minded Group. When my case arrived at last I had been four days in the same suit and the group around the table might have been of like mind to ask me to withdraw.

The conference met in the Palais des Nations, that graveyard of failed hopes. The panoply of international meetings rolled by, with speeches in plenary, caucusing in groups, the circulation of draft resolutions and a carefully worded result. The ASEANs had every reason to be satisfied. They won widespread support, kept the debate focused on the fact that the solution lay in Vietnam's hands and got international sympathy for their difficulties. After the conference the flow of refugees slowed to a trickle and stopped.

While in Geneva I had instructions to make secret contact with Phan Hien, the Vietnamese representative, to see whether Vietnam might take a more conciliatory attitude towards a Cambodian settlement and to signify New Zealand's willingness to help if it did. A car picked me up and drove to a modest flat in a working-class suburb. Phan, beaming again, was at the top of the stairs and with perfect symbolism began by offering me coffee and cigarettes. Then we talked for over an hour, Phan's easy manners equalled only by his skill in handling awkward points.

On refugees he agreed that Vietnam would have to do something but it needed 'a reasonable period of time'. On Cambodia his justification was weak. He claimed that his country had been forced to invade because China was threatening a pincer movement against its own existence. The immediate need was to rebuild, 'more time was needed before political changes could be considered'. The conversation revolved around China. When I suggested that Prince Sihanouk might play a part in a settlement he retorted that 'Mr Sihanouk' was too closely connected to China which, he argued, had designs on Vietnam and in time on South East Asia. His smooth tone dropped for a moment and he said sharply, 'Don't try to play the China card'. I said we weren't and he endeavoured to repair the lapse with less than his usual subtlety, contrasting New Zealand's tone and posture at the conference as being 'more rounded, more *moelleux*' than Australia's. The coffee had cooled and I went back to the hotel and on to Wellington to report.

By now I was coming to the end of my term. Seniority meant a slow rise up the local diplomatic rankings but then the Soviet ambassador, who was Dean of the Diplomatic Corps, had a heart attack and I found myself Dean. This was not a very onerous position in Singapore, where the corps was well behaved and had few disputes with the authorities. However the custom was that departing ambassadors were presented by their colleagues with an engraved silver tray and a small fund was maintained to pay for these. The trouble was that the stricken Russian, who had been flown to Moscow, was the only signatory to the bank account, and a sudden exodus of ambassadors left me scrambling to fund the trays. The Singapore Prime Minister was unsympathetic: how typical of diplomats, he said, not to have two signatories to the account.

In Sri Lanka time had made me Vice-Dean. The Dean was the Cuban ambassador, a lively and worldly woman who bought her clothes and shoes in Paris and whose conversation I greatly enjoyed as we stood side by side at the airport when arriving dignitaries were welcomed. This occasionally raised delicate questions. Wellington asked me to attend a meeting of the Non-Aligned in Colombo in June, three weeks before the Bali meeting. High though the bar had been set in the past, this conference managed to set a new world record in fat-headed compromises. After hours of wrangling over Cambodia it decided to seat the representative of the Pol Pot government on condition he did not speak and Cambodia was not mentioned by anyone else. So the Foreign Minister of the Vietnamese-backed government, Hun Sen, found himself an observer like me. We circled uneasily round each other in the lobbies outside the conference hall and on one occasion I had to turn my back rather than be introduced, nervous that any photograph of us shaking hands might be taken as New Zealand recognition of the invasion.

The work of the Dean seemed more demanding in Sri Lanka but the affair of the Burmese ambassador was perhaps exceptional. His wife had become enamoured of a player in a night-club band. One night, as she was returning from the club, the ambassador waited with a pistol and shot her as she got out of the car. The next morning the neighbours in Cinnamon Gardens were surprised to see the ambassador stacking wood on the back lawn and, connoisseurs of cremation, quickly grasped that he was building a pyre. When the police were called the ambassador opened the metal front gates just enough to say that there was no trouble and to remind them that his house was Burmese territory. Then he went back to work. The houses around his long back garden were now alive with fascinated spectators as he emerged with the body of his wife, placed it on the pyre and set it alight. He was, said the Dean, well connected at home but after an awkward interval he was recalled.

In September I had a visit from Bernard Galvin and his partner, Professor Margaret Clark. Bernard was on crutches, joking that he was the only person ever to have broken a toe falling *upstairs*. He was on his way to England and stopped off to ask if I would be willing to succeed him as Head of the Prime Minister's Department. The Prime Minister was agreeable though he had yet to mention it to Cabinet. The Foreign Ministry was also in favour. I looked out the window at the sun on the lawn. Diplomatic life had been fun and Bernard's health spoke of the demands of the position, but what could be said about this unexpected offer? I said yes, and life changed forever.

The end of my time in Singapore was increasingly taken up with the consequences. At Christmas 1979 the Soviet ambassador in New Zealand, Sofinsky, broke a prime rule of the diplomatic game. In the absence of his KGB man who normally did these chores he went to Auckland himself and in a motel room handed over an instalment of the regular subsidy paid to the Soviet-aligned Socialist Unity Party which had been pressing with increasing urgency for the money. He was caught by our security service, leaving Moscow embarrassed and the government to decide what to do about it.

The young foreign affairs adviser from the Prime Minister's Department, Simon Murdoch, flew to Singapore to brief me. The only course was to expel the unfortunate Sofinsky but New Zealand sold large quantities of mutton (which few others would buy) and butter to the state trading corporations in Moscow and the Prime Minister wanted to take further advice on the risks to our trade.

The next morning I was on the Concorde, looking at the curvature of the earth high over the Indian Ocean and on my way to London which had long experience of handling diplomatic expulsions. Arriving on a bleak January afternoon I went straight to the Foreign Office and explained the position. Come back at teatime, was the kindly advice. I returned in the winter darkness to find a full bench of mandarins sitting around the tea table. Their view was straightforward: if we expelled Sofinsky the Russians would expel our ambassador but there the matter would rest unless we wished to take it further. It would take stronger measures than this to lead Moscow to imperil its purchases of food. That was clear enough, and I had only to break the news to our Moscow ambassador, Jim Weir, who had come to London to hear the verdict. He was likely, I had been told, to have only forty-eight hours to leave the country; the only consolation I could offer was that he buy a packet of round red stickers and put them on all the possessions that would have to be shipped after him. The next day I was back in Singapore, having travelled to London essentially for afternoon tea.

Later in the month I accompanied the Prime Minister on an official visit to the Philippines, my first acquaintance with some of the perennial features of these journeys. One was the overriding importance of news from New Zealand. As we crawled along in Manila traffic, even with motorcycle outriders, he would start to fret, asking me where the news summaries were and why they were late. The party travelled with a primitive fax machine the size of a small suitcase whose performance this far from home was erratic to say the least. In an effort to ensure the quickest service I took the machine into my bedroom – a mistake never repeated. At intervals during the night it would burst into a noisy clatter, spewing out a stream of smudged cuttings. In a daily ritual the PM would go carefully through them all at breakfast, before calling in the New Zealand journalists to berate them for their poor coverage.

Talks with President Marcos were more like an audience, with the President and Mrs Marcos on high-backed chairs while Muldoon, the ambassador and I sat on sofas. After a state banquet that night at the Mala-canang Palace the PM suggested a nightcap. It was nearly midnight and I would have preferred to go to bed. This, too, was a recurrent feature of his travel. He liked to wind down and we would have (in my experience) one glass of whisky and twenty minutes or so of free-flowing conversation. This was an opportunity to raise thoughts beyond his usual tight concentration on the day's issues, but there were perils to being too free-flowing. On this occasion he asked my view of Bill Sutch, a senior civil servant who had been tried and acquitted under the Official Secrets Act for contacts with the KGB. As it happened his first wife, a progressive lady who passed her long life waiting for the Red Dawn, was a cousin of mine. I said frankly that I thought he was as guilty as sin. The next morning, after the press had been summoned, the PM worked the talk around to Bill Sutch and then declared that he was 'as guilty as sin'. This led to a little flurry of headlines at home and a private vow by me to be more careful.

We made an excursion out of town, to Tarlac in the north. A place of scrub-covered eroded hills, it was the scene of a joint New Zealand–ASEAN reafforestation project. I could not help feeling that our visit was a mixed blessing. The President had lent us his large cream-coloured helicopter. As it settled gingerly on to the ground outside the PM's window, I could see a brigadier and guard of honour presenting arms while a band burst into a patriotic welcome. From my window on the other side I could see families scrambling to save their pots and bedding as the downdraft blew over their flimsy huts.

Before the packers arrived we made a last visit to Colombo, with a short stay at the Hill Club in Nuwara Eliya high above the tea-growing slopes and frosty at this time of year.* The club, once the social centre of the British tea-planters, was an uninhibited expression of their nostalgia. It was built of stone with mullioned windows in the style of a Tudor country house. Inside the impression was maintained with oak furniture, large bowls of flowers and cases of stuffed trout from Taupo among other places. Our bedroom was large, with chintz-covered armchairs and that luxury of tropical exiles, a wood fire. As we left the aged servant who had lit the fire and managed the water for a bath on our earlier stays came up for a quiet word. Did I think, he said, that the *sahibs* would ever come back? He received my answer with the grim dignity of one who has had a bad diagnosis confirmed and shuffled off, remembering belatedly to come back for his tip.

Then in the customary fashion we had to eat and drink our way out of Singapore, the last days and nights passing in a blur of lunches, dinners, receptions and affectionate goodbyes. The cat was given to the commander of the battalion, Colonel Bestic. Quarantine regulations would not allow the corgi to be repatriated and he was buried in the garden. Once in the air we looked down at the dwindling island republic. I said to Julie, 'They will be richer than us in seven years'. She was disbelieving but so they were – in six.

---

* While on a chilly early-morning walk I met a man carrying a lumpy sack which had a curious ripple. When I enquired he said, 'They are cobberas, sir' and disappeared into the mist.

# CHAPTER EIGHT

# *The Last Years of Muldoon*

THE DOOR OPPOSITE MY DESK OPENED. GERRY SYMMANS, THE Prime Minister's press secretary, stood there and announced, 'I've been round the traps and there's a possum in every one'. His choice of door marked the significance of the occasion for this alternative entrance, like the Holy Year door of St Peter's, was used only on the rare and august occasions when the Prime Minister looked in.

It was the middle of October 1980 and I had been head of the Prime Minister's Department for a month. The Prime Minister, Robert Muldoon, was away on an extensive series of overseas visits which took in India, China, Bermuda, Washington, New York and Mexico. In his absence members of his parliamentary caucus were plotting to remove him. They were naturally reticent about their activities and no word had leaked out, even I think to the peripatetic Prime Minister, but Gerry had good contacts and came in every few hours to brief me on his enquiries.

The next day he was back in the doorway to give the results of his latest count: there was now a majority in the caucus willing to replace Muldoon. 'He's gone,' said Gerry dramatically. But it was more accurate to say that he had not yet arrived. On his way home from Mexico the Prime Minister, who had been alerted to his danger, spent a day's stopover in Honolulu almost continuously on the phone to his colleagues. As soon as he was back in New Zealand he plunged at once into the fight for his political life.

The plotters, discontented with the Muldoon style of personal government and looking to the general election in a year's time, hoped to replace him with his deputy, the able and soft-spoken Brian Talboys.

He too was travelling and was in Bonn when asked to lead the revolt. He declined, saying he had never wished to be Prime Minister. While some still hoped that he could be drafted, this left the rebels nonplussed and the campaign without a candidate. While things drifted, Muldoon, whose willpower was remarkable (indeed it was a prime reason for the restlessness of his colleagues), worked tirelessly to quell the mutiny. He spoke to members of the caucus, to senior members of the National Party and used a television interview to rally his supporters throughout the country. Within a week he was back on top, but the effort of will left the Prime Minister exhausted. For ten days after he yawned, had to have things repeated, and even fell asleep during his weekly meeting with the Advisory Group.

By this time I had been six months in the Beehive, the aptly named building which housed Ministers, the Prime Minister and his department, first as Deputy Head while I tried to learn from my predecessor, Bernard Galvin, how things were done. This was not simple; a department built to serve a prime minister was inevitably shaped around his style and needs and the view from the top of this circular building covered the whole panorama of government. The flow of unrelated issues and minor crises took some getting used to. Contemplating an especially intractable problem I muttered, 'This is a stinker'. The Prime Minister cheered up immediately. 'Mr Hensley,' he said, 'that's what we are here for. Anything easier gets solved before it reaches the ninth floor.'

The Prime Minister's Department had had a separate existence only since Muldoon had come to power at the end of 1975, when the Prime Minister's Advisory Group was added and Galvin appointed as head. Bill Rowling told me some years later that had he been re-elected then he would have done the same thing, and appointed the same able Treasury official.

In the China of the Ming emperors the equivalent department was housed in the Pavilion of Literary Depth. We had no such ambitions, Muldoon liking his papers succinct and businesslike. The traditional tasks continued. The Cabinet Office, honours system and Press Office largely ran themselves; supervision of the intelligence agencies meant chairing the Intelligence Council and Terrorism Committee and meeting weekly with the heads of the three agencies (though the Director of the Security Service reported direct to the Prime Minister). The heart of the new department, though, was the Advisory Group.

Muldoon, never amenable to the thought of being advised, preferred to call it his Liaison Group; the press nicknamed it the Think-tank. Its main functions were to keep the Prime Minister informed about all important issues affecting the government, and to provide a quick response when he wanted something done. It was thus more of a fire brigade than a think-tank. When I asked Bernard how far ahead they planned he thought for a moment and said, 'as far as tomorrow afternoon'.

The Advisory Group had only seven members, people in their thirties, drawn half and half from government and the private sector, who served for two years. This meant that I was constantly looking for replacements but the two-year limit enabled me to persuade chief executives to lend me their best for the experience to be gained, and also prevented the group from putting down roots and becoming another layer of bureaucracy. The risk to be avoided was that it might evolve into a White House staff, coming between the PM and his Ministers and devoting itself to second-guessing the work of others. Keeping it small and informal meant that it had to work through and maintain good relations with government departments, business, trade union and farmer groups or the flow of information would dry up.

For the same reason it seemed essential that the group be strictly non-political. Candidates were required to have no public political associations. Early on Bernard had fought and won this battle. Muldoon had thought of adding promising backbenchers but had been persuaded that departmental and other sources were less likely to cooperate with political appointees. Thereafter he exerted no influence on group appointments, content simply to be briefed on who was joining. On one occasion he saved me from myself. I mentioned someone I was planning to approach. Looking over his glasses he said, 'I have heard nothing but good of her'. A twinkle in his eye made me suspicious and on checking I found she had been an active member of the National Party. I chose someone else and Muldoon never mentioned my near-miss again.

The only other occasion when he raised his eyebrows was the appointment of Tim Groser as foreign affairs specialist. A photo of Tim peering out through a forest of hair and beard appeared in a magazine, with the snide comment that Tim's old radical colleagues on the Committee on Vietnam were bemused at his defection. The PM asked me about it and I had to confess that, though Tim had worked for me in

Foreign Affairs in 1973, this was news to me. I talked to Tim and told the PM I had every confidence in him. Muldoon nodded and dismissed the matter.

The fact was he had no interest in the private opinions of his staff. The issue for him was ability not politics and the barrier between party and government was scrupulously respected. He thought that both his departmental heads voted Labour and remarked to me on the eve of the 1981 general election in a tone of mild regret that if the election depended on the Advisory Group he doubted he would get a majority. He was not in the least troubled. He valued the civil service for information and analysis, not emotional support. He said once with feeling that the difference between Opposition and Government was access to officials, but he did not depend on them for guidance. He knew what he wanted and his people were there to deliver it. Provided they were competent and loyal he was indifferent to what else they thought.

In a private glossary of Muldoonisms prepared by some of the group 'a senior and experienced official' was defined as 'one who agrees with me' and 'a junior and inexperienced official' as 'one who does not'. This was uncomfortably close to the mark and I had hastily to suppress the paper in case it leaked to the parliamentary press gallery. Those he trusted could argue with him, provided they had a command of the subject. They did not necessarily win: the best you could hope for was 'Perhaps we'd better look at that again'. More often the only acknowledgement was a resigned grunt.

On one occasion he asked me to look into a course he was proposing to take. When I reported back that it could not legally be done in that way he became irritated and said, 'I don't agree. We'll go ahead anyhow.' There was a silence. I drew a breath and said, 'In that case, Prime Minister, I will have to put my advice in writing'. There was an even longer silence. Then he turned and said, 'It's as bad as that, is it?' I nodded and after a grunt nothing more was heard of the proposal.

When his department's view differed from his, as it did on some aspects of the 'Think Big' development projects, he simply ignored it. At a Cabinet Committee meeting, reading from a briefing note I had given him, he exclaimed in surprise, real or affected, 'For once I agree with my own department'. Once he publicly disagreed. In Napier giving a speech we had drafted on labour market policy his brow suddenly darkened and he said, 'I don't agree with this'. When he complained I told him that it had been cleared with the Minister of Labour; left unspoken was the thought that perhaps he should read his speeches in advance.

The Advisory Group was divided into broad 'portfolios' – economics, foreign affairs, agriculture, business, social affairs and transport – into which all the concerns of government were packed. Members had one thing in common with diplomatic practice: they were out every day doing a round of their contacts. The PM was normally briefed in a steady flow of notes which he read and if necessary commented on with characteristic speed. On quiet days a note could make the round trip seemingly without a pause.

A flow of information on business activity, economic data, and farming conditions could be assumed. Less predictable was his interest in social policy. He had of course no interest in theory; it was always the personal, the practical touch. Coming into his office could sometimes be a surprise, with a crowd of roughly dressed gang members sitting on the floor deep in conversation with the PM in his armchair. One of the Advisory Group's perennial tasks was finding jobs and accommodation for the gangs. It was not for the faint-hearted. When a house was found for the Mongrel Mob on Hill Street, near the Beehive, the members celebrated by burning down their old accommodation and committing two rapes. Their new neighbours included two Opposition Members of Parliament who not unnaturally complained. Muldoon was indulgent.

Once a week, usually on Friday afternoons, the Advisory Group had a two-hour meeting with the PM – virtually sacrosanct however crowded his schedule – around the coffee table in his office. Each member reported on the week's events and issues coming up while the PM sat slumped in his armchair. Muldoon's manner was benevolent, almost paternal with a group the age of his children, but his questioning could be sharp and anyone who had not marshalled their facts carefully could be quickly discomfited. So there was always a slight after-examination air as we filed out of his office and adjourned to mine where we went through the next week's Cabinet papers and I could pour a relaxing drink for everyone.*

---

* At one Group meeting the PM produced a bottle of gin he had been sent. It had been made from whey, a by-product of the dairy industry. He wondered what it might be called: 'My whey', said George Green.

The result of all this was that the PM was formidably well informed. Notes would be shot off to Ministers enquiring what they were proposing to do about a problem of which in some cases they were not yet aware. This knowledge was a power which made possible his steadily tightening grip on government business. After the coup attempt he never quite trusted his Cabinet colleagues again; good information together with his powers of concentration and grasp of detail gave him an increasing ascendancy over them to the point of their sometimes seeming mesmerised. Some of the more nervous Ministers had occasionally to be discouraged from trying to communicate with the PM through his department.

My own relationship with him was correct, even formal. It was always 'Mr Hensley', especially when about to deliver one of his more weighty thoughts. Working with him was businesslike; wider conversations were kept to the car or aircraft. I would see him early on most days with a list of issues which would be briskly ticked off within fifteen minutes at the most. The art when briefing him was to keep the crocodile's jaws open long enough to poke in enough information before they would snap shut on a decision. Once taken a decision was hard to reverse. On one occasion he sent out a press release on the coolstore in Bahrain which I thought, with some reason, would cause resentment there. I took it back to him on some excuse and he said, 'You think I am wrong, don't you?' He was silent for a moment and then said, 'You may well be right. But if we stop to reconsider everything we will never get on. Let it go.'

He enjoyed chewing steadily through the pile of paper on his desk and was at a loss on the rare occasions when it ran out. He would then prowl the ninth and eighth floors, making everyone uneasy. The door of my room would open and the PM would stand there, peering round the room as if he had never seen it before, to make some inconsequential remark. On Bernard's advice I tried to keep a few papers in a bottom drawer which could be produced to relieve his boredom at these times.

Normally it was I who in the course of the day went up and down the corkscrew staircase (in my disillusioned moments it seemed like a metaphor for the business of government) which connected the department with the PM's office on the floor above. Sometimes he would be fretful – 'this is not tidy, see what you can do'; sometimes impatient over a delay. Sometimes he felt he was being pressed too hard – 'don't you Sir Humphrey me' he once said alluding to a British television comedy which in New Zealand tended to be taken as a documentary on civil service cunning. Occasionally the best way of managing the PM was to keep out of his way entirely. From time to time he liked to have a convivial lunch with a close friend and on those days I made sure that nothing went to him after 3.30 when the sky was likely to darken and the mood change.

He could display an equally unpredictable good humour. I made the mistake of giving a background briefing to a journalist on the scientific monitoring mission being sent to Mururoa atoll. I came back to the office to find it splashed as the front page lead. I went straight up to the PM whom I discovered to my horror standing up and contemplating the paper spread out on his desk. I said, 'It was me, Prime Minister'. He dismissed this, saying that he had rung the Minister of Foreign Affairs to complain. When I finally persuaded him that I was the culprit, a silence fell. It was hard to know what else to say. Finally he turned to me with a hint of a smile and said, 'I bet you won't do it again'.

Once he even made amends, if only indirectly. At the early morning briefing he made a complaint which was in my view quite unjustified. We both got testy and I left, closing the door behind me fairly firmly. I was away for the rest of the morning but when I returned, still heated, I found a note on my desk asking Julie and me to his lunch for the Prince and Princess of Wales – in several months' time.

His prime-ministership was now in its second half. Years in office always take their toll. He was becoming less resilient, and more defensive. He ate and drank too much and took no exercise whatever. I raised it with him once and he said, 'Mr Hensley, I take my exercise from the neck up' – a fact which a glance at his shape confirmed. He was as methodical and hard-working as ever, his powers of concentration undiminished, but the government was on a downward slope.

The oil shock of 1979 and fast-rising inflation sharpened the struggle to keep the protected New Zealand economy afloat. The modest economic reforms of his first term were now only a memory. Instead there was a growing feeling of being under siege. Ever the pragmatist, uninterested even sceptical of theoretical frameworks and their uncertain outcomes, he resorted more and more to meeting difficulties as they arose. Underpinning this was an increasing reliance on government borrowing to tide the economy over until better times returned.

He saw himself as a manager, a political manager. His aim was always, in a favourite phrase, to keep things 'tidy' and a grumble to those around him that this or that was untidy was a signal to get to work. He was cautious about risk but disliked doing nothing. Contemplating a set of equally unattractive options he said to me, 'Let's get it moving and then we can see better how to steer it'. For such a powerful personality he could be surprisingly resigned, even fatalistic: people let you down, things turned out badly, the only thing to do was accept the situation and make do. Told of an act of black treachery by someone he had favoured, he simply stared out the window for a while. Then he turned and delivered a memorable Muldoonism: 'You know, Mr Hensley, there's an awful lot of human nature in people.'

Because government was management, and management by him, he was weak on the forms of government, the rules and conventions which help parliamentary government work in an orderly way. This contributed a large share to New Zealand politicians' growing indifference to constitutional convention. His dominating nature made him impatient of restraint. Because he believed he understood what New Zealanders wanted done he could be careless about how he did it. When I referred to a legal impediment to a proposed course he said, 'Mr Hensley, we keep a little room down there [pointing to the dome of the legislative chamber] to change the law'.

Yet if he was a tyrant, he was not a dictator. However much he over-whelmed disagreement by the force of his strong personality he was and always saw himself as a democrat. On one of the infrequent occasions when we had a wider discussion I urged the benefits of a four-year par-liamentary term. He firmly disagreed: 'I can have an idea while shaving, have it endorsed in Cabinet that morning, put it into the House in the afternoon and have it become law by midnight. While I have that power – and I should – it needs to be kept on a three-year leash.'

Policy was worked over in energetic detail but he had a genial fatalism about outcomes. Discussing an appointment, he commented that however much trouble he took a third of his choices turned out poorly. So worrying about the future was pointless. Whatever you did it was uncertain; the human nature in people could upset the most careful plans. Once when we were having dinner in Suva before returning to New Zealand he saw that I was thoughtful and said, 'I will give you some advice that Keith [Holyoake] gave me. Never worry about possibilities. Half of them never happen and the half that do are so changed that you wasted your time worrying about them in the first place. Since taking that advice I have never lost a night's sleep.' I could not give the same unqualified testimonial but it was a helpful thought.

His political views were those of his generation. He had returned from the war like many servicemen to start a career and marriage. Like many of them he felt that New Zealand in the 1950s was about as good as human society could be. His premiership was a painstaking but ultimately losing battle to keep it that way, in a changed world where New Zealand's prosperity could no longer be sustained by its traditional exports. So he was conservative in his instincts, conservative in his loyalty to the mixed economy and high degree of state control which had grown up in the 1930s and '40s, conservative ironically in his desire to preserve the main legacy of the first Labour Government. He claimed that his aim was to leave the country no worse than he found it but in the end could not manage even this modest goal.

He was no charmer – 'an unlovely man' was Julie's comment in her diary after welcoming him for the first time in Singapore. His own description was 'a counter-puncher'. To bystanders it often seemed that he got his retaliation in first but there was a certain truth to his view. If he sensed a threat or challenge he could be pugnacious. Like many politicians he made snap judgements about those he met and if he instinctively disliked someone he could be very rude. As the *Daily Telegraph* put it, with exquisite tact, 'the fairy of sycophancy' had failed to bless him in the cradle.

Politics especially administration was his whole life: 'I have been in government and in opposition, Mr Hensley, and believe me government is better'. It left a bleakness in his private life. He knew a lot about gardening but the practice had dried up. On weekends at Vogel House he would not be in the well-tended gardens but sitting inside with papers on the chairs around him. If there were no public engagements other weekends in Auckland would be spent in a comfortless hotel suite, again with only official papers for recreation.

This was a rather cheerless life for Dame Thea but she never complained. Coming home from the Commonwealth meeting in New Delhi she was told in Sydney of the death of her beloved father, but as Prime Minister's wife still had to go on to Wellington before joining her family in Auckland. Yet it was a successful marriage and stayed so, despite the pressures of political life. There were rumours of course to entertain Wellington dinner parties; I fended off all enquiries by saying firmly, 'That is a party matter'. 'Tam', as she was always called, helped organise his nomadic political life and her importance to him was made clear to everyone around him. But he was not a demonstrative man. At that Commonwealth meeting the Indian authorities closed off the Taj Mahal in Agra so that she, Hazel Hawke and Julie could walk through in peace, all three perhaps reflecting on what real husbandly devotion could manage.

Muldoon had the most formidable willpower of the ten prime ministers for whom I worked. When concentrating he radiated a field of force which made anyone tingle who stepped into it. His staff usually saw a more benign Muldoon. Like the birds which peck in the open jaws of basking crocodiles those around him enjoyed a certain immunity but however frequently they stepped into his office, no one did so without mentally tightening the belt and bracing the neurons.

Outside this circle many, especially urban liberals whom he disliked whatever their party allegiance, found him overbearing and dominating. His quickness of retort when attacked, the almost involuntary anger which rose in him, heightened this. On a rowdy Thursday evening in the House he destroyed the career of a former Labour Cabinet Minister, Colin Moyle, by referring to police suspicions of his homosexuality. Years later talking as we flew home from Japan and everyone around us slept in the darkened cabin, he told me that this was the action he most regretted in his life. The private and the public Muldoon could be very different persons. Tupuola Efi, a former Samoan prime minister, responded to a kindly letter from Muldoon on his election defeat by saying, 'I hope you will forgive my saying as a friend that I wish this side of your character was exhibited more frequently to public exposure'.

He himself saw his benevolence reserved, not for those who could look after themselves, but for the ordinary New Zealander, the little man. He said he received 25,000 letters a year and all were methodically answered. Sometimes he revealed a remarkable patience: 'Dear Mrs ——, Thank you for your letter about the trouble you are having with your husband. I am afraid there is little that the Government can do ...' Others revealed an unexpected talent for apology, as when at a press conference he compared someone's proposal to a belief in the tooth fairy and had to write to several children to say that he had not meant at all to express doubt about the tooth fairy. One or two flashed with the Muldoon counter-punch, as when a Texan wrote rather pompously to say that trouble over air traffic controllers meant he would not visit New Zealand. In two lines the Prime Minister commended his decision: 'Someone as arrogant as you would not like New Zealand'.

Urgings for more vigorous economic reform from his advisers were tested against the vulnerability of the ordinary citizen, and declined. He had an old-fashioned streak of populism: when told that controlled mortgage rates were weakening the banks, he said coldly that the banks could look after themselves but homeowners could not. Like many long-serving prime ministers he gradually left his party behind him, preferring to rely increasingly on his proclaimed 'feel' for the ordinary New Zealander. But cut off from ordinary life, high on the ninth floor of the Beehive, this instinct too began to atrophy and in the end became an excuse for self-justification. The economic stopbanks had to be raised higher and higher. The Treasury and Prime Minister's Department found their time increasingly devoted to racing about sticking fingers in an ever-growing number of leaks, drafting regulations, Orders in Council, prime-ministerial commands, in a losing battle to command the waters. Still the tide rose and New Zealand the way he (and many others) wanted it could no longer be preserved.

Like most prime ministers he became increasingly interested in foreign affairs, welcoming overseas travel as a break from the burdens at home. His approach was practical rather than intellectual. He never in my experience set out any world view more elaborate than that you should stick by your friends. He had little interest in the United Nations or the complexities of multilateral diplomacy and looked on international gatherings mainly as an opportunity to exchange views with fellow heads of government.

Diplomacy for him was a personal affair, as scrappy, instinctive and matter-of-fact as the man himself. As a result he distrusted his Foreign Ministry which he suspected, with some justification, of deploring his methods. He had no systematic view of New Zealand's interests abroad, indeed would have distrusted such an approach. The world was divided into people he respected and liked – Margaret Thatcher, Lee Kuan Yew, Takeo Fukuda, whose economic experience stretched back to attendance at the London Conference in 1932, George Shultz in the Reagan Administration, Emeka Anyaoku, who later became Commonwealth Secretary-General, and several Pacific leaders such as Ratu Mara of Fiji. Then there were the people he did not admire – Malcolm Fraser,

Jimmy Carter, Shridath Ramphal, Robert Mugabe and Walter Lini of Vanuatu.

Had he ever thought about it he would have agreed with Lord Curzon's view that there are only two requirements in foreign policy: to know what you want and then to make sure that others know it too. By that definition he excelled. His blunt opinions went round the world, ensuring that his press conferences were always well attended, but he was largely indifferent to any but the domestic reactions. An unkind colleague of mine called it 'foreign policy by blurt' and though Muldoon learnt some restraint he never acquired the habits of discretion desired by his diplomatic advisers. His reference to President Carter as 'a peanut farmer', an offhand comment which implied his suspicion of the President's foreign policies, naturally irritated Washington. Since Muldoon was looking forward to a White House visit some hasty repair work was required. Some time later he said to me plaintively, 'But I was right about Jimmy Carter, wasn't I?'

He famously said that foreign policy was trade. For a government often preoccupied with issues like sporting contacts with South Africa, nuclear ship visits, the South Pacific and Third World debt, this was barely a half-truth. It would have been more accurate to say that the Muldoon foreign policy was home policy travelling beyond the twelve-mile limit. His forays into external affairs were almost always in pursuit of domestic objectives. With congenial leaders he could make his points as comfortably as any diplomat, and his experience and clear mind meant he was listened to with respect. On unfamiliar ground, however, his impatience and aggressiveness made him less predictable.

His most useful contribution to New Zealand's diplomatic machinery was the dinner party. He was the first prime minister to entertain regularly, at his official home Vogel House. His dinners were carefully structured affairs with good wine and food, both of which he liked. He did not necessarily expect to enjoy himself, or that others would either; the important point was that things had to be done properly. The start could be rather constrained as people circled around one another, but if he was cheerful at the table the evenings could be very successful. Either way, however, they had to finish at ten when he liked to watch the television news upstairs. If I was there, one of my unstated tasks was to look at my watch a quarter of an hour beforehand, make noises of the 'Goodness gracious, is that the time?' sort and like our corgi in Singapore gently move the guests towards the door. As soon as everyone was out the door bolt would be shot home and the PM would dash upstairs. On gloomier occasions the guests could find themselves outside in the dark by nine-thirty.

He was not a subtle negotiator; he tended like a bull terrier to sink his teeth into a position and not let go. This showed when the time came to clinch a round of negotiations with the European Commission on sheepmeat. The Commission wished to impose a quota on New Zealand lamb exports to the Community. The GATT rules meant that a tariff reduction had to be offered to New Zealand in compensation. Any limit on our shipments was unwelcome but for the time being the point was academic since actual exports were well within the proposed quota. On the other hand reducing the tariff would substantially increase returns to the farmer.

Negotiations rose up the chain to the point where the Agricultural Commissioner from Brussels, Finn Gundelach, came to settle a deal. The two delegations met all day in the Cabinet Committee room. After lengthy discussions, the point was reached where we could all see the outline of an agreement: we would accept a revised quota and they would almost halve the tariff to 10 per cent. Everyone was getting their papers together when the PM suddenly said 8 per cent and could not be moved. The subsequent dinner at Vogel House was a chilly affair, Gundelach went home furious, and after a decent interval we accepted the 10 per cent.

Similar memories hovered around the first official visit I made with him to Japan and Korea in April 1981. In his foreign-policy-by-blurt days he had announced that the Japanese would be excluded from our fishing grounds unless they provided better access for our beef. This certainly gained the attention of the Japanese but it also irritated them and the result was a draw. Now his aim was more modest. Given the steady growth in New Zealand's sovereign borrowing, he hoped to secure easier access to Japan's capital markets. To add weight he brought with him his Deputy, Duncan MacIntyre, and no less than three heads of departments. He made the rounds of senior ministers explaining why our shaky economy needed further forbearance and spent part of an afternoon with Prime Minister Suzuki in his official residence, a strikingly squat and dark house built after the 1923 earthquake. The Japanese were amiable but cautious; they were not about to agree to any hasty relaxation of their controls.

After that it was a round of sightseeing. The Prime Minister travelled in a car, the rest of us in a bus which, as always happens, led a group of middle-aged departmental heads to behave like schoolboys on an outing. We drove to the Toshogu Shrine which housed a sacred white horse. The previous horse, a gift from New Zealand, had died what from the Chief Priest elliptically called 'an unfortunate accident' and we were there to present a replacement. The new incumbent was still in quarantine so we handed over a photograph, inspected the horse's sacred home and drove on to the Ise Peninsula. There we toured ancient temples and the pearl fishery and returned to Tokyo on the pleasantly named Kinki Nippon Railway. The visit at least achieved a limited allocation of samurai bonds; in Korea, though the sightseeing was just as agreeable, the government was impervious to urgings for greater market access.

The following month brought the decisive point in what proved to be one of the major achievements of his government – the free trade (CER) agreement with Australia. Negotiations had been under way for well over a year, pushed on by the Australian Trade Minister, Doug Anthony, and his New Zealand counterpart, Hugh Templeton. The Australians, nervous about the future of their neighbour's economy, took the lead; New Zealand was more cautious, worried about the possible effects on its protected industries. A joint committee of permanent heads met alternately in Canberra and Wellington to do the spadework.

Muldoon made it clear that he was not bound by this. His instructions to Bernard Galvin, now Secretary to the Treasury, and me were that he was happy for officials to explore and map the outlines of a possible agreement but that he remained uncommitted. While the meetings and detailed discussions went on back and forth across the Tasman he kept in careful touch with the Manufacturers Federation and with leaders of business. His concerns were not eased by his justified suspicion that any free-trade agreement would undermine the highly protected economy he had inherited. In my own early days of blurt I was unwise enough in a discussion to urge that this was a longer-term advantage of CER, a gaffe hastily covered over by my colleagues.

Now we had reached a fork in the road; a decision had to be made. Anthony came over in May for two days of talks to review progress. Fortunately Muldoon respected him and the two got on well. This in no way softened the PM who spent some time outlining the difficulties for New Zealand of 'eventual free trade'. When Anthony complained about Wellington's recent decision to *raise* the tariff on wine, saying that there had been a strong reaction at home, the PM said blandly that his government got letters like that too. But he came off the fence. That evening, tidying the papers in his office, he said to me in a phrase that was the nearest he came to enthusiasm, 'I think we can bring this together'. There was still a year of negotiations ahead, and some difficult issues to resolve (like import licensing and export incentives), but with his backing it was never likely that the effort would fail.

Another of the remaining issues was whether the Australian state governments would extend to New Zealand the same preference on government purchases which they gave themselves. Canberra said it was powerless to help and so immediately after these talks Lance Adams-Schneider and I set off to make the rounds of the state capitals. The premiers, wary of giving up their powers, tended to feel that CER was the Federal Government's business and no particular concern of theirs. We returned with ambiguous results and Cabinet was not happy, taking the view that if the agreement could not deliver trade which was directly under governmental control New Zealand manufacturers would have little confidence about the rest.

So a few months later Hugh Templeton and I set off on another round. This time the outcome was more promising: Victoria and New South Wales (much the most important) were still reluctant, but Tasmania and Western Australia agreed on the spot. Queensland's Joh Bjelke-Petersen was hard to pin down – 'Don't you worry about that' – but at least undertook to take a paper to his Cabinet, as did South Australia's Premier, David Tonkin. Whether Dr Tonkin remembered is another matter. He gave us lunch in the panelled oval library of an old Adelaide house and asked me what South Australian wine I would like. I knew of only one, Grange Hermitage. We drank a bottle of the 1971 and then the 1974, after which I rather lost track. In mid-afternoon the Premier remembered that he was supposed to be meeting the Federal Treasurer, John Howard. A message was despatched summoning him to the library and when he peeped cautiously round the door he was hailed by us all with shouts of welcome. We emerged in the late afternoon from the merriest government lunch I ever attended but sadly Tonkin proved a better host than politician, losing the next election.

The Springbok rugby tour of that year was the most painful issue the country had grappled with for decades. In form it was a foreign policy matter, though the undoubted damage it did to New Zealand's international reputation proved to be temporary. It was in fact a domestic dispute, about morality and the law, about how New Zealanders defined themselves and their society, and it divided the country into two bitterly opposed halves.

Like all serious quarrels it had been building for years as a growing disapproval of the apartheid regime in South Africa tangled with the longing of a rugby-playing population to play the only other country where rugby was king. In 1973 Norman Kirk had gone back on earlier undertakings and banned a projected Springbok tour. Two years later Muldoon pledged in the election campaign to allow sporting bodies freedom of choice. He insisted on this when all Commonwealth Governments undertook in the Gleneagles Agreement to 'take every practical step to discourage sporting contacts'. Voluntary restraint worked in New Zealand for four years until the Rugby Union invited the Springbok team for a mid-year tour in 1981.

The Government wrote to express its disapproval; Parliament passed a unanimous resolution opposing the tour. None of this had any effect on the elderly executive of the Rugby Union. I went to the house of the widowed chairman, Ces Blazey, a lonely old man who held stubbornly to the view that politics were not his business. When I brought the PM the Union's final word he stared down at his desk for some time and then said gloomily, 'I see nothing but trouble in all this, nothing but trouble'. He decided to make a last effort, doing so on television rather than behind closed doors so that there could be no subsequent misunderstanding. It was, though, a curiously ambivalent speech, reflecting perhaps his own feelings as well as the fact that polls showed the country to be almost evenly divided, with a slight majority opposed to the tour. He asked the Union to consider carefully the impact on the country but he also talked of the South African war graves alongside New Zealanders in Italy and said sternly that it would be cowardice to back down in the face of threats. With that, and just as the tour began, he departed on a tour of Europe and North America, only partly explained by the need to attend the wedding of the Prince and Princess of Wales.

The first games saw serious clashes with the police as the demonstrations became an overt effort to stop the tour and the organisers promised, with a little understatement, to 'go to the edge of the law'. Football fields were ringed with security fences and even rows of shipping containers and both police and protesters worked hard on their tactics. Matters came to a head at the game in Hamilton on 25 July when in a carefully planned move a column of protesters broke through the fence at a prearranged point and 400 of them led by Father Terry Dibble occupied the ground just before kick-off. Arrest procedures for the trespassers were too slow as more poured into the terraces and anger rose in the 30,000 crowd. When someone of uncertain mental health stole a plane and was reported to be on his way to the ground the Police Commissioner, Bob Walton, called off the game.

Immediately afterwards, with one eye still on the television screen, I telephoned the PM in Washington to describe the events, ending with the comment that I thought the country owed a considerable debt to Walton for a brave decision that had probably averted bloodshed. In the ensuing silence the temperature on the line fell to cryogenic levels: 'You do, do you', said the PM, 'well I don't'. He asked me to impress on Walton what was at stake – it could lead to an immediate general election – and to ensure that he took the time to consult his senior officers and to exercise a mature judgement before concluding that the police were incapable of maintaining order.

Early the next afternoon, a Sunday, we met in the Acting Prime Minister's office and later that evening at his house. Walton was still troubled: he had had an hour's discussion with Blazey of the Rugby Union, who was unmoved. The Commissioner had 'grave doubts' about future matches. If the tour went on general policing would be virtually non-existent. The use of greater force was technically simple but would the Government accept the consequences? MacIntyre, who had been one of the youngest brigadiers in the war, was calm and told him to take all the time he needed to make up his mind. Late at night I suggested to the Acting PM that he should brief Muldoon. I dialled the number for him and then handed it across the desk when it was ringing. A newly awakened and grumpy PM answered, whereupon MacIntyre said, 'Gerald would like to have a word with you', and handed the phone back. After I had reported on the day's inconclusive steps he asked me to issue a curious press statement, saying that he had seriously considered returning home but he was now satisfied that Ministers could do all that was required and 'I propose to continue with my programme'.

The next day a more considered response began to evolve as MacIntyre issued a statement saying that the issue was no longer the merits of the tour but what was permissible in a democratic society. To ease the strain on the police the Defence Force was instructed to provide logistic support and to help get 700 police to the next game, at New Plymouth. A group of Ministers met in the early evening to hear – and reject – a rather hopeful proposal to wind up the tour; meanwhile Father Dibble was threatening self-immolation if it proceeded.

A day later the same group sat down in the Cabinet Committee room with a large group of trade unionists and concerned churchmen, led by Jim Knox, President of the Federation of Labour. Jim delivered one of his baffling remarks, saying that it was wrong to say the Government could not let the protesters win: 'it was the responsibility of the Government to govern in the interests of all the people'. Pat Kelly, an Irish Marxist, said it was part of our British heritage to resort to illegal action on a moral issue. The Reverend Mr Walpole said he felt bad about breaking the law but decided he had to because the country was suffering internationally. Everyone called for a roundtable of all the parties to get the tour called off but despite an invitation from Ministers no one was prepared to urge that protesters stay off the grounds.

Attitudes were hardening, in the country as well as in the Ministry. After Hamilton there was a significant shift; a slight majority as reflected in the polls now disapproved less of the tour than of attempts to halt it by force. The country was taken aback by the violence that had been loosed; playing football with white South Africans might be wrong but it was not illegal. The Prime Minister, now back home, promised to convene a meeting immediately after the tour to discuss what lessons could be learnt. When urged to ensure a good representation of 'the very large middle ground concerned about the tour', he asked about the very large middle ground attending the matches. 'They too have their views and I am in the middle of it.' He liked the idea of a domestic Gleneagles signed by all New Zealand sports bodies, because it preserved the voluntary principle, but in the excited atmosphere it was not practicable.

The protest movement was perhaps sobered by the results of its own success. The games and the accompanying clashes went on but only the match at Timaru was cancelled, on police advice. The atmosphere was tense before the second test in Wellington. Touring the police dispositions with Commissioner Walton that morning was like visiting the trenches before a battle. However, no serious effort was made to halt another game. Only at the final test in Auckland did history repeat itself, predictably as farce, when Marx Jones stole a plane, buzzed the packed stands at Eden Park and flour-bombed the scrum. I telephoned the PM to relay a series of bulletins, each more bizarre than the last. Then after eight weeks of what felt like a siege, the tour was over and the country was left to lick its wounds.

The Prime Minister, however, was now in battle order, hunched down where his advisers could no longer reach him, following his own internal radar. He was angry because he felt he had been humiliated by the Commonwealth Secretary-General's decision, as the tour got under way, to move the meeting of Commonwealth Finance Ministers – one of his favourite gatherings which he was looking forward to chairing – from Auckland to Nassau in the Bahamas. He was out to make trouble. By ill-fortune the Commonwealth heads of government were meeting in Melbourne at the end of September and he began to drop hints that he was preparing files (never seen by me) on the domestic record of some of his Commonwealth critics.

Julie and I had been enjoying a ten-day break travelling around the country with Lee Kuan Yew and Mrs Lee. The Singapore Prime Minister came to Melbourne with us on the Air Force Boeing together with Lord Carrington, the British Foreign Secretary, who had been sent by Mrs Thatcher to have a tactful word with her friend. He had no more success than anyone else. When I joined the plane in Christchurch, after the delights of tramping through the snow on Mount Cook, the mood was sombre and the PM uncommunicative.

As soon as we reached the hotel in Melbourne he savaged the unfortunate High Commissioner (his own appointment) for a confusion over the site of his opening press conference. Disregarding convention he upstaged the Secretary-General, who was traditionally the first to meet the press, and thereafter his conferences were so frequent that he spoke more in public than he did to his fellow heads of government. In this combative mood and with his instinct for publicity he controlled the headlines throughout the conference. An Indian newspaper concluded that the 'Muldoon sideshow' proved more interesting to the media than the meeting itself.

Since the Australian Prime Minister, Malcolm Fraser, was chairing the gathering the main story became a kind of cartoon contest between the lofty, rather ponderous Fraser and the stumpy, quick-witted Muldoon. The centrepiece of the mid-conference retreat in Canberra was to be a 'Melbourne Declaration on World Poverty', but before Fraser could release it Muldoon had dismissed it in a speech to the National Press Club as 'a collection of pious platitudes'. Regrettably it was, and that was the story which ran all day: 'Muldoon Wrecks Fraser's Coup'.

Fraser had hoped to avoid his conference being dominated by the Springbok tour and a wrangle over the Gleneagles Agreement. On the evening he arrived Muldoon had a half-hour meeting with him. The dislike between the two men made the conversation stiff. Fraser said that he had been talking to other heads of government and they were not going to make a fuss over Gleneagles. Muldoon accepted that but 'our people want to know what it means'. Fraser must have been dismayed; Muldoon was signalling that for him this meeting was going to be about the meaning of Gleneagles.

What Fraser could hardly have foreseen was that most of the discussion would be in public. Muldoon talked frequently and aggressively to the press but, isolated in the Commonwealth, he talked much more mildly in the meeting itself. He insisted though that there was a fundamental misunderstanding about the Agreement which he had helped to draft. Everyone had undertaken to *discourage* sporting contacts 'by means consistent with their laws'. New Zealand was a free country and where there is freedom of choice 'some people make the wrong choice'.

Most of his hearers had difficulty accepting that New Zealand could not have refused visas to the Springboks. Among others Mugabe of Zimbabwe was critical, leading Muldoon to dismiss his views publicly as coming from someone 'just out of the bush'. There was uproar and the PM explained to the meeting in a polite but none too convincing retraction that after years as a guerrilla Mugabe perhaps did not see a game of football as especially important. The Commonwealth's own crystal ball was just as clouded: the Melbourne communiqué gave warm praise to Mugabe's government which 'had earned the respect of the world community and fully justified the trust placed in it by the Commonwealth'.

The general assumption was that he was addressing the New Zealand electorate (an election was due in two months' time) rather than the Commonwealth. There was no doubt an element of truth in this but it was not clear to me or to others that his 'antics' (a favourite word with reporters) went down well at home. If anything they may have unsettled that part of his political base which disapproved of violent protest but liked New Zealand to look respectable. His personality was always aggressive when he felt himself on the defensive. Now there was a lasting resentment as well. He was deeply angered over what he saw as the 'insult' given to him by the shift of the Finance Ministers' meeting. At bottom I think this was the mainspring of his behaviour.

He was certainly difficult to get through to, or even to live with, over these nine days. No one wished to incur the shelling which the luckless High Commissioner had endured; members of the delegation moved about their tasks as unobtrusively as possible. As an experiment we had brought a couple of walkie-talkies with us to keep everyone in better contact with the PM's movements. Towards the end, when the PM was away from the meeting for a time, several of us were relaxing in the delegation office, with feet on desks and plastic cups of beer in hand. The walkie-talkie stood upright on a table of its own. Suddenly like a Greek oracle prophesying trouble it spoke. 'The Prime Minister', it said in the voice of Inspector Jock Munro, the PM's bodyguard, 'is now thirty yards away.' Feet vanished from desks and cups from sight and everyone was sitting at their desks when the PM entered, as if waiting for the headmaster.

He did not speak, merely beckoned me outside. He had decided, for no pressing reason that I could think of, to leave the conference a few hours early and wanted me to draft a letter to leave behind as a contribution to the communiqué. Sitting behind him at the morning session I scribbled some thoughts which he toughened up. The resulting letter said that New Zealand would continue to carry out its obligations under the reaffirmed Gleneagles Agreement, but would withdraw if there were any more boycotts of its sportsmen – meaning at the forthcoming Commonwealth Games in Brisbane.

Then, as everyone was preparing to leave for the airport, he asked me to take the letter to Fraser as chairman. Fraser's exasperation boiled over. He said angrily, 'I'm not going to accept this'. I argued, with more conviction than I felt, that he was obliged to convey its contents to the meeting. In the end he read it out; the meeting then rejected it as being out of order at that stage. By that time the New Zealand delegation was flying home, in glum silence.

The election campaign a few weeks later was always going to be close. After six years Muldoon's popularity had waned and the economic outlook was uncertain. He himself seemed pessimistic. I had gone on leave to clean up the garden – government was virtually suspended and it was prudent to be out of the Beehive – but he clearly implied to me, a night or two before the vote, that he did not expect to win. Indeed, it might have been better for the country if he had not. In the end a handful of votes in Taupo gave him a one-seat majority. Watching him on television I could see him becoming progressively more relieved and progressively more tight as the results came in. I went to the phone to suggest that he might become less available to the cameras but his press secretary, now Brian Lockstone, had anticipated this. Though the television commentators kept up a hopeful refrain, 'We will be crossing to the Prime Minister shortly', it was as well for the public proprieties that he was not seen again that night.

The most pressing task after the election was economic: wages and prices were chasing each other in a spiral which was threatening to get out of control. Inflation was now in the high teens. The trade union leadership could not think of any better response than the traditional insistence that wages be allowed to catch up. This was not only fruitless but damaging to the interests of everyone. However, as the guardian of a highly protected economy, the Government was equally short of effective responses. Muldoon too thought only within the traditional framework; more radical answers were only just emerging in Britain and the United States and in any case they were incompatible with the mixed and regulated economy he was trying to preserve.

This left some form of voluntary restraint as the best hope and here Muldoon did have a new idea. For over a year talks had been going on between the employers, unions and government on the possibility of a trade-off between wages and taxes. The proposal was that the Government would reduce taxes on the lower paid in return for an equivalent reduction in claims at the annual wage round. The employers had no difficulty with this but the Federation of Labour wanted full compensation for inflation, which meant a much larger tax cut than the Government could contemplate. The talks straggled on, with better progress when we met at official level, but the FOL could not overcome its distrust of anything which suggested a 'wage path'. Jim Knox was not a flexible man and felt safer with the soapbox oratory of the past. Muldoon did not help. Jim's harrumphing brought out in him an apparently irresistible urge to tease. The meetings slipped by in wrangling between the two until the Budget and the start of the wage round overtook them.

By the beginning of 1982 the situation had worsened. Everyone agreed that a resumption of the wage–tax talks was urgent and there was a growing hope that some sort of tripartite wage-fixing mechanism might grow out of them. In the meantime the Government was struggling to get its own finances under better control. The Prime Minister (who was also the Finance Minister) decreed a cut of 3 per cent in all departmental spending. In a highly inflationary climate this was something of a challenge, particularly for a small department like my own whose spending was almost entirely on salaries. However, the Prime Minister's own department could hardly plead hardship. We could do without the tea lady – most people made their own tea or coffee whenever they wished – and though the saving was small when added to others it put us over the top. Another position was found for Millie Cottam at the National Library but this assault on one of the sacred institutions of bureaucracy caught the interest of the media. Cartoonists went to work, Millie gave interviews, and the PM was delighted with the publicity it provided for his savings campaign.

A side effect, though, was to revive the FOL's fears that any tax cut would be offset by cuts in government services, what was called the 'social wage'. A working party within the tripartite talks had made considerable technical progress in equating various levels of tax relief for the lower paid with levels of restraint in the wage round later in the year. The PM also gave an undertaking in writing that social services would not be affected. In the end the unions could not overcome their suspicion of the unknown and Ken Douglas, the intelligent Secretary of the FOL, told us that even if the trade-off were accepted he was doubtful the Federation could deliver it. This was never put to the test; in late May the FOL Conference rejected the proposal by an overwhelming majority. The result was telephoned to me in the early evening. The PM was still there and I went upstairs to give him the figures. His mild response was unexpected: 'You know, Mr Hensley, after two years of work you would have thought we might have got more votes than that'.

There was now no Government wages policy. In January I had given the PM a note which looked at other possibilities if no agreement could be reached, including a statutory guideline, centralised indexation or a wage freeze. Nonetheless no work had been done on any of these notions and I was alarmed three or so weeks after the FOL vote when the PM told me he had decided on a wage freeze and was calling a Cabinet meeting to approve it. I got hold of Bernard Galvin and we hastily drafted a paper setting out all disadvantages of a freeze, emphasising that the effect was always temporary and that none had held more than a hundred days. When I took it to the PM, he snapped, 'I know what you're going to say and I don't agree'. Asked to read it anyhow, he did so rapidly and then passed it back, saying that he still did not agree.

He must, however, have read it more carefully than appeared. Three months after, in late September, he said to me with suspicious mildness, 'Do you know what day it is?' I could attach no special significance to the date but grasped that I was being teased. It was a hundred days since the freeze, which was still watertight and indeed remained so for the lengthy period it remained in force. It delivered the short-term goals the PM wanted: inflation came down from 17 per cent to less than 2 per cent, and average disposable income at the end of 1983 was well above the levels recorded in mid-1982. This did not alter the fact that the longer the freeze continued the greater the cumulative distortions and the more difficult the challenge of dismounting from the tiger.

So the focus shifted to what form of wage-fixing should follow the freeze. There was a general disinclination to go back to the old disorder but only vague ideas on what might replace it. After the freeze had been in place for a year a Long-Term Wage Reform Committee was established, chaired by the Secretary of the Treasury, with the Secretary of Labour and me on the government side, and representatives of the unions and employers, to seek agreement on a new system. Progress was as ever like wading through treacle but by the end of the year the outline of a new system had emerged. Before the start of the annual wage round tripartite consultations would be held to decide what the economy could bear, and if necessary set a guideline for the level of settlements. Despite the implications for the existing union structure, the FOL had also come some way towards acceptance of industry or enterprise bargaining. This was probably the best that could be hoped for within the current economic framework. The tripartite formula existed in theory for two years but it was never seriously implemented and was swept away by the next Government.

In 1982 the Prime Minister had more success with his foreign policy, although here he was reacting to events. At the beginning of April Argentina invaded and occupied the Falkland Islands. The PM acted at once, even before Britain had formally declared war, and Cabinet decided to expel the newly arrived Argentine ambassador and withdraw the landing rights of its airline. The ambassador was summoned to the PM's office followed by a surge of cameras and reporters who camped outside. It was a solemn occasion. Muldoon launched into his introduction: 'Ambassador, I would not like you to think that what I am about to say is in any way a reflection on you personally . . .' He was halted by anxious cries from the ambassador who, it became apparent, could not understand English. A Spanish interpreter was hastily sought from the Foreign Ministry. She took twenty minutes to arrive. We sat there in awkward silence, watching the sun move over the carpet, from time to time exchanging sickly smiles with the ambassador. The sound of the media crush on the other side of the double doors came intermittently like the roaring of surf. Finally the interpreter was ushered in, a little breathless. We all leant forward and the PM began again, 'Ambassador, I would not like you to think . . .'

A month later I happened to be on the phone to our High Commission in London when they relayed the news that HMS *Sheffield*, struck by Exocet missiles, was on fire and sinking. I told the PM, who immediately decided to offer a New Zealand frigate, not as a replacement but to join the Royal Navy squadron patrolling in the Gulf and thus free a British ship for redeployment to the Falklands. Both decisions, at the time and since, have been decried as an embarrassingly knee-jerk reaction when the Mother Country called. This is plausible. In fact the Mother Country had not called but Muldoon was of the generation whose closest sympathies were with Britain. There was more to it than that however. His instinct was that you stood with your friends. Margaret Thatcher was one and the generals in Buenos Aires were not, and he was never unmindful of the fact that New Zealand needed the firm support of Britain in its annual battles with the European Community over access for butter and cheese. His actions were widely praised in Britain; months later when crossing the Atlantic on British Airways the pilot announced, 'I think you might all like to know that today we have the Prime Minister of New Zealand, Robert Muldoon, with us' and the entire cabin burst into applause. More lasting was the negotiating coin that British Ministers and officials continued to spend on our interests in Brussels.

Towards the end of July the Mother Country, in the form of the Judicial Committee of the Privy Council, came up with a startling conclusion of its own. The judges decided that two New Zealand statutes from 1923 and 1928 if read together meant that everyone born in Samoa after 1924 was a New Zealand citizen. At a stroke almost all the citizens of one independent state had become citizens of another. This seemed (especially to the New Zealand Court of Appeal which was reversed) a rather frivolous decision. The Parliaments which had passed the two laws had clearly intended no such thing; indeed it would have been contrary to the League of Nations mandate under which New Zealand then governed Samoa. Nonetheless it had now been declared to be the law. The PM handed me the cables from London and said rather wearily, 'See what you can do'.

I convened a group of knowledgeable people from the relevant departments and we set to work in a room on the top floor of the Beehive where the wind played like a bassoon round the metal windows. For several days we worked through the international precedents and the possible options. None of them was especially attractive, bearing out Muldoon's dictum that the task for governments was always to choose the lesser evil. The Samoan Prime Minister suggested it might be better to do nothing and see what developed, but this was unacceptable to both sides of the New Zealand Parliament. Different types of passport would have created two levels of citizenship. In the end we recommended a rough but simple form of justice: all Samoans who were in New Zealand at the time of the Privy Council's decision, whether legally or as over-stayers, would become citizens; all future arrivals would have to meet the established immigration rules. When the PM read the report his only comment was, 'I wondered how you were going to get out of this'.

He talked it over with the Samoan Prime Minister, who was in New Zealand. He had no personal objection but went home to consult his Cabinet. The Samoan Government preferred to stay out of the matter but New Zealand was equally reluctant to be seen to impose a solution. In the end it was decided to embody the new arrangements in a protocol to the existing Treaty of Friendship between the two countries, and the Attorney-General, Jim McLay, and David Lange for the Opposition secured approval for this in a visit to Apia.

There were one or two demonstrations outside the Beehive but so small as to signify fairly wide acceptance of the new arrangements. Economic pressures and the rising political temperature were bringing more frequent and larger protests to the grounds of Parliament Buildings.

Muffled chants and megaphone cries floated into the office and each week I could check the Government's standing by looking down to see what banners were in the forecourt below. The demonstrators remained if not good-tempered certainly peaceable but they highlighted the fact that the Beehive containing the entire Cabinet had no security and could be freely entered by anyone willing to open the door.

I raised it with the Prime Minister, pointing out that an exhibitionist suicide who had blown himself up at the Wanganui Computer Centre would have caused more of a bang, so to speak, by doing so in the lobby of the Beehive. Muldoon dismissed this, but a few days later I walked in through the basement, went up nine floors to his office and on an impulse walked through the rarely used double doors to confront him. He looked up, startled, as I pointed out that not a single person had seen me until I appeared in his office. Now I had his attention and could suggest some simple safeguards. He shied at the thought even of bag searches, claiming that the wives of his colleagues would not put up with them. I expressed scepticism and he said, 'Mr Hensley, you should know that there are the wives of Ministers and there are Ministers' Wives'. In the end we settled for a few restrictions on entry to the basement. He was indifferent to security, claiming on another occasion that he had never been frightened since the war. He drove himself to and from work each day and on one occasion when his ageing car broke down he waited on the side of the road for some time.

Another sign that the ship of state was weakening was the growing number of leaks, all politically inspired. Any controversial issue was likely to turn up in public, often selectively edited (Muldoon's practice with these last was immediately to release the whole document, however sensitive). It got to the point where I told a member of the Advisory Group drafting a paper on the environment to do so as if for the front page of the morning paper. Sure enough it turned up a week or two later, but on the front page of the evening paper. Whatever the rights and wrongs of a particular issue, public debate could not be allowed to be manipulated in this way, or the civil service to take part in it.

At the PM's request I undertook a number of investigations into serious leaks. No leaker was ever caught; the best hope was that a police detective walking the corridors and interviewing those with access to a particular document might frighten once and future leakers. Once we got close enough to identify the department, and once in a surprising turn I found myself talking to the actual culprit. I entered the PM's office to find him reading a well-connected weekly newsletter and looking a little pale. He said he thought there had been a Budget leak and after reading the paragraph I agreed. At that time Budgets were prepared in high secrecy, advance knowledge could be very profitable and a leak was a resignation matter for the Minister concerned. He asked me to look into it at once. There were no obvious leads and after I had made an initial report he suggested it was pointless to continue. In a flash of understanding I realised that I was talking to the leaker. Now it was my turn to tease. I kept it up for a couple more days, reporting that I had narrowed the field down to the upper floors of the Beehive while the PM continued to urge that it was a waste of my time.

At the turn of the year the country was threatened with a more serious fallout. At Christmas the PM, as a part of his invariable routine, would retire for three weeks to his beach house at Hatfields, near Auckland, and I would go south to Akaroa. All would be blissfully quiet for ten days until the PM became bored. At first the local policeman would be sent round with a message and I would ring Hatfields from the station, until my father-in-law reluctantly installed a phone. Muldoon would enquire whether I had read some article in the Auckland morning paper and would be disappointed when I reminded him, as I did every year, that the paper did not reach a small fishing town on Banks Peninsula. This was just an initial offering: if the boredom continued the phone calls would come every day on a variety of subjects until I offered to go back to Wellington.

In January 1983, however, there was an emergency. A Soviet satellite, Cosmos 1402, was nearing the end of its life. A malfunction meant that the small nuclear reactor which powered it had not been boosted into a higher orbit but would enter the atmosphere with the other pieces. A few years earlier a similar reactor had strewn a trail of radioactive debris across part of northern Canada. Since the decaying orbit of the satellite passed over New Zealand roughly once a day, the PM was understandably worried about public fears.

I went back to Wellington, invented something called the Satellite Re-Entry Committee and as information became available began issuing bulletins in its name. In a quiet time it attracted considerable media attention and I had to convene a real committee so that pictures could be taken of it hard at work. It was not until the end of January that, with the help of intelligence sources, we could track its last orbits. The news was about as bad as it could be. I rang the PM at Hatfields to say that it looked as if the final orbit would arrive over Invercargill, track up the East Coast of the South Island, pass up the middle of the North Island and, if it got that far, exit from the Bay of Plenty. He listened in silence and then said, 'I'll bet it passes over every marginal seat on the way'. We alerted Civil Defence and issued warnings about staying away from any space debris. However, after traversing the length of the country the satellite managed to stagger on and collapse into the Indian Ocean. The Satellite Re-Entry Committee disappeared with it.

In March the Australian Government changed and Bob Hawke became Prime Minister. A few days before the election my counterpart in Canberra, Sir Geoffrey Yeend, rang to say that if defeated Malcolm Fraser intended to step down as party leader and retire from Parliament. I passed this unsurprising news to Muldoon who seemed taken aback. 'Will he? Will he?' he kept saying, as if he could hardly credit that anyone would do such things. I felt a premonitory chill; clearly we were going to have difficulties when the time came here.

The future cast another shadow in that month. My phone rang in the middle of the night: the new Australian Government had decided to devalue its dollar. I drove out to Vogel House, thinking that this was an excellent opportunity to make a much larger adjustment to our over-valued currency. In the darkened courtyard outside the front door I met Bernard Galvin and we had a whispered consultation. 'How much do you think?' he said. My wet finger had suggested 15 per cent; he with more knowledge had settled on the same figure. The door opened and we went inside.

It quickly became clear that the PM would not contemplate a devalu-ation of this size, was reluctant indeed to contemplate any devaluation at all. He regarded devaluation, not as one of the tools of economic management, but as a victory for speculators and an admission of weak-ness by him. The discussion went on into the small hours as Bernard and I searched for fresh angles to persuade him. In the end he agreed to take a paper to Cabinet the next morning but would not commit himself to a figure.

A paper hastily drafted setting out the pros and cons of a devaluation caused the worst falling-out the PM and I ever had. Because time was so short before Ministers met I circulated the paper to them as soon as it was ready. Muldoon was furious: didn't I know the Cabinet rule that only he had the authority to do so. I did, but thought it sensible that Ministers should have as long as possible to read and digest the contents. He saw an infringement of his control of information, and on an issue where he knew his advisers disagreed with him. He emerged with Cabinet having agreed to the smallest possible devaluation – 6 per cent. Bernard put his head in his hands: 'The life of a permanent head', he said, 'is one of rejection and dejection'.

Three months later Muldoon flew to Canberra to meet the new Government. He lunched at the National Press Club, where he was always comfortable, and made a thoughtful speech on transtasman relations. He saw a growing integration spurred on by external events but no union: 'I rarely make predictions but I predict absolutely . . . no New Zealand Prime Minister will go to Premiers' meetings as the Premier of the state of New Zealand'. Cheered by their hospitality he went on his rounds, to see the Deputy Prime Minister and then the Treasurer, Paul Keating. On our way to Keating's office I glanced at my watch and realised that we were about to strike the after-lunch downturn.

Even so I was unprepared for the row which ensued. Things started calmly enough as the two Finance Ministers exchanged polite comments about the first six months of CER, but then Keating complained that Australian investment proposals were not getting fair treatment in New Zealand. Suddenly, like two Irish street-fighters in a bar, it was all on. They shouted at each other, getting hotter by the minute, and when the Australian Treasury Secretary, John Stone, or I tried a soothing comment, they both turned on us, saying 'You keep out of this'.

The discussion with Bob Hawke was much calmer, calmer indeed than those with his predecessor. Both Hawke and Muldoon were practical managers, and neither much interested in doctrine, though in some respects the New Zealand PM was at least as much to the left. This was certainly so on Pacific affairs in which Muldoon had always taken a deep interest. His main aim at this meeting was to persuade Hawke to soften Australia's dislike of the Pacific Forum Line, a government-funded shipping service which linked the small island states. He was unsuccessful and this led to a distinct cooling in their relationship at the next meeting of the South Pacific Forum.

The South Pacific was one of Muldoon's enduring interests. Perhaps it was because he had spent part of his war service there, perhaps because he felt an obligation to help the small states overcome the handicaps of size and isolation. At any rate he was a strong supporter of the Forum, which brought together the heads of government of all the independent island states, together with Australia and New Zealand, and never missed an annual meeting. On these occasions a different Muldoon appeared. His briskness and impatience were left behind in New Zealand and instead he became a benign Pacific leader. Each year he took pleasure in briefing his delegation on the 'Pacific way', solemnly advising them that pushing for decisions was not the way business was done. 'We will have a bit of a chat about things', he liked to say, and though he joked about the restful silences which marked Forum discussions, he was happy to sit there while the issues were slowly talked through.

The first I went to, in the newly independent Kiribati in July of 1980, was in some ways the last of the traditional, easy-going Forums. We lived on the naval survey ship *Monowai*, anchored in the Tarawa lagoon. On the first afternoon a swim was arranged from an islet in the lagoon. The PM attired in capacious swimming-shorts seated himself under a palm tree, his globular form overshadowed by an enormous straw sombrero at least three feet across which made him look irresistibly like the Parsee man. Sessions of the Forum were held in an open-sided meeting-house, cooled by the trade wind blowing across the atoll. Chickens wandered in and out, undisturbed by the undemanding discussion about shipping, air services and the possible dumping of nuclear waste.

The following year the leaders gathered in Vila, capital of the new state of Vanuatu which had at last freed itself from the awkward rule of a dual British and French condominium. These experiences changed the tone. Father Walter Lini, the new Prime Minister, pressed hard for action on New Caledonia and brought forward resolutions in UN-style language. The moderate majority was uncomfortable with this and in the end decided only to send Ratu Mara of Fiji to Paris 'in a spirit of helpfulness rather than antagonism'. Muldoon too disliked the UN jargon and had taken one of his instinctive dislikes to Lini; on one occasion Muldoon spread a New Zealand newspaper on the table and pored over it while Lini was speaking.

As a slight justification for this calculated rudeness, we were still in the middle of the Springbok tour and he was keen to see every scrap of news. I had brought with me a secure phone, a rather primitive machine called the Brahms which had only one channel; after speaking a handle had to be pushed to allow the other person to speak. This was a challenge for politicians. On the way home we set it up in a house on Norfolk Island, just across from Bishop Patteson's lovely mid-Victorian mission church. The Brahms handle variations baffled Muldoon until I leant forward and pushed the handle whenever he paused. At the other end the Acting Prime Minister was less well served and as the jerky briefing proceeded the PM noted with unjustified pride, 'I don't think MacIntyre has any idea how to work this thing'.

At Rotorua in August 1982 the rising temperature in New Zealand over the Treaty of Waitangi also gave a slight edge to proceedings. At the opening Sunday church service, in St Faith's at Ohinemutu ('the girl cut off from the world') a handful of protesters spat as the leaders walked in. The service was partly in Maori with Muldoon and Father Lini reading the lessons; as they did so through the open windows floated non-traditional exhortations from people in a small boat out on the lake, such as 'Tom Davis, get out of bed with Muldoon'.*

The most pressing issue for many of the leaders was the uncertain future of the Forum's shipping line. Undercapitalised from the start, after three years of operation mounting losses meant it was having trouble paying its bills. Without it states like Tuvalu and Kiribati would have no regular services and Muldoon was determined to keep it afloat. He worked hard at the meeting, pledging that New Zealand would meet half of the $12 million needed. Australia, sceptical of the line's viability, was persuaded to allow the island states to use some of its aid money if they wished and the crisis seemed over.

It was not. At the next Forum in Canberra the traditional opening church service was the calmest interval. Everyone went, except the Australians who had organised it. Sitting in the Duntroon chapel listening to Tudor anthems I felt a long way from the Pacific. The meetings, though, were dominated by a blazing row between New Zealand and Australia over the future of the line. The Rotorua deal had come unstuck, with some governments being dilatory in their payments and the Australian aid bureaucracy being allegedly slow in approving disbursements. New Zealand again undertook to meet half of the continuing shortfall but Bill

---

* Davis was Premier of the Cook Islands.

Hayden on the Australian side looked at the accumulating losses and saw further assistance as a waste of money.

Muldoon, increasingly short tempered, was ready for a fight and Hawke who was never shy of a challenge was happy to meet him. After increasingly angry exchanges at the end of the last day the Forum found itself still deadlocked and Hawke's farewell reception had to be abandoned. With the issue threatening to spill over into a serious quarrel between the two countries, Geoff Yeend and I (still on reasonable terms) ducked into a room to see if we could draft a compromise. Muldoon was not much pleased with what we achieved – the Australians agreed to allow their aid money to be used for one more year – and complained about the 'dead hand of Australian bureaucracy'. He returned home saying that it was the end of the Forum line but ironically the line had turned the corner. Fortified with a European loan it moved into the black and slipped off the agenda.

The rest of his term was dominated by another international campaign, to reform the Bretton Woods system which had set the framework for international trade and payments since the end of the war. With New Zealand's internal economic management largely immobile his thoughts turned more and more to the problems faced by developing countries after the oil shocks. His list of the main problems was clear enough: the new protectionism revealed in the rise of non-tariff barriers and 'voluntary' restraint agreements; the rising burden of debt with an increasing number of countries having to seek relief; and what he saw as the dangerous over-exposure of the international banking system.

The international community, he argued, should start the search for a comprehensive solution, akin to a new Bretton Woods, before the outlook deteriorated further. Friends like Margaret Thatcher and George Shultz did not discount the risks but were confident that the existing international institutions could be adapted to handle them. Muldoon disagreed; he felt with increasing concern that a new and more responsive system was needed. His thinking had been evolving for some time. In mid-1982 he urged an early version on Fraser who had his own four-part plan for World Economic Recovery. Like a pair of young mothers the two sat in Kirribilli House and insincerely admired each other's offspring.

Circumstances led him to use the Commonwealth as the main vehicle for his campaign. As it gained momentum the UN Secretary-General wrote to urge him not to overlook the United Nations; the Davos Economic Forum asked him to speak at its meeting in January 1983; the American journal *Foreign Affairs* requested a major article. The fluent pens of his Advisory Group, principally Tim Groser, were kept busy. He talked about it wherever he travelled and his force and experience ensured that he was listened to carefully. The American Secretary of the Treasury, Don Regan, was even sufficiently persuaded to issue (and then hastily withdraw) a statement supporting his views. But a succession of Commonwealth meetings gave him the best continuing platform. A year after Melbourne he found himself being fervently commended by some of his old African critics. At the Finance Ministers' meeting in 1982 all the old resentments were forgotten as they praised his initiative and ordered an expert study into the issues he had outlined.

The following year the Commonwealth heads of government met in New Delhi. The New Zealand delegation travelling there in the Air Force Boeing was unusually large because our High Commission in Delhi had been the Foreign Ministry's sacrifice to the 3 per cent cuts. On board was our High Commissioner (now resident in Wellington), communications and secretarial staff, a press contingent and, at the PM's invitation, Professor Margaret Clark (Bernard's wife) and Julie. We also for the first time took a doctor, though in the event the physician was needed only to heal himself and some innocents of the press party who renewed their supplies of the hotel's bottled water with the help of an obliging man in the corridor who promptly refilled the empties from the nearest tap.

Mrs Gandhi, chair also of the Non-Aligned Group, saw the call for a 'new Bretton Woods' and the relief this implied for developing countries as the main purpose of the meeting. At first, however, outside events intervened. The Americans invaded the little Caribbean state of Grenada and deposed the increasingly unpredictable Marxist who was Prime Minister. The British were peeved, even though the Governor-General had called for help, and the anti-American members (including Mrs Gandhi) were highly censorious about this interference with a Commonwealth member. The arguments went back and forth across the floor for a day and Muldoon's address had to be deferred until after the retreat. It was, however, a real debate; in Hawke's view the best he had ever heard. The Eastern Caribbean states retorted with a spirited defence of the intervention, the redoubtable Eugenia Charles of

Dominica pointing out that a launch full of armed men could overthrow her government. The Commonwealth decided to look into the security of small states.

Then the leaders flew down to their retreat in Goa where the plan was that they could relax and talk among themselves away from their advisers. Muldoon, though, wanted me to be on hand, and so Julie and I spent a pleasant weekend, wandering undisturbed around the ornate churches of Old Goa while the leaders, or so Muldoon claimed with some irritation, were worked eleven hours a day. There was little to show for it. The inevitable Goa Declaration on International Security expressed such instantly forgettable views as that 'the world is threatened with a general break-down of order in the international community' but could not bring itself to mention Grenada.

The next morning Muldoon opened the economic debate. He referred to the expert group's study 'Towards a New Bretton Woods', but argued that there was no shortage of technical analysis; what was needed now was political leadership to get a process under way. He cautioned that careful consultation and preparation was the key; it was important not to convene an unwieldy conference which might seek hasty or premature remedies. This was well received. African leaders who had been so critical in Melbourne lined up to shake his hand and Julius Nyerere regretted that he had not gone to Davos to hear him there.

A New Delhi Statement on Economic Action was called for. We had tabled a draft before the retreat; the Indians had tabled another; and the Secretariat had a third under the table. At the start of the day the Secretary-General asked me to chair a drafting group to reconcile the competing drafts, stipulating that this would have to be completed before the end of that day's session. As a veteran of long communiqué nights I paled at the thought of what the Commonwealth doctors of pedantry could do with at least three drafts to play with. Work started at a leisurely pace until a hopeful enquiry about lunch gave me an opportunity. I said lunch would be deferred until we had finished. This caused some grumbling but also a marked increase in the pace. By mid-afternoon the group were eating their lunch while I brought the agreed text to the meeting. It was adopted with little dissent and a Commonwealth consultative group including New Zealand was appointed to carry on the effort. As it was being introduced there was a tap on my back. Lee Kuan

Yew bent down and whispered, 'It is excellent but it won't do any good, you know'.

He was right. As sometimes happens many of the risks were easing even as the international community was wondering what to do about them. The surge in the American economy, the widening effects of trade liberalisation, and the replenishment of international liquidity, especially through enlargement of the IMF's quotas, all tackled some of the symptoms which had alarmed Muldoon. Instead of a comprehensive approach the issues were being dealt with piecemeal, but in the end they covered most of the worries on his checklist – except debt. As this was more generally perceived the interest in a new Bretton Woods began to slacken.

This trip home was a cheerful one, undented even by a birdstrike coming into Darwin. We boarded the plane ready to leave Delhi; then time ticked by as we sat on the tarmac in the roasting heat. Asked to enquire what the difficulty was the PM's Private Secretary returned with the news that the airport was very crowded with departures and we would have to wait. It took a few minutes to grasp the meaning of this: 'Ask him, how much?' I said to Harold Hewett. He came back to say US$300. The plane door was open, the PM was tilted back apparently dozing with a magazine over his face, and everyone was increasingly uncomfortable. I whispered, 'Pay him', but Harold, ever the perfect secretary, whispered back, 'Under what item?' A voice rumbled from under the magazine, 'Put it down to disbursements'. Harold handed over the money, the doors closed and we took off. Four months later, 'unsupported expenditure' of $371.70 on 'gratuities' was retrospectively allowed by Treasury.

Sir Robert (as he became in the New Year honours) continued to press his argument at the OECD in Paris the following February, and with Mrs Thatcher in London. His manner with her was slightly arch and almost gallant. He admired her robust approach and political toughness, while she saw him, with perhaps a little more detachment, as 'one of us'. She remained politely sceptical about his Bretton Woods views. At the dinner he gave for her at the New Zealand High Commission he spoke about the then current split in the British Cabinet between Wets and Dries and said confidingly, 'I am with the Dries'. This was something of a surprise since Sir Robert's economics were considerably more moist than the wettest of Mrs Thatcher's Wets, but it says something of his regard for her, and something of hers for him that she insisted on coming despite having a feverish cold. Sitting next to her husband, I noticed that while carrying on the conversation he kept an anxious eye on his wife. Half way through the pudding he said, 'Excuse me, but I think I must take Margaret home' and whisked her off without a murmur.

As it happened the next time we were in London, for a meeting of the Commonwealth Bretton Woods group in May, I was the one coming down with a cold. As we sat upstairs at No 10 Downing Street, in a room which seemed to become brighter with flowers and chintzes on each visit, Mrs Thatcher fixed her eye on me and said, 'You have a cold'. I admitted this weakness and she said to her Private Secretary, 'Robert, bring the pills from the left-hand side of the bathroom cupboard'. She dropped two into a glass of water and kept her eyes intently on me as I drank. Then she said briskly, 'That's better, isn't it?' It wasn't, but my willpower was not Dry enough to do other than agree.

In February Muldoon paid his last official visit to the United States. We crossed the Atlantic by Concorde and were then flown to Washington on one of the President's aircraft. For the next two days the PM held a kind of court in the Embassy Row Hotel. The Secretary of the Treasury, Don Regan, was the first caller. American lamb producers were lobbying for countervailing duties to be levied on New Zealand imports on the grounds that they were subsidised. Indeed they were, and that prevented us from seeking the protection of the GATT Subsidy Code. Muldoon argued that New Zealand should be treated as an exception and given the protection anyway. Regan protested that the Administration had to be even-handed and could not favour a particular country. 'Go on, Don, you can do it', said Muldoon as they parted – and he did.

Then the Secretary of State, George Shultz, arrived in the sitting-room of the PM's little suite. They were easy with each other and, after a little fencing about a new Bretton Woods and the Subsidy Code, the two ranged comfortably over the international situation. Then Shultz glanced at his watch and said that he would have to get to the White House to brief the President before the PM's call.

Half an hour later we sat down at the Cabinet table, President Reagan flanked by Shultz and his Defence Secretary, Caspar Weinberger, with his index cards before him. The discussion was a touch laborious as the President studied his cards with little enthusiasm and contemplated the Subsidy Code with even less. Observations made from crib notes on a card rather lacked spontaneity but with the help of his two advisers the conversation kept moving.

Then we went upstairs to lunch in the old Family Dining Room, and saw a different President. As a host his conversation flowed easily, in reminiscences, funny stories, discussions about the judiciary and moonshine liquor, comparisons between our two countries, without a card in sight. After the two had appeared in the Rose Garden to meet the press and we were on our way home in the car Muldoon asked me for my impressions. They were not what I had expected: the weight of the presidential charm and the force with which he held a few simple ideas were surprising. Mrs Thatcher was a more sophisticated thinker, but both shared this ability to simplify and the unbending willpower to make it happen. I could now grasp how the two were shifting the world's political agenda. Muldoon liked to say that in public life it was necessary to strip an issue down to its barest essentials but he was no reformer and lacked – perhaps just as well – the unblinking vision that they had.

Dinner that evening was given by Vice-President Bush and his wife at their house in the old Naval Observatory near our embassy. Defense Secretary Weinberger turned out to be a dog-lover but even he blanched a little when I told him the family bred Staffordshire bull terriers and that the first litter had been stolen by the Mongrel Mob.* On my other side Barbara Bush talked about life in Beijing ten years earlier when the newly built New Zealand embassy had one of the few courts and Bryce Harland would invite the Bush family for tennis in the weekends. She was still grateful to Bryce for his kindness but when I offered to pass on her regards she said, 'Oh, he won't remember us now'. Then after a busy time in New York we left for an extensive tour of the southern United States, going to the Mardi Gras in New Orleans, calling on Lady Bird Johnson in Austin and giving a seminar on world economic reform at Berkeley.

The fact was Sir Robert's zest for politics at home had gone. The mechanics of extricating the economy from the freeze were as difficult as everyone else had predicted and his interest was fading with his resilience. His control over Parliament was crumbling as well. When

---

* After the second litter we received a curious message from the Mob guaranteeing the puppies' safety.

the Opposition introduced a bill to ban nuclear ship visits two members of his caucus announced an unwillingness to vote against it. This did not directly affect his majority since two members of the Labour Party moved the other way, but his thoughts turned to an election.

We were at a family dinner in a Wellington restaurant celebrating Sarah's birthday when he made his move. It came after a confrontation with one of his errant members which has been portrayed as a drunken and foully abusive tirade. If so, it was highly uncharacteristic. He never used bad language. 'My goodness' was the strongest I could remember, though Jenny Edwards Officer, his appointments secretary, recalled him once saying 'C'est la bloody vie!' in a moment of exasperation. When he was angry he became not noisier but colder and more deadly. Neither of the other two who were present at this confrontation could recall such language being used, so the question must remain open.

As the evening wore on, however, there was no question that the PM became progressively less sober. The Governor-General accepted some responsibility for this. When Muldoon drove to Government House to seek a dissolution, Sir David Beattie was holding a dinner party which included editors and some members of the Opposition. In this awkward situation he asked that the PM be shown into the study and given a drink until he could quietly slip away from the table. This delicate task took time and Sir Robert had been served two hefty whiskies before the Governor-General was able to join him and grant the dissolution.

Whatever the proof levels reached in the course of the night, this was not an impulsive move. Sir Robert had been considering the possibility for some time; at the beginning of May he asked me to find out the shortest time possible between dissolving Parliament and a general election. In the end the prospect of continuing difficulties in holding his majority made up his mind. In his fatalistic way he preferred to die on his feet than be nibbled to death by a restless caucus.

The election campaign was marked by an accelerating run on the New Zealand dollar. Given the distorted state of the economy and its over-valued currency this was probably inevitable. It became a certainty when a policy paper by the shadow Finance Minister, Roger Douglas, revealed that he favoured a devaluation. Speculators grasped a riskless chance to make money and the Advisory Group's daily briefings for the campaigning PM became a doleful account of the day's foreign exchange losses. In the last few days the outflow became an unsustainable flood.

His election defeat was decisive. The next morning, a Sunday, Bernard Galvin and I met with Spencer Russell, the Governor of the Reserve Bank, in his office to consider the next steps. It was clear that the country's remaining reserves would not last for more than seven days. Either a substantial devaluation or a closure of the foreign exchange markets was essential. We would have to go and see the Prime Minister. There was, however, a definite reluctance to disturb the wounded lion in his lair. As this was a money matter I thought that one of his financial advisers should ring him; they took the firm view that it was the job of the head of his department and I was outvoted.

It was midday. The telephone rang for some time until answered by the PM in a sleepy and surly voice. I explained the situation and said that we would like to see him that afternoon. 'I don't want to see you', he said, a response so disconcerting (he was always ready to talk at any hour) that I said rather rudely, 'What do you mean, you won't see us?' 'What I just said', with a flash of his old fire. I pointed out that it would be impossible in the circumstances to reopen the money markets. 'You can do what you like', he snapped and hung up. No one quite knew what the legality was, but on the principle that the safety of the state is the first law a statement was put out that evening closing the exchange markets until further notice.

Early the next morning the three of us gathered in the PM's office. The Governor and Bernard advised an immediate and large devaluation, though they did not name a figure. Muldoon was as resistant as ever, berating us for being badly briefed: a devaluation would add to the internal deficit and the cost of living and present a huge gift to speculators. He was convinced that if the incoming government was as resolute as he it could be avoided. When Galvin and Russell left for Auckland to brief the incoming Prime Minister, David Lange, Muldoon told me that he would ring Lange and explain why a devaluation was 'unnecessary'.

When he did so, Galvin and Russell were already explaining to Lange that the proposal for a united stand would not be credible; a devaluation of 20 per cent was now required. Lange thereupon rejected any joint statement as futile and the two returned to Wellington. Bernard rang me after three to report the outcome but was vague about when they would tell Muldoon. After nearly two hours had ticked by I rang Bernard again to say that the poor man was sitting there waiting to hear what had happened. Bernard's view was that David Lange should tell him but he did then telephone the PM. In the meantime Muldoon had learned of Bernard's earlier conversation with me. On an issue of this magnitude I thought the PM should hear the outcome from those who had been there and not hearsay from me. He however felt that, turning to face the rising sun of the new government, I had withheld information from him; it caused a coolness between us for some time.

That evening was the annual dinner of the Bankers' Association, held in the dark panelling and red plush of a traditional French restaurant, Le Normandie. The bankers had bad luck with their dinner; the previous year it had coincided with our largest anti-terrorist exercise and proceedings had been regularly disrupted by reports to the PM who was guest speaker. This year the Governor-General was guest and the situation from a banker's point of view was much worse.

No one's nerves were improved by the news that the PM was going to make a statement on television. Le Normandie had nothing as untraditional as a television set so I rang young Gerald at home and he relayed the main points. Sir Robert had restated his view that firmness would hold the currency and then flung down his challenge: 'I am not going to devalue, so long as I'm Minister of Finance'. So we now faced not just a liquidity crisis but a constitutional crisis as well. By law the government could not change for another ten days but the long-established convention was that in this period an outgoing government would act on the advice of its successor in any urgent matter.

Bernard, Spencer Russell and I retired to the bar to ponder. It was however too noisy and too full of bankers wishing to offer advice and so we moved on to the lavatory. This provided privacy but was also a gift to cartoonists who played variations on the 'penny wise, dollar foolish' theme. Sir Robert's defiance of the constitutional convention had raised the stakes considerably. I briefed the Governor-General in the hall and he said that he was ready to act if it was deemed to be necessary.

The deadlock had to be broken, if need be by dismissing the PM and reconstituting his colleagues as a government for the remaining few days. Urging this, though, was stretching the duty of an unelected civil servant to the limit. Sir Keith Holyoake's advice was not much use to me in sleeping that night but I decided first thing next morning to consult the Solicitor-General, Paul Neazor. I walked into his office as the clock was chiming eight. 'You're too late,' he said, 'the Attorney has decided to act.' Jim McLay, the Attorney-General and Muldoon's deputy, had telephoned earlier after talking to some of his colleagues and was on his way to present an ultimatum to Sir Robert. Cabinet met a few hours later and the devaluation was approved.

Political careers, Enoch Powell thought, by their nature end in failure. There are exceptions – Ronald Reagan and Lee Kuan Yew spring to mind – but this was not one of them. As the bustle went on preparing for a new government, Muldoon sat on in gloom in his office until I wondered if he was ever going to depart. On the day he was to go to Government House to resign I went upstairs, feeling I could not leave him on his own. We sat down and I searched for some consoling thoughts. 'History will remember you as one of the most, err, remarkable prime ministers of the century' was the best I could manage, hoping that he had not noticed the pause while I groped for the right adjective. We sat on in uneasy silence waiting for the summons; I felt like a chaplain at an execution. Then the door opened and he got up heavily and walked out of the room which had been the centre and reason for his life. Even after the events of the preceding week it was a sad moment: there was an awful lot of human nature in Sir Robert Muldoon.

# CHAPTER NINE

# The Elusive David Lange

THE NEW PRIME MINISTER, DAVID LANGE, WAS GIVING A morning tea. It was his first day in the office. The room was packed with his newly selected Ministers, campaign staff, party members, secretaries and people who had just wandered in. It was a day of triumph; after nine years Labour was back in power and owed this in a significant measure to the Lange touch – his charm, his wit and his easy ability to communicate. Flushed with excitement and clutching a cup of tea and a cake, the Prime Minister moved constantly around the room, surging up to people to make a joke, rolling away again and then looking back to see whether it was appreciated or not. It was a happy scene. Clutching my own cup and propped on the edge of the PM's desk, I watched his joyous face and thought, 'You will never be as happy again'.

Perhaps I suddenly felt the weight of my years; for the first time I was working for a prime minister younger than me. Perhaps it was the influence of the room, where carefree gatherings like this were rarer than a windless week in Wellington. Or perhaps it was half-conscious forebodings; like an elderly relative at a wedding I felt that such unclouded joy could not endure. The Government was young in both years and experience. In a single election we had overflown a whole age group, dropping from the RSA generation to the baby boomers. Of the new Cabinet only two or three had been in government before, and this did not include either the PM or his deputy.

This did not dent the confidence of those settling behind their desks. Experience had not won them such a triumphant victory. What the Government had was energy and brains; it was the brightest Ministry for many years. With a clear win and not many commitments it could break out of the narrowing gorge of the last Muldoon years and range over a wide plain of reform. But first there was the business of learning how to work the system. Labour had been in power for only three of the preceding twenty-four years and much of its institutional memory of policy formation and the use and limitations of the public service had gone. Time was needed to settle the internal map of the Government, the network of personal links, antipathies and informal pathways that – whatever the formal arrangements – determines how each administration works.

My own position on the new internal map was imprecise, not to say ambiguous. Mike Moore, one of the new Ministers, noted that Labour had always a tribal wariness about the public service. Certainly Norman Kirk had it. This time, though, the distrust was especially marked. For the party enthusiasts the black rule of Muldoon had been banished and a new order of the ages begun. All the more strange then that someone who had frequently been at his side and no doubt supported his failed policies should still be there. Political distrusts might make it necessary to have a new head of the Prime Minister's Department. A week before the change of government, however, Lange wrote to me to say that 'I wish you to continue in your present position for the time being', commenting that the transition would be sufficiently difficult without a change at the top.

On this rather equivocal note we began working together. We got on easily enough, after an initial tussle over his desire to be called 'David'. This was not appropriate for a professional relationship; after two weeks or so my disapproval prevailed and everyone, even the cleaners, began addressing him as 'Prime Minister'. My morning briefings changed too, from a brisk exchange of fire to an entertaining conversation stretching over three-quarters of an hour. Despite firm resolutions made going up the stairs I was never able to get through my list without the PM retailing diverting stories, reminiscences or titbits of gossip about his colleagues. When I was put to bed in early September with a diagnosis of exhaustion, a handwritten letter arrived from him apologising for holding too many meetings, saying that he had not realised the effect on his staff until he read the newspaper stories.

His desire to entertain and win approval was marked, more so even than for most successful politicians. He liked an appreciative audience and one of the duties of those around him was to provide it. The Chief Justice called to protest against possible delay in completing a new High Court building. A lengthy search through his briefcase revealed he had left behind the document he was supposed to present, so he made his case orally, ending with the plea that unless something was done, 'my colleagues and I face the prospect of spending the rest of our judicial lives in the DIC'.* I looked out the window, knowing that the PM was trying to catch my eye; it was the sort of establishment solemnity he particularly relished.

On another occasion I took him to meet Oleg Gordievsky, the KGB colonel who had been a British double agent. Gordievsky's seniority and experience made him a good guide on the Soviet Union's spying operations abroad, and in particular its use of agents of influence to work on public opinion in Western countries. (He, like an earlier KGB visitor, Stanilaus Levchenko, was impressively intelligent; it was clear that the Soviet Union put some of its best minds into intelligence-gathering.) His British code-name had been 'Ovation'. He stood up as the PM entered the room and David Lange grinned with pleasure and said, 'Ah, a standing Ovation'.

The shape of his personality unfolded over time. He was not a methodical worker and had all the administrative ability of the one-man law office (an elderly practitioner I had known in Christchurch kept all his files in a washing basket, an informal filing system which might well have interested David Lange). He could mislay a clutch of papers in a phone booth and it was always wise to have a spare copy of any important paper handy. He was physically restless and mentally also, reading papers quickly and initialling the bottom of each page in legal style. Listening to a briefing he would do the morning's crossword, jotting down the answers as if copying from a crib; when I challenged this split concentration, he repeated the gist of the briefing with complete accuracy.

This quickness of mind was not matched by similar force of will. Political leadership hinges mostly on willpower but it was a different force of personality which had propelled him to the top only a few years after he won Colin Moyle's seat in 1977. His booming and confident

---

* A department store with office accommodation above.

oratory, quick wit and personal charm underwrote his leadership because they had been the planks of his electoral victory. He lacked more traditional resources as a party leader. He had no deep roots in the party or the trade union movement, and no easy familiarity with the party machinery, which never wholeheartedly accepted him.

So keenly did he like to have the approval of those he spoke with that over time the suspicion grew that he sometimes tailored his message to avoid discomforting his hearers. He hated confrontation, preferring to delegate to others the communication of even those minor disappointments which prime ministers have to deliver. When this could not be avoided his uneasiness was made plain in the volume of his voice, the fervent assurances and the billowing of subordinate clauses. On one occasion he made a proposal to me, at such length and with such a mixture of warmth and obfuscation that it was four hours before I realised that he was offering me the ambassadorship to the UN. I rang him at home and declined; he sounded almost relieved.

At bottom he was deeply ambivalent about himself and his worth. Hence he had a defensive view of the outside world. It was necessary to get in first, not with a counter-punch like his predecessor, but with a put-down, a diversion or a distraction. At times he could seem like a network of raw nerves stretched tightly over his ample skin. It is too pat to blame his mother but that unbending Methodist lacked maternal fondness. When he became Leader of the Opposition Julie said to her, 'You must be proud of your son'. 'No, why should I?' was the stern reply. Her son was quite capable of getting his own back. Speaking at the opening of the restored Pompallier House in Russell he suddenly confided that the place had a special significance for him; he had been conceived in the garden. His mother gave an outraged denial. I never liked to ask how Russell had come to be his middle name.

He was a gifted storyteller but his stories could undergo considerable improvement, and were often used as weapons of ridicule. His anarchic streak made him edgy about authority and rank. Mrs Thatcher's choice of Admiral Sir John Fieldhouse to intercede with him on ship visits was thus not a good one. The PM retaliated by spreading the story that when the Admiral left his cap was carried before him on a cushion. This was quite untrue but it eased Lange's discomfort over the call.

He was uncomfortable even with the usual social restraints. He disliked formal dinners because they tied him down; he preferred to move around, bouncing thoughts off people, seeking (and gaining) their delighted recognition. The official residence, Vogel House, he found a strain. He would complain almost every day about some awkward feature of life there. The most heartfelt of these complaints was that the domestic staff folded the edge of the lavatory paper in neat triangles. For such a sociable man the evenings alone in that big house must have been oppressive. His wife, Naomi, stayed in Auckland, with the children and her church. Joe Walding, who acted as a mentor for the PM for a time, expressed forebodings to me about this, making a rueful comparison with Norman Kirk's family arrangements.

The annoyance over the lavatory paper touched his deep dislike of being watched. His worries about bugging amounted to a mild paranoia. We had his office swept periodically and even installed curtains to prevent sophisticated listening from afar. Then in one of those odd occurrences which seemed to match his restless spirit, a member of the Advisory Group reached down the side of one of the couches in the office and pulled out a small round metal object with a wire attached. Despite this there was never any evidence of bugging and the standard precautions were in any case pointless in an office like his where anyone could wander in. On one occasion when we were deep in discussion a window-cleaner whom I had not noticed offered a thought.

He presided over his government rather than directing it. The domestic direction was set by his Finance Minister, Roger Douglas, who had become a convert to the economics of the 'new Right'. He found in the Treasury a partner which had been reading and thinking along the same lines in the last years of the Muldoon administration. Sharing the same intellectual framework the partnership was ready to move boldly on a series of radical policy changes. So was Lange. 'Welcome to Yugoslavia', was his greeting to Tony Tan, the Singapore Finance Minister, a month before the election. He was too intelligent not to grasp how close to the economic reefs New Zealand had drifted, and too young to have any conservative nostalgia for the remedies of the 1930s.

So he was a warm backer of the Douglas reforms, soon termed Rogernomics, but as a public presenter rather than a detailed participant. When in December he commented at a press conference that removing exchange controls was 'not a starter', the young Treasury ideologues were angered, telling us that the PM should not have spoken when the Finance Minister had not formulated a position and threatening to cut off further information on the question. This was high-handed but not a forerunner of the open warfare which was to break out between the two three years later. During the most rapid period of economic change in the country's history the Lange–Douglas bond was solid. The clearest evidence of this was from David Lange himself: he loved telling stories about the foibles of his ministerial colleagues, but there was never a single one about Roger Douglas. That respect was the axle on which the Government ran and when it broke the Government did too.

With his other colleagues he could sometimes seem more an amused bystander than the head of their Government. His wit bubbled up as oil once did from stony ground. A paper from the Cabinet Office discussed the bureaucratic aspects of establishing a Ministry of Women's Affairs at considerable length and complexity. It came to me with a note from the PM: 'Mr Hensley, I have gone to lie down'. Once when we were travelling he tried a machine that spoke your weight and claimed that it had said, 'One at a time please'.

Occasionally his comments could cause trouble. A female correspondent found her letter returned to her with 'Who is this shrew?' written on it by the PM. When a Russian cruise ship the *Mikhail Lermontov* was wrecked in the Marlborough Sounds, he observed casually that New Zealand was the only Western nation ever to sink a Soviet ship, only to learn that the vessel had indeed been under the direction of a New Zealand pilot. Social embarrassment was one thing but he was also Foreign Minister and this exuberance and light-heartedness of speech was to deepen the difficulties of our new foreign policy.

Two weeks after he took office we set off on his first foreign visit, to Papua New Guinea, which was celebrating the tenth anniversary of its independence, opening an eye-catching new Parliament building and hosting the last of the experiment in Commonwealth regional conferences. It was an uneventful occasion. We visited the start of the wartime Kokoda Trail where crocodile-meat kebabs were cooked. Their taste was compared to the inevitable chicken but the PM enjoyed his, calling to his wife, 'Quick, Naomi, take a picture of a man eating crocodile'. The climax was a dinner in Port Moresby where the guest of honour was Gough Whitlam, Prime Minister of Australia when the former trust territory had become independent. The celebration became rather noisy, especially when a provincial premier began heckling the speakers. When Whitlam spoke he had to raise his voice: 'I am glad to be speaking to you on this convivial occasion'. There was a crash as the premier fell to the floor – 'this *increasingly* convivial occasion', Whitlam continued imperturbably.

Then there was scarcely time to wash our aloha shirts before in late August the South Pacific Forum met in Tuvalu, a chain of Polynesian atolls once known as the Ellice Islands. Funafuti, the capital, boasted a wartime airstrip which took up most of the centre of the island, but no hotel. *Monowai* was once again anchored in the lagoon while the PM and I lived in a little bungalow vacated by a government family.* We took turns at making breakfast. When it was David Lange's turn I had to be there to make sure he put the kettle on; when it was my turn he would have wandered off through the bananas to talk to someone just when the toast was ready.

The first two nights were made sleepless by a rooster which crowed repeatedly in the bright moonlight. At last I got up, with murder in my heart. Moving quietly around the side of the house I met, not the rooster, but the PM coming the other way. 'You too?' he said. The bird meanwhile had fallen silent and made a prudent withdrawal. Next morning I found that we had been issued with a bicycle and made a shaky journey through the palm trees and houses of the little town in the cool of the dawn. Despite breakfast being on the table the PM went off to try it. I discovered later that he had somehow got on to the airstrip. The Samoan delegation was waiting there with their bags for an RNZAF plane to take them to Fiji when the Prime Minister of New Zealand wobbled into view, waved and said, 'The plane's been cancelled – we're going by bike'.

The Forum was back to its customary style, with prayers and hymns in a white coral-cement church festooned with hibiscus and frangipani, and a feast with drumming and dancing each night. The shipping line was no longer an issue; New Caledonia was on autopilot; but there were ripples over the Australian proposal for a nuclear-free zone. Criticised by Father Lini for being insufficiently anti-nuclear, it was still going through a fairly leisurely drafting stage and there was no disposition to take any decisions this year. Lange floated the suggestion that the coming UN General Assembly might be asked to bless the zone and this

---

* Known in radio communication with the ship as Camp David.

irritated Hawke. They had already had a terse exchange in Port Moresby when Hawke had warned that mishandling the issue of nuclear ship visits could mean the end of ANZUS. Things did not improve in Funafuti; when asked how he found working alongside David Lange, Hawke said, 'I didn't work alongside him. He was at the other end of the table. I found it fairly congenial.'

The question of visits by nuclear-armed or nuclear-powered ships was now the dominant issue in New Zealand's foreign policy. Anti-nuclear resolutions had become the chief concern of Labour Party conferences and an anti-nuclear bill had indirectly caused the election. David Lange had from his youth and time with Lord Soper and the Methodist Mission in London shared this opposition to the weapons. He was less bothered about nuclear propulsion but accepted that emotionally the two were linked. One of the planks of the Labour election campaign was 'to make New Zealand and its territorial waters nuclear free'. The country was already nuclear-free in terms of the Nuclear Non-Proliferation Treaty so this applied to visiting ships, in practice those from the United States or Britain. In turn this threatened the ANZUS alliance relationship with the US and Australia, which was the cause of Hawke's concern.

The alliance, sought earnestly by Australia as a result of its wartime vulnerability, was just over thirty years old. It had no standing structure or bureaucracy and for half that time was a helpful but barely visible security guarantee. The Vietnam War, however, gave it a public profile as the two countries sent modest troop contingents in support of the US intervention. Those who were opposed to the war came to oppose the alliance and what they saw as its tendency to tie New Zealand to the aims of American foreign policy and involve the country in other people's wars.

By an unlucky chance the ANZUS Council (the three Foreign Ministers) was scheduled to meet in Wellington in what turned out to be the days immediately after the election. The outgoing Muldoon Government insisted on going through with it but an informal meeting arranged between David Lange and George Shultz was much more significant. Misunderstanding dogged their discussion. The PM was conciliatory, apparently saying that over the next six months he would be discussing the issue at branch meetings of the Labour Party. The Americans took this as an indication that he would work to soften his party's policy on ship visits. Given the Lange habits of seeking the approval of his hearers and becoming ever more elaborately obscure when uneasy, their mistake was not surprising.

In talking to me and to other officials in the following weeks the PM made clear both his unalterable opposition to nuclear weapons and his commitment to remaining within ANZUS. We understood that our task was to find a means of reconciling the two. This would be difficult but not impossible; finding the right balance between two conflicting positions was what the art of diplomacy was about. There was no need for haste; the Americans had made it clear at the meeting that they had no desire to force the issue. My understanding was that we had at least to the end of the year and perhaps beyond to seek a solution.

So at irregular intervals a group, the core of which was the Secretary of Foreign Affairs, the CDS, the Secretary of Defence and me, met with the PM in his office to explore the possibilities.* The two fixed points were that the Government would not make any substantial changes to its electoral undertaking (there would be no turnaround as the Australian Labor Government was felt to have done); and the Americans would not accept any weakening of their policy of 'neither confirm nor deny' (NCND), maintaining silence on the presence of nuclear weapons on their ships – to do so would not only be tactically unwise but might undermine their basing arrangements in countries such as Japan and the Philippines and their port calls elsewhere.

In August we attempted a sketch, groping our way towards a possible agreed statement which might be made in a few months' time. The Americans would recognise that in present circumstances there was little strategic need for nuclear weapons in the South Pacific, and they understood New Zealand's wish not have nuclear weapons in its ports. For its part New Zealand would reiterate its understanding of NCND and its desire to continue as a full ANZUS partner. The wording shifted and reformed under the political pressures from both sides, but in essence it was a variant of the 'don't ask, don't tell' policy followed by the Scandinavian countries and everyone else who was opposed to nuclear weapons but accepted American naval visits.

---

\* To amuse him on one occasion I showed him an Australian cartoon of someone stumbling ashore on a Pacific island and being told, 'I can smell the uranium on your breath'.

This seemed a reasonable approach in the circumstances because the PM in the privacy of his office was still firmly repeating that New Zealand should remain in ANZUS. He was saying this not only to his advisers but also to Hawke and to the other heads of government he met. At the beginning of October he went to Singapore 'to sit at Mr Lee's feet' (Lee's response was that this would be 'quite a bundle'). He told the Singapore PM that Labour Party conferences did not determine government policy and that the Government had no intention of leaving ANZUS.

Ambiguities were creeping in, however. It was not clear that David Lange's definition of alliance membership was the previously accepted one. And while he was presiding at our discussions on a possible formula, his public statements and speeches sounded a different note. Addressed solely to his domestic audience they expressed absolute rejection of nuclear weapons and when not actually critical of the Americans did not show much understanding of their position. Differences in a long-standing alliance, as in any close relationship, were better explored and tested in private rather than repeatedly underlined in public.

These public statements, their emotional tone and occasional witty ridicule, were going to test the faith of the Americans in our assurances that we were looking for a mutually satisfactory answer. So was the growing pressure from anti-nuclear lobbyists that New Zealand should reject even the *possibility* that a nuclear weapon might occasionally visit its harbours. The scope for an amicable solution was narrowing. The aim shifted from the search for an agreed statement to looking to buy time, gaining a longer period during which calm could return and a solution might become more practicable. If a patently non-nuclear ship could make a visit within the next few months the issue could be laid away for two or so years without our alliance responsibilities being questioned. This had happened a decade or so earlier when there had been a deadlock over who would accept accident liability for nuclear-powered ships.

Thinking along these lines was interrupted by the murder of Indira Gandhi and the PM's departure for her funeral. He loved India but I was alarmed when he appeared in my hotel room on our first evening in New Delhi looking distressed, pale and sweating. His stapled stomach was giving him some pain. He swallowed a piece of banana and was comfortable again. We went off to view Mrs Gandhi's body, lying in semi-chilled darkness but with dark blotches already appearing on her gaunt face.

The next day the cremation took place outside the old city on the banks of the Yamuna. Mrs Gandhi's assassination by Sikh extremists had triggered outbreaks of communal violence. Several hundred died in New Delhi and in a sinister echo of the Partition killings trains were arriving at the station there with dead passengers lolling in their seats. Despite the deployment of large numbers of troops in the centre of the city and around the funeral site the atmosphere was jittery.

We sat in rows facing a stage on which the high funeral pyre had been built, with Mrs Gandhi's body resting on the top, covered with garlands of marigolds and other flowers. The midday sun was hot and there was no shade in the dry scrubland of the riverbank. Helicopters circled low above us, raising dust, occasional gusts of hot air and a persistent apprehension. Rajiv Gandhi, now Prime Minister himself, recited some prayers, circled the pyre and touched the fire to it. The flames crackled and rose high. Time went by; the sun beat down; and the helicopters circled lower, with heavily armed soldiers peering watchfully out. The PM wondered when it would be proper to leave. Not having attended an outdoor cremation before, I asked the colonel looking after us: 'Sir, when the head explodes'. I regretted having asked. We sat on, the fire burnt less fiercely and suddenly the ceremony was over. There was confusion as everyone tried to scramble into the parked buses. The Canadian Secretary of State for External Affairs and I managed to get standing room in one, he claiming rather improbably to have beaten a leper and a pregnant woman for the places.

Even here, though, the ANZUS problem cast its shadow. The Japanese Prime Minister, Nakasone, asked for a meeting to have a look at this newcomer who might be going to complicate Japan's long-standing conventions for hosting US ships. The atmosphere in his hotel room was cool. Nakasone sat aloof with his eyes half-closed and said little; Lange was nervous and talkative but his jauntiness froze in the air. We left in silence and I did not think the assessment was favourable.

Back home again the plan to buy time firmed up. In the middle of November the PM told the American ambassador that he was looking for a means of dealing with the differences 'in a politically feasible and therefore gradual way'. The CDS, Air Marshal Jamieson, went secretly to Honolulu to seek the cooperation of CINCPAC, Admiral Crowe, in finding a suitably uncontroversial ship to make the first visit. The American admiral could give no assurances but he understood the delicacy of the situation and offered an oil-fired destroyer, *Buchanan*, which had visited Auckland five years earlier. Its advanced age and class made any nuclear armament unlikely, as did the fact that it would be making a special journey to New Zealand rather than coming off a regular patrol. The PM appeared to be happy with this. Because the timing of the visit had not yet been fixed the ship's identity was closely held among no more than half a dozen. We were anxious about a possible leak to the newspapers: Julie was now a leader-writer and to avoid difficulties if the name surfaced I did not disclose it even to her.

Then the calendar took a hand. A tri-nation naval exercise, *Sea Eagle*, was to be held in the Tasman Sea in the following March. It would look strange if an American ship did not visit then and awkward if it was to be one of the possibly nuclear-armed participants. *Buchanan* would have to fill the gap. It was suggested to the Americans in December that they submit a request for a port call by this ship. As a precaution they submitted their note in draft and I was with the PM when he discussed this with the ambassador.* He jibbed at a phrase which implied a return to the status quo before the election but otherwise raised no difficulty with the wording. He promised a prompt reply and suggested that the *Buchanan* visit should be considered at the first Cabinet of the new year. The Americans not unnaturally took this as a broad hint that it would be approved. So did his advisers: 'I think we've got it licked', said one of my colleagues.

Engrossed in what was being worked out in the PM's office, we paid little heed to his public rhetoric, which continued to be uncompromising and dismissive of the Americans' concerns. Nor were we aware, as Washington was, that the PM was not keeping his Cabinet Ministers or his caucus informed. He declined the offer of Cabinet papers, saying that he would brief his colleagues orally but there was no evidence that he did so. When the embassy checked with senior Ministers in December it found no sign that the PM had discussed the *Buchanan* visit with them.

Over the Christmas and summer holiday season at the start of 1985 the proposed visit became known (probably from Washington) and a lobby of anti-nuclear activists, the peace movement and members of

---

\* In the late afternoon of 12 December. Ambassador Browne was about to leave for Washington.

the left wing of the Labour Party mounted a campaign in the media to keep pressure on the government. The risks of a visit were imaginatively stressed, from Soviet missiles in time of war to nuclear explosions in our harbours; fears about the alliance relationship with the United States were dismissed as groundless; and David Lange was nominated for a Nobel Peace Prize.

The prospective recipient had meanwhile left for a holiday in the Tokelau Islands, north of Samoa and as remote a place as anywhere in the wide Pacific, where he was out of communication with his government or anyone else. In his absence preparations went ahead for Cabinet consideration of the visit on 28 January. Departments had prepared a bundle of papers for the discussion, though it was never clear how far they were circulated. The key judgement on *Buchanan's* armament had to be made by Air Marshal Jamieson and we spent some time over the wording. None of us was in any doubt that the ship was not nuclear-armed but a flat assurance to this effect could hardly be given unless every part of it had been personally inspected. We settled for the view that it was 'highly unlikely'.

Unknown to us, members of the Labour Party executive had also been at work. At a meeting five days before Cabinet they had made a radical shift in the government's position. The ban on the entry of nuclear-armed vessels in the election manifesto was extended to cover *nuclear-capable* vessels. This was refining New Zealand's anti-nuclear stance to a pharmaceutical purity. In more practical terms it was clearly designed to block the possibility of any American ship visits; the definition of 'nuclear-capable' was so wide it could be stretched to fit any naval vessel.

An air force plane brought the PM back from Pago Pago half way through the Cabinet meeting. I saw him at six that evening. He sat slumped in his chair and said, 'Gerald, you have no idea how difficult it was in Cabinet this afternoon. I was in a minority of one.' I was surprised, having previously worked for a prime minister who regarded being in a minority of one as a comfortable working majority. Lange implied that there had been overwhelming opposition to the *Buchanan* but gave no details of the discussion (much later several Ministers had difficulty recalling any, except a vague statement by Lange that another ship should be sought). Instead he wanted to ask the Americans for another type of ship, an Oliver Hazard Perry-class frigate, which was considered to be less nuclear-capable. It seemed most unlikely that the Americans would allow us to pick and choose among their fleet but the request was duly passed on to a dubious ambassador.

Early the following morning the phone rang beside my bed. It was Merv Norrish, the Secretary of Foreign Affairs: had I read the paper? I had not, having just been woken up, but the Wellington newspaper led with the story that the PM had asked for a Perry-class frigate. Such a serious leak would not have come from the embassy, nor from the three officials who had been with the PM at the meeting. It looked highly likely that the PM's ship had leaked from the top. Indeed it had; David Lange in expansive form briefing reporters the evening before had let slip enough detail to allow the quick-witted to work out what sort of ship he had in mind.

It had little effect. Later that day we assembled in the PM's office to hear the ambassador's reply. As predicted, it was a firm no. After approving the wording of their request in draft, we had rejected it when formally presented; they would not make another. Indeed the shift to banning nuclear-capable ships, which the parliamentary caucus was to endorse a day later, made any other offer equally open to rejection. It was the end of six months of effort to reconcile the anti-nuclear policy with our long-standing alliance relationship with the United States. The Americans felt they had been deceived by us and were angry; ten years later Paul Wolfowitz was still angry, complaining to me in Honolulu that, 'I went out on a limb for you guys'.

The more immediate question for the group of officials who had worked with the PM was whether we had been deceived, or had simply deceived ourselves. Opinion was divided between those who thought that David Lange had been content to preside over a contest between the anti-nuclear purists and the ANZUS alliance until pushed by the Labour Party executive into backing their view. Others pointed to his speeches and the growing influence of his speechwriter, Margaret Pope, to argue that his anti-nuclear convictions had always been predominant and he had failed to be frank with his advisers. 'I think we have been led up the garden path,' said one.

Whatever the truth, the next step was to limit the fallout on our national interests. We knew that a list of presidential sanctions on intelligence and defence cooperation was close to completion and it seemed sensible to make our case against unwise or drastic moves before the draft hardened into decisions. The PM decided that I should go to Washington 'without publicity'. First however there was our silver wedding party. David Lange arrived at the house clutching a huge bouquet of flowers which Thaddeus McCarthy had sent to Julie at the Beehive and had a happy time carving the pig which, following Samoan custom, was the centrepiece in the dining-room. At dawn I was on my way.

I spent a long day making the rounds of the Washington agencies where the atmosphere was cooler than the winter weather. In one sense I was too late: the President had already taken his decisions and all that was left was to urge the Administration to step carefully in their implementation. My arguments were not well received. Senior officials felt that they had been deliberately misled by Lange. An alliance could not function when the ships of one partner could not visit another. Michael Armacost, the Under Secretary of State, said they had tried to look on the bright side for months but the PM had done nothing to push what he said was his preferred solution. It was not the US which was filing for divorce, he said; it had been told it could not come into the bedroom.

Simon Murdoch (counsellor in the embassy) and I spent the rest of the day going round the other agencies, including the CIA and National Security Council, to a similarly bleak reception. In the evening we were back in the State Department to see the head of the Bureau of Intelligence and Research, Morton Abramovitz. A long acquaintance encouraged Mort to be even franker. He thought my colleagues and I had been deluding ourselves over the prospects of a solution; after a visit the previous November he said, 'I thought you guys must have been smoking pot, you were in some dreamland'. The PM had made no effort and had 'let events decide his policy'. The overriding American interest now was to protect its other alliances. When I asked if this was a wise way to end a relationship of fifty years, he said, 'So be it', and Simon and I were out in the dark on D Street.

I flew to Los Angeles to meet the PM, who was on his way to England to speak in the Oxford Union debate. His stopover in California was for a strange little ceremony; the list of presidential decisions were to be read out to him. There was no bell, book or candle as we gathered round the Consul-General's dining-room table, but a definite air of excommunication. Bill Brown, a Deputy Assistant Secretary of State (and also an old acquaintance), made the now familiar complaints that both the *Buchanan* and the timing of its visit had been chosen on New Zealand's advice. He then gave details of cutbacks in defence and intelligence cooperation but made it clear that there would be no trade retaliation.

I complained that when the US was accusing us of not understanding the international situation it hardly seemed logical to shut us out of their sources of information, but the PM was relieved – he had been fearful about trade. He emphasised more than once that New Zealand was absolutely committed to the Western alliance and to being a good ally, but also made an ambivalent point he had once mused on in his office: enhancing his domestic constituency was easier than preserving the relationship with the US – but he would not, he said, succumb to this temptation.

On that note Brown left and ten minutes later we did too, to find Bill standing carless on the suburban pavement. It said something about the relationship that he accepted our offer of a lift and together with those he had just cast into outer darkness rode into town in comfortable conversation. The PM was on his way to give a lunchtime address on 'The New Zealand Connection' at the Ambassador Hotel. We made our way in through the kitchens and past where Robert Kennedy had been assassinated, with Lange making slightly nervous jokes. He departed from his text to comment on the morning's events, saying the measures amounted to a drastic scaling down of cooperation with New Zealand in those areas, but again reaffirmed that 'New Zealand is committed to the ANZUS alliance'.

Then he left for London and I went on to Ottawa to discuss the alterations to our relationship with the Canadians. There was an awkward moment on the tarmac. As we stood at the foot of his plane, and I again expressed a concern that the Oxford Union debate be handled carefully, someone arrived with a leader from the *Evening Post*, Julie's paper, which made a stinging attack on the Government's American policy. There was a polite silence while I explained that writing leaders rotated among a team, but being rung up at four in the morning by some irate reader, in the days when Julie was a television critic, began to look more attractive.

When I reached London the Oxford debate was over, a triumph in the eyes of everyone but the British Government. Joe Walding, just installed as High Commissioner, took me aside to berate me for allowing the ANZUS muddle to develop as it did. I told him that he should rather seek an explanation from his old colleagues in the parliamentary party.

But another of Joe's warnings was brought home to me that day. I went to the Howard Hotel that evening to report to the PM. The police guard on the floor confirmed that he was in but there was no answer when I knocked on the door. When I returned two hours later the PM opened the door at once and when I mentioned the earlier call said that he and Margaret had been walking in the park. Whether it was because his manner was a little hesitant I suddenly understood that an affair was under way. When I had earlier given a routine warning about bugged hotel rooms he seemed discomfited; my warning must have reverberated for a more weighty reason.

The British like the Canadians did not disguise their disagreement with our policy on ship visits but were also concerned about the possible impact of the American measures on the long-standing five-power relationship. Mrs Thatcher's Intelligence Coordinator, Sir Antony Duff, had gone to Washington in early February to argue with the Americans and Mrs Thatcher herself had stressed to President Reagan the importance of maintaining New Zealand's intelligence flow ('the British have been all over us,' Abramovitz said to me). Within the new rules the British would do what they could to help but reduced access by our diplomats had to be accepted and we withdrew from the weekly meetings of the Joint Intelligence Committee in Whitehall. I spent the weekend at his house in Dorset with Tony Duff, who had just become head of the Security Service. I was woken in the dim dawn by the sight of the Director of MI5 standing beside my bed with a cup of tea. I must have looked surprised because he said, 'I'll taste it first if you like'.

The concern about ANZUS rumbled on at home (78 per cent of those polled supported it – and almost the same number believed New Zealand should also be nuclear-free) but, though spasmodic efforts were made from time to time, the issue was dead. Years later a member of the Cabinet said to me, 'You know, if we had taken the *Buchanan* decision eighteen months later it would have been different'. He may have been right; the inexperience and airy confidence of that time faded as the months went by. But other things would have been different too. The dispute touched off a wave of New Zealand nationalism; a professor of political science went so far as to call it New Zealand's Declaration of Independence – what could be more independent than quarrelling with our old friends and our wartime saviour. It also distracted attention from the radical changes to the country's statist economy that were gathering speed. There was no conscious trade-off between the reforms and the anti-nuclear policy – public affairs do not work in such a neat way – but had the *Buchanan* been accepted the full weight of the Left's discontent would have fallen on the Government's domestic policies.

Nationalist excitement mixed with some apprehension was just beginning to subside in mid-1985 when a bizarre crime reignited both. Near midnight on 10 July the Greenpeace vessel, *Rainbow Warrior*, in Auckland on her way to the French nuclear test site at Mururoa, was struck by two explosions which sank the ship at her moorings and drowned a photographer. It seemed a police matter until in the course of the following day some anomalies began to emerge. One bomb had been skilfully placed at the stern to skew the ship's frame so that she could not have sailed again.

The next day the Terrorism Committee convened to hear a strange story. The outboard motor club in Auckland harbour had suffered from vandalism and members were taking turns to stay there overnight, keeping all the overhead lights on. On this night the watcher was interested to see a man dressed in a diving suit and red woollen hat paddle a Zodiac inflatable up to the club's ramp (now in a blaze of light) where he was met by a man and a woman in a rented stationwagon. The equipment was loaded and the three drove away.

The couple were picked up when they returned the car. They had Swiss passports identifying them as the Turenges. They were held over the weekend and the bug we were rude enough to place in their motel room revealed, from the woman's anxiety not to take the marital deception too far, that they were not married. Some quick work by the SIS over the weekend proved the passports, issued in Lyons, to be false, while the Zodiac, from which all identifying marks had been removed and some other items of kit also, pointed to the French. It seemed inconceivable that any arm of the French government would have been involved but a group of right-wing adventurers seemed plausible.

The Terrorism Committee went into high gear, meeting seventeen times in all. The discussions were practical and informal; the PM liked to drop in from time to time to be briefed and to offer some suggestions. Day by day the puzzle began to be pieced together, and it increasingly looked like a high-level military or secret-service operation. An outboard motor dropped in the harbour from the Zodiac was recovered, as was a sophisticated military rebreathing apparatus, which allowed a diver to work without creating air bubbles. The 'Swiss couple' turned out to be Major Alain Mafart, second in command at the Combat Divers Training Centre in Corsica, and Captain Dominique Prieur of the French Army. The explosives had been brought to New Zealand aboard the *Ouvea*, a yacht chartered in Noumea by Xavier Maniguet, a naval physician and diving specialist. The yacht had landed at Parengarenga, a remote bay in the Far North, and only declared itself to Customs three days later.

The bombs and the expert divers who were to place them on the *Rainbow Warrior* travelled in the rented stationwagon down to Auckland. They were perhaps unaware of how conspicuous they appeared in a small community but it proved entertainingly easy to trace their progress. Dozens of people remembered them – in the easygoing Northland fashion they were assumed to be smuggling drugs. At lunch in Whangarei they flirted with the waitress, who was delighted to recall them; elsewhere they enquired about night lights for a Zodiac and where they could get a repair kit (when examined by the police the inflatable had a slow puncture); a roadside rendezvous was noted; even when they stopped in a forest clearing at Kaiwaka a passer-by remembered one and possibly two outboard motors in the car. Most entertaining of all, they turned out to have stayed on three occasions, the last the day before the bombing, at a motel near Helensville which was part-owned by David Lange.

At the end of a week it was clear that we were looking at a professionally organised and well-funded operation, and with the help of some hints from a rival French intelligence agency with whom we had good relations we identified the prime suspect as the DGSE, the French external intelligence group which had something of a cowboy reputation. The 'Turenges' were in jail, charged with immigration offences. We had ample evidence of their links with the actual bombers, the crew of the *Ouvea*, whose real names were also being uncovered. The yacht, however, had sailed for Norfolk Island on its return journey to Noumea and as yet we had no evidence on which to arrest them.

When *Ouvea* arrived there I telephoned my counterpart in the Prime Minister's Department in Canberra to say that we planned to search the boat and take samples of bilge water which might contain traces of explosives. It would be helpful if the yacht's departure could be delayed as long as possible. The Australians protested that they had no power to hold the yacht. I understood this but suggested that the Administrator might be away from the office that afternoon, playing golf perhaps (though I remembered giving up golf forever after playing on the Norfolk Island course) or otherwise hard to find – anything which might delay the yacht for a few vital hours during which we might get our evidence and seek the arrest of the crew. The Administrator did his best, the police went over the boat very thoroughly, but we still did not have the evidence and the boat sailed at the end of the day.

The next day we picked up a message from the *Ouvea* which had had a powerful radio specially installed: 'We have a problem. We have certainly caught a bug, a big bug' and went on to mention the full check-up in Norfolk Island. Three days later the yacht gave its position, close to New Caledonia, and talked of a rendezvous. We put up an Orion maritime patrol aircraft to make sweeps over the area (courteously informing the French naval commander in Noumea that we were doing so) but the yacht was never seen or heard from again. Subsequent information suggested that it was scuttled and the crew taken on board the French nuclear submarine *Rubis* which was nearby.

Unaware of this at the time, we had to assume that the yacht had landed its crew quietly somewhere along the New Caledonian coast. The bilge water had indeed tested positive for explosives and we now had our arrest warrants. Using diplomatic channels we hastily constructed a net over South East Asia, reaching as far afield as Tokyo, Honolulu and even Santiago. It covered every possible stopover point for flights from Noumea; with the help of cooperative local authorities we hoped to get our suspects as they stepped from the plane. The effort was in vain, but we nearly got Xavier Maniguet.

He had left the yacht in Norfolk Island, possibly spooked by the attention it was receiving there. He flew to Sydney and in the afternoon he went to the movies where we had the pleasure of sitting nearby as he found himself by chance next to a French couple who had shadowy links to the French embassy. After an interview with the New Zealand police he moved on to Singapore where he stayed for a few days, perhaps waiting (as we thought) to meet his boating colleagues. He ended his stay abruptly when he met a New Zealand journalist who mentioned that there was a warrant for his arrest. After much jocularity over such an absurd misunderstanding he waved goodbye to the reporter and an hour and a half later was a late boarder on the UTA flight to Paris.

By then we had a better understanding of the background to the crime. It was said that a neutron bomb was to be tested at Mururoa in the southern spring. The French Ministry of Defence (of which the DGSE was a part) had received information that equipment to monitor and analyse such a test was being installed on the *Rainbow Warrior*. Initial thoughts of sinking the vessel at sea were abandoned, for humanitarian or practical reasons, and instead its last port call at Auckland was chosen. The DGSE mounted a carefully organised operation. A thirty-year-old woman, Frédérique Bonlieu, was sent to infiltrate Greenpeace, posing as an ecologist. The head of the Corsican diving base, Major Louis Dillais, spent a month in New Zealand to direct the operation and enjoy some river rafting. At least ten agents moved in and out of the country but in the end we caught only Mafart and Prieur.

In Paris military sources continued to spread the story that the bombing had been carried out by the extreme right with connections in New Caledonia (as an alternative they also hinted that the British had been involved). The cover was unravelling, though, as the French press with the help of talkative sources in the New Zealand police fingered the DGSE. On 8 August President Mitterand sent a message to the PM noting with mild surprise that a link might exist between the two under arrest and 'French services': 'I intend that this affair be treated with the greatest severity and that your country be able to count on France's fullest support'. The same day the French Prime Minister announced an urgent enquiry.

Counsellor of State Tricot set to work and two weeks later was able to report that agents of the DGSE had indeed carried out the bombing but the government had not been involved and all the agents were innocent, including the crew of the *Ouvea* now admitted to be back in France, and 'probably' Major Mafart and Captain Prieur. 'Tricot washes whitest' said the French press. Paris may still have suspected that we were bluffing about how much we really knew. It was perhaps not easy to understand the intimacy of a small country like New Zealand, from the watcher at the boat club (the father of a well-known TV journalist) to the list of sightings of the bombers on their travels.

Our ambassador, John Macarthur, suggested a bold step – that in effect we bundle up our file of all these details and send it to Paris. This was unorthodox and the lawyers had misgivings but the Terrorism Committee met on a Friday night and with the PM's agreement sent off the file. A silence fell after it was handed over and thereafter there was a readier acceptance of the facts by the French Government. And also at the Cordon Bleu school in Paris where our daughter Sarah was studying cooking. Her teacher, Chef Bernard, would lift her ponytail, kiss the nape of her neck and announce, 'Mademoiselle Sarah and I will go to prison in place of the terroreests'. In the press, though, there was a rising tide of nationalist, anti-Anglo-Saxon sentiment, with disdainful references even in the quality papers to New Zealand as a remote sandbank with a crude and unrefined society. Guards were placed on the embassy and the consulate in Noumea. There were rumours of an attempt to free Mafart and Prieur and they were moved to special quarters at Ardmore, near the SAS base, where counter-terrorist teams could keep watch on the perimeter.

In France the familiar script of a state scandal was solemnly played out. Charles Hernu, the Minister of Defence, in mid-September angrily objected to 'the campaign of rumours and insinuations' about him. Four days later the Prime Minister, Laurent Fabius, said frankly on TV, 'It was agents of the DGSE who sank this boat. They acted under orders' and Hernu resigned. By tacit consent no one mentioned the authorisation given by Mitterand; in a monarchical presidency it was more convenient to maintain the pretence that the king could do no wrong.

In New Zealand the 'Swiss couple' were tried and convicted of manslaughter, after the Crown changed its plea from murder. Influenced perhaps by public indignation, the Chief Justice imposed the unexpectedly severe sentence of ten years. Discreet discussions had already begun in New York about compensation. The French intimated a wish to be generous, and also the hope that the convicted couple would be able to spend part of their sentence in France. David Lange's oratory was uncompromising: there would be no 'sordid haggling or selling of prisoners'. The French, unlike the Americans, applied pressure on our trade. The clearance of lambs' tongues and other New Zealand imports was mysteriously held up and the Government backed down. The prisoners were deported to Hao atoll in French Polynesia whence, after a barely decent interval, they returned to France, and David Lange never forgave the Ministry of Foreign Affairs or the able international lawyer who had helped him get the settlement.

Before that we had set off in August on another journey around the South Pacific. After a night in Niue, whose population had largely leaked away to New Zealand, and a dawn fishing expedition which did not manage even a bite, we went on to Samoa. The talks there were not contentious; the Privy Council decision was no longer an issue, and the

PM spent some time drawing a distinction between regional conflicts, which would be dealt without super-power involvement, and global conflicts, for which the ANZUS Treaty was relevant. He complained that the Samoan Prime Minister, Tofilau Eti, did not understand the distinction, but then neither did I.

There was a kava ceremony, speech-making in front of a stack of pigs roasted whole (I carefully avoided the PM's eye), and he was invested with the title of Matautia. (Several weeks later when my Estimates were being debated in the House an Opposition member asked whether it was true that the PM's Samoan title was Tulongalofa.) Then we sailed to Savai'i in considerably more comfortable style than my first trip twenty-five years earlier. At lunch in a plantation at Lata, Tofilau, who had been at our wedding, asked me anxiously if he had said something wrong. As he was speaking in Samoan my expression must have changed because as if a shutter had opened I was able for a time to follow what he was saying without effort.

We flew on to the South Pacific Forum in Rarotonga, where it was also the twentieth anniversary of self-government. The main business of the Forum was the adoption of the South Pacific Nuclear-Free Zone which the lawyers drafting it had come to call Spinfizz. The last obstacle, though, was still Father Lini; his party had committed itself to a zone so comprehensive that it would have banned everything from bombs to wrist watches, and some hard work was required behind the scenes to head off a Vanuatu veto. Eight countries, including Australia and New Zealand, signed the treaty at a little ceremony under the palm trees and work continued on protocols which it was hoped the five acknowledged nuclear powers would sign.

This was only the world's second nuclear-free zone but perhaps because of the Cooks' celebrations and the South Pacific Games also being held there the atmosphere was one of light-hearted fun. This infected the New Zealand delegation. Our alphabetical neighbour at the Forum table was the President of Nauru, Hammer de Roburt. At each sitting Hammer tended gently to doze off and his neighbours started a book on how long it would take. After lunch all New Zealand eyes were on Hammer who after only nine minutes gave an unmistakable snore. Chris Beeby, an international lawyer, who had gone short on the President against all earlier form found himself the winner, and the excitement in the New Zealand seats was such that Hammer woke up.

Then in the pre-dawn darkness we left for Tonga where we were accommodated at Tufumahina, the royal guest house, along with a dubious-looking American pastor (the King, though not an early riser, was a strong supporter of the prayer-breakfast movement). In the afternoon the PM and I went to the palace, a pleasantly rambling Victorian house, to call on the King. We sat in a silk-furnished drawing-room, balancing elegant china on our knees with tea and cucumber sandwiches, while through the open sash windows came a medley of tunes being played by the royal band. Conversation languished in the afternoon warmth. The King roused himself to ask the PM who in turn asked me the name of the song being played. I could not help. Silence fell again, silence of the tranquil Pacific kind. Finally it was time to leave. The band struck up 'God Defend New Zealand' and we were on our way to see the Prime Minister, Prince Tuipelehake, who was the King's younger brother.

The PM was now wary of Tongan conversational habits. I suggested that if all else failed he ask Tuipelehake about growing vanilla, a topic on which in the past I had found the prince almost unstoppable. The three of us sat at one end of the Cabinet table. The talk again flowed as readily as laughter in a funeral home. After another long silence the PM looked across the table and I nodded: it was time to play the ultimate card. David Lange leant forward and said, 'I understand Prime Minister that you are very interested in vanilla'. 'Yes,' said the prince and lapsed into silence again.

In the car driving to our next engagement, the opening of our new High Commission office in Nukualofa, the PM was understandably derisive about my advice. After the speeches there was a tour of the building. Seeing Tuipelehake sitting alone on a sofa (his legs did not allow him to follow the official party upstairs) I joined him – and received a full ten minutes on vanilla, its cultivation, marketing and lamentably low price. The PM, however, declined to believe me and took a revenge at the dinner which the High Commissioner, Priscilla Williams, gave that night.

After we had eaten I sat down with the King in another room. Always a good talker on these informal occasions (as at Vailima years before when he was Crown Prince), the King was in entertaining form. After almost two hours had passed, however, I was beginning to feel that it had been a long day when the PM loomed in the doorway behind the King, made merry goodbye motions with his hands and left. I explained to His Majesty that Mr Lange had left Rarotonga before dawn and needed his sleep. The King said he entirely understood; fortunately he himself had only got up at noon. Gloom descended on me; I was a royal prisoner. Time ticked by into the small hours and though the King's talk was never dull it was an increasing struggle to stay awake. Then chance brought an unexpected deliverance. The British High Commissioner came into the room with photographs of a recent picnic. His Majesty stood up to examine them under the light, the royal band stationed in the shrubbery outside burst with relief into the national anthem and the King said, 'I suppose I will have to go now'.

The next day the King gave a large outdoor feast, on the grounds in front of the palace, and we left for home. On the way the Air Force Andover had to make a refuelling stop on Norfolk Island. The Chief Minister had hospitably arranged a tour around the island but I strongly advised Chris Beeby to skip the tour and make for the bond store where casks of Australian wine were available (CER had not yet widened the choice at home). We each bought a ten-litre cask of Brown Bros cabernet sauvignon, encountering as we did so the others who had abandoned the tour to try the attractions of the store.

The PM and most of the party were dropped off in Auckland, leaving only Chris and me to go on to Wellington in the little four-seat cabin at the back of the plane. On the way Chris decided to open his cask and in doing so managed to pull off the plastic tap. Red wine squirted out over the walls and the ceiling, making the cabin look like the scene of a chainsaw massacre. We seized sheets of newspaper and were attempting to mop up when the door opened and the steward surveyed the gory sight. 'I'll clean that up,' he said, 'if you just tell me how you did it.'

The ANZUS row and the *Rainbow Warrior* bombing unsettled public opinion in New Zealand, leaving it feeling vulnerable and prone to conspiracy fears. In January 1986 Customs uncovered a load of arms and ammunition concealed on a French-owned ship, the *Ile de Lumière*, berthed at Auckland. It quickly became apparent that the clandestine shipment was destined for New Caledonia, not New Zealand; the quantity and range was not consistent with an assault operation. Nonetheless excitement ran high, or as high as was possible in the depths of the holiday season. It was alleged that the ship's cook, the owner of the cache, had military training and links with the *Rainbow Warrior* and that an Entebbe-style operation to free the two French prisoners had been planned. These wild speculations were not dampened by comments by the Customs rummagers that there was 'enough to start a small war' and that rifles and other weapons would probably be found (they were not). It took several phone calls and finally a letter from Lange to halt these official statements which looked as if the Government was trying to whip up anti-French feeling.

The PM himself, however, was far from immune to this underlying sense of vulnerability. Some years later he said that I had 'padded into his office' to announce that Soviet missiles were heading for the United States, and though I padded back twenty minutes later to say that it was a false alarm nothing the US ever did frightened him as much as this inadvertent warning. I had no recollection of this and I would almost certainly have remembered an outbreak of nuclear war and even more certainly have warned others (including my wife) during that twenty-minute interval.

On reflection I concluded he must have conflated in his mind two much more harmless occasions. In his early months, briefing him about the safeguards against an accidental launch, I mentioned that the Distant Early Warning radar line in Arctic Canada had once picked up what appeared to be a flight of incoming missiles. The system immediately rebalanced itself by checking other sensors and within seconds the alert was over – possibly the work of a flight of geese. In September 1986 we received a flash that a Soviet submarine missile had gone astray on a test flight. It was unarmed and not intercontinental but there was a risk that it might land in China and cause an awkward diplomatic incident and I told the PM. Half an hour later word arrived that it had been located in Siberia. David Lange's lively imagination had created a fright where none existed.

His nervousness was widely shared: polls showed that after a drum-beat of alarmist stories (the clock creeping ever closer to midnight) 44 per cent of New Zealanders thought nuclear war likely. Money was set aside from the *Rainbow Warrior* compensation fund to make a study of the consequences for the country of a nuclear war which, thankfully, was to be confined to the northern hemisphere. The group concluded that there would be huge disruption from 'fear, panic and a massive sense of grief and loss' and recommended that 'high priority must be given to prevention'.

In the manner of such studies they urged a much more expensive Phase II to look at dreamier matters – the word 'strategies' was freely used – including the preparation of home-grown medicines, alternative fuels, recycling lubricating oils, decentralising government and re-establishing 'southern trade'. A year on the initial enthusiasm had faded and the PM decided that this should not be considered in isolation from other disaster planning. My committee could not reach agreement and the issue lapsed.

Then excitement was renewed when a real if minor conspiracy turned up. The 'Maori Loans Affair' was an attempt by the Maori Affairs Department to raise $600 million offshore to fund a Maori Development Bank. Attracted by the scent of this naivety a flock of vultures gathered to feed on it. What emerged was a variant of the 'brokered loan confidence game' which had proliferated with the flow of petrodollars and dreams of dipping into it. So there was naturally an Arab connection, who claimed to be a former Kuwaiti Finance Minister, and a rich cast of other rogues. They ranged from a retired American air force general described succinctly as 'a playboy and drunk', someone who hinted of links with the CIA, a fashionable interior decorator, to a raft of convicted fraudsters, bankrupts and promoters of collapsed companies.

The sharp end was a man named Raepple, regarded by overseas currency and fraud protection services with a marked distaste increased by the fact that in a series of dubious operations no one had been able to fasten a criminal conviction on him. Raepple worked on an ambitious scale in the Pacific. In July 1986 he was in the Cooks as 'a Californian philanthropist with an interest in low-cost housing'; four months later he was in Vanuatu offering to raise funds from Middle Eastern sources for a new airport. There was a fiasco in Tonga over an unbuilt 'Crown Prince Hotel' and talk of setting up an International Bank of the South Pacific.

In a series of meetings in Hawaii senior officers from the Maori Affairs Department had been introduced to this strange crew by an entrepreneur from Rotorua who had persuaded the Minister to give him a letter authorising him to negotiate on behalf of the department. By law loans could not be raised on the credit of the New Zealand government without the consent of Treasury which finally discovered what was going on in November. The loan was never made; the PM declared that the Minister had acted 'unwisely'; the State Services Commission enquired into the doings of the department; and the PM asked me to trace the international networks involved.

I gathered a small group from the Reserve Bank, Police, Foreign Affairs and intelligence agencies and with help from the FBI and Washington's currency-protection office we lifted the turf long enough to gaze upon the convoluted rat-run of money-launderers, criminals and snake-oil salesmen who had descended on the Pacific and our own Maori Affairs Department in the wake of the petrodollar boom. It was a sad enough spectacle. The gaze of Television New Zealand, however, saw something more sinister. Ronald Rewald had opened a branch of his Hawaiian investment firm in Auckland. He claimed to have been financed and employed by the CIA and though he was convicted of perjury on this (and on 93 other counts) the TV cameras looked lovingly at the Auckland building as evidence of an American plot to destabilise New Zealand.

The mood of New Zealanders was unsettled by more than these stories. A sequence of major changes dismantled forty years of the country's economic geography. Farm subsidies were abolished at a stroke; import licensing phased out and tariffs lowered; an indirect goods and services tax introduced; the dollar floated (against the expectations of many of us it went up rather than down); government departments corporatised; and thousands of their former employees laid off. In all this turmoil the Post Office struck an unexpected blow: for what must have been the first time in its history it delivered a number of papers a day early. Since they were advance copies of the 1986 Budget this was serious enough for the Minister of Finance to offer his resignation. The PM asked me to investigate but there was no evidence that anyone had profited from their unexpected windfall and the resignation was not accepted.*

As the months turned into years, however, the suspicion grew that in some mysterious way David Lange contributed to the general uncertainty. He was a sort of political poltergeist: a restless and perhaps unhappy spirit around whom strange things happened, the equivalent of pictures falling off the wall and objects rising from the table. Bugs and

---

* The PM wanted an interim report which he could table quickly. I spent a day interviewing the participants from the Minister down, and settled down at night to dictate the report to my PA, Kath Parkinson, finishing after midnight. When I returned at 8 the next morning the report, flawlessly typed, was waiting on my desk.

nuclear war came and went, ships were blown up or sunk by their pilots, terrorists stayed in his motel, airliners were hijacked, he fell asleep in his flat and set fire to it; nothing not even travel in the South Pacific was ever quite straightforward with him.

You might come to work in the morning and find that the political furniture had been silently rearranged and some upended. Policies declared to be firmly in place might move in the night or disappear – his repudiation of the flat-tax plans which he had previously announced, for example, or his abrupt announcement at Yale that New Zealand should withdraw from ANZUS. The Royal Commission on Social Policy was another example. By 1986 there was a growing feeling that the aims and scope of social policy had grown rather haphazardly and should be re-examined, though agreement on this covered a deep divide between those who advocated tighter definition of government policy and those who sought a wider social justice.

The PM discussed the matter with me among others. He agreed that the terms of reference would need to be firmly drawn to discourage the commission from pondering on the entire human condition. Apart from this the key to a workable programme was finding the right person to head the commission secretariat and he accepted my suggestion of a young but experienced Treasury official. As chairman he in turn proposed an Auckland barrister, Ted Thomas. I did not know him so the PM arranged for him to call and I thought him an excellent choice. After a last discussion I left the PM's office believing that only the details remained to be settled. Then silence fell, the PM came under pressure from others and Thomas withdrew. The Royal Commission was finally established on quite different lines.

By then my own position had come to look distinctly shaky. In the middle of 1985 John Henderson, a political science lecturer who had worked for Lange in Opposition, was appointed Director of the PM's Office and took over the Advisory Group. His calm and practical nature helped this novel arrangement to work well enough but in the mistier reaches of the Left the mistrust of my background did not ease. A chemistry lecturer at Auckland University published an article in Australia asserting that I was of uncertain loyalty, owing a higher allegiance to the five-power intelligence arrangements. It ended with a dark warning to the PM: 'He should beware the Ides of March'. Thinking it was slightly ridiculous to have to do so, I went upstairs to assure the

PM of my undivided loyalty to my country. He brushed this away; the lawyer in him was much more interested in the libel and he urged me warmly to bring an action. I had no inclination to commence a lawsuit in another country but the question of my allegiance was forgotten as he sketched out my case.

For the next eighteen months hints continued to be dropped by others of a reorganisation of the Prime Minister's Department or a change in its Permanent Head. In this unsettled atmosphere I pressed on with the intelligence review which the Government had requested in the wake of the American restrictions. In the course of this lengthy process an opportunity turned up to deal with the problem of the Prime Minister's Department. The State Services Commission became attracted by the then fashionable concept of 'comprehensive security'. This held uncontroversially that there was more to security than defence and external intelligence but went on to argue that, since natural disasters were more likely in New Zealand than aggression, dealing separately with these events risked a misallocation of resources.

The Commission believed that too much effort was being spent on external intelligence rather than on studying dangers at home and the PM was persuaded that it would be more efficient to bring domestic and external risks under one office. I was unconvinced by the logic that such disparate responsibilities as military threats and volcanic eruptions could be better handled together but logic may not have been the only consideration as the way was opened for organisational change. At the end of March 1987 New Zealand became the only Westminster democracy to abolish its Prime Minister's Department, leaving three separate agencies in its wake like the fragments of an exploded asteroid: the Prime Minister's Office, the Cabinet Office and the Office of the Coordinator for Domestic and External Security.

I moved to an office in the Government Communications Security Bureau and set about coordinating. The scope was extensive but ill defined; in the meantime there were changes in the intelligence structure to put in place. The new weekly assessments committee did not get off to the most auspicious start. There was a new government in Fiji and though the Prime Minister was Fijian his Labour Party was widely seen as Indian-dominated. We concluded that it would have difficulty establishing its authority and might not last its full term. Richard Prebble, who had better Fijian sources, thought this too optimistic and he was proved right. Two weeks later we had a flash message saying that armed soldiers had entered the parliamentary chamber in Suva. I phoned the PM at once and he announced to the world that a coup had overthrown the elected government of Fiji.

This was a shock to those in New Zealand who had hoped that Fiji's racial tensions had calmed sufficiently to allow an orderly change of power through the ballot box. The disappointment was particularly sharp for the Labour Party, which had provided some fraternal support for its namesake in Fiji, and for David Lange. In the days following the coup his statements were not always carefully considered. In conversation I (and others) urged him to condemn the coup but to be wary of too much comment on Fiji's internal politics, especially the high-chiefly leadership. Instead he called for the troops on peacekeeping duty in the Lebanon to be brought home to stage a counter-coup – an invitation to civil war if it had been heeded – and said the respected Ratu Mara (who had played no part in the coup) was guilty of treachery. This dimmed any hopes that New Zealand might be able to influence events and clouded the atmosphere just as the crisis was about to turn on us.

I had just arrived at my desk on the morning of 19 May, five days after the coup, when my phone rang: an Air New Zealand 747 returning from Tokyo had been hijacked while refuelling at Nadi. I told the Beehive basement to put the lights and the kettle on for a meeting of the Terrorist Emergency Group (TEG) and went straight across to see the PM. Organisationally we ought to have been in good shape to meet this test. Two years earlier (ironically it had received Cabinet approval in the middle of the *Rainbow Warrior* affair) we had simplified the rather cumbersome anti-terrorist machinery. The core idea, the TEG, I borrowed from the British who seemed unhappily to have the most frequent experience: a simple group of the relevant Ministers and officials, normally chaired by the Prime Minister and with a membership geared to the particular crisis, which could coordinate the effort, whether military, police or diplomatic, and provide speedy direction. Communications and the necessary intelligence and other support were sited in the Beehive basement. We had exercised all this several times, including as it happened a hijacking at Wellington Airport which initially only the PM and I knew was simulated.

So the second surprise of the morning was when I walked into the PM's office to tell him that everything was ready in the basement. He said that he did not intend to convene the TEG. I protested that without the group it would be impossible to coordinate our response. The PM could not be moved: 'You'll manage it', he said.

There was no time seek his reasons or argue further; the phones outside were already shrilling. For the next hour or so I worked from his outer office, moving from one phone to another while one or two more kept ringing around me. At one point the Minister of Police, Ann Hercus, came by and asked if I needed help. Talking on one phone I gestured to another which she answered, to find herself talking to her own Commissioner, and for a time her efforts relieved the pressure.

It was impossible to let my other colleagues know what was going on, though I did manage to send a message to the CDS. At the beginning of any emergency like this the most daunting enemy is the unknown – who the hijackers are, what their aims are and how much support they have – and so the first and most urgent task was to learn the nature and scope of the challenge. Air New Zealand in Auckland could speak to the pilot through a single side-band radio in the cockpit, and in the course of the morning we found that a competent Fiji police officer, Inspector Govind Raja, in the control tower could also communicate through a loudspeaker in the cockpit roof.

The outlines of what had happened gradually became clearer. Amjad Ali, employed by the air terminal services and known to the pilots, had come on to the flight deck in the usual way. He seemed strained and as the passengers were boarding and the refuelling was nearly complete he suddenly revealed four sticks of dynamite with six-second fuses and announced the hijack. As he did so, a quick-witted pilot on the jump seat darted out the door and down the stairs to get the passengers off. The hijacker found himself controlling only the flight crew and the plane itself.

His first demand, relayed to us by the pilot, was to be flown to Libya. Our aim had to be to keep the aircraft where it was; if it took off with a full load of fuel it could go anywhere and we would lose whatever tenuous hold we had on the situation. We could communicate with the pilot through his cockpit radio but it was he who was on the flight deck, not us, and he would have to be the final judge of the hijacker's determination. All we could hope to do was to keep the talk going, first to calm the hijacker and then perhaps to start negotiations.

He had no Libyan connections and after a time admitted to the pilot that he did not want to go to Libya at all. His demands, or more accurately wild talk, revolved around the situation in Fiji, the need to restore democracy and for New Zealand to help. He had notes for President Reagan, one for Bob Hawke, calling him 'a good traitor' and puppet of the CIA, and one for David Lange: 'At this moment your aircraft is under Fiji Liberation Organisation. In the name of Her Majesty the Queen I request to you, Sir, to the immediate military action against Kernel Rambuka's dictatorship.' The pilot persuaded him to ask to be flown to Auckland, where the plane had been headed, but any takeoff was still a worry. Sympathetic discussion, slowed down by having to pass through Auckland, went back and forth but the strain of keeping it going was beginning to tell on the pilot, the hijacker and everyone else.

Inspector Raja came on the phone to say that he had Amjad's parents with him in the control tower – should he put them on to make a personal appeal to their son? It seemed a good idea but the parents struck a dispiriting note, weeping and pleading, 'Oh son, you have brought eternal shame on us; nothing can wipe out the stain of your deed'. Not surprisingly Amjad again became agitated, once more lighting a cigarette and waving it near the fuses of the dynamite strapped to his body. The pilot came on the side-band radio: 'Get them off' and Mum and Dad were hastily removed from the microphone.

By now, after ten o'clock, we knew what we were dealing with. There was only one hijacker, who had already retreated from his initial demand, and though there were sympathisers at the airport there was no organised support, apart perhaps from a brother who had hung about mournfully for a time. The talks had to be kept going and something could still go wrong; otherwise time and the need for sleep would settle the issue. I stepped back into the PM's room to tell him. He then produced his next surprise. He asked me to go to Nadi 'to coordinate the negotiations there'. I argued that this made no sense; my place was in Wellington not at the hijack where the pilot, Inspector Raja and Air New Zealand were coordinating well. He repeated his request and I demurred but when he did so a third time any further misgivings would have been insubordinate. I turned to leave the room.

As I did so, a discussion with a group in the office, which included a deputy secretary from Foreign Affairs but no military advisers, resumed. I heard a reference to sending a Hercules with troops to Nadi. When we were dealing with a lone hijacker even contingency preparations to storm the aircraft made no sense at all, let alone the fact that the Fijian troops positioned at the airport (who had dispersed the sympathisers) might well take exception to the arrival of New Zealand forces. I stepped back to ask the PM for his assurance that no military aircraft would land at Nadi while the hijack negotiations were going on. He gave this unhesitatingly and I went home to pack.

While I was on the plane which Air New Zealand had provided to take me, a police team and some aircraft engineers to Nadi, another act in the drama was taking place in the Beehive. The CDS, unable to find out what was going on, came to the Beehive to see me, only to be told I had just left. He had been directed by his Minister to send an aircraft and counter-terrorist troops to Nadi as soon as possible. He found eight or more people in the PM's office. After some discussion he was given in writing by the PM a rather broader directive to despatch an aircraft immediately with sufficient troops 'to act as required to protect New Zealand's interests in Fiji'. What actions might be required was never spelt out and when he pointed out the delicacy of sending armed troops to a foreign country he was told that the Governor-General (whose authority did not extend far beyond Government House) had given the necessary permission.

These murky manoeuvrings ended when the hijack did. While we were in the air the flight engineer, 'a tough little nut', went aft ostensibly to the lavatory and hit Amjad from behind with a full bottle of Teachers Whisky. When I stepped on to the tarmac the hijacker was being wheeled off to Lautoka Hospital with a suspected fracture of the skull and the flight engineer had reluctantly handed his bottle to the police. (His reluctance was justified; when it was returned after the lengthy judicial processes though still sealed it had mysteriously been emptied.) I talked to the pilot and other members of the flight crew, to Inspector Raja and some airport staff, and reported the results to the PM by telex.

That evening the PM asked me to go on to Suva to help out in the High Commission which he said was under some pressure. So the next morning I rented a small car and drove along the south coast, with the windows open to the on-shore breeze and the 'Goon Show' playing on Fiji's state radio. At a little bridge that marked the western entry to Suva there was what appeared to be a traffic jam. I had just joined the queue when an agitated gentleman leant in the passenger-side window and said, 'Sir, I must ask you to turn back, I must ask you to turn back immediately'. While I was still absorbing this unusual request, the front and rear windshields of the car in front dissolved into fragments and it became clear that a major riot was taking place in the market-place just ahead.

I wrenched the car to the left, with my agitated friend leaping nimbly out of the way, and bumped across a stretch of waste land until it was possible to reach another road and drive along the ridge to reach the High Commission residence above Laucala Bay where I was expected for lunch. Along the way I saw restless groups milling about and signs of some disorder but the traffic was moving unhindered. (The 'Goon Show' had finished; it was starting to seem disturbingly realistic.) When I arrived I was met outside by Patricia Gates, the High Commissioner's wife, not to remonstrate with me for lateness but to say that the ousted Prime Minister, Dr Timothy Bavadra, his wife and private secretary had just taken refuge in the house.

Bavadra, a kindly country doctor, seemed dazed but his chiefly wife, Adi Kuini, was composed. News came that a large mob was moving along Laucala Bay's main avenue towards the house; if it was known he was there they might well try to seize Dr Bavadra. Some sort of escape plan was needed. By chance the New Zealand frigate *Wellington* was in the harbour and both the house and the High Commission were guarded by detachments of sailors. They could not hold back a crowd but if trouble came the tiny Wasp helicopter could be summoned from the ship to lift the Bavadras to safety. The rest of us would have to scramble down the hillside to the beach. The private secretary was unhappy at being assigned this undignified mode of departure but the helicopter was too small and was unlikely to have the time to make two trips. The sailors prepared to fell some palms to make a larger landing pad but half a mile away the mob was checked and dispersed by the army. The Bavadras were later able to leave the house and made their way safely to the Western Division where he had his political base.

It was a day of random racial violence. Mobs armed with clubs and bush knives seemed to form spontaneously and roam through the city. As the High Commissioner and I sat talking in his office later that afternoon the noise of such a mob could be heard. I hurried down to move my car. The crowd laughing and singing were moving down the road, smashing the windows of the parked cars as they did so. Suddenly a file of armed soldiers moved out from the central police headquarters opposite me and across the road. They dropped on to one knee and levelled their weapons directly at the crowd. There was a tense silence in which the only sound was the click of safety-catches being removed. I took a step back to the shelter of a buttress provided by St Patrick's Cathedral. Then the crowd silently dissolved, flooding on to the footpaths and back up the hill.

Trouble peaked that night as police and army struggled to restore order. Indian shops were looted and burnt and passers-by attacked on the street. The mindlessness of racial violence is peculiarly sickening and deeply shocked a group of New Zealand journalists who had taken refuge in a hotel. I walked cautiously through the darkened streets to offer some reassurance and to brief them on how to get to the ship if the disorder became uncontrollable. On my way back I paused outside a familiar shop. It was closed and barred with steel shutters firmly down. A voice within asked me what I wanted. On impulse I said, a pair of khaki shorts. There was a murmured conference inside but the spirit of commerce was not easily cowed. What size? said the voice. Then there was a wait, during which I moved into the shadows as a police Land Rover came by – this was no time to be picked up for loitering with intent on a Suva pavement. Then a hatch opened and a hand came through the bars with my purchase.[*]

Both power and telephones were intermittently cut, sometimes for lengthy periods. The High Commission wives, isolated in houses scattered across Suva, were apprehensive about what might happen if they could not communicate with their husbands in the office. An army engineer had been assigned to the office after the coup and I asked him whether we could set up our own network. The city was still locked down but a few hours later the resourceful Major Beaver was back with boxes of small marine radios (they came, he said, 'out the back door' of a large firm). He dropped them off around the town with some quick instruction and morale rose again as everyone could talk on the network and report any emergency to the office.

Over the next two days there was still sporadic rioting but the army gradually imposed some semblance of order. It became possible to plan a final and delicate task. Dr William Sutherland, Dr Bavadra's senior adviser, had been obliged to go into hiding when the coup occurred and had later taken refuge with his wife and children in the High Commission,

---

[*] Known in the family as the 'coup trews', they lasted for years.

where the family were living in the library. This was a burden to everyone and I was asked to help get him safely out of the country.

I still had my little car and the plan was simple enough. The Bank building housing the High Commission was just across the road from the central police station, now occupied by the army. Leaving by the front door would therefore be awkward. It was decided that the sailors guarding this door would stage an altercation with their relief and while the Fijian army looked with fascination at this breach of service discipline we could quietly drive away from the back. I walked over the ground in the evening and it seemed negotiable for my car – a large green lawn belonging to a neighbouring convent.

Before dawn the next day we loaded as much luggage as we could take into the back seat of the car where it provided useful cover for Sutherland. His New Zealand wife, Helen, sat in the front with me and I hoped we looked like a holidaying couple returning with their children. At six the sailors staged their fight and we sneaked off. Unexpectedly, however, the nuns had done their washing overnight and what had been lawn the day before was now filled with large quantities of sheets, habits and less describable articles. I bumped through this blindly, brushing sheets aside while waving in a reassuring way to two startled nuns and calling out 'Lovely morning' through mouthfuls of underwear.

We finally emerged on to a leafy and quiet side street but my relief was cut short when I checked the rear-vision mirror. Behind us was an army truck with a six-man patrol in the back. I kept up a cheery burble with my passengers, who were perhaps already losing what little confidence they had in their Pimpernel and took the next turning to the left. So did the truck. I drove on and turned right, and so did the truck. Helen Sutherland, wary about being betrayed, said sharply, 'This is not the way to the main road'. I pleaded a convincing ignorance of Suva's streets but after the next turning the truck disappeared and we were on the road to Nadi.

For the first time in days I looked at the petrol gauge. It showed empty. I could see an ignominious end, all of us being arrested as we waited beside a car which had run out of gas. We drove, with my chatter becoming more and more abstracted as I tried to calculate how many more miles we might have.

I was relieved when a large petrol sign showed over the palm trees. I drove into the forecourt and pulled up. Outside the driver's window was a sturdy pair of brown legs. My eyes travelled up past a navy *sulu* to the face of a large and benign police constable. 'Ah there, Sergeant,' I said, jumping out and leaning against the car hoping that my male passenger had the sense to crouch even lower under the luggage. Unbelievably I had stopped at what must be the only combined petrol and police station in the world. A rather nervous Indian attendant took what seemed an age, fumbling with the cap and spilling some petrol, going back for rags to clean it up, apologising profusely and then going back for change. 'We have had a delightful holiday, Inspector,' I said, suppressing the impatient urge simply to drive off. Instead we chatted about the tourist attractions of Fiji until everything was done. 'Nice to have met you, Superintendent,' I said driving away with exaggerated calm.

After that it was relatively straightforward. The only obstacle was the military checkpoint on the Sigatoka bridge. The best way to manage this was to play the idiot tourist, a role which my passengers might have felt came fairly naturally. I drove straight through with a cheery wave; there were shouts from the soldiers but no shots. I put my charges into a motel near Nadi, bought them what I hoped was a soothing lunch and went off to see what could be arranged at the airport.

I went to an acquaintance made during the hijacking whom I felt could be trusted and asked for his help in getting the family on the Sydney flight. It was arranged that they would arrive just as the flight was closing, after all the others had gone through, to minimise the risk of being recognised. We waited until the last minute, I saw them through the gate and then retired to the concourse in case there was trouble. Time ticked by (the flight was delayed; they were recognised walking across the tarmac) and the paperback I had chosen to read was less than suitable – *Life among the Cannibals, or Two Years in Feejee, by a Lady*. While pretending to read it I became aware of a young man standing before me. He said, 'Mr —— (my contact) has asked me to tell you that the Sydney flight has left and that unfortunately there were no empty seats'. From this oblique message I knew that my charges were safely away, and this time my relief lasted.

The general election held later that year was on the face of it a triumph for the Lange Government. Although its traditional support was eroded it gained enough other votes to be returned after three years of bold reform with an increased majority. It was surprising, then, that when I went to congratulate the PM on the following Monday morning the atmosphere was more that of someone who had lost. His manner was subdued almost to the point of gloom and congratulations seemed out of place. The strain of office was beginning to tell, but underlying this was his increasing disenchantment with the Douglas reforms and the widening split with his Finance Minister.

The old ebullience in foreign relations was also fading and he became more careful about preserving important relationships. To smooth our links with Australia he approved a joint venture between the two countries to build the Anzac-class frigates. There was considerable public feeling and some doubts in Cabinet about this. Some Ministers wanted the engines of the New Zealand frigates derated so that they could not keep up with the American battle fleet. The PM asked me to report on the project: installing slower engines turned out to cost more. More realistically he was concerned about possible cost overruns. At my suggestion he approved the baseline characteristics with the proviso 'subject to overall cost ceiling of $300 million in 1986 NZ$' – a target which was met.

He was ready to work with the Australians in even more sensitive ways. International communications were shifting to satellites and intelligence-gathering would have to follow or dwindle to irrelevancy. We bought 30 hectares of stony ground in the Waihopai Valley in Marlborough as the site for a satellite station. It turned out to be perfect for grapes as well as reception and a local winemaker asked me if he could lease the large part not needed for the dish and buildings. A GCSB wit suggested that if the site was planted we would not need to build the dish – everything would come in on the grapevine. It was an attractive thought but bureaucratic caution prevailed.

Lange was regularly briefed by me and despite his later claims knew exactly what was involved and why the station was needed if we were to keep up with technological change. The Australians were building a similar one at Geraldton and their Defence Minister explained to the PM why the two installations separated by five time zones would enhance the benefit to both countries. The proposal did not go to Cabinet: I took the PM's authorisation across to the Finance Minister to counter-sign. Then the PM balked at announcing it, despite my urging that the longer he waited the greater the risk that it would leak. The weeks went by; when reminded he would say that he was waiting until after Hawke's visit (though that would have looked worse), or some other excuse. In the end it leaked to the local (Opposition) Member of Parliament and the PM was furious.

He also showed an unexpected willingness to work with the British government over the publication of *Spycatcher*. Despite signing a confidentiality agreement a disgruntled former member of MI5 published recollections which were exceedingly frank about some of the agency's operations and methods. It was naturally a bestseller and sales were not in the least hindered by the British government's efforts in the courts to halt publication. We were approached to support its argument in the New Zealand courts and whether it was the lawyer in him or the desire to mend fences with London the PM was firmly in favour. I told the British High Commissioner that we would support their case on the duty of confidentiality but not on any damage to New Zealand from publication since the book already had a worldwide circulation.

Along with the British Cabinet Secretary, Sir Robert Armstrong, I gave evidence in the High Court that New Zealand had an interest in the action since it too relied on the confidentiality of its servants. Outside, the secretary-general of the Communist Party, Ron Smith, gave less relevant testimony, handing out leaflets saying 'Hensley Supports Nuclear War'. In allowing a newspaper to continue serialising the book the Chief Justice did not find my evidence persuasive but I received belated encouragement from the Court of Appeal, which held that where state secrets were concerned 'the New Zealand Government can unlock the door to New Zealand Courts for a foreign government by appropriate evidence of its support'.

In between these excitements the office for Domestic and External Security Coordination (the DESC) – now doubled in size when I recruited a part-time assistant, Jim Rolfe – turned its attention to natural disasters. We prepared a paper on the principles to guide a recovery process and the ink was hardly dry on Cabinet's approval when tropical cyclone Bola struck the north-eastern part of the North Island with such force over three days that floods and mud largely destroyed the region's economy in what was described as the worst disaster ever to hit New Zealand.

There was not much to be done while the rain was still falling and the civil defence emergency was in force, but we starting planning and found a retired stock and station agent, Jock McKenzie, to act as man on the spot – he proved to be the key to the operation. As soon as the sun came out the PM and I toured the region in an Air Force helicopter. From the air the damage done by torrents of water on the soft slopes of the East Coast was dramatically visible. We stopped at damaged villages, farms and schools, distributing boxes of fresh milk, bread, orange juice and other comforts. At Tolaga Bay a *tangi* was in progress for four elderly women who had been swept away in a car. We sat on the *marae* for an hour while speakers addressed the dead: 'We have loved you in life, now go and leave us in peace'.

At Te Araroa, an isolated coastal village, we were given lunch which was served on long tables down the main street. Large buckets of boiled potatoes were joined by equally large supplies of *paua*, the native abalone which had been swept up on the beaches, and indeed down the main street, by the storm. 'Unbridled paua' said the PM as he munched away, looking around to make sure I had heard the joke. As we made our way back to Gisborne in the late afternoon there was still one box of supplies in the helicopter and I suggested to the pilot that we drop it off at some remote farm. He pointed down to one where the river had risen and cut off all road access and the helicopter came down gently on the back lawn. Hearing the clatter the farmer's wife emerged from the back door wearing only a short pink nightie and gumboots, to be met by the Prime Minister of New Zealand advancing upon her with a box of gifts. She did the only thing possible; she burst into tears. In the plane the local MP grumbled that they were two of the worst Tories in his electorate. 'Well, there's one less now,' said the PM cheerfully.

It was harvest time and over a million dollars worth of grapes, tomatoes, avocados and other perishable crops smothered in the silt would be lost without quick action. The morning after the visit we invented the Disaster Recovery Employment Scheme (DRES). Its name was more complicated than the concept which was simply that local bodies and tribal *runanga* could recruit teams of the unemployed to dig out crops, fences and houses and we would meet the bill. The PM was in Auckland, about to go to a Samoan church service, but he agreed at once and we put out a press statement in his name.

The DRES worked better than we could have hoped. Five hundred were employed for over six months at a cost of under $5 million. After the horticultural crops had been salvaged they worked on clearing fallen trees, cleaning up roads and houses and any tasks that could be handled with pick and shovel. We found a tough ex-Works foreman to oversee the scheme. I attended the dawn rollcall in Gisborne twice and the appearance of our workers would have scared a commando sergeant. 'The police are looking for half,' said the foreman proudly, 'and their wives for the other half.' I hoped it was coincidental but the number of burglaries in Gisborne declined markedly over the six months. But they enjoyed being needed and having the gratitude of the community; one of the gang members we hired in Wairoa told me that people now waved to him in the street.

Wairoa, bisected by its river, had a problem of its own. The flood had swept away the bridge carrying the main road and the town was cut in two, the only crossing requiring a lengthy detour upstream. Many lived on one side and worked on the other; the hospital for example was cut off from the nurses' home. We stood on the stump of the bridge watching the river boiling past. It was too wide for any temporary bridging and there was no one to operate a ferry. Someone suggested trying the army and though the army had nothing as civilian as a ferry, within five days it had a Light Tactical Raft shuttling back and forth across the river. Normal life was restored to the town and the raft ran for months. Each day's final trip coincided with the end of a shift for the nurses. There were rumours of a riverine equivalent of the Mile High Club which we firmly, and possibly even correctly, dismissed.

The biggest difficulty was how to restore the rural economy on which the whole region depended. Three-quarters of all farms had suffered loss of stock and buildings; many had also lost land and grazing to slips. Fifty volunteers and others, grouped into teams, carried out the most comprehensive survey of its kind ever done in New Zealand. Armed with this data we sat down to work out a compensation package. The traditional approach of paying for damage was abandoned – it would take too long to pay out and it did not make sense to require the replacement of buildings, fences and farm roads in flood-prone places.

Instead, working through the second weekend, we settled on a more radical scheme which covered loss of income whether from erosion, structural damage or other effects of the storm. To avoid delay farmers were asked to submit their own claims which were checked by random visits and the use of a French satellite's imagery. Farmers could use the money as they wished; to rebuild the farm, sell up and buy another, or take the money and retire to Tahiti, as I explained slightly nervously to the PM. There were special arrangements for Maori leasehold land. We tried it out on the President of Federated Farmers on a Sunday after he had returned from church and then on the PM who took it straight to Cabinet the next day. It cost about $56 million but it worked. Farmers liked the freedom to change their farming pattern, and the speed: within four weeks almost half of those who had claimed knew what they were to receive and we aimed to complete the payouts by midwinter.

More than anything else this restored confidence and raised spirits crushed by the shock of loss. There was anecdotal evidence of depression and even suicidal reactions. With the help of volunteers we cobbled together a simple counselling service to respond to calls from families or neighbours. This could only be sustained for a month so I asked Social Welfare to take over. A week later a lengthy proposal arrived, replete with academic references, which called for fourteen new cars, nineteen staff to drive them, and a director and receptionist. People wanted the reassurance of action rather than words and Jock reported that the need was falling. We put counselling aside; compensation turned out to be the best therapy.

In the meantime slips had carried away the main pipeline and Gisborne's water supply had been reduced to a trickle. Repairs would take months. Our first thought was to charter a tanker and fill it with fresh water but the harbour basin was too small for it to turn. Drilling artesian bores seemed the quickest answer and the PM immediately approved $2 million for this. The water was not perfect – it was said to predate Captain Cook – but it tided the town over and enabled industry to restart while the normal system was rebuilt.

A month after the storm the recovery was well under way. Army bulldozers, though, were still working to reopen some of the back roads and with winter coming on we tried to accelerate the repair of houses. An unorthodox approach was sometimes needed. Houses at Tolaga Bay had silt above their floorboards but the Maori Affairs Department which had been given the task of restoration had not got beyond removing the lower weatherboards, which made them draughtier than ever. I met a young man, Parekura Horomia, who described himself as a kind of junior whip of the Ngati Porou, the largest *iwi* in the region. On a snap judgement I offered to pay for time and materials if he could organise their repair within six weeks. He did and the widows of Tolaga Bay were warm and dry for the winter.[*]

---

[*] He later became Minister of Maori Affairs in the Clark Government.

It was a busy year for natural disasters. The DESC found itself building a long stretch of river wall to enable the business district of Greymouth to be reoccupied after two major floods. In the following dry summer the rural fire service was rebuilt on a new basis after two forest fires in Canterbury. Each of these and other tasks could be tackled with fresh enthusiasm because there was no DESC bureaucracy to work through. The key to the system was the close link to the PM and David Lange's quick decision-making. He enjoyed the immediate action, the human side of disaster relief, and on Mondays would get retrospective Cabinet authority for several spending approvals which he had given us over the weekend. Treasury was later to purse its lips over the amount spent on Bola but the PM's boldness put a whole region back on its feet.

In other respects his hold on power was steadily loosening. He became disillusioned with the economic achievements of his own government and when, at the beginning of 1988, he abruptly vetoed moves towards a flat tax, the differences in Cabinet broke into open warfare. He did not have the steely will needed to manage dissension. Politics for him was the theatre of public attention, not the mastery of committee discussions. The strain began to show; I noticed a tinge of self-pity creeping into his stories.

He became a ghost in his own administration. A loner by nature he had never taken colleagues or advisers into his confidence, as the *Buchanan* affair and the Fiji hijack showed. Now that confidence was increasingly withheld from him. The beginning of the end came in April 1989 when in a speech at Yale he called for New Zealand to formally withdraw from ANZUS. It was Anzac Day in New Zealand and his proposal was singularly ill timed. The Acting Prime Minister rang in some heat to ask if I had known in advance. It became apparent that no one had. The PM had given us copies of his speech before he left but none contained the offending paragraph. While travelling he seemed to have decided on his own to make the call without consulting any of his colleagues, and with it went the last of his loyal supporters in Cabinet. In early August he resigned and his deputy, Geoffrey Palmer, took over. When I went to say good-bye I was looking at a sad and exhausted man; the dizzy ride of five years was over.

The Prime Minister's Department was reconstituted along its old lines and the little domestic and external security establishment sensibly went back into it. Some years earlier Harvard University had offered me a fellowship which had to be declined since it was hardly possible to tell the PM that I proposed to be away for a year. Now they generously renewed the offer and I left in September to spend the academic year there.

The Centre for International Affairs found me a comfortable flat opposite the Law School, where I could keep an eye on the periodic demonstrations to which the law students seemed addicted. Cooking for myself was eased by a book of not-too-ambitious recipes assembled by my daughters. The recipes all started with the word Daddy – 'Daddy, cut up one onion . . .'. Breakfast, though only tea and toast, took almost an hour. I pored over the newspaper accounts of the fall of the Berlin Wall and the disintegration of the Soviet empire and sometimes forgot the toast. At 8.40 the bell rang for prayers. The university had given up starting the day with public prayers but for people like me it was the signal to fold up the papers and walk through the autumn leaves or winter snow to my office in the Centre.

The Centre (always abbreviated to CFIA to avoid the embarrassment of its more logical initials) was in effect a small college within the university. The fellows were expected to help with the graduate students and take part in a programme of seminars; otherwise your time was your own. Most were engaged in writing a book or major scholarly articles. Some were like tired seabirds, resting for a time on the rigging of the university before flying back to their own countries. One was a former President of Lebanon who had spent much of the previous months of civil war taking refuge from the shelling in a cellar and found university life especially restful. Another was a quiet Israeli major-general who later led the Labour Party for a time. In the springtime demonstration season we stood together in the common room watching a noisy student crowd outside. When I mused on what it was about he said modestly, 'I think it's me'.

Learning to use the little IBM personal computer given to me by the Centre turned out to be the most valuable knowledge I acquired at Harvard. It was like learning to ride a bike: I went through a painful three weeks, wrestling with the perverse distinction computers make between logic and sense and losing large parts of the article I was writing for a Wellington newspaper at one in the morning, but one day I wobbled off without falling and never looked back.

Reading and listening were the two great pleasures. As an honorary faculty member I had access to the stacks in the huge Widener Library, where an afternoon could be spent in the slotted-steel shelves, dipping into books, adding to the pile to take back to the flat. The most pressing gaps in my knowledge were on Asia and the Centre organised a reading list and arranged for me to attend lectures and seminars on China and Japan. For fun there were the lectures on Bach by the great Christoph Wolff, whose pronunciation of the word Bach, bouncing off the panelled walls at the back of the hall, was worth the admission alone.

Overshadowing all this were the extraordinary events taking place in Eastern Europe. The fellows held a monthly breakfast (a leisurely affair, even by my standards, lasting from 9 to 11) to which one of the notables passing through Harvard would be invited. It was the Czech Foreign Minister whose sad words have remained most with me. The Velvet Revolution was fine if you were young and had a future to look forward to, he said, but people of his generation had lost forty years which could never be recovered.

The force of what was happening was finally brought home to me by a small gathering called to consider (a very Harvard concern) why no one had predicted the precise timing of this collapse. We sat upstairs in the Faculty Club while the snow fell outside and a log fire burned in the grate. What warmed everyone most though was a fierce denunciation of the CIA's over-credulous estimates by two senior Russian officials. The CIA analysts defended themselves lamely as the Russians said that no half-intelligent person in Moscow had ever believed Soviet statistics and how could the CIA have been so taken in? The world was turning upside down. A few nights later I looked down at the Beaux Arts Trio taking their bows after a concert and was struck by the tradition they represented – three dumpy figures with the light gleaming on their white hair and shirt-fronts who had helped carry the values of civilisation through the long totalitarian shadow cast by the twentieth century.

It was time to go home. At six one morning a phone call from New Zealand suggested the position of Secretary of Defence. The winter sun outside the window was rising in a dull red ball as I once again reflected that in government business you should go with the flow. The flow turned out to have some turbulence and I set some sort of record for Defence, being fired before I even got to the office. After some months, from which my garden and new Labrador puppy greatly benefited, I finally managed to get there and lived happily ever after.

# INDEX

Abramovitz, Morton 280, 282
Aburi 105, 106
Accra 106, 108–9
Adams-Schneider, Lance 238
Adeel, Omar 63–6, 68, 69
Adelaide 238
Adu, Yaw 74, 75, 106, 107, 108, 112, 116, 126, 127
Africa: colonialism in 48, 55; East and Central, Commonwealth Secretariat visit 72–82. *See also* specific countries and place names
Agnew, Spiro 160
Agriculture, Ministry of (N.Z.) 189
Aikman, Colin 5, 14, 55
Air New Zealand 747 hijacking 296–9, 309
Aitutaki 53, 65, 66, 67, 68
Akaroa 208, 251
*Akatere* 64
Algeria 56
Ali, Amjad 297–8, 299
Alley, Rewi 170–1
Amachree, Godfrey 66–7
Amazon River 89
Amin, Idi 122, 184
Ankrah, General 106, 108–9, 116
Anthony, Doug 237–8
Anuradhapura 211
Anyaoku, Emeka 106, 109, 129, 234
ANZUS treaty 204, 218, 273–5, 276–83, 288, 290, 294, 309
APEC 176
Apia 1, 5, 6–7, 13–7, 18–23, 26–8, 31, 37, 38, 41, 43, 186, 249
Argentina 247–8
Armacost, Michael 280
Armstrong, Neil 134, 150
Armstrong, Sir Robert 305
ASEAN 176–7, 203–4, 207–8, 214–8, 219, 223
Asia-Pacific region 175–6
Astor, David 86
Atafu 24–5
Atiu 65
Atlanta 155
Auckland 62, 97, 178, 221, 232, 241–2, 263, 270, 277, 283–4, 284, 286, 290, 293, 306
Australia 46, 141, 165, 166; and ASEAN 177, 204, 207, 217, 218, 219; and Commonwealth 72, 75, 79, 96, 97, 101; and phosphate business 187, 189–90; and South Pacific 11, 18, 22, 52, 59, 253, 255–6; and Vietnam 138, 143, 217, 218, 219; and Waihopai Valley satellite station 304; CER agreement 237–8, 253, 290; devaluation 252–3; frigates joint venture with NZ 304; nuclear-free policy 272–3, 274, 288. *See also* specific states and cities
Awolowo, Chief 108
Ayida, Allison 111, 119
Ayub Khan, Mohammad 94, 96

Bahamas 242
Bahamas Constitutional Conference 130
Bahrain 229
Balewa, Sir Abubakar Tafawa 83, 84–5, 86, 104
Bali 217
Ball, George 145
Banaba (Ocean Island) 187, 188, 189
Banda, Hastings 80–1, 91
Bandaranaike, Anura 198
Bandaranaike, Chandrika 198–200, 209, 210
Bankers' Association 264
Barbados 88
Bavadra, Kuini 300
Bavadra, Timothy 300
Beattie, Sir David 262
Beeby, Chris 288, 290
Beijing 155, 156, 157, 167–72, 218, 261
Beira 85, 87
Beit Bridge 99
Bengal 94
Benghazi 83
Benin 109
Bernhardt, Prince 135
Betham, Fred 21, 36
Betham, Olive 21
Bethesda, Maryland 149–52, 153
Bhutto, Zulfikar Ali 73
Biafra 107, 109–31
Bjelke-Petersen, Joh 238
Black September terrorists 162–4
Blazey, Ces 239, 240
'boat people' 215–6, 217–9
Bonlieu, Frédérique 286
Botswana 97
Bottomley, Arthur 75
*Bounty* 53
Brazil 89
Bretton Woods system 256, 257, 258, 259, 260
Brisbane 244
Britain 3, 11, 18, 48, 59, 69, 75–104 *passim*, 108, 110, 114, 117, 128, 129, 130, 155, 161, 174, 196, 198, 204, 212, 245, 247–9, 273, 282, 305. *See also* London
British Honduras 70
British Phosphate Commission 187–8
Brockway, Lord Fenner 116
Brougham, Lord 14
Brown, Bill 280–1
Brown, George 99
Browne, H. Munroe 277
Bruce, David 170
Brundle, Frank 18–9
*Buchanan* 277–8, 280, 282, 283, 309
Buchwald, Art 153
Buckingham Palace 99–100
Bunker, Ellsworth 52
Burma 220–1

Burnett, Shorty 19
Burnham, Forbes 89
Bush, Barbara 261
Bush, George 261

Cabinet Office (N.Z.) 225, 271, 295
Cairo 94
Cambodia 138, 144, 145, 203, 205, 215, 216–7, 218, 219, 220
Canada 71, 75, 79, 83, 85, 90, 96, 97, 98, 101, 116, 128, 129, 149, 166, 281, 291
Canberra 189–90, 218, 237, 242–3, 252, 253, 255, 284
*Canterbury* 161
Canton, *see* Guangzhou
Caribbean 257–8
Caribbean Community 185
Carrington, Lord 242
Carter, Jimmy 198, 203, 235
Castro, Fidel 50
Central African Federation 79
CER agreement 237–8, 253, 290
Ceylon 94, 97, 98, 101. *See also* Sri Lanka
Charles, Eugenia 257
Chatham Islands 178
Chenault, Anna 155
Chequers 91
Chevrier, Lionel 87
Chiang Kai-shek 155
Chidzero, Bernard 97
China 49, 94, 97, 139–40, 141–2, 148, 154–8, 165, 167–74, 175, 176, 195, 214, 219, 224, 291, 311.
*See also* specific place names
Chittagong 94
Cholon 215
Chou En-lai 156, 158
Christchurch 2, 22, 184, 185, 242, 268
Christmas Island 189
CIA (U.S. Central Intelligence Agency) 136, 137–40, 146, 156–7, 159, 164, 280, 293, 298, 311
CINCPAC 141, 276
Clark, Margaret 221, 257
Cleveland, Harlan 51
Coleman, Governor 10–1
Collins, Sir John 11
Colombo 175–6, 209, 210, 211, 212, 220, 223
Comecon 215
Commonwealth 70, 73, 74, 75, 81, 82, 83, 90, 93, 96, 103. *See also* specific countries
Commonwealth Education Conference 116, 117
Commonwealth Finance Ministers' meetings 185, 242, 244, 257
Commonwealth Fund for Technical Cooperation 98
Commonwealth Games 244
Commonwealth Heads of Government meetings 75, 83–6, 88, 89–93, 97–8, 100–3, 183–5, 232, 233, 242–4, 257–9
Commonwealth Relations Office 99
Commonwealth Sanctions Committee 85–6, 87, 89, 94, 99, 102
Commonwealth Secretariat 70–2, 73–131; and

war in Nigeria 104–31; visit to East and Central Africa 72–82
Confucius 169
Congo 44, 49, 75, 116, 122, 128
Cook Islands 53–6, 59–60, 61–8, 97, 186–7, 255, 292
Cook Islands Party 67, 68
Corner, Frank 3, 4, 5, 12, 28, 32, 58, 60, 62, 135, 141, 167, 178, 181–2
Cosmos, Soviet satellite 251–2
Cottam, Millie 246
Council of Commonwealth Societies 77
Cranston, Bill 72
CREEP (Committee for the Re-Election of the President) 159
Croudace, Mary (Auntie Mary) 6–7, 23, 25, 26, 39, 152
Crowe, Admiral William 276–7
Cuba 220
Cuban missile crisis 49–52
Cushing, Cardinal 58
cyclone Bola 305–8, 309

Dakar 118, 119
Dare, Ollie 64
Dar-es-Salaam 81
Darwin 259
Davidson, J. W. 55
Davis, Tom 255
Davos Economic Forum 257
de Gaulle, General Charles 58
De Roburt, Hamme 288–9
Defence Ministry (N.Z.) 311–2
Deng Xiao-ping 214, 215
Department of… *see* name, e.g. Island Territories Department
devaluation 252–3, 262–5
Dhaka 94
Dhaulagiri, Mount 95–6
Dibble, Terry 240, 241
Dike, Kenneth 111
Dillais, Louis 286
Disaster Recovery Employment Scheme 306–7
disaster relief 305–9
Distant Early Warning radar line 291
Dodan Barracks 107–8, 116
Dodd, Thomas 141
Domestic and External Security Coordination Office (N.Z.) 295, 305–9
Dominica 258
Dorticos, President 50
Douglas, Ken 246
Douglas, Roger 262, 270–1, 293, 304
Duff, Sir Antony 95, 282

East African Common Services Organisation 74
East Coast 305–8
ECAFE (Economic Commission for Asia and the Far East) 175–6
Economist Intelligence Unit 131
Edmonds, Paul 5
Education Ministry (N.Z.) 202

Edward, Lake 128
Effiong, Philip 131
Efi, Tupuola 233
Ehrlichman, John 140
Elizabeth II, Queen 55, 70, 79, 99–100, 184, 201
Ellsberg, Daniel 147
Enahoro, Chief Anthony 117–8, 119, 120, 121,
    122, 123, 124–5, 126, 127, 128
Entebbe 74, 76, 103
Enugu 106
Eti, Tofilau 288
Europe 174; Eastern 311
European Community 236, 248
*Evening Post* 281
Everett Academy 58
External Affairs Department (N.Z.) 2, 13, 16, 23,
    32, 131. *See also* Foreign Affairs Ministry

Fabius, Laurent 287
Falealupo 9, 17
Falkland Islands 247–8
FBI 293
HMS *Fearless* 100, 102
Federal Palace Hotel 84
Federated Farmers 307
Federation of Labour 245, 246, 247
Fergusson, Sir Bernard 61, 62, 97, 131, 139
Festus, Chief 86
Fieldhouse, Admiral Sir John 269
Fiji 11, 59, 187, 234, 254, 272; 1987 coup 295–303,
    309
Firth, R. M. 135
Forbidden City 171–2
Ford, Charlotte 56
*Foreign Affairs* 257
Foreign Affairs Ministry (N.Z.) 54, 55, 59, 60, 167,
    189, 190, 221, 227, 230, 287, 293, 298; Asian
    Division 165, 167; Economic Division 181, 190.
    *See also* External Affairs Department
Fort McNair 139
France 44, 139, 283–7, 290–1
*France* (liner) 132–3
Fraser, Malcolm 119, 234, 242–3, 244, 252, 256
frigates, joint venture with Australia 304
Fukuda, Takeo 234
Funafuti 272

Galvin, Bernard 179, 221, 225, 226, 229, 237, 247,
    252, 253, 263–4
Gandhi, Indira 101, 257, 275–6
Gandhi, Rajiv 276
Garner, Sir Savile 74, 86
Gates, Patricia 300
GATT 236, 260
Geneva 217, 218–9
Georgetown 162
Ghana 51, 69, 82, 83, 84
Gibraltar 93, 109
Gilbert and Ellice Islands 188. *See also* Kiribati;
    Tuvalu
Gisborne 306–7, 308
Gleneagles Agreement 239, 241, 243, 244

Goa 53, 258
Goa Declaration on International Security 258
Goh Keng Swee 197, 204, 205
Gold Coast Colonial Service 74
Gordievsky, Oleg 268
Gorton, John 101
Government Communications Security Bureau
    295–303
Gowon, Major-General 104, 105, 106, 107–8, 109,
    111, 114–5, 116, 117, 118, 129
Grand Pacific Hotel, Suva 1
Grant, Ulysses S. 136
Green, George 228
Green, Marshall 149
Greenberg, William 56
Greenpeace 283, 286
Grenada 257
Grey, Aggie 6, 18–9, 26
Greymouth 308–9
Groser, Tim 226–7, 257
Guangzhou 165, 167; train journey to 172–4
Gundelach, Finn 236
Guyana 88–9, 184, 185

Haiphong 148
Haldeman, H. R. 140
Hamilton 240, 241
Hammarskjold, Dag 44, 45, 52
Hanan, Ralph 62
Hanoi 142, 145, 147, 148, 149, 158, 215, 217
Hao atoll 287
Harland, Bryce 55, 167–8, 261
Harriman, Governor 59
Hartke, Vance 179
Harvard University, Centre for International
    Affairs 310–1
Hatfields Beach 251, 252
Hawaii 292, 293. *See also* Honolulu
Hawke, Bob 252, 253, 256, 257, 273, 275, 298, 304
Hawke, Hazel 233
Hayden, Bill 255–6
Heath, Edward 92
Heber, Bishop 198–9
Helms, Richard 159
Henderson, John 294
Henry, Albert 63, 67–8
Hensley, Caroline (To'oa Caroline) 33, 58, 60, 150,
    152–3, 193
Hensley, Gerald
    career: Commonwealth Secretariat, London
        70–131; Cook Islands 63–8; Harvard
        University 310–2; High Commissioner,
        Singapore 191–223; United Nations, New
        York 40–59; Washington, D.C. 132–64;
        Wellington 2–6, 60–2, 69, 164, 165–90,
        224–310, 311–2; Western Samoa 1–2, 6–39
    personal life: marriage to Juliet 2, 12–3, 22–4,
        25–6, 95, 112, 152–3, 280; homes 32–5, 37–8,
        41, 56–7, 61, 71, 72–3, 133, 134–5, 138, 162,
        191–5; children and family life 33, 37, 51,
        60–1, 68–9, 97, 98–9, 132–4, 149–53, 191,
        192, 195, 208–9, 262, 287, 310; holidays

46–7, 97, 251; home leave 97, 152; attack on house in Georgetown 162–4

Hensley, Gerald (junior) 47, 61, 150, 151, 153, 195, 264

Hensley, Juliet (née Young): marriage to Gerald 2, 12–3, 22–4, 25–6, 112, 152–3, 280; life in Western Samoa 32–5, 37–8, 39; children and family life 33, 47, 51, 60–1, 68–9, 72–3, 97, 98–9, 149–53, 191, 192, 208, 262, 287; life in New York 40–1, 44, 46–7, 56–7, 58; life in Wellington 61, 178–9, 180, 230, 242, 262, 269, 277, 281; life in London 72–3, 92, 99–100, 101; visits home while living abroad 97, 105, 152; peritonitis on journey to Washington 132–4; life in Washington, D.C. 134–5, 136, 138, 149–52, 153, 162–4; life in Singapore, Sri Lanka and the Maldives 191–5, 198, 201, 202, 203, 206, 208–9, 212, 223; visit to Taj Mahal 233; visit to New Delhi and Goa 257, 258

Hensley, Sarah 68–9, 150–1, 262, 287

Hensley, Sophie 98, 132, 133, 150, 153, 163–4, 208

Hercus, Ann 297

Hernu, Charles 287

Hewett, Harold 259

Hewitt, Sir Lennox 103

Hickory Hill 153

Ho Chi Minh trail 144–5

Hoare, Major ('Mad Mike') 116

Hoffman, George 124

Holbrooke, Richard 198, 217, 218

Holdridge, John 148, 156, 168, 204

Holyoake, Lady Norma 44, 140

Holyoake, Sir Keith 36, 50, 54, 60, 61, 84, 91, 102, 140, 143, 147, 204, 206, 231, 264

Hong Kong 165, 167

Honolulu 276, 279, 285

Horomia, Parekura 308

Howard, John 238

Hue 148

Hughes, Cledwyn 83

Hun Sen 220

Ibadan 108

Ibos, Nigeria 105, 106, 109, 112

Ieng Sary 217

Ikoyi Hotel 86

*Ile de Lumière* 290–1

India 49, 53, 73, 83, 94, 97, 101, 155, 224, 275–6

Indonesia 52–3, 56, 177, 207, 216

International Monetary Fund 185, 209, 259

Ironsi, General 105

Island Territories Department (N.Z.) 4, 5, 37, 54, 55

Italy 110

Jaffna 210, 211–2

Jagan, Cheddi 89

Jahnke, Alfred 20–1

Jamaica 97, 98, 183–5

James, Sir Morris 93

Jamieson, Air Marshal Sir Ewan 276, 278

Japan 165, 175, 176, 181–2, 189, 191, 196, 205, 207, 217, 233, 236–7, 274, 276, 311

Jayewardene, J. R. 209

Johnson, Lady Bird 261

Johnson, Lyndon 44, 140, 146, 147

Johore 205

Joint Intelligence Committee 282

Jones, Marx 242

Jones, Sir Glyn 79–80

Juliana, Princess 135

Kaduna 117

Kahana 95

Kamanga, Vice-President 85

Kampala 74, 119, 120, 121–8

Kandy, 176, 212–4

Kano 87; Emir of 116

Kap'yong 166

Kapwepwe, Simon 79, 89–90, 91

Karachi 96

Kariba Dam 78

Karnaphuli River 94

Kathmandu 94–5

Katsina, Colonel 117

Kaunda, Kenneth 78–9, 83, 90, 98, 103

Keating, Paul 253

Kelly, Pat 241

Kempthorne, Bishop 7

Kennedy, Ethel 153

Kennedy, Jacqueline 44, 58, 153

Kennedy, John F. 44, 50, 57–8, 140, 153

Kennedy, Robert 281

Kent State University 145

Kenya 77–8, 98. *See also* specific place names

Kenya Game Park 97

Kenyatta, Jomo 77, 80, 98

KGB 221, 222, 268

Khyber Pass 96

Kingston, Jamaica 183–5

Kingston, Ontario 88

Kiribati 189, 254, 255

Kirk, Norman 151, 167, 175, 176, 177–81, 184, 186, 239, 267, 270

Kirk, Ruth 178, 179, 180

Kissinger, Henry 136, 140, 142, 148, 149, 156, 157, 182

Knox, Jim 241, 245

Kogbara, Ignatius 118, 119, 129

Kokoda Trail 271

Korea 141, 165–7, 175, 236, 237

Krushchev, Nikita 45, 50

Kuala Lumpur 207

Kuwait 12

Kyoto 181–2

Lagos 83, 84–7, 104, 106, 107, 108, 109, 110, 111, 112, 113, 114, 116–8, 120, 122, 123, 125, 128, 130, 131

Lahore 96

Landi Kotal 96

Lange, David 180, 249, 263–4, 266–309

Lange, Naomi 270, 271

Lange, Phoebe 269

Langley, Virginia 137, 138
Langstone, Frank 135, 162
Laos 144, 145
Laucala Bay 2
Le Duc Tho 148, 149
leaks, political 250–1, 279
Lebanon 296
Lee Chin Koon, Mrs 209
Lee Kuan Yew 85, 91–2, 102, 115–6, 177, 184, 197–8, 203, 206–7, 234, 242, 258–9, 265, 275
Lennox-Boyd, Alan 18
Levchenko, Stanilaus 268
Levestam, Ash 25
Liberia 56
Libya 297, 298
Lin Biao 157, 169
Lin Ping 169–70
Lini, Walter 235, 254, 255, 272
Lisbon 107, 121
Lockstone, Brian 245
London 71–4, 78, 82, 87–8, 89–93, 98–103, 109–21, 128–31, 132, 134, 170, 187–8, 221–2, 248, 259–60, 273, 281–2
Long-Term Wage Reform Committee 247
Los Angeles 152, 280–1
Lowu 165
Lusaka 78, 83
Luxembourg 107

Macarthur, John 286
Macdonald, Audrey 77
Macdonald, Malcolm 77
Macdonald, Sir Thomas 84, 85
MacIntyre, Duncan 236, 240–1, 255
Mafart, Alain 284, 286, 287, 291
Makarios, Archbishop 87
Makindi 126
Malawi 74–5, 79–81
Malaysia 73, 94, 141, 143, 177, 195, 196, 204, 207, 215, 216, 218
Maldives 12, 191, 200–3
Malietoa Tanumafili II 14, 28, 30, 33, 153
Mangaia 64, 67
Manhattan, *see* New York
Maniguet, Xavier 284, 285
Manihiki 66
Manila 222
Manley, Michael 184
*Manu'atele* 10
Manyara, Lake 81–2
Mao Tse-tung 139–40, 155, 157, 168, 169
Maori Affairs Department 292–3, 308
'Maori Loans Affair' 292–3
Mara, Ratu 234, 254, 296
Marcos, Ferdinand 222
Marlborough House 71–2, 73, 84, 90, 99, 109, 110, 111, 112, 116, 129
Marlborough Sounds 271
Marsack, Judge 33
Mata'afa, Fiame 15, 31, 35, 36
Mau movement 7, 16
Mauritius 97

Mayday Tribe 145
Mbanefo, Sir Louis 119, 120–1, 122, 123, 124–5, 126–7, 128–9, 130, 131
McCain, Admiral 141–2
McCarthy, Thaddeus 280
McGovern, George 160
McIntosh, Alister 2–3, 6, 13, 16, 61, 68, 70–1
McIntyre, Alister 185
McKay, Alan 9–10, 17
McKay, Cyril 37
McKenzie, Jock 305, 308
McLay, Jim 249, 264–5
McLean, Donald 138
MEDSEA 165, 175
Melbourne 242–4, 257, 258
Menzies, Sir Robert 72, 73, 84
*Mikhail Lermontov* 271
Ministry of ... *see* name, e.g. Foreign Affairs Ministry
Mitchell, John 141
Mitchell, Martha 141
Mitterand, François 286, 287
Mojekwu, Christopher 110, 111, 112, 113, 118
Mongolia 157
Mongrel Mob 228, 261
*Monowai* 254, 272
Monroe, Marilyn 47
Moore, Mike 267
Moors, Harry 35
Morgan, Henry 184
Moscow 107, 221, 222
Moyle, Colin 233, 268
Mugabe, Robert 235, 243
Muldoon, Dame Thea 232–3
Muldoon, Sir Robert 191, 203, 206–7, 221, 222–3, 224–65
Mulinu'u 29, 31
Mulivai 25
Munro, Jock 244
Murchison Falls 75
Murdoch, Simon 221, 280
Mururoa atoll 230, 283, 285–6

Nadi 1, 296, 298–9, 302, 303
Nairobi 74, 76, 77, 93, 97–8, 103
Nakasone, Yasuhiro 276
Napier 227
Nash, Walter 2–3, 6
Nasir, President 201, 202
Nassau 242
National Press Club, Canberra 243, 253
National Security Council (U.S.) 136, 140, 280
Nauru 187, 288
Neazor, Paul 264
Nelson, O. F. 21
Nepal 94–6
Netherlands 52–3, 212
New Caledonia 254, 272, 284, 285, 286, 290
New Delhi 177, 232, 257–9, 276
New Delhi Statement on Economic Action 258–9
New Guinea 180; Dutch 52–3
New International Economic Order 183, 186

New Plymouth 241
New South Wales 238. *See also* Sydney
New York 4, 5, 39, 40–59, 64, 133, 151, 153, 185,
    217, 224, 261, 287
*New York Times* 136, 147
New Zealand Communist Party 170
NIBMAR (no independence before majority rule)
    92, 93, 94, 100, 102
Nicaragua 49
Niger 49
Nigeria 93; civil war in 99, 104–31. *See also* Lagos
Nile River 75, 76
Niue 287
Nixon, Richard 136, 137, 139, 140–8, 149, 154–61,
    167, 181
Njoku, Eni 125
Nkrumah, President 74
Nobel Peace Prize 149, 278
Norfolk Island 255, 284, 285, 290
Norrish, Merwyn (Merv) 279
Noumea 284, 285
Nuclear Non-Proliferation Treaty 273
nuclear-free policy 235, 262, 272–5, 288, 291
Nukualofa 289
Nukunono 24
Nyerere, Julius 79, 81, 98, 102, 103, 258

Obote, Milton 70, 74, 85, 91, 98, 119, 121–2,
    123–4, 126, 129
Ocean Island (Banaba) 187, 188, 189
Odaka, Sam 121, 123, 124, 126
OECD 182, 183, 259
Officer, Jenny Edwards 262
Officials Economic Committee 208
oil shocks 137, 181, 182–3, 230, 256
Ojukwu, Colonel 105, 106, 108–9, 115, 116, 126,
    127, 129, 130, 131
Okpara, Michael 114, 117, 119, 127
Organisation for African Unity 82, 120
Oswald, Lee Harvey 58
Ottawa 88, 100, 135, 281
*Ouvea* 284–5, 286
Oxford Union debate 280, 281

Pacific, *see* South Pacific
Pacific Forum Line 253, 255–6
Pago Pago 10, 25, 278
Pakistan 73, 94, 96, 98, 156
Palmer, Geoffrey 309
Panama 184
Panmunjom 166
Papauta 23, 24, 26, 32–5
Papeete 60
Papua New Guinea 11, 271–2
Paraa Lodge 76
Paris 129, 130, 139, 140, 147, 170, 182, 220, 259,
    285, 286, 287
Parkinson, Kath 293
Peacock, Andrew 217, 218
Pearl Harbor 141
Pearson, Lester 85, 88, 90, 91, 93, 100, 116
Peel, Sir John 98

Penrhyn 65
Pentagon 146
Pentagon Papers 136, 147
Peren, Caroline *see* Hensley, Caroline
Peshawar 96
Pham Van Dong 214–5
Phan Hien 214, 219
Philippines 218, 222–3, 274
Phnom Penh 203
phosphate mining 187–90
Pokhara 95
Pol Pot 216, 217, 220
Police Department (N.Z.) 293, 297
Pompallier House 269
Pope, Margaret 279, 282
Port Moresby 271
Portugal 48, 53, 102, 212. *See also* Lisbon
Poumau, Papali'i 8, 9, 35–6
Powles, G. R. 3, 5, 13, 14, 15–6, 17, 18, 19–20, 22,
    26, 27, 32, 39
Prebble, Richard 296
Prieur, Dominique 284, 286, 287, 291
Prime Minister's Advisory Group 225–7, 228, 250,
    257, 262, 270, 294
Prime Minister's Department (N.Z.) 178, 221,
    224–95, 310
Prime Minister's Office (N.Z.) 294, 295
Privy Council 248–9
Punjab 96

Queensland 189–90, 238
Quentin-Baxter, Quentin 40, 43

Radziwill, Lee 44
Raepple, Max 292
*Rainbow Warrior* 283–7, 290, 291, 296
Raja, Govind 297, 298, 299
Rajaratnam, Sinnathamby 197, 217, 218
Rakahanga 66
Rambuka, Sitiveni 298
Ramphal, Sir Shridath (Sonny) 89, 235
Rana family 95
Rarotonga 53, 55, 63, 64, 66–8, 288, 290
Rata, Matt 178, 179
Rata, Nellie 178
Reagan, Ronald 260–1, 265, 282, 298
Red Cross 124, 129
Regan, Don 257, 260
Reserve Bank 263, 293
Rewald, Ronald 293
Rhodesia, Northern 44
Rhodesia, Southern 48, 73–5, 76–7, 78, 81, 82, 83,
    84–6, 87–8, 90–4, 98, 99, 100–1, 102, 103. *See
    also* Salisbury
Riddiford, Daniel 61, 62
Rifai, Najmuddine 38
Rift Valley 82
Rockefeller family 56, 58
Rogernomics 270–1
Rolfe, Jim 305
Rotorua 255, 292
Rowling, Bill 183, 184–5, 225

Royal Commission on Social Policy 294
*Rubis* 285
Rupununi 89
Rusk, Dean 204
Russell 269
Russell, Spencer 263, 264
Ruwenzori mountains 128

Saigon 138, 146, 147, 148, 149, 203, 204, 215
Salisbury 73, 76, 78, 92
Salote, Queen of Tonga 19
Samoa, American 10–1
Samoa, Western (Samoa) 280, 287–8; and
    New Zealand citizenship 249; banana crops
    186–7; the Beach 20–2, 26, 38, 39; German
    community in 20–1; transition from trusteeship
    to independence 1–39, 43, 55; Treaty of
    Friendship with New Zealand 28, 32, 249;
    wedding anniversary visit 152–3. *See also* Apia
São Tomé 118
Satellite Re-Entry Committee 251–2
Saud, King of Saudi Arabia 94
Savai'i 8–10, 17, 35, 288
Scandinavia 274
*Sea Eagle* exercise 277
Seddon, Richard 53
Selassie, Haile 44
Senanayake, Dudley 101
Senanayake, Mr (Kandy) 212–3
Seoul 165–6
Shalimar Gardens 96
Shanahan, Foss 42–3
HMS *Sheffield* 248
Shepherd, Lord 128, 129–30
Shultz, George 234, 256, 260, 273
Sidwell Friends' School 150–1
Sihanouk, Prince 219
Singapore 73, 85, 141, 143, 170, 177, 189, 191–8,
    202, 203–9, 214–23, 232, 270, 275, 285
Sinhalese 209, 210, 212
Sinkiang 140
Smith, Arnold 71, 73, 74, 75, 76, 77, 78, 80, 81, 82,
    84, 88–9, 90, 91, 92, 94–7, 98, 99, 100, 101, 102,
    106, 107–30, 134, 184
Smith, Ian 73, 75, 85, 88, 92, 93, 100
Smith, Lin 206
Smith, Ron 305
Social Welfare Department (N.Z.) 308
Socialist Unity Party 221
Sofinsky, V. N. 221–2
Soper, Lord 273
South Africa 48, 74–5, 78, 83, 87, 88, 92, 99, 102,
    235; sporting contacts with 235, 238–42, 243
South Australia 238
South East Asia 44, 143, 146, 176–7, 196, 203, 207,
    214, 215, 216, 218, 219, 285. *See also* specific
    countries
South Pacific 4, 11, 12, 20, 43, 52, 53, 59–60, 186,
    202, 235, 253–6, 274, 287–90, 294. *See also*
    specific countries
South Pacific Forum 253–6, 271–3, 288–9
South Pacific Nuclear-Free Zone 288

Soviet Union 41, 43, 44–5, 48, 50–2, 138, 139, 140,
    148, 155, 156, 157, 158, 214, 215, 220, 221–2,
    260, 271, 278, 291, **311**
Springbok rugby tour, 1981 238–42, 243, 254
*Spycatcher* 305
Sri Lanka 175–6, 191, 198–200, 209–214, 220. *See
    also* Ceylon
State Department (U.S.) 136, 138, 142, 146, 147,
    157, 158
State Services Commission 292, 295
Stevenson, Adlai 51, 56
Stevenson, Robert Louis 1, 13, 33, 35
Stone, John 253
Strong, Anna Louise 170
Stuyvesant, Peter 57
Suharto, President 207
Sukarno, President 52
Sumatra 177
Sutch, Bill 222
Sutherland, Helen 302
Sutherland, William 301–3
Suva 1, 16, 231, 296, 299–303
Suzuki, Zenko 236–7
Sydney 285
Symmans, Gerry 224

Taihape 97
Taiwan 155, 156, 157, 158, 167
Taj Mahal 233
Talboys, Brian 218, 224–5
Tamasese, Tupua (d. 1929) 7
Tamasese, Tupua (Fautua) 12, 14, 21, 25, 26, 28,
    30, 31, 36, 38, 39
Tamils 210–2, 213
Tan, Peter 198
Tan, Tony 270
Tanzania 81–2, 83, 84, 126, 130
Tarawa 188–9, 254
Tarlac 223
Tasmania 238
Taufa'ahau Tupou IV, King of Tonga 19, 289–90
Television New Zealand 293
Templeton, Hugh 237, 238
Terrorism Committee 225, 283, 286
Terrorist Emergency Group 296–7
Thailand 141, 203, 214, 215, 216
Thant, U 45, 52, 63, 99
Thatcher, Margaret 79, 234, 242, 248, 256, 259–
    60, 261, 269, 282
'Think Big' development projects 227
Thomas, Miss F. Comyns 100
Thomas, Ted 294
Thomson, George 102
HMS *Tiger* 93, 94
Tizard, Bob 185
*Tofua* 11
Tojo Hideki 205
Tokelau Islands 24, 33, 278
Tokyo 165, 181, 285, 296
Tolaga Bay 306, 308
Tonga 2, 3, 19, 186–7, 289–90, 292
Tonkin, David 238

Toshogu Shrine 237
Treasury (N.Z.) 1, 189, 234, 237, 247, 259, 270, 292, 294, 309
Treaty of Waitangi 255
Trend, Sir Burke 84
Tricot, Bernard 286
Trinidad and Tobago 88
Trudeau, Pierre 100, 101, 102
Truman, Harry S. 155
Tuipelehake, Prince Fatafehi 289
Tungi, Prince 19
Tupouniua, Mahe 176
Tutuila 10
Tuvalu 189, 255, 272–3

Uganda 70, 74, 75, 93, 98, 119. *See also* specific place names
United Arab Republic 51
United Nations 11–2, 38, 90, 185–6, 234, 254, 257, 269; Cook Island elections, observer at 63–6, 68, 69; Declaration on Colonialism 47–8, 53–4; General Assembly 4, 15, 29, 36, 41, 42, 44, 45–6, 47, 49, 52–3, 69, 157, 176, 183, 184, 217, 272; General Assembly, Fourth (Colonial) Committee 49, 54, 55, 69, 78; Mission to Western Samoa 3–4, 5, 6; New Zealand Mission to 39–46; Security Council 43, 44, 50, 51–2, 87, 88, 93, 94, 217, Special Committee on Colonialism (Committee of Twenty-Four) 48, 53, 58–9, 63, 69; Special Committee on Colonialism, Sub-Committee for the Pacific 58–60; Trusteeship Council 4, 6, 27–8, 43
United States 10–1, 50–2, 53, 59, 69, 83, 89, 99, 114, 128, 129, 176, 182, 183, 203, 207, 215, 217, 218, 235, 245, 257, 291; and ANZUS treaty / NZ nuclear-free policy 204, 218, 273–5, 276–83, 290, 294, 309; and China 139–40, 141–2, 148, 154–8; and Vietnam War 138, 139, 140, 141–9, 159, 160, 181; Muldoon's last visit to 260–1; southern 46–7, 261; Watergate Affair 141, 158–61. *See also* CIA; FBI; National Security Council (U.S.); New York; State Department (U.S.), Washington D.C.; White House; names of presidents; and names of other cities and states
Upolu 8, 39
Ussuri River 140

Vailima 13–4, 15–6, 17, 18, 24, 25, 27, 33, 37, 38, 39, 289
Vaimoso 7
Vance, Cyrus 217, 218
Vanuatu 235, 254–5, 288, 292
Victoria 238. *See also* Melbourne
Vietnam 91, 102, 119, 130, 136, 138, 139, 140, 141–9, 159, 160, 175, 18, 203–4, 205, 214–9, 226, 273
Vietnam Mobilisation 144
Vietnam Moratorium 143

Vila 254–5
Vogel House 232, 235–6, 270

wage freeze 246–7
Waihopai Valley satellite station 304
Waimate 179
Wairoa 307
Waitangi Day 205
Walding, Joe 178, 179, 270, 281–2
Walker, Patrick Gordon 106
Walpole, Rev. 241
Walters, General 139
Walton, Bob 240, 241
Wanganui Computer Centre 250
Washington D.C. 110, 132–64, 224, 240, 260, 280, 282
Watergate Affair 141, 158–61
Watt, Hugh 163
Waugh, Auberon 130
Weinberger, Caspar 260, 261
Weir, Jim 222
Weld, Sir Frederick 206
Wellington 2–6, 60–2, 68–9, 164, 165, 176, 178–81, 224–309, 311–2
*Wellington* (frigate) 300
Western Australia 238
Western Samoa, *see* Samoa, Western
White House 136, 140, 143, 144, 145, 146, 154, 159–60, 161, 235, 260–1
Whitlam, Gough 271–2
Williams, Eric 88
Williams, John 53
Williams, Priscilla 289
Wilson, Harold 81, 83, 85, 86, 88, 90, 91, 92–3, 94, 97, 100–1, 102, 103, 116, 130, 131
Wilson, Michael 72, 73, 84, 97, 128
Withers, Reg 190
Wolff, Christoph 311
Wolfowitz, Paul 279
Women's Affairs Ministry (N.Z.) 271
World Fertiliser Fund 176
Wren, Sir Christopher 71
Wriggins, Howard 198
Wright, Jack 26–7, 36, 43, 55

Yahya, President 155, 156
Yeend, Sir Geoffrey 252, 256
Yoruba 104, 108, 109
Young, Austen 178, 179, 180
Young, Juliet, *see* Hensley, Juliet (née Young)

Zambesi River 74, 78
Zambia 74, 78, 79, 82–3, 84, 85, 86, 89–90, 126, 130
Zanzibar 82
Zaria 117
Zimbabwe 243
Zomba 80
Zorin, Valerian 51